Characteristics of men, manners, opinions, times, etc

Shaftesbury, Anthony Ashley Cooper, Earl of, 1671-1713, J M. 1856-1933 Robertson

Nabu Public Domain Reprints:

You are holding a reproduction of an original work published before 1923 that is in the public domain in the United States of America, and possibly other countries. You may freely copy and distribute this work as no entity (individual or corporate) has a copyright on the body of the work. This book may contain prior copyright references, and library stamps (as most of these works were scanned from library copies). These have been scanned and retained as part of the historical artifact.

This book may have occasional imperfections such as missing or blurred pages, poor pictures, errant marks, etc. that were either part of the original artifact, or were introduced by the scanning process. We believe this work is culturally important, and despite the imperfections, have elected to bring it back into print as part of our continuing commitment to the preservation of printed works worldwide. We appreciate your understanding of the imperfections in the preservation process, and hope you enjoy this valuable book.

SHAFTESBURY'S
CHARACTERISTICS

CHARACTERISTICS

OF

Men, Manners, Opinions, Times, etc.

By the Right Honourable
ANTHONY EARL OF SHAFTESBURY

EDITED, WITH AN INTRODUCTION AND NOTES, BY
JOHN M. ROBERTSON

IN TWO VOLUMES

VOL. I

London
GRANT RICHARDS
1900

EDITOR'S PREFACE

This edition of Shaftesbury's *Characteristics* reproduces all the essays he himself so entitled, with strict adherence to his text, as corrected by him for a reissue. Of that corrected copy I have collated a large part with the reprints, and I find that his alterations were scrupulously given effect to, down to the smallest particulars. A few of the footnote references to corroborative passages in the book itself have here, as a matter of convenience, been altered back to their first form, specifying titles and sections of the essays rather than pages of the book; but no liberty has at any point been taken with the text beyond the modernising of the spelling and disregard of the old italics and capitals.

This external change has been made with some reluctance, but with a conviction that it is really a service to the author. The profuse use of italics and capitals in English books of Shaftesbury's day, though in exact reprints it lends a certain agreeable local colour to such books as the *Spectator*, and though it might lend an analogous element to an exact reprint of Shakspere, is a positive hindrance to the fluent reading of an argumentative treatise. Those who have read the *Characteristics* in an old edition will find the modernised text distinctly easier to follow. As with variations of type, so with spelling. One hesitates to put "them" for the modish "'em" commonly used, even by some theological writers, about 1700 ; but the usage is become so quaint in its virtual foppery, like the spelling "aukard," as to be disconcerting to the reader's thought. It may interest moderns, however, to know that Shaftesbury wrote "specter," "center," and "theater," thus giving to these "Americanisms" the classic English paternity established for so many others.

In the interest of a large part of the reading public it has been thought advisable to append footnote translations of the Latin and Greek extracts in the original. Some of them, doubtless, hardly needed translating ; but others would have given trouble to all but readers who had not let their classics rust ; and the usage has been made uniform. In this matter the editor has been relieved by a much better scholar. Elucidatory notes, which at some points in the text had become necessary, and at others may not be supererogatory, have been invari-

EDITOR'S PREFACE

ably put in brackets, a course recommended by the fact that in Mr. Hatch's unfinished edition of 1869 some of Shaftesbury's own notes have been marked "Ed."

Save for that edition, unfortunately stopped by its editor's death when only one of three volumes had been printed, the present is believed to be the first reprint of the *Characteristics* for over a century. It is hoped that it does not unworthily reproduce a set of treatises which once had almost classic status throughout Europe, and in our own day have been made the subject of two elaborate German monographs.

EDITOR'S INTRODUCTION

In his *Pensées Diverses*, Montesquieu has a surprising phrase, giving an obsolete view of more than one reputation. "The four great poets," it runs, are "Plato, Malebranche, Shaftesbury, Montaigne." Probably the idea came from Shaftesbury himself, who often discusses poetry as identical with good moral teaching. The author of the *Spirit of Laws*, on his part, was not exactly a connoisseur of poetry, for he is further committed to the view that "Pope alone has felt the greatness of Homer"; and in any case his praise of a thinker as a poet does not necessarily imply approval of his teaching, since he affirms in another page that Malebranche has fallen into a thousand sophisms through missing the principle of relativity. Since, however, he makes no such charge against Shaftesbury, he must be supposed in his regard to have intended high praise; and as a matter of fact his eulogy of the author of the *Characteristics* would be echoed, with whatever differences of phrase, by multitudes of instructed men in France, Germany, and England, at the time he wrote. As late as 1794 we have Herder praising our author as a "virtuoso of humanity," who had "signally influenced the best heads of the eighteenth century."[1] Such a reputation seems worth looking into.

[1] Cited by G. von Gizycki, *Die Philosophie Shaftesbury's*, 1876.

SHAFTESBURY'S CHARACTERISTICS

I

Anthony Ashley Cooper, third Earl of Shaftesbury, was born in London on February 26, 1671 (New Style). Connected by direct descent with the famous "Achitophel" of Dryden, who was his grandfather, he is associated in literary history no less closely with John Locke, who had been charged by the first earl to find a wife for his invalid son, and who acted thereafter as supervisor of the training of the seven children born of the marriage. Under Locke's eye and method, Anthony, the firstborn, was taught Greek and Latin, on the plan of conversation, by an accomplished woman, Elizabeth Birch, daughter of a schoolmaster. He had thus the rare fortune to be able to read both languages with ease at the age of eleven. Yet it was thought fit to send him to the Winchester public school at that age, presumably by way of toughening him for practical life. Professor Fowler, his most thorough biographer, has seen a letter in which, at the age of nineteen, he gives a startling account of the ways of the school; and the biographer's conclusion is that "the English public-school education of those days probably left fewer traces of culture, and inspired boys less with the love of letters, than it does even in our own." Shaftesbury, however, had been well grounded under Locke; and three years (1686-89) spent in foreign travel added a perfect mastery of French to his skill in the classics, and gave him a love of the arts which solaced him till his death. On his return to England he gave nearly five years to quiet study.

It was not, however, to letters but to politics that he gave himself when he felt he had intellectually come of age In 1695 he entered Parliament as member for Poole; and in that

EDITOR'S INTRODUCTION

year he—he and not the Earl of Halifax, of whom the story is sometimes told—made the often-cited stroke of advocacy for the Bill which provided that men indicted on charges of treason should be allowed the use of counsel. Finding himself at a loss for words, he had yet presence of mind enough to say: "If I, sir, who rise only to speak my opinion on the Bill now depending, am so confounded that I am unable to express the least of what I proposed to say; what must the condition of the man be who is pleading for his life without any assistance, and under apprehensions of being deprived of it?"[1] The Bill passed; but Shaftesbury did not often so conciliate the House. It was then in one of its most factious periods; and Shaftesbury's hereditary Whiggism and personal independence were not to the taste of either side. In any case, his health soon worsened to a degree that forced him to give up his seat after the dissolution of 1698. His malady was Locke's—asthma, to which London smoke then, as later, was peculiarly deadly; and to relieve it he spent a year in Holland, returning to England at the end of 1699, when, on his father's death, he succeeded to the title. Macaulay, in his specific manner, asserts that after leaving the Commons Shaftesbury "gave himself up to mere intellectual luxury." As a matter of fact he exerted himself so greatly on the Whig side in the two elections of 1701 as to receive the special thanks of the king, with repeated offers of high office; and though he declined these, it was only the complete change of men and measures at the accession of Anne that drove him back into private

---

[1] Macaulay (ch. xxi.) gives a much more elaborate version of the appeal. If it had been worded as he gives it, it would justify his suspicion that the whole episode was premeditated. But his version is plainly a composition of a later date. That in the text is the report authorised by Shaftesbury's son.

life. Even thereafter, his letters show him constantly and deeply interested in current politics, though he became ere long a confirmed invalid.[1]

It was in this state of health that he at length addressed himself to deliberate authorship, and to no less deliberate marriage. Those of his letters unwarrantably published by Toland show him desirous of marrying, in 1708, the daughter of a certain rich "old lord," who (the father, that is,) would not take a favourable view of him or his suit, though he was willing to forego a dowry. One plan failing, he formed another, and in 1709 married Miss Jane Ewer, a distant family connection, with very little fortune. Ten years earlier he seems to have put aside the suggestion of Locke, that he should propose to a certain young lady with a fortune of £20,000. In private life he cared above all things for quiet happiness, and he seems to have found it, as he humorously testifies to his friend Molesworth that after marriage he finds himself "as happy a man now as ever."

In 1708 had been published his anonymous *Letter Concerning Enthusiasm*, which had the distinction of speedily eliciting three angry replies, each bulkier than his pamphlet—one being twice its size. His only previous venture had been an edition in 1698 of some sermons of the Cambridge Latitudinarian, Dr. Whichcote, to which he put a laudatory preface. In 1699 Toland had published without his permission his remarkably precocious *Inquiry Concerning Virtue or Merit*, in some respects his most weighty performance; but not till he had put his ethical doctrine afresh, with a lighter and more unsystematic

---

[1] In June 1703 he writes of "my health, which I have mightily impaired by my fatigues in the public affairs these last three years" (*Original Letters of Locke, Sidney, and Shaftesbury*, ed. by T. Forster, 1830, p. 198).

EDITOR'S INTRODUCTION

touch, in his *Essay on the Freedom of Wit and Humour* and his *Moralists*, both published in 1709, and produced his *Advice to an Author* (1710), did he proceed to publish the revised version of his early treatise with the others.

It was in 1711 that he put forth his collected essays as *Characteristicks of Men, Manners, Opinions, Times*, including among them the *Inquiry*, and adding, as third volume, *Miscellaneous Reflections on the preceding Treatises, and other Critical Subjects*. It may be surmised that the *Moralists*, the *Wit and Humour*, and the *Advice to an Author*, or some of them, had been begun before 1708; and that his industry from that year onwards was motived partly by his success, partly by his consciousness of rapidly failing strength, and the need to husband time. Only two more years were left him. In July 1711 he set out for the warmer clime of Italy; and there, at Naples, he died early in 1713, barely forty-two years old.[1] His last literary labours were the careful revision of his *Characteristics* and the writing of two essays in aesthetics, a *Letter on Design*, and a *Notion of the Historical Draught or Tablature of the Judgment of Hercules*; with some note-making for a general essay on the arts.

II

Of this short literary career the success was rapid and far-reaching. It was hardly an exaggeration in 1733 to say, as did the preface to the pocket-edition of that year, that "all

---

[1] Various errors are current as to the above dates. I have been elsewhere misled by a standard authority which gives 1711 as the year of Shaftesbury's death; the editions of 1733 and 1737 (and presumably others) describe the *Miscellaneous Reflections* as having been first printed in 1714; Mr. Hatch's edition represents the whole collection as first appearing in 1713; and Dr. Gideon Spicker in his work on Shaftesbury dates it 1709.

the best judges are agreed that we never had any work in the English language so beautiful, so delightful, and so instructive as these *Characteristicks*." On the title-page of a clerical *Cure of Deism*, published in 1736, Shaftesbury and Tindal figure as "the two Oracles of Deism"; and this was perhaps the high-water period of the Deistic agitation. Nor was it only a popular acceptance that was thus indicated: the praise of Leibnitz had reached the Earl before his death; Hutcheson, the most considerable philosopher between Berkeley and Hume, was his professed champion, and declared that his writings "will be esteemed while any reflection remains among men";[1] while Mandeville, Berkeley, and Butler testified to his importance in criticising him. Abroad, his status was equally high. The *Essay on the Freedom of Wit and Humour*, issued in 1709, was translated into French before 1713; a German translation of the essays was begun in 1738; Diderot, then in his first Deistic stage, issued his adaptation of the *Inquiry Concerning Virtue and Merit* in 1745; Montesquieu panegyrised him as we have seen; a complete French translation of his works and Letters appeared at Geneva in 1769; and a complete German translation of the *Characteristics* in 1776-79. By that time, Shaftesbury's form of optimism had even carried the day in Germany over that of Leibnitz,[2] who had admitted its measure of congruity with his own; and there are clear traces of his influence in both the ethics and the aesthetics of Kant.[3] As regarded his general vogue, the facts that his philosophy was the basis of

[1] Preface to the later editions of *An Inquiry into the Original of our Ideas of Beauty and Virtue*. The passage is not in the first edition (1725).
[2] Cp. Lange, *History of Materialism*, Eng. tr. ii. 146, 147.
[3] Zart, *Einfluss der englischen Philosophen seit Bacon auf die deutsche Philosophie des 18ten Jahrhunderts*, 1881, S. 219, 231. Kant, of course, never committed himself to optimism.

EDITOR'S INTRODUCTION

Bolingbroke's, and therefore of Pope's *Essay on Man*, and that at least eleven English editions of his book (the last appearing at Basel) had been produced by the year 1790, may be taken to signify that he held a classic standing before the beginning of the reaction against the French Revolution, in which so many popularities were undone. The publication of Brown's *Essays on the Characteristics* in 1751 was a proof that forty years after publication they were reckoned dangerously influential; and the prompt production of three replies to Brown testified to the rightness of his estimate of Shaftesbury's vogue.

The decay of this reputation in the present century has been ascribed by one critic alternately to the unattractiveness of Shaftesbury's style and to the inconclusiveness of his thinking; as if profundity conferred popularity, or charm of style philosophic influence. Certainly the fashion of style has changed since Shaftesbury's passed as specially delightful. Its main defect is that which differences it so entirely from Montaigne's, its constant preoccupation with the labour of being at ease. Lamb has done it a certain injustice in calling it "genteel"; for though Shaftesbury seeks to "regulate his style or language by the standard of good company, and people of the better sort,"[1] he is really concerned less to be superior than to seem natural; and when he is fairly judged he must be admitted to have substantially reached his aim. Yet, withal, his very conception of the natural had a certain gentility; so that, though his prose is really not inferior to Addison's, with which it is so often contrasted by way of condemnation, it is inferior in both energy and ease to Dryden's, which lay to his hand as a model. Addison is indeed more transparent, but only because he is so much shallower. Something depends on the depth of

[1] *Advice to an Author*, part i. § 1.

what a man has to say. What deprives Shaftesbury of litheness and large-limbed vigour as a writer is his derivative ideal of propriety, which perhaps correlates with his invalidism; though on the other hand it goes by the ruling standards of his age. A generation before, Dryden's own gift, no less than the heritage of spacious and imaginative prose which still remained to compensate Englishmen for the loss of great dramatic verse, had availed to reveal to him, after Rapin and Rymer had done their worst, the supremacy of Shakspere and the doom of the classic French tragedy, as well as to preserve stride and stature in his own prose. But the *âme damnée* of James II., the Romanist pervert, and the venomous assailant of the first Shaftesbury, was nearly the last man to whom the accomplished and scholarly third Earl, Whig of the Whigs, was likely to look for either example or instruction.[1] In these matters Locke could not guide his pupil, and he formed his taste on the French critics of the periwig period, reading the classics partly through their spectacles.

Thus we find him praising the Elizabethans and Milton at most for their choice of blank verse and their ethical quality, finding Shakspere devoid of grace, finish, polish, and ornament, but a good moral teacher so far as *Hamlet* went; and Milton as an artist no better—this after poor John Dennis had shot his bolt on the right side, and just before Addison took up Milton's cause in the *Spectator*. Shaftesbury, again, had enough of the fine gentleman in him to make him concerned to tell his readers[2] that he allowed the printer to sell as many copies of the book as he could for his own profit, the author taking no money;

---

[1] See the long note in the *Miscellaneous Reflections*, Misc. v. ch. ii., where Dryden is not unskilfully pilloried for some of his petulances.

[2] *Advice to an Author*, part iii. § 2.

and that his *Letter Concerning Enthusiasm* was really a private letter, which got into print by accident.[1] The punctilio about money survived in the peerage till Byron's day, so that we must not charge it specially to Shaftesbury; but the whole attitude smacks more of Beau Brummel than of Montaigne. And with all his lordship's severity on his professional fellow-authors for "aiming at a false sublime, with crowded simile and mixed metaphor (the hobby-horse and rattle of the Muses)," he could proceed in the next breath after that very protest to speak of the Elizabethans as having "happily *broken the ice* for those who are to follow them; and who, *treading in their footsteps*, may at leisure *polish our language*, lead our ear to finer pleasure, and find out the true rhythmus and harmonious numbers which alone can satisfy a just judgment and Muse-like apprehension"[2]—one of the most comprehensive mixtures of metaphor on record, and a tolerable specimen of crowded simile, if not of the false sublime.

Some of his canons of style, further, were pettily pedantic, and pedantically held. In his own carefully corrected copy of the *Characteristics*, now in the British Museum, he notes that a friend has suggested the substitution of a "though" for a "notwithstanding" at a place where such a change would create a succession of ten monosyllables, "an offence," he declares, "which I am resolved never to commit." In another page, finding he has actually committed it, he deliberately creates a tautology by way of cure, and the clause "for any one to take the chair who is not called to it" is made to run "neither called nor invited."[3] For once he seems to have been bowing to Dryden, who in the *Essay on Dramatic Poesy* derides a

---

[1] *Misc.* i. chs. ii. iii.; *Misc.* iv. ch. i.
[2] *Advice to an Author*, infra, p. 142.
[3] *Infra*, p. 53.

poetaster of his day as "creeping along with ten little words in every line." Dryden's judgment seems to have become canonical, since Pope in the *Essay on Criticism* repeats it:—

And ten low words oft creep in one dull line.

But that Dryden had no notion of forbidding every succession of ten monosyllables either in prose or in verse is clear from his own practice in the same *Essay*; for not only does he at times put ten successive monosyllables in his prose, but he renders thus a bad line of Ovid:—

Now all was sea, nor had that sea a shore;

and, as everybody will remember, he begins his translation of the *Aeneid* with the ten monosyllables—

Arms and the man I sing, who, forced by fate.

What he was condemning was the eking out of a verse with weak redundant particles, as "for," "to," "unto," to the entire loss of sonority and strength; and Pope had in view the same kind of thing. Categorically obeyed, the veto accepted by Shaftesbury would have quashed Shakspere's

> We are such stuff
> As dreams are made on, and our little life
> Is rounded with a sleep;

and Tennyson's

> Break, break, break,
> On thy cold gray stones, O Sea!

and

> When the dumb hour, clothed in black,
> Brings the dreams about my bed.

It is not thus that the great masters of speech are ruled:[1] and Shaftesbury's acceptance of such an arbitrary bondage in

---

[1] In Bacon's essay *Of Gardens* (par. 6) there is a sequence of twenty-four monosyllables.

EDITOR'S INTRODUCTION

style, while standing for "free thought" in all things, must be granted to take him out of the magistral rank. At times, as in the *Miscellaneous Reflections*, he is even dilettantist enough in his manner and matter to justify Professor Fowler's complaint that his tone becomes "falsetto."

All this however proves only that Shaftesbury is not a great or an impeccable artist: it does not amount to destroying his credit as a good writer. Before he was classed as a Deist, nobody seems to have denied that he wrote very well indeed. On the first appearance of the *Letter Concerning Enthusiasm* it was credited to Swift by all his friends; and Swift himself, believing it to be by his accomplished friend Hunter, pronounced it "very well writ."[1] This praise it certainly deserves. Though Shaftesbury can at times sink below Addison—who, however, was capable of chronic bad grammar as well as of much slipshod—he is normally above him in point of sheer vivacity and intension, to say nothing of his intellectual impact on a reader's sense. Even as critics the two men are pretty much on a par, since Addison's admiration of Milton was mainly based on religious sentiment, and was freely extended to the impossible Blackmore. And though Shaftesbury's elegant manipulation of his rapier often makes us wish for the clean cut and thrust of Hobbes's mightier blade, yet he can at times write, and that in criticism of Hobbes,[2] with a swift sureness and spontaneous power that the other could not excel, and that Addison could not approach.

---

[1] Forster's *Life of Swift*, p. 220.

[2] See the *Essay on the Freedom of Wit and Humour*, part iii. § 1, end. As regards the criticism there passed upon Hobbes, it should be remarked that he himself anticipates it in the admission (*Leviathan*, part i. ch. xiv) that religious fear "hath place in the nature of man before civil society"; and again (part ii. ch. xxx.) in the insistence that men must know before law the obligation to keep faith. But Hobbes never properly colligated his principles, and he is substantially open to Shaftesbury's attack. Temple

SHAFTESBURY'S CHARACTERISTICS

It was not literary imperfection, then, that lost the *Characteristics* their one-time credit. Rather their very literary art may have counted somewhat to that effect, since the students to whom finally Shaftesbury's audience was restricted would be apt to be impatient with his gentlemanlike discursiveness and want of visible method, in contrast with the businesslike progression of Locke. Nor can it well have been the logical insufficiency of his philosophy that lost him his status as a serious classic in the sense in which Locke may be said to have kept his; for Locke is at least as pervious to criticism. The explanation, however, though different from those above considered, is perhaps fully as simple. In any case it is properly to be reached by way of a view of his doctrine.

III

The *Letter Concerning Enthusiasm*, with which Shaftesbury began his few years of diligent authorship, gives clear clues to all the essentials of his thought, though it is properly a political pamphlet aiming at influencing immediate action. As we have seen, he was a highly-principled Whig, and as such he disliked at once the fanaticism of "enthusiasm" and the fanaticism which would forcibly suppress it. In the case of the "French prophets," both forces were at work; and though he did not anticipate any serious convulsion from their clash, he saw in their emergence an excellent opportunity for inculcating a counsel of perfection—a counsel which, as it happened, he must first have given to himself before passing it on. For as urbane

---

had already put the two sides of the case shrewdly enough in the phrase: "Nor do I know, if men are like sheep, why they need any government, or, if they are like wolves, how they can suffer it" (*Essay upon the Original and Nature of Government*, 1672; Works, ed. 1814, i. 9, 10).

EDITOR'S INTRODUCTION

as he is—to use one of his favourite idioms—in his plea for good-humour in all matters of religious discussion, it happens that he came to that view by way of self-discipline, having become aware in himself of "those defects of passion, those meannesses and imperfections which we acknowledge such in ourselves, which as good men we endeavour to be superior to, and which we find we every day conquer as we grow better." Serenity was the prescription of his early *Inquiry Concerning Virtue*; but he had not always fulfilled his ideal. In the first of his *Letters to a Student*, under date February 24, 1706-7, he is anything but good-humoured about the "enthusiasts" who, then as always, decried the "cold dead reasoning" which put them at a disadvantage; and on that score he warmly champions Locke, whom on other grounds he was later to criticise with some asperity. It was later in the same year that he wrote his plea for ridicule as the proper regimen for "enthusiasm," having in the interim doubtless found it the more comfortable frame of mind. As his Letter to Somers avows, we are all capable of some sort of "enthusiasm"; and as he elsewhere urges, the only safeguard against miscarriage is vigilant self-judgment. The very self-consciousness of the Letter might alone suggest the manner of its inception. It does not employ banter, but prescribes it: a man spontaneously given that way would have made the fun he recommended.

And that Shaftesbury went through a process of self-discipline in serenity as a part of his progress to (or in) a philosophy of optimism, may be gathered from one of his letters to his friend Molesworth, dated November 4, 1708:—

You may think me melancholy if you will. I own there was a time in public affairs when I really was; for, saving yourself, and perhaps one or two more (I speak the most) I had none that acted with me against the injustice and corruption of both parties: each of them enflamed against me, particularly one, because of my birth and principles; the other, because of my pretended apostasy, which was only adhering to those principles on which their party was founded. . . . But the days are long past since you and I were treated as Jacobites.

Yet even in the very year in which he published his Letter on Enthusiasm and his Essay on Wit and Humour we find him writing to his student *protégé* with extraordinary heat against Lucian as "a wretch who was truly the most profane and impious";[1] a deliverance so surprising as to make us feel afresh that the critic's leaning to humorous methods was a rather artificially cultivated mood with him.

Having declared, however, for ridicule as the proper protection for the State and the spirit against fanaticism, he must needs argue, as a consistent optimist, that there was nothing to be feared from the resort to such an instrument. It could check folly, but it could not hurt truth. Thus his humane prescription led him subtly into a position not tenable without paralogism; and he duly paralogised, albeit pleasantly, even making Aristotle say, what Aristotle never said, that ridicule is the test of truth. No right-thinking person, Shaftesbury goes on, can endure ridicule of the truth. But the right-thinking person, who thus admittedly apprehends the truth without the help of ridicule, has nothing to do with the case; since the business in hand is to enlighten the wrong-thinking, the enthusiast who takes error for truth. And as this person errs about what is truth, he can obviously err about the rightness of ridicule; so that for him it is no test; while the other man, in the terms of the case, does not need this test in particular.

[1] Letter of January 28, 1708-9.

EDITOR'S INTRODUCTION

Forty years later, "Estimate" Brown took much time and space to put some such refutation of the false formula into which Shaftesbury unwittingly expanded his very sensible counsel to the politicians of his day. In the criticism, the practical good wrought by Shaftesbury's challenge receives small recognition. The trouble was that by Brown's time the test of ridicule had come to be rather freely applied in directions where others than enthusiasts were disturbed by it. Voltaire was now in session. Brown was probably wrong in arguing that the ridicule of Aristophanes contributed to the death of Socrates—a question still discussed—but he was of course safe in saying that any doctrine whatever may be ridiculed by a qualified opponent, and that the worse may so be made to appear the better reason. Shaftesbury had indeed implied as much in the somewhat odd passage in which, while professing orthodoxy, he argued concerning the hostility of the Jews to Jesus that "had they but taken the fancy to act such puppet-shows in his contempt as at this hour the Papists are acting in his honour," they "might possibly have done our religion more harm than by all their other ways of severity." Paul, he proceeded to say, had fared ill at urbane and critical Athens. Believing Christians might be excused for inferring that a man who wrote thus, and who had previously urged that no right-thinking person could enjoy "ridicule wrong placed," was not a believer.

As to this there has been some forensic dispute, though his express compliments to Christianity as a "witty and good-natured religion" have not as a rule given satisfaction to the serious. Of his way of life it is told by his son that "whenever his health permitted, he was constant in attending the services of the Church of England, and received the Holy Communion regularly three or four times a year"; and in a letter to his brother he blessed Providence for a church "where zeal was not frenzy and enthusiasm; . . . religious discoveries not cant and unintelligible nonsense; but where a good and virtuous life . . . joined with a religious performance of all sacred duties and a conformity with the established rites, was enough to answer the highest character of religion." As Dr. Fowler says, "the language is not very fervid"; and one is moved to pronounce his lordship pious in a Pickwickian sense,[1] the more so when we have his own avowal as to the calculated way in which, after a youth of some outspokenness, he decided to alter his outward demeanour, without professing to have altered his opinions. In a letter to his brother under date January 19, 1701-2, printed by Mr. Hatch (App. II.), Shaftesbury gives a striking account of a visit he had received from a set of charlatan "enthusiasts," whom he specifies as "my old acquaintance Chrysogenes and Chrysogeneia his accomplished spouse," and a woman in Quaker's dress who accompanied them. Telling how he did his best to receive their vaticinations with respectful religious comment, he mentions that he asked his friend "if he thought this discourse any way strange in me, or if he judged of me now at this time by my character of early days and in the heat of youth,[2] when he first knew me, though even then he knew very well the awful impression I had of a Deity. And here I appealed to him concerning my much altered character

---

[1] Compare the cautiously ironical passage in the *Miscellaneous Reflections*, Misc. v. ch. iii., with what follows.

[2] Shaftesbury probably had leanings to Deism early instilled into him by his grandfather, of whom is first told, by Toland, the familiar story of the statesman's saying that all wise men are of one religion, the nature of which wise men never tell. Toland (*Clidophorus*, ch. xiii.) says he had the story from "a near relation to the old Lord Shaftesbury."

EDITOR'S INTRODUCTION

of late years, my greater deference to all things sacred, or that carried but the shadow of religion." It may be doubted whether such a declaration, could it have been read by Berkeley, would have induced him to withhold from its presumed application to Shaftesbury [1] his remark that "an infidel who sets up for the nicest honour shall, without the least grain of faith or religion, take any test, join in any act of worship, kneel, pray, receive the Sacrament, to serve an interest."[2] And yet, apart from the gratuitous implication of the last clause, Shaftesbury would in that case only be doing what Berkeley constantly and passionately called upon unbelievers to do. Again and again he urges on them the "usefulness" of Christianity, and the recklessness of any course which takes away existing moral motives and menaces. There is no reason to doubt that Shaftesbury in his conformities acted on some principle of giving a good example to "the vulgar"; and yet Berkeley is only the more exasperated.

Between the two men there is perhaps little to choose on the point of principle, since Berkeley implicitly justifies the subordination of truth to supposed public utility;[3] and on the point of temper and bearing the advantage is almost wholly with Shaftesbury, who does seem to have attained a due philosophic tranquillity, where Berkeley grows more and more embittered during some thirty years of strife with the new ideas. What he thought of the philosophy of his friend Pope's *Essay on Man*, which is in large part pure Shaftesbury,[4] filtered

---

[1] Professor Fowler is satisfied that all the insinuations at the outset of the third Dialogue of *The Minute Philosopher* were directed against Shaftesbury. This is probable, but not certain on the face of the composition.

[2] *Minute Philosopher*, Dial. iii. § 2.

[3] Cp. Dial. iii. end, and Dial. iv. § 4.

[4] This was noted by Voltaire (*Lettres sur les Anglais*, xxii.); but even

through Bolingbroke, is not recorded.¹ The first two epistles of the *Essay* appeared in 1732, the very year of the issue of the *Minute Philosopher;* and they brought upon Pope charges of pantheism and immorality. His rehabilitation at the hands of Warburton is a good illustration of the chances of opinion-making. Warburton, we are assured, on first reading the *Essay* declared that it taught rank atheism.² When the French academician Crousaz said the same thing, Warburton took Pope's side, declared that he spoke "truth uniformly throughout," and went about to prove as much in an elaborate com-

in Professor Ward's excellent edition of Pope the inspiration of the *Essay* is credited solely to Bolingbroke and Leibnitz, though Pope denied having ever read anything by Leibnitz, and Bolingbroke dismissed him with contempt, as chimerical and unintelligible (*Letter to Mr. Pope*, in volume with *Letter to Wyndham*, 1753, p. 476). Specific parallels between Shaftesbury and Pope are traced by Warton, *Essay on Pope*, 4th ed., ii. 64-66, 93-95, 97-98. But there are many others: compare, for instance, the thesis, "true self-love and social are the same," with the *Inquiry Concerning Virtue*, bk. i. part ii. § 2; bk. ii. part ii. § i.; the passage "Shall gravitation cease?" with Shaftesbury's "The central Powers . . . must not be controlled to . . . rescue from the precipice a puny animal" (*Moralists*, part i. § 3); and the passage—

> Opinion gilds with varying rays
> Those painted clouds that beautify our days,

with the engraving on the title-page of the later editions of the *Characteristics*, and its legend, πάντα ὑπόληψις—a thesis often returned to in the text. So general, indeed, is the parallel, that we must suppose Bolingbroke's silence on the subject to be due to the sharp political opposition between him and Shaftesbury in the war period, and to Shaftesbury's unanswerable indictment of his career in the *Characteristics* (see the *Miscellaneous Reflections*, Misc. iii. ch. ii., and editor's note).

¹ Warton (ii. 123, 124, 295) has an odd story, derived from Spence, to the effect that Berkeley persuaded Pope to omit from the *Essay* an address to Jesus Christ, on the score that "the Christian dispensation did not come within the compass of his plan"—the very circumstance, it might have been supposed, which to Berkeley would be most objectionable.

² Mr. Stephen's *Pope*, p. 178; Warton, ii. 125, citing Bishop Law.

EDITOR'S INTRODUCTION

mentary. Later, Pope told this precious champion that "to his knowledge the *Characteristics* had done more harm to revealed religion in England than all the works of infidelity put together";[1] and Warburton passed on to Brown the mission of confuting Shaftesbury. Finally, Pope, in reply to the complaint of the younger Racine that his *Essay* was Spinozistic and irreligious, wrote repudiating alike Spinoza and Leibnitz, and claiming to be on the side of Pascal and Fénelon.[2] Yet, even after Warburton demonstrated to him his orthodoxy, he had written his "Universal Prayer," which passed current as "The Deist's Prayer"; and it had contained at first a stanza asking whether any act could "offend great Nature's God which Nature's self inspires?" Compared with the prudent poet, the most untruthful man of his age, and the accommodating if blusterous bishop, the author of the *Characteristics*, whom they utilised and impeached, comes out fairly well for posterity, as a man and as a propagandist.

His course, however, involved distinct penalties. By putting forth an ethical philosophy which plainly impugned the reigning creed, and embroidering it with sarcasms against the priests thereof, he put himself in the position of owing his literary vogue to the vogue of heresy, and of losing it when that went out of fashion. To speak of him as unwarrantably indirect in his way of impugning the argument from miracles,[3] is to make unduly small account of the risks which in 1711 still attended any direct attack on the popular religion. Under the Blasphemy Law of 1697, the author of such an attack could be

---

[1] Chalmers' *Biog. Dict.*, art. on Brown, cited by Professor Fowler.

[2] Warton, ii. 121. The letter is dated 1742. Pascal, it may be noted, is copied in the lines of the *Essay* describing man as the "glory, jest, and riddle of the world"; but he would certainly have repudiated it as a whole. [3] So Professor Fowler, *Shaftesbury*, p. 121.

imprisoned; and in 1713 Anthony Collins actually found it expedient to fly to Holland during the storm aroused by his *Discourse of Freethinking*. Shaftesbury was quite direct enough to be instantly ranked with the unbelievers. He had indeed declared for a Church Establishment, on Harrington's ground that "'tis necessary a people should have a public leading in religion."[1] But Hobbes before him had failed to win by such a view any forgiveness for direct hostility to the intellectual claims of Churchmen; and Bolingbroke in the next generation was disowned by the Church he had politically championed, when, after his death, the views they knew him to hold on religion were by his directions put in print. It was a matter of ecclesiastical police. And as Shaftesbury and Bolingbroke among the older writers mainly represented the deistic position at the date of the French Revolution for English people of heterodox culture, they passed together from fashionable popularity to disgrace as soon as the upper classes realised that rationalism of every sort had begun to mean democracy. Shaftesbury in particular was notable as a rather pronounced Whig, though he did speak of monarchy with much complaisance. The *Characteristics* accordingly have not been reprinted in full from that day to this. The explanation is, broadly speaking, that when "free" views were again able to force a hearing, they were put by new writers in a current idiom, and in terms of the ideas accumulated during a hundred years of research. Relatively to modern philosophy, Shaftesbury is but a pioneer. But after two German monographs such as those of Spicker[2] and Gizycki[3] have been devoted to showing his im-

[1] *Letter Concerning Enthusiasm*, § 2.
[2] *Die Philosophie des Grafen Shaftesbury*, 1872.
[3] *Die Philosophie Shaftesbury's*, 1876.

portance in the line of progress of moral philosophy; and after two such culture-historians as Hettner and J. H. Fichte have pronounced him a most important writer, whom our century does ill to neglect; even if we smile at Dr. Spicker's unsmiling reminder [1] that it needed the Germans to teach us to appreciate Shakspere, it may be assumed that a knowledge of an English author of such repute will be generally admitted to be a part of a liberal English culture.

IV

We come now to a study of Shaftesbury's philosophy without any preoccupying concern as to why it first succeeded and then failed. As exhibiting a way of thought which prevailed widely in Europe throughout the eighteenth century, and affected even the orthodox theology which repelled it, the ethic and *Welt-Anschauung* of the following essays deserves undistracted attention. Put with much graceful reiteration throughout the *Characteristics*, it may be briefly stated thus:—

1. Not only is the world providentially ruled by a Mind; but that rule is as absolutely beneficent as in the nature of things it can be. Nothing in the universe is "ill," relatively to the whole, and everything is as it must be.[2]

2. The ruling Mind may be alternately conceived as the Soul of the universe and as a personality external to the universe.[3] Disbelief in such a Mind need not necessarily do

---

[1] Work cited, S. 53.

[2] *Inquiry Concerning Virtue*, bk. i. part i. § 2; part ii. § 1; part iii. § 3; *Moralists*, part i. §§ 2, 3; part ii. § 4; part iii. § 2; *Letter on Enthusiasm*, §§ 4, 5.

[3] Cp. *Moralists*, part iii. § 1; *Inquiry Concerning Virtue*, bk. i. part iii. § 3.

harm, but does no active good; right belief can do much good, and wrong belief much harm.[1]

3. The ruling Mind being absolutely beneficent, Benevolence is the proper frame of mind in Man, who is so constituted as to find happiness in all his benevolent affections and in all beneficent action, and misery in the contrary.[2] Delight in evil does exist, but is "unnatural."[3]

4. This being so, all cajolery and terrorism in religion are vicious and fallacious. God is to be loved without hope of reward or fear of punishment.[4] Immortality is likely enough; but future happiness is not to be held out as a bribe to right action when right action is in itself happiness; and future punishment is for the same reasons not to be held out as a menace, especially seeing that such considerations weaken the appeal of the natural moral interests, and that there is no virtue in doing right from fear. Yet the *strong* hope of future reward and *strong* fear of future punishment may lead men into habits out of which true virtue may grow; though a *weak* belief in a future state is again entirely injurious.[5]

5. While virtue is thus in every way natural to Man, there is an art or refinement in that as in other expressions of natural preference. Perfect virtue, then, is perfected taste in morals. "All Beauty is Truth"; "Beauty and Good are one and the same." Misconduct, accordingly, is bad taste in morals; and it is not surprising that ill-educated people err in ethics as in

[1] *Inquiry*, bk. i. part iii.
[2] *Inquiry*, bk. i. part ii. § 2; *Moralists*, part ii. § 1; *Essay on Wit and Humour*, part iii. § 1.
[3] *Inquiry*, bk. ii. part ii. § 3.
[4] *Inquiry*, bk. i. part iii. § 3; *Moralists*, part ii. § 3. *Letter on Enthusiasm*, § 5.
[5] *Inquiry*, bk. i. part iii. § 3; *Moralists*, part ii. § 3; *Essay on Wit and Humour*, part ii. §§ 3, 4.

EDITOR'S INTRODUCTION

aesthetics. To be good-humoured and truly cultivated is to be right in religion and in conduct, and consequently happy. To be malevolent or maleficent, in the same way, is to be miserable.[1]

Merely to state these articles of philosophic faith in context, of course, is to show their inconsistency. But we shall best appreciate their influence by remembering that they share that defect with all philosophies which have ever been popular, and by reflecting that the defect followed inevitably on their purpose as a reform of religious theory from within. If we ask why Shaftesbury in effect affirmed that "whatever is, is right," that the universe is beneficently controlled, and that man is naturally virtuous, while avowing that most things need rectifying, that the ruling Mind is normally misconceived by its creatures, and that bad taste in morals abounds, the first answer must be that Shaftesbury set out with some philosophic conclusions entailed on him by previous thought.

His critics and commentators in general have rather oddly overlooked the fact that his philosophy, as regards its bases, is drawn more or less directly from Spinoza. It is customary to point to *The Moralists* as the enunciation of his optimism that presumably influenced the *Theodicée* of Leibnitz, which appeared a year later; but the main positions of *The Moralists* are laid down in the *Inquiry Concerning Virtue*, and the whole argument of that essay is contained in the version published by Toland in 1699,[2] the later alterations being in the main

---

[1] *Wit and Humour*, part iii. § 4; part iv. §§ 1, 2; *Advice to an Author*, part iv. § 3; *Moralists*, part iii. § 2.

[2] Archbishop King's Latin essay on the *Origin of Evil*, to which Zart thinks Leibnitz owed more than to Shaftesbury (*Einfluss der englischen Philosophen seit Bacon auf die deutsche Philosophie des 18ten Jahrh.*, 1881, S. 15, 16), appeared in 1702.

mere improvements in style. Now, that Shaftesbury should at the age of eighteen have produced from his own meditations a finished and formal philosophical treatise, of which the theses were capable of influencing European thought for a century, would be an extravagant assumption. It is morally certain that his main ideas were given him; and as a matter of fact they are nearly all explicit or implicit in Spinoza, whose teaching Shaftesbury was sure to hear of in his sojourn in Holland in 1698, if he had not studied it before. That there can be nothing essentially evil in the universe as a whole; that sin and evil are "not positive"; that men cannot properly be said to sin against God; that blessedness is not the reward of virtue but the state of virtue; that acts done from fear of punishment are not virtuous; that benevolence involves happiness; that things which are evil relatively to us are to be borne with tranquillity, since nothing in the universe can be otherwise than it is; that angry passions constitute a state of misery—all these doctrines are to be found in Spinoza's *Ethics* or in his correspondence.[1] Some of them are also to be found, in less explicit form, in the *De Legibus Naturae* of Cumberland (1672), who like Shaftesbury oppugned Hobbes; some (with other favourite ideas of Shaftesbury's such as that of the beauty of virtue) in the ethic of the ancients — Platonic, Stoic, Epicurean; some in Charron and Locke. With some of these debts Shaftesbury was reproached by clerical assailants; but not one of them, I think, noted that he echoes the Book of Proverbs (xi. 17), and none of them seems to have known his

---

[1] Cp. the *Ethics*, part i. Prop. xvii., Coroll. and Schol.; Prop. xxxiii. and Scholia; Prop. xxxvi. and Appendix; part ii. Prop. xlix. Schol.; part v. Prop. xlii. Letters to Blyenbergh, Jan. and Feb. 1665 (Ep. 32, 34, 36, ed. Gfrörer).

EDITOR'S INTRODUCTION

relation to Spinoza, his chief forerunner.[1] It seems regrettable that he himself should never have avowed his chief sources; but as regards Cumberland he may have been unaware of his coincidences; and as regards Spinoza he probably had cause to apprehend being specially attacked as atheistic if he professed any agreement with the great Jew, since his *Inquiry* seems to have been actually so stigmatised.[2]

The ethical ideas thus variously traceable Shaftesbury puts formally but simply and lucidly in the *Inquiry*; and in the *Moralists* he develops them with that urbane strategy of exposition which he regarded as best ensuring attention and comprehension on the part of those whom he wished to reach. And the central inconsistency as well as the practical insufficiency of the scheme as a whole inheres in the great structure of Spinoza as well as in the lighter framework set up by Shaftesbury and the flimsy erection of Pope. Needless to add, Spinoza in his beginnings proceeds on Descartes; and Descartes in the very act of claiming to begin a philosophy without presuppositions had presupposed the idea of God. Thus the whole series of efforts to deal philosophically with the problem of evil were but revisions of the immemorial theological effort, with the problem still conceived as theology had put it,[3] and as it was envisaged ages ago in the drama of Job and his cold comforters.

---

[1] Some suggestions Shaftesbury may also have had from the *Enchiridion Ethicum* of Henry More, which he highly praises in one of his Letters to a Student (December 30, 1709); and it is to be noted that Hobbes himself, as against the passages (*e.g. Leviathan*, part i. ch. vi.) in which he seems to make moral distinctions arbitrary, expressly states their natural basis in social utility (part i. ch. xv. near end).

[2] See *The Moralists*, part ii. § 3.

[3] The direct passage of the problem from theological hands to those of Spinoza can be readily seen from the *Disputatio de Malo* of Robert Baronius, § 5 of part i. of his *Metaphysica Generalis*, described on its title-

SHAFTESBURY'S CHARACTERISTICS

For us to-day, the criticism of all alike is that the attempt to prove the essential rightness of an infinite universe as such is not so much fallacious as meaningless. As some of our discerning ancestors must have gathered from the battles of Irish bishops soon after Shaftesbury's day,[1] every expedition to reconcile "divine goodness" with earthly evil ends in trouble, for it has to be finally admitted that infinite goodness cannot be as human goodness; that is to say, that infinite goodness has no meaning for men. Thus every optimistic philosophy ends in verbally explaining to an uncomprehended infinitude, in terms of finite thought, the necessity of its infinite perfection from its own point of view: a laudably disinterested undertaking, but one which men might profitably forego in the pursuit of their own concerns.

Theory apart, the undertaking has this special bane, that inasmuch as any doctrine, to be held at all intelligently, must needs be construed with a meaning rather than as meaningless, the optimistic view of evil is always tending to paralyse ethics. Normally, no doubt, the theorem that evil is *non-ens*, that whatever is is right, that wrong is so only relatively to the finite, is held as a philosophic verbalism, out of touch with conduct.

page as *ad usum theologiae accommodata* (Leyden, 1657). The proposition as to the nonentity of evil was also taken over by Spinoza from Descartes: see the *Principia philos. Cartes.*, Pars i. Prop. xv. and Schol., and the *Cogitata Metaphysica*, Pars i. c. vi. Dr. Martineau, indeed (*Spinoza*, p. 56), finds that in this one case of the doctrine that evil is *non-ens* Spinoza may have been indebted to rabbinical philosophy—in particular to Maimonides. But for that matter the thesis is at least as old as Gregory of Nyssa, who anticipated St. Augustine in using it against the Manicheans; and it reappears clearly in the Pseudo-Dionysius; and again, long afterwards, in Giordano Bruno. (Ueberweg, Eng. tr. i. 330, 343, 351; ii. 27.)

[1] See Mr. Leslie Stephen's account of the feud of Bishops Browne and Berkeley, *English Thought in the Eighteenth Century*, i. 114-118. Archbishops King and Synge were implicated.

EDITOR'S INTRODUCTION

In the hands of Pope the insincerity of it becomes preposterous. Spinoza and Shaftesbury, like their predecessors, affirm in one breath the universal harmony of things, and in the next denounce the discords. In our own day, Mr. Browning has with unique vivacity repeated their procedure, reminding us in one set of poems, in the ancient fashion, that we who see only a minute fraction of the scheme of things have no right to an opinion; and in others darkly explaining how Deity "unmakes but to remake" its moral misfits. "It's better being good than bad," sings the poet, face to face with evil; going on to inform us that his "own hope is, a sun will pierce the thickest cloud earth ever stretched," and that what God blessed once cannot prove accurst. On that airy footing, perhaps, little harm is done to anything but the logical sense. But whether or not Mr. Browning ever made of his optimism a deafening medium between his sensibilities and

> the fierce confederate storm
> Of sorrow, barricadoed evermore
> Within the walls of cities,

there is always an even chance that the less sensitive will so employ the theorem.

In the case of Shaftesbury as in that of Pope, it is plain, the optimist and the moralist are always tending to neutralise each other. If partial ill be universal good, how shall the man who thinks so be zealous to alter any ill save, by reflex action, the pinching of his own shoe? If he be really concerned to mend human things, to what end does he insist that it is only from the ignorant human point of view that they need mending, and that a Benevolent First Cause has done all things well? For the mere comfort of resignation under ills that cannot be altered, such a moral price seems excessive, to say nothing of the philosophical vertigo involved. Haunted by the old dilemma, and hemmed in by the adversary, Mr. Gladstone in our own day took the prudent course of avowing that evil in general is a mystery, though like his teachers he could always salve any particular evil by the argument from finite ignorance. Two hundred years ago, in the first enchantment of naturalistic exploration, away from the theological close, the pioneering theists did not feel the need for reserves, else Shaftesbury and Pope had not had such an easy time of it in criticism.

We can but note, then, that Shaftesbury saddled his ethic with optimism on the pressure of his theistic presuppositions, and that he did his work winningly enough to satisfy the liberal majority for two or three generations. If he repelled Christians where Locke sought to conciliate them, on the other hand he seemed to Deists to give a new footing to theistic ethics by rejecting Locke's polemic against innate ideas as irrelevant,[1] inasmuch as moral ideas are none the less inevitably developed. It was his form of optimism, as we saw, that carried the day in the land of Leibnitz; he inspired the Deism of France, through Diderot and Voltaire; and it may well have been by lineal literary descent from him that Browning drew his creed; for we find it accepted, apparently from the *Characteristics*, by Priestley,[2] who passed it on to the Unitarian Cogan and to W. J. Fox, from whose preaching in South Place Chapel Browning would seem to have partly derived it.[3]

At the same time, the ethic of the *Characteristics*, considered apart from its theistic frame, was no less widely influential. The appearance of the book, says our historian of ethics, "marks

---

[1] See the *Letters to a Student*, under date June 3, 1709.
[2] *Essay on the First Principles of Government*, 2nd ed. 1771, pp. 257-261.
[3] Cp. Dr. Conway's *Centenary of the South Place Society*, 1894, pp. 80, 89.

EDITOR'S INTRODUCTION

a turning-point in the history of English ethical thought." "Shaftesbury is the first moralist who distinctly takes psychological experience as the basis of ethics. His suggestions were developed by Hutcheson into one of the most elaborate systems of moral philosophy which we possess; and through Hutcheson, if not directly, they indirectly influenced Hume's speculations. . . . Moreover, the substance of Shaftesbury's main arguments was adopted by Butler."[1] In this aspect, again, our author compels our critical attention.

V

The gist of Shaftesbury's doctrine of morals, later systematised by Hutcheson, lies in his claim that is self-evident "that in the very nature of things there must of necessity be the foundation of a wrong and a right taste, relish, or choice, as well in respect of inward characters and features as of outward person, behaviour, and action."[2] Its immediate controversial bearing lay in its relation to the ethics of Hobbes and Locke, of whom the former, though he did incidentally note clearly enough that moral law is an expression of a surmised social utility, was led by his reaction against rebellious fanaticism to place all moral authority in a political head; while the latter, rejecting political absolutism, placed the source of morals in the will or command of Deity. To force moral philosophy from these bases to that of human nature and rationally conceived utility was no small service; and this Shaftesbury virtually accomplished. The previous effort of Cumberland, who was in

[1] Sidgwick, *Outlines of the History of Ethics*, 3rd. ed. p. 190.
[2] *Advice to an Author*, part iii. § 3; *infra*, pp. 216, 217.

the main not only utilitarian but psychologically materialistic,[1] but who still made Deity a concurrent factor in morals, seems to have come to nothing, apparently for lack of adhesiveness of statement. His book, whether in the original Latin or in the English abridgment or complete translation, seems never to have been widely circulated; whereas Shaftesbury became instantly popular; and ever since his day, through the succession of Hutcheson, Butler, Hume, Smith, Bentham, Mill, and Spencer, the rationalistic view has held its ground in English thought. Even Brown's clerical criticism of the *Characteristics* expressly aimed at putting a thorough in place of an imperfect utilitarianism.

Imperfections apart, Shaftesbury's teaching broadly promoted rational morals, not only against the political and theological forms of dogmatism, but against the anarchism which they had generated. Locke's dogma that rightness and wrongness depend on God's will, left small theistic standing-ground against his own demonstration that all moral ideas are acquired, and vary accordingly. As Hutcheson remarked, "Nothing is more ordinary among those who after Mr. Locke have shaken off the groundless opinions about innate ideas, than to allege that all our relish for beauty and order is either from advantage, or custom, or education;"[2] and the argument as to morals was on all fours. Mandeville made it classic; but Shaftesbury's remarks[3] show that it was popular before Mandeville published the prose commentary on his *Fable of*

---

[1] See the account of his doctrine by Whewell, *Lectures on Moral Philosophy*, ed. 1862, pp. 75-83.

[2] *Inquiry into the Original of our Ideas of Beauty and Virtue*, 1st. ed. pp. 73, 74.

[3] *Inquiry*, bk. ii. part ii. § 1; *Wit and Humour*, part ii. § 2; part iii. § 3; *Advice to an Author*, part iii. § 3.

EDITOR'S INTRODUCTION

the Bees. Against that Nihilistic line of attack Shaftesbury's defence would have been distinctly stronger if, instead of affirming the infinite rightness of things and loosely attaching to that concept the further formula that the infinite order is absolute beauty, to which it is our business to approximate, he had squarely put it that the relations involved in ethics *are* subjectively variable, like those involved in aesthetics. Moral opinions clearly enough root in the nature of things; they therefore vary with all variations and developments in human relations. As Brown irreligiously put it, right or beautiful actions "have not any absolute and independent but a relative and reflected beauty."[1] And as Shaftesbury himself admitted the greater need for self-study and criticism in morals than in aesthetics, he should in just sequence have proceeded to teach that the right adjustment of human relations all round is a matter of endless and anxious calculation. This much he might have recognised even without the light of that concept of evolution which prepares us to find in men an endless diversity of adaptation to social conditions, from the best to the worst. As it was, he gave a standing-ground against moral anarchism; but his optimism put his adherents very much at their ease in Zion, and left not a little logical room for the play of the dogmatisms which avowedly recognised the difficulties he ignored. Life was too plainly a less simple matter than he made it out.

Two criticisms typify the resistance against which Shaftesbury failed to provide. Mandeville in his grimly humorous way pointed to the enormous force of egoism in human affairs, and in effect decided for the theoretic solution of Hobbes. Brown, while sharply repugning Mandeville, whose humour he

[1] *Essays on the 'Characteristics,'* 1751, p. 136.

appreciated as little as he did Shaftesbury's, dwelt equally with him on the stress of evil, and theologically insisted on the necessity of a hope of reward and fear of future punishment as a restraint on human action, declaring such a belief to be "the essence of religion."[1] Such theological utilitarianism, dignified by Butler and confused by Paley, became the ruling English orthodoxy. The upshot was that while Shaftesbury was in favour with leisured and irresponsible men of rational culture, the semi-pessimism of the cynic and of the theologian held its ground with the majority,—all the more easily because Shaftesbury himself allowed that "the mere vulgar of mankind often stand in need of such a rectifying object as the gallows before their eyes."[2] Between Mandevillism and the Church, despite the revulsion of many, there grew up a curious sympathy. It is indeed a mistake to take seriously, as does Professor Fowler, the closing sentence of Mandeville's book, in which, with a sardonic humour all his own, he speaks of Shaftesbury as designing "to establish heathen virtue on the ruins of Christianity." There was certainly small serious concern for Christianity in the author of the *Fable of the Bees*. None the less there arose, as Henry Crabb Robinson wrote to Schlosser, a "sneaking kindness" towards Mandeville on the part of Churchmen,[3] who felt that if he did not believe in them he at least damaged their adversary, the optimistic pantheist.[4] The

---

[1] *Essays*, p. 210.
[2] *Essay on the Freedom of Wit and Humour*, part iii. § 4, end.
[3] Schlosser, *History of the Eighteenth Century*, Eng. tr. ii. 51, note.
[4] Mandeville observed that no two systems could be more opposed than his and Shaftesbury's. Yet there is a point of concurrence, at which Shaftesbury's is left undeveloped. In general he argued for the pleasurableness of virtue, where Mandeville founded on the old Christian doctrine that there is no virtue without self-sacrifice. In the *Inquiry*, however, Shaftesbury expressly admits that there is more virtue in governing a bad

EDITOR'S INTRODUCTION

due subjection of "the vulgar," however, was sufficiently agreed upon all round, down till the last decade of the century, to make it possible for Shaftesburyan deists and pantheists to maintain themselves as good friends of the reigning order; and when that was suddenly and vehemently assailed they seem promptly to have joined the party of authority and repression.

VI

When all is said, however, Shaftesbury is found to leave to our own age the legacy of a rarely tolerant judgment, a deeply rational bias, and many a shrewd hint towards the understanding of that social evolution which his formula of optimism as a whole unduly glosed. He deserves, among other things, to rank as one of the very first of our sociologists; since ideas which afterwards seem fresh in Hume and Ferguson are to be found clearly enough set forth in his pages. Not only does he confute with masterly force the Hobbesian fallacy that a political compact first gives validity to moral obligations,[1] but he expresses in a singularly modern way the continuity and ubiquity of the associative principle in man, from the primordial herd onwards to societies within society.[2] While humorists and paradoxers of Mandeville's school were obscuring the truth by their exaggerations, witty or otherwise, he puts his finger accurately on the economic principle in religious evolution.[3] And though Mandeville on the whole did more for the analysis of con-

disposition than in following a good one (*Inquiry*, bk. i. part ii. § 4). "There seems," he confesses, "to be some kind of difficulty in the case."

[1] See the *Wit and Humour*, part iii. § 1; *infra*, pp. 73, 74.
[2] *Id.* part iii. § 2.
[3] *Miscellaneous Reflections*, Misc. ii. chs. i. ii.

temporary social problems, he rendered no better social service than did Shaftesbury in the *Letter Concerning Enthusiasm*, of which the paralogism did no harm, seeing that men always did and always will ridicule what they do not believe; while the practical plea for a literary and humorous instead of a physical and malignant inquisition into popular heresy was more persuasive and more practically effective than any other of that age, not even excepting Locke's. At a time when we are imprisoning the "Peculiar People" for doing without doctors for their children, it is still well worth reading. And at a time when "empire" is becoming once more a popular ideal in an advanced civilisation, it is no less worth while to read the arguments in the *Characteristics*[1] as to the affinity of the arts and sciences for the life of free states, and as to the diseases incident to overgrown ones.

Not that Shaftesbury was a sworn friend of peace. His faith in the rule of infinite goodness, and in the dependence of human happiness on the play of the benevolent affections, left him a very warm partisan of the war against Louis XIV.; and his last days seem to have been darkened by disappointment at the stop put to hostilities by the new Ministry. That "the fatal villainy of the priest Sacheveril, and the fall of the old Ministry and Whigs," should reduce a devout theistic optimist to serious dejection,[2] and that he should die full of a sense of "shame" over such a national "calamity" as the granting of an easy peace to a half-ruined enemy, are notable psychological facts. The onlooking mind craves a closer adjustment of philosophy to life, and grows more than ever doubtful of the

---

[1] *Advice to an Author*, part ii. §§ 1, 2; *Wit and Humour*, part ii. § 2.
[2] Letter to Furly, July 19, 1712, in T. Forster's vol. of *Original Letters of Locke, Sidney, and Shaftesbury*, 1830, p. 270.

EDITOR'S INTRODUCTION

value of optimistic theories of things. It is only fair, however, to remember that it was a dying man who thus desponded with his optimistic essays under his pillow; and for the rest, that throughout his life Shaftesbury had very well fulfilled his principle that happiness lies in the exercise of the benevolent affections. The student Michael Ainsworth, son of his butler, to whom he addressed the letters collected and published in 1716, was one of many beneficiaries of his. Among the others was the deist Toland, to whom he accorded a pension somewhat against his own bias, Toland's vivacious temperament being lacking in some of the merits he most appreciated.

It is this spirit of practical benevolence, finally, that best countervails the aesthetic shortcomings of Shaftesbury's aesthetic essays, the *Notion of the Historical Draught or Tablature of the Judgment of Hercules*, and the *Letter Concerning Design*. It is with regret that I dissent from Professor Fowler's verdict that these papers, which were incongruously included in the later editions of the *Characteristics*, show him to have had a good taste in the arts. They rather show him, I think, to have had no breadth of taste in architecture, since he despised St. Paul's as "Gothic," and to have held the typically Anglican view that painting is properly not a source of delight to the sense, but a vehicle of moral instruction. His aesthetic, as we have seen, was like his ethic Platonist and *a priori*; and when Baumgarten in the next generation began to lay the bases of a truly inductive aesthetic, he had to negate the principle on which Shaftesbury most insisted. Shaftesbury was in fact false to his own rules of *expertise*, for if he had consulted the trained tastes, those of the artists, not even in England would he have found them in accord with his. In the closing paragraph of the *Notion* he expressly insists that painting "has nothing more wide of its real aim, or more remote from its intention, than to make a show of colours, or from their mixture to raise a separate and flattering pleasure to the sense"; and though in a footnote he adds a possibly sounder plea that "it is always the best when the colours are most subdued," it is evident that he did not value a picture as a composition in colour, but as a fingerpost to right conduct. From that hopeless standpoint one turns with satisfaction to his appeal, in the *Letter Concerning Design*, for an inclusion of the whole people in the artistic culture that he hoped England would thenceforth develop. "In reality the people are no small parties in this cause. Nothing moves successfully without them. There can be no PUBLIC but where they are included." There spoke the man with a gift for morals, the "virtuoso of humanity," who advised authors to "add the wisdom of the heart to the task and exercise of the brain, in order to bring proportion and beauty into their works."[1]

And though the delicate copperplates of curious design which adorn the old octavo editions published after the author's death cannot be said to observe even his own relatively judicious stipulation that multiplicity of detail should never be allowed to perplex the eye in any design, yet their careful scrupulosity of symbolism and of execution has a certain coeval congruity with the text, while reminding us that that in turn carried in it so much more of new life. In an age of mostly restrictive and pedestrian artistic ideals, and of thinking that was apt to be splenetic when it was not commonplace, Shaftesbury rises, despite his aesthetic chains, to intellectual levels of serenity and sincerity where, though aliens and predecessors may transcend him, no English contemporary stands by his side—not the

[1] *Advice to an Author*, part ii. § 3; *infra*, p. 180.

EDITOR'S INTRODUCTION

exasperated Swift, nor the otherwise embittered Berkeley, who stand on cloudier heights; and not the esteemed Addison, whose ideas are to-day so entirely negligible. Given fair play, the *Characteristics* can still hold their own with most of the books with which they competed in their generation.

JOHN M. ROBERTSON.

CONTENTS

PREFACE 1

TREATISE I

A Letter concerning Enthusiasm to My Lord *****

Section	I	.	.	.	.	.	.	5
,,	II	.	.	.	.	.	.	9
,,	III	.	.	.	.	.	.	17
,,	IV	.	.	.	.	.	.	24
,,	V	.	.	.	.	.	.	28
,,	VI	.	.	.	.	.	.	31
,,	VII	.	.	.	.	.	.	37

TREATISE II

Sensus Communis; An Essay on the Freedom of Wit and Humour

Part	I.—Section	I	.	.	.	.	.	43
	,,	II	.	.	.	.	.	44
	,,	III	.	.	.	.	.	46
	,,	IV	.	.	.	.	.	48
	,,	V	.	.	.	.	.	51
	,,	VI	.	.	.	.	.	54

SHAFTESBURY'S CHARACTERISTICS

		PAGE
PART II.—Section	I	57
,,	II	63
,,	III	65
PART III.—Section	I	69
,,	II	74
,,	III	77
,,	IV	81
PART IV.—Section	I	85
,,	II	89
,,	III	94

TREATISE III

Soliloquy or Advice to an Author

PART I.—Section	I	103
,,	II	112
,,	III	124
PART II.—Section	I	137
,,	II	150
,,	III	170
PART III.—Section	I	182
,,	II	197
,,	III	212

TREATISE IV

An Inquiry concerning Virtue or Merit

BOOK I

PART I.—Section	I	237
,,	II	239

CONTENTS

		PAGE
PART II.—Section I	. . . . . .	243
,, II	. . . . . .	247
,, III	. . . . . .	251
,, IV	. . . . . .	255
PART III.—Section I	. . . . . .	258
,, II	. . . . . .	261
,, III	. . . . . .	265

BOOK II

PART I.—Section I	. . . . . .	280
,, II	. . . . . .	282
,, III	. . . . . .	285
PART II.—Section I	. . . . . .	293
,, II	. . . . . .	317
,, III	. . . . . .	330
CONCLUSION	. . . .	336

PREFACE

IF the Author of these united Tracts had been any friend to prefaces, he would probably have made his entrance after that manner, in one or other of the five treatises formerly published apart. But as to all prefatory or dedicatory discourse, he has told us his mind sufficiently in that treatise which he calls "Soliloquy." Being satisfied, however, that there are many persons who esteem these introductory pieces as very essential in the constitution of a work, he has thought fit, in behalf of his honest printer, to substitute these lines under the title of a Preface; and to declare "That (according to his best judgment and authority) these presents ought to pass, and be received, construed, and taken, as satisfactory in full, for all preliminary composition, dedication, direct or indirect application for favour to the public, or to any private patron or party whatsoever: nothing to the contrary appearing to him from the side of truth or reason." Witness his hand, this fifth day of December, 1710

A. A. C. A. N. A. Æ. C.
M. D. C. L. X. X. I.[1]

[1] [These initials presumably signify as follows:—"Anthony Ashley Cooper, Armiger, Natus Anno Aetatis Christi (*or* Aerae Christianae) 1671"—that being the year of his birth.]

TREATISE I

A LETTER
CONCERNING ENTHUSIASM

TO

MY LORD *****.

Ridentem dicere verum
Quid vetat?   Hor. *Sat.* I.

Printed first in the year MDCCVIII.

[* The name "Sommers" is added in the sixth edition, 1737.]

A LETTER CONCERNING ENTHUSIASM[1]

Sept. 1707.

MY LORD,

Now you are returned to . . ., and before the season comes which must engage you in the weightier matters of state, if you care to be entertained a while with a sort of idle thoughts, such as pretend only to amusement, and have no relation to business or affairs, you may cast your eye slightly on what you have before you; and if there be anything inviting, you may read it over at your leisure.

It has been an established custom for poets, at the entrance of their work, to address themselves to some muse: and this practice of the ancients has gained so much repute that even in our days we find it almost constantly imitated. I cannot but fancy, however, that this imitation, which passes so currently with other judgments, must at some time or other have stuck a little with your lordship, who is used to examine things by a

---

[1] [The words "enthusiasm" and "enthusiast" normally carried in the seventeenth and eighteenth centuries the significance of "fanaticism" and "fanatic," especially of the emotionally demonstrative kind. Churchmen and Deists alike disparaged all such manifestations. Compare Locke, *Essay*, bk. iv. ch. xix. § 7. Shaftesbury accepts the normal sense of the terms, but endeavours in this Letter and elsewhere to widen and elevate their application. Compare the end of the present Letter with the *Moralists*, part iii. § 2, and the *Miscellaneous Reflections*, Misc. ii. ch. i. Dr. Henry More had previously urged such a modification; but Shaftesbury appears to have given the first effective lead to the modern and commendatory use of the terms.]

better standard than that of fashion or the common taste. You must certainly have observed our poets under a remarkable constraint, when obliged to assume this character: and you have wondered, perhaps, why that air of enthusiasm, which sits so gracefully with an ancient, should be so spiritless and awkward in a modern. But as to this doubt, your lordship would have soon resolved yourself; and it could only serve to bring across you a reflection you have often made on many occasions besides, that truth is the most powerful thing in the world, since even fiction itself must be governed by it, and can only please by its resemblance. The appearance of reality is necessary to make any passion agreeably represented; and to be able to move others we must first be moved ourselves, or at least seem to be so, upon some probable grounds. Now what possibility is there that a modern, who is known never to have worshipped Apollo, or owned any such deity as the muses, should persuade us to enter into his pretended devotion and move us by his feigned zeal in a religion out of date? But as for the ancients, 'tis known they derived both their religion and polity from the muses' art. How natural therefore must it have appeared in any, but especially a poet of those times, to address himself in raptures of devotion to those acknowledged patronesses of wit and science? Here the poet might with probability feign an ecstasy, though he really felt none: and supposing it to have been mere affectation, it would look however like something natural, and could not fail of pleasing.

But perhaps, my lord, there was a further mystery in the case. Men, your lordship knows, are wonderfully happy in a faculty of deceiving themselves, whenever they set heartily about it· and a very small foundation of any passion will serve us, not only to act it well, but even to work ourselves into it beyond our own reach. Thus, by a little affectation in love-matters, and with the help of a romance or novel, a boy of fifteen, or a grave man of fifty, may be sure to grow a very natural coxcomb, and feel the *belle passion* in good earnest. A

ENTHUSIASM

man of tolerable good-nature, who happens to be a little piqued, may, by improving his resentment, become a very fury for revenge. Even a good Christian, who would needs be over-good, and thinks he can never believe enough, may, by a small inclination well improved, extend his faith so largely as to comprehend in it not only all scriptural and traditional miracles, but a solid system of old wives' stories. Were it needful, I could put your lordship in mind of an eminent, learned, and truly Christian prelate you once knew,[1] who could have given you a full account of his belief in fairies. And this, methinks, may serve to make appear how far an ancient poet's faith might possibly have been raised together with his imagination.

But we Christians, who have such ample faith ourselves, will allow nothing to poor heathens. They must be infidels in every sense. We will not allow them to believe so much as their own religion; which, we cry, is too absurd to have been credited by any besides the mere vulgar. But if a reverend Christian prelate may be so great a volunteer in faith, as beyond the ordinary prescription of the catholic church to believe in fairies, why may not a heathen poet, in the ordinary way of his religion, be allowed to believe in muses? For these, your lordship knows, were so many divine persons in the heathen creed, and were essential in their system of theology. The goddesses had their temples and worship, the same as the other deities: and to disbelieve the *Holy Nine*, or their Apollo, was the same as to deny Jove himself, and must have been esteemed equally profane and atheistical by the generality of sober men. Now what a mighty advantage must it have been to an ancient poet to be thus orthodox, and by the help of his education, and a good-will into the bargain, to work himself up to the belief of a divine presence and heavenly inspiration? It was never surely the business of poets in those days to call *revelation* in

[1] Dr. Edward Fowler, Bishop of Gloucester. [Note to ed. of 1733. One of the replies to the Letter deals excitedly with this passage, and is plausibly ascribed to Bishop Fowler.]

question, when it evidently made so well for their art. On the contrary, they could not fail to animate their faith as much as possible; when by a single act of it, well enforced, they could raise themselves into such angelical company.

How much the imagination of such a presence must exalt a genius we may observe merely from the influence which an ordinary presence has over men. Our modern wits are more or less raised by the opinion they have of their company, and the idea they form to themselves of the persons to whom they make their addresses. A common actor of the stage will inform us how much a full audience of the better sort exalts him above the common pitch. And you, my lord, who are the noblest actor, and of the noblest part assigned to any mortal on this earthly stage, when you are acting for liberty and mankind;[1] does not the public presence, that of your friends, and the well-wishers to your cause, add something to your thought and genius? Or is that sublime of reason, and that power of eloquence, which you discover in public, no more than what you are equally master of in private, and can command at any time, alone, or with indifferent company, or in any easy or cool hour? This indeed were more godlike; but ordinary humanity, I think, reaches not so high.

For my own part, my lord, I have really so much need of some considerable presence or company to raise my thoughts on any occasion, that when alone I must endeavour by strength of fancy to supply this want; and in default of a muse, must inquire out some great man of a more than ordinary genius, whose imagined presence may inspire me with more than what

[1] [The high eulogy here passed on Somers was not overstrained, according to the literary standards of the time. Addison dedicated to him the *Spectator* in nearly as high a strain; and Swift's humorous dedication of the *Tale of a Tub* goes as far; though on changing parties Swift changed his tone. The detailed estimate in Macaulay's twentieth chapter substantially bears out all these panegyrics on the great Whig statesman. In religion he seems to have been nearly if not quite as advanced as Shaftesbury, for whom he had a great regard.]

ENTHUSIASM

I feel at ordinary hours. And thus, my lord, have I chosen to address myself to your lordship; though without subscribing my name: allowing you as a stranger the full liberty of reading no more than what you may have a fancy for; but reserving to myself the privilege of imagining you read all, with particular notice, as a friend, and one whom I may justifiably treat with the intimacy and freedom which follows.

Section II

If the knowing well how to expose any infirmity or vice were a sufficient security for the virtue which is contrary, how excellent an age might we be presumed to live in! Never was there in our nation a time known when folly and extravagance of every kind were more sharply inspected, or more wittily ridiculed. And one might hope, at least from this good symptom, that our age was in no declining state; since whatever our distempers are, we stand so well affected to our remedies. To bear the being told of faults is in private persons the best token of amendment. 'Tis seldom that a public is thus disposed. For where jealousy of state, or the ill lives of the great people, or any other cause, is powerful enough to restrain the freedom of censure in any part, it in effect destroys the benefit of it in the whole. There can be no impartial and free censure of manners where any peculiar custom or national opinion is set apart, and not only exempted from criticism, but even flattered with the highest art. 'Tis only in a free nation, such as ours, that imposture has no privilege; and that neither the credit of a court, the power of a nobility, nor the awfulness of a Church can give her protection, or hinder her from being arraigned in every shape and appearance. 'Tis true, this liberty may seem to run too far. We may perhaps be said to make ill use of it. So every one will say, when he himself is touched, and his opinion freely examined. But who shall be judge of what may be freely examined and what may not? Where liberty may be used and where it may not? What remedy shall we prescribe to this in general? Can there be a better than from that liberty itself which is complained of? If men are vicious, petulant, or abusive, the magistrate may correct them: but if they reason ill, 'tis reason still must teach them to do better. Justness of thought and style, refinement in manners, good breeding, and politeness of every kind can come only from the trial and experience of what is best. Let but the search go freely on, and the right measure of everything will soon be found. Whatever humour has got the start, if it be unnatural, it cannot hold; and the ridicule, if ill-placed at first, will certainly fall at last where it deserves.

I have often wondered to see men of sense so mightily alarmed at the approach of anything like ridicule on certain subjects; as if they mistrusted their own judgment. For what ridicule can lie against reason? or how can any one of the least justness of thought endure a ridicule wrong placed? Nothing is more ridiculous than this itself. The vulgar, indeed, may swallow any sordid jest, any mere drollery or buffoonery; but it must be a finer and truer wit which takes with the men of sense and breeding. How comes it to pass, then, that we appear such cowards in reasoning, and are so afraid to stand the test of ridicule? O! say we, the subjects are too grave. Perhaps so: but let us see first whether they are really grave or no: for in the manner we may conceive them they may, peradventure, be very grave and weighty in our imagination, but very ridiculous and impertinent in their own nature. *Gravity* is of the very essence of imposture. It does not only make us mistake other things, but is apt perpetually almost to mistake itself. For even in common behaviour, how hard is it for the grave character to keep long out of the limits of the formal one? We can never be too grave, if we can be assured we are really what we suppose. And we can never too much honour or revere anything for grave, if we are assured the thing is grave, as we apprehend it. The main point is to know

ENTHUSIASM

always true gravity from the false: and this can only be by carrying the rule constantly with us, and freely applying it not only to the things about us, but to ourselves; for if unhappily we lose the measure in ourselves, we shall soon lose it in everything besides. Now what rule or measure is there in the world, except in the considering of the real temper of things, to find which are truly serious and which ridiculous? And how can this be done, unless by applying the ridicule, to see whether it will bear? But if we fear to apply this rule in anything, what security can we have against the imposture of formality in all things? We have allowed ourselves to be formalists in one point; and the same formality may rule us as it pleases in all other.

'Tis not in every disposition that we are capacitated to judge of things. We must beforehand judge of our own temper, and accordingly of other things which fall under our judgment. But we must never more pretend to judge of things, or of our own temper in judging them, when we have given up our preliminary right of judgment, and under a presumption of gravity have allowed ourselves to be most ridiculous and to admire profoundly the most ridiculous things in nature, at least for aught we know. For having resolved never to try, we can never be sure.

> Ridiculum acri
> Fortius et melius magnas plerumque secat res.[1]

This, my lord, I may safely aver, is so true in itself, and so well known for truth by the cunning formalists of the age, that they can better bear to have their impostures railed at, with all the bitterness and vehemence imaginable, than to have them touched ever so gently in this other way. They know very well, that as modes and fashions, so opinions, though ever so ridiculous, are kept up by solemnity; and that those formal notions,

---

[1] ["A jest often decides weighty matters better and more forcibly than can asperity."—Hor. *Sat.* I. x. 14, 15.]

which grew up probably in an ill mood and have been conceived in sober sadness, are never to be removed but in a sober kind of cheerfulness, and by a more easy and pleasant way of thought. There is a melancholy which accompanies all enthusiasm. Be it love or religion (for there are enthusiasms in both) nothing can put a stop to the growing mischief of either, till the melancholy be removed and the mind at liberty to hear what can be said against the ridiculousness of an extreme in either way.

It was heretofore the wisdom of some wise nations to let people be fools as much as they pleased, and never to punish seriously what deserved only to be laughed at, and was, after all, best cured by that innocent remedy. There are certain humours in mankind which of necessity must have vent. The human mind and body are both of them naturally subject to commotions: and as there are strange ferments in the blood, which in many bodies occasion an extraordinary discharge; so in reason, too, there are heterogeneous particles which must be thrown off by fermentation. Should physicians endeavour absolutely to allay those ferments of the body, and strike in the humours which discover themselves in such eruptions, they might, instead of making a cure, bid fair perhaps to raise a plague, and turn a spring-ague or an autumn-surfeit into an epidemical malignant fever. They are certainly as ill physicians in the body-politic who would needs be tampering with these mental eruptions; and under the specious pretence of healing this itch of superstition, and saving souls from the contagion of enthusiasm, should set all nature in an uproar, and turn a few innocent carbuncles into an inflammation and mortal gangrene.

We read[1] in history that Pan, when he accompanied Bacchus in an expedition to the Indies, found means to strike a terror through a host of enemies by the help of a small company, whose clamours he managed to good advantage among the echoing rocks and caverns of a woody vale. The hoarse bellowing of the caves, joined to the hideous aspect of such dark and

[1] Polyaeni *Strateg.* i. 2.

ENTHUSIASM

desert places, raised such a horror in the enemy, that in this state their imagination helped them to hear voices, and doubtless to see forms too, which were more than human: whilst the uncertainty of what they feared made their fear yet greater, and spread it faster by implicit looks than any narration could convey it. And this was what in after-times men called a *panic*. The story indeed gives a good hint of the nature of this passion, which can hardly be without some mixture of enthusiasm and horrors of a superstitious kind.

One may with good reason call every passion panic which is raised in a multitude and conveyed by aspect or, as it were, by contact of sympathy. Thus popular fury may be called panic when the rage of the people, as we have sometimes known, has put them beyond themselves; especially where religion has had to do. And in this state their very looks are infectious. The fury flies from face to face; and the disease is no sooner seen than caught. They who in a better situation of mind have beheld a multitude under the power of this passion, have owned that they saw in the countenances of men something more ghastly and terrible than at other times is expressed on the most passionate occasion. Such force has society in ill as well as in good passions: and so much stronger any affection is for being social and communicative.

Thus, my lord, there are many panics in mankind besides merely that of fear. And thus is religion also panic; when enthusiasm of any kind gets up, as oft, on melancholy occasions, it will. For vapours naturally rise; and in bad times especially, when the spirits of men are low, as either in public calamities, or during the unwholesomeness of air or diet, or when convulsions happen in nature, storms, earthquakes, or other amazing prodigies: at this season the panic must needs run high, and the magistrate of necessity give way to it. For to apply a serious remedy, and bring the sword, or *fasces*, as a cure, must make the case more melancholy, and increase the very cause of the distemper. To forbid men's natural fears, and to endeavour the overpowering them by other fears, must needs be a most unnatural method. The magistrate, if he be any artist, should have a gentler hand; and instead of caustics, incisions, and amputations, should be using the softest balms; and with a kind sympathy entering into the concern of the people; and taking, as it were, their passion upon him should, when he has soothed and satisfied it, endeavour, by cheerful ways, to divert and heal it.

This was ancient policy: and hence (as a notable author[1] of our nation expresses it) 'tis necessary a people should have a *public leading* in religion. For to deny the magistrate a worship, or take away a national church, is as mere enthusiasm as the notion which sets up persecution. For why should there not be public walks as well as private gardens? Why not public libraries as well as private education and home-tutors? But to prescribe bounds to fancy and speculation, to regulate men's apprehensions and religious beliefs or fears, to suppress by violence the natural passion of enthusiasm, or to endeavour to ascertain it, or reduce it to one species, or bring it under any one modification, is in truth no better sense, nor deserves a better character, than what the comedian declares of the like project in the affair of love—

> Nihilo plus agas
> Quam si des operam ut cum ratione insanias.[2]

Not only the visionaries and enthusiasts of all kinds were tolerated, your lordship knows, by the ancients; but, on the other side, philosophy had as free a course, and was permitted as a balance against superstition. And whilst some sects, such as the Pythagorean and latter Platonic, joined in with the superstition and enthusiasm of the times; the Epicurean, the Academic, and others, were allowed to use all the force of wit

---

[1] Harrington.

[2] ["You will manage it no better than if you undertook to be rationally insane."—Terence, *Eunuchus*, Act i. Sc. 1.]

and raillery against it. And thus matters were happily balanced; reason had fair play; learning and science flourished. Wonderful was the harmony and temper which arose from all these contrarieties. Thus superstition and enthusiasm were mildly treated, and being let alone they never raged to that degree as to occasion bloodshed, wars, persecutions, and devastation in the world. But a new sort of policy, which extends itself to another world and considers the future lives and happiness of men rather than the present, has made us leap the bounds of natural humanity; and out of a supernatural charity has taught us the way of plaguing one another most devoutly. It has raised an antipathy which no temporal interest could ever do; and entailed upon us a mutual hatred to all eternity. And now uniformity in opinion (a hopeful project!) is looked on as the only expedient against this evil. The saving of souls is now the heroic passion of exalted spirits; and is become in a manner the chief care of the magistrate, and the very end of government itself.

If magistracy should vouchsafe to interpose thus much in other sciences, I am afraid we should have as bad logic, as bad mathematics, and in every kind as bad philosophy, as we often have divinity, in countries where a precise orthodoxy is settled by law. 'Tis a hard matter for a government to settle wit. If it does but keep us sober and honest, 'tis likely we shall have as much ability in our spiritual as in our temporal affairs: and if we can but be trusted, we shall have wit enough to save ourselves, when no prejudice lies in the way. But if honesty and wit be insufficient for this saving work, 'tis in vain for the magistrate to meddle with it: since if he be ever so virtuous or wise, he may be as soon mistaken as another man. I am sure the only way to save men's sense, or preserve wit at all in the world, is to give liberty to wit. Now wit can never have its liberty where the freedom of raillery is taken away: for against serious extravagances and splenetic humours there is no other remedy than this.

SHAFTESBURY'S CHARACTERISTICS

We have indeed full power over all other modifications of spleen. We may treat other enthusiasms as we please. We may ridicule love, or gallantry, or knight-errantry to the utmost; and we find that in these latter days of wit, the humour of this kind, which was once so prevalent, is pretty well declined. The crusades, the rescuing of holy lands, and such devout gallantries, are in less request than formerly: but if something of this militant religion, something of this soul-rescuing spirit and saint-errantry prevails still, we need not wonder, when we consider in how solemn a manner we treat this distemper, and how preposterously we go about to cure enthusiasm.

I can hardly forbear fancying that if we had a sort of inquisition, or formal court of judicature, with grave officers and judges, erected to restrain poetical licence, and in general to suppress that fancy and humour of versification; but in particular that most extravagant passion of love, as it is set out by poets, in its heathenish dress of Venuses and Cupids: if the poets, as ringleaders and teachers of this heresy, were, under grievous penalties, forbid to enchant the people by their vein of rhyming; and if the people, on the other side, were, under proportionable penalties, forbid to hearken to any such charm, or lend their attention to any love tale, so much as in a play, a novel, or a ballad—we might perhaps see a new Arcadia arising out of this heavy persecution: old people and young would be seized with a versifying spirit: we should have field-conventicles of lovers and poets: forests would be filled with romantic shepherds and shepherdesses: and rocks resound with echoes of hymns and praises offered to the powers of love. We might indeed have a fair chance, by this management, to bring back the whole train of heathen gods, and set our cold northern island burning with as many altars to Venus and Apollo, as were formerly in Cyprus, Delos, or any of those warmer Grecian climates.

ENTHUSIASM

Section III

But, my lord, you may perhaps wonder, that having been drawn into such a serious subject as religion, I should forget myself so far as to give way to raillery and humour. I must own, my lord, 'tis not merely through chance that this has happened. To say truth, I hardly care so much as to think on this subject, much less to write on it, without endeavouring to put myself in as good humour as is possible. People indeed, who can endure no middle temper, but are all air and humour, know little of the doubts and scruples of religion, and are safe from any immediate influence of devout melancholy or enthusiasm, which requires more deliberation and thoughtful practice to fix itself in a temper, and grow habitual. But be the habit what it will; to be delivered of it at so sad a cost as inconsiderateness, or madness, is what I would never wish to be my lot. I had rather stand all adventures with religion, than endeavour to get rid of the thoughts of it by diversion. All I contend for, is to think of it in a right humour; and that this goes more than half-way towards thinking rightly of it, is what I shall endeavour to demonstrate.

Good-humour is not only the best security against enthusiasm, but the best foundation of piety and true religion; for if right thoughts and worthy apprehensions of the Supreme Being are fundamental to all true worship and adoration, 'tis more than probable that we shall never miscarry in this respect, except through ill-humour only. Nothing beside ill-humour, either natural or forced, can bring a man to think seriously that the world is governed by any devilish or malicious power. I very much question whether anything besides ill-humour can be the cause of atheism. For there are so many arguments to persuade a man in humour that, in the main, all things are kindly and well disposed, that one would think it impossible for him to be so far out of conceit with affairs as to imagine they all ran at adventures; and that the world, as venerable and wise a face as it carried, had neither sense nor meaning in it. This however I am persuaded of, that nothing beside ill-humour can give us dreadful or ill thoughts of a Supreme Manager. Nothing can persuade us of sullenness or sourness in such a being, beside the actual sore feeling of somewhat of this kind within ourselves; and if we are afraid of bringing good-humour into religion, or thinking with freedom and pleasantness on such a subject as God, 'tis because we conceive the subject so like ourselves, and can hardly have a notion of majesty and greatness without stateliness and moroseness accompanying it.

This, however, is the just reverse of that character which we own to be most divinely good when we see it, as we sometimes do, in men of highest power among us. If they pass for truly good, we dare treat them freely, and are sure they will not be displeased with this liberty. They are doubly gainers by this goodness of theirs. For the more they are searched into, and familiarly examined, the more their worth appears; and the discoverer, charmed with his success, esteems and loves more than ever, when he has proved this additional bounty in his superior, and reflects on that candour and generosity he has experienced. Your lordship knows more perhaps of this mystery than any one. How else should you have been so beloved in power, and out of power so adhered to, and still more beloved?

Thank heaven! there are even in our own age some such examples. In former ages there have been many such. We have known mighty princes, and even emperors of the world, who could bear unconcernedly, not only the free censure of their actions, but the most spiteful reproaches and calumnies, even to their faces. Some perhaps may wish there had never been such examples found in heathens; but more especially, that the occasion had never been given by Christians. 'Twas more the misfortune indeed of mankind in general, than of Christians in particular, that some of the earlier Roman emperors were such monsters of tyranny, and began a persecution, not on religious men merely, but on all who were suspected of worth or virtue. What could have been a higher honour or advantage to Christianity than to be persecuted by a Nero? But better princes, who came after, were persuaded to remit these severe courses. 'Tis true, the magistrate might possibly have been surprised with the newness of a notion, which he might pretend, perhaps, did not only destroy the sacredness of his power, but treated him and all men as profane, impious, and damned, who entered not into certain particular modes of worship; of which there had been formerly so many thousand instituted, all of them compatible and sociable till that time. However, such was the wisdom of some succeeding ministries, that the edge of persecution was much abated; and even that prince[1] who was esteemed the greatest enemy of the Christian sect, and who himself had been educated in it, was a great restrainer of persecution, and would allow of nothing further than a resumption of church lands and public schools, without any attempt on the goods or persons, even of those who branded the State religion and made a merit of affronting the public worship.

'Tis well we have the authority of a sacred author in our religion to assure us that the spirit of love and humanity is above that of martyrs.[2] Otherwise, one might be a little scandalised, perhaps, at the history of many of our primitive confessors and martyrs, even according to our own accounts. There is hardly now in the world so good a Christian (if this be indeed the mark of a good one) who, if he happened to live at Constantinople, or elsewhere under the protection of the Turks, would think it fitting or decent to give any disturbance to their mosque-worship. And as good Protestants, my lord, as you and I are, we should consider him as little better than a rank

---

[1] [Julian. The subject is recurred to in the *Miscellaneous Reflections*, Misc. ii. ch ii. note.]

[2] 1 Cor. xiii. 3.

enthusiast, who, out of hatred to the Romish idolatry, should, in time of high mass (where mass perhaps was by law established), interrupt the priest with clamours, or fall foul on his images and relics.

There are some, it seems, of our good brethren, the French Protestants, lately come among us,[1] who are mightily taken with this primitive way. They have set afoot the spirit of martyrdom to a wonder in their own country; and they long to be trying it here, if we will give them leave, and afford them the occasion: that is to say, if we will only do them the favour to hang or imprison them; if we will only be so obliging as to break their bones for them, after their country fashion, blow up their zeal, and stir afresh the coals of persecution. But no such grace can they hitherto obtain of us. So hard-hearted we are, that notwithstanding their own mob are willing to bestow kind blows upon them, and fairly stone them now and then in the open street; though the priests of their own nation would gladly give them their desired discipline, and are earnest to light their probationary fires for them; we Englishmen, who

---

[1] [These were refugees from the Cevennes, where had occurred the war of the Camisards, as a sequel to the Revocation of the Edict of Nantes. Frightful cruelties, recalling the Languedoc massacres of four centuries before, awoke in the persecuted people a spirit of mystic frenzy, and hundreds declared themselves inspired by the Holy Ghost to prophesy. It was some of these "prophets" who reproduced in London the ecstatic phenomena of their warfare in the Cevennes. In 1707 the refugees petitioned the English court for succour for their destitute; and £1000 a month were allowed them. In the same year (July) a number of the prophets were tried for publishing books containing predictions of trouble for England, and were ultimately sentenced (November) to be fined 20 marks, with the alternative of imprisonment, and to be pilloried at Charing Cross and Cornhill. Shaftesbury's Letter, which in the collected edition is dated Sept. 1707, remains without reference to the sentence in question. A number of contemporary pamphlets deal with the proceedings of the "French prophets"; and fairly full details as to the literature of the subject will be found in Appendix I. to the unfinished edition of the *Characteristics* by the Rev. W. M. Hatch, 1870.]

are masters in our own country, will not suffer the enthusiasts to be thus used. Nor can we be supposed to act thus in envy to their phoenix sect, which it seems has risen out of the flames, and would willingly grow to be a new church by the same manner of propagation as the old one, whose seed was truly said to be from the blood of the martyrs.

But how barbarous still, and more than heathenishly cruel, are we tolerating Englishmen! For, not contented to deny these prophesying enthusiasts the honour of a persecution, we have delivered them over to the cruellest contempt in the world. I am told, for certain, that they are at this very time[1] the subject of a choice droll or puppet-show at Bart'lemy Fair.[2] There, doubtless, their strange voices and involuntary agitations are admirably well acted, by the motion of wires and inspiration of pipes. For the bodies of the prophets, in their state of prophecy, being not in their own power, but (as they say themselves) mere passive organs, actuated by an exterior force, have nothing natural, or resembling real life, in any of their sounds or motions; so that how awkwardly soever a puppet-show may imitate other actions, it must needs represent this passion to the life. And whilst Bart'lemy Fair is in possession of this privilege, I dare stand security to our National Church that no sect of enthusiasts, no new venders of prophecy or miracles,

---

[1] Viz. *Anno* 1707.

[2] [*i.e.* St. Bartholomew's Fair, then at the height of its popularity and disrepute. In 1708 was made the first of a series of attempts to confine it within its original bounds of three days, which it had so far exceeded as to last a full fortnight. No reference is made in Professor Henry Morley's *Memoirs of Bartholomew Fair* to the particular "droll" mentioned by Shaftesbury; but such a performance was sure to be popular, being a return to a favourite species of ridicule, dating from Ben Jonson's day. It is to be feared that the puppet-show was not conducted in the spirit of Shaftesbury's essay; but the "prophecies" seem rapidly to have degenerated into money-getting imposture. See, in Mr. Hatch's edition, p. 33, extracts from a satirical handbill on the pilloried prophets, preserved in the Bodleian, also his Appendix, pp. 380, 381.]

shall ever get the start, or put her to the trouble of trying her strength with them, in any case.

Happy it was for us, that when popery had got possession, Smithfield was used in a more tragical way. Many of our first reformers, 'tis feared, were little better than enthusiasts; and God knows whether a warmth of this kind did not considerably help us in throwing off that spiritual tyranny. So that had not the priests, as is usual, preferred the love of blood to all other passions, they might in a merrier way, perhaps, have evaded the greatest force of our reforming spirit. I never heard that the ancient heathens were so well advised in their ill purpose of suppressing the Christian religion in its first rise, as to make use, at any time, of this Bart'lemy Fair method. But this I am persuaded of, that had the truth of the Gospel been any way surmountable, they would have bid much fairer for the silencing it, if they had chosen to bring our primitive founders upon the stage in a pleasanter way than that of bear-skins and pitch-barrels.

The Jews were naturally a very cloudy[1] people, and would endure little raillery in anything, much less in what belonged to any religious doctrines or opinions. Religion was looked upon with a sullen eye; and hanging was the only remedy they could prescribe for anything which looked like setting up a new revelation. The sovereign argument was Crucify, Crucify.[2] But with all their malice and inveteracy to our Saviour, and his apostles after him, had they but taken the fancy to act such puppet-shows in his contempt, as at this hour the papists are acting in his honour, I am apt to think they might possibly have done our religion more harm than by all their other ways of severity.

[1] [*i.e.* gloomy.]

[2] Our author having been censured for this and some following passages concerning the Jews, the reader is referred to the notes and citations in the *Miscellaneous Reflections*, Misc. ii. ch. i. [See also, hereinafter, the *Advice to an Author*, part iii. § 1.]

ENTHUSIASM

I believe our great and learned Apostle found less advantage [1] from the easy treatment of his Athenian antagonists, than from the surly and curst spirit of the most persecuting Jewish cities. He made less improvement of the candour and civility of his Roman judges, than of the zeal of the synagogue and vehemence of his national priests. Though when I consider this apostle as appearing either before the witty Athenians, or before a Roman court of judicature, in the presence of their great men and ladies, and see how handsomely he accommodates himself to the apprehensions and temper of those politer people, I do not find that he declines the way of wit or good-humour; but, without suspicion of his cause, is willing generously to commit it to this proof, and try it against the sharpness of any ridicule which might be offered.

But though the Jews were never pleased to try their wit or malice this way against our Saviour or his apostles, the irreligious part of the heathens had tried it long before against the best doctrines and best characters of men which had ever arisen amongst them. Nor did this prove in the end any injury, but, on the contrary, the highest advantage to those very characters and doctrines, which, having stood the proof, were found so solid and just. The divinest man who had ever appeared in the heathen world was in the height of witty times, and by the wittiest of all poets, most abominably ridiculed, in a whole comedy writ and acted on purpose. But so far was this from sinking his reputation, or suppressing his philosophy, that they each increased the more for it; and he apparently grew to be more the envy of other teachers. He was not only contented to be ridiculed; but, that he might help the poet as much as possible, he presented himself openly in the theatre; that his

---

[1] What advantage he made of his sufferings, and how pathetically his bonds and stripes were set to view, and often pleaded by him, to raise his character, and advance the interest of Christianity, any one who reads his Epistles, and is well acquainted with his manner and style, may easily observe.

real figure (which was no advantageous one) might be compared with that which the witty poet had brought as his representative on the stage. Such was his good-humour! Nor could there be in the world a greater testimony of the invincible goodness of the man, or a greater demonstration, that there was no imposture either in his character or opinions. For that imposture should dare sustain the encounter of a grave enemy is no wonder. A solemn attack, she knows, is not of such danger to her. There is nothing she abhors or dreads like pleasantness and good-humour.

Section IV

In short, my lord, the melancholy way of treating religion is that which, according to my apprehension, renders it so tragical, and is the occasion of its acting in reality such dismal tragedies in the world. And my notion is, that provided we treat religion with good manners, we can never use too much good-humour, or examine it with too much freedom and familiarity. For, if it be genuine and sincere, it will not only stand the proof, but thrive and gain advantage from hence; if it be spurious, or mixed with any imposture, it will be detected and exposed.

The melancholy way in which we have been taught religion, makes us unapt to think of it in good-humour. 'Tis in adversity chiefly, or in ill health, under affliction, or disturbance of mind, or discomposure of temper, that we have recourse to it. Though in reality we are never so unfit to think of it as at such a heavy and dark hour. We can never be fit to contemplate anything above us, when we are in no condition to look into ourselves, and calmly examine the temper of our own mind and passions. For then it is we see wrath, and fury, and revenge, and terrors in the Deity; when we are full of disturbances and fears within, and have, by sufferance and anxiety, lost so much of the natural calm and easiness of our temper.

We must not only be in ordinary good-humour, but in the

best of humours, and in the sweetest, kindest disposition of our lives, to understand well what true goodness is, and what those attributes imply which we ascribe with such applause and honour to the Deity. We shall then be able to see best whether those forms of justice, those degrees of punishment, that temper of resentment, and those measures of offence and indignation, which we vulgarly suppose in God, are suitable to those original ideas of goodness, which the same Divine Being, or Nature under him, has implanted in us, and which we must necessarily presuppose, in order to give him praise or honour in any kind. This, my lord, is the best security against all superstition: to remember that there is nothing in God but what is godlike; and that he is either not at all, or truly and perfectly good. But when we are afraid to use our reason freely, even on that very question, "whether he really be, or not," we then actually presume him bad, and flatly contradict that pretended character of goodness and greatness; whilst we discover this mistrust of his temper, and fear his anger and resentment, in the case of this freedom of inquiry.

We have a notable instance of this freedom in one of our sacred authors. As patient as Job is said to be, it cannot be denied that he makes bold enough with God, and takes his providence roundly to task. His friends, indeed, plead hard with him, and use all arguments, right or wrong, to patch up objections, and set the affairs of providence upon an equal foot. They make a merit of saying all the good they can of God, at the very stretch of their reason, and sometimes quite beyond it. But this, in Job's opinion, is flattering God, accepting of God's person, and even mocking him.[1] And no wonder. For, what merit can there be in believing God, or his providence, upon frivolous and weak grounds? What virtue in assuming an opinion contrary to the appearance of things, and resolving to hear nothing which may be said against it? Excellent character of the God of truth! that he should be offended at us for

[1] ch. xiii. 7-10.

having refused to put the lie upon our understandings, as much as in us lay, and be satisfied with us for having believed at a venture, and against our reason, what might have been the greatest falsehood in the world, for anything we could bring as a proof or evidence to the contrary!

It is impossible that any besides an ill-natured man can wish against the being of a God; for this is wishing against the public, and even against one's private good too, if rightly understood. But if a man has not any such ill-will to stifle his belief, he must have surely an unhappy opinion of God, and believe him not so good by far as he knows himself to be, if he imagines that an impartial use of his reason, in any matter of speculation whatsoever, can make him run any risk hereafter; and that a mean denial of his reason, and an affectation of belief in any point too hard for his understanding, can entitle him to any favour in another world. This is being sycophants in religion, mere parasites of devotion. 'Tis using God as the crafty beggars use those they address to, when they are ignorant of their quality. The novices amongst them may innocently come out, perhaps, with a "good sir," or a "good forsooth"; but with the old stagers, no matter whom they meet in a coach, 'tis always "good your honour!" or "good your lordship!" or "your ladyship!" For if there should be really a lord in the case, we should be undone (say they) for want of giving the title; but if the party should be no lord, there would be no offence; it would not be ill taken.

And thus it is in religion. We are highly concerned how to beg right; and think all depends upon hitting the title, and making a good guess. 'Tis the most beggarly refuge imaginable, which is so mightily cried up, and stands as a great maxim with many able men, "that they should strive to have faith, and believe to the utmost; because if, after all, there be nothing in the matter, there will be no harm in being thus deceived; but if there be anything, it will be fatal for them not to have believed to the full." But they are so far mistaken that, whilst they have this thought, 'tis certain they can never believe either to their satisfaction and happiness in this world, or with any advantage of recommendation to another. For besides that our reason, which knows the cheat, will never rest thoroughly satisfied on such a bottom, but turn us often adrift, and toss us in a sea of doubt and perplexity, we cannot but actually grow worse in our religion, and entertain a worse opinion still of a Supreme Deity, whilst our belief is founded on so injurious a thought of him.

To love the public, to study universal good, and to promote the interest of the whole world, as far as lies within our power, is surely the height of goodness, and makes that temper which we call divine. In this temper, my lord (for surely you should know it well), 'tis natural for us to wish that others should partake with us, by being convinced of the sincerity of our exemple. 'Tis natural for us to wish our merit should be known; particularly if it be our fortune to have served a nation as a good Minister; or as some prince, or father of a country, to have rendered happy a considerable part of mankind under our care. But if it happened that of this number there should be some so ignorantly bred, and of so remote a province, as to have lain out of the hearing of our name and actions; or hearing of them should be so puzzled with odd and contrary stories told up and down concerning us, that they knew not what to think, whether there were really in the world any such person as ourself; should we not, in good truth, be ridiculous to take offence at this? And should we not pass for extravagantly morose and ill-humoured if, instead of treating the matter in raillery, we should think in earnest of revenging ourselves on the offending parties, who, out of their rustic ignorance, ill-judgment, or incredulity, had detracted from our renown?

How shall we say then? Does it really deserve praise to be thus concerned about it? Is the doing good for glory's sake so divine a thing? or is it not diviner to do good even where it may be thought inglorious, even to the ungrateful, and to those who are wholly insensible of the good they receive? How comes it then, that what is so divine in us, should lose its character in the Divine Being? And that according as the Deity is represented to us, he should more resemble the weak, womanish, and impotent part of our nature, than the generous, manly, and divine?

Section V

One would think, my lord, it were in reality no hard thing to know our own weaknesses at first sight, and distinguish the features of human frailty with which we are so well acquainted. One would think it were easy to understand that provocation and offence, anger, revenge, jealousy in point of honour or power, love of fame, glory, and the like, belong only to limited beings, and are necessarily excluded a being which is perfect and universal. But if we have never settled with ourselves any notion of what is morally excellent; or if we cannot trust to that reason which tells us that nothing beside what is so, can have place in the Deity; we can neither trust to anything which others relate of him, or which he himself reveals to us. We must be satisfied beforehand that he is good, and cannot deceive us. Without this, there can be no real religious faith or confidence. Now, if there be really something previous to revelation, some antecedent demonstration of reason, to assure us that God is, and withal that he is so good as not to deceive us; the same reason, if we will trust to it, will demonstrate to us that God is so good as to exceed the very best of us in goodness. And after this manner we can have no dread or suspicion to render us uneasy; for it is malice only, and not goodness, which can make us afraid.

There is an odd way of reasoning, but in certain distempers of mind very sovereign to those who can apply it; and it is this: "There can be no malice but where interests are opposed. A universal being can have no interest opposite; and therefore can have no malice." If there be a general mind, it can have no particular interest; but the general good, or good of the whole,

ENTHUSIASM

and its own private good, must of necessity be one and the same. It can intend nothing besides, nor aim at anything beyond, nor be provoked to anything contrary. So that we have only to consider whether there be really such a thing as a mind which has relation to the whole, or not. For if unhappily there be no mind, we may comfort ourselves, however, that Nature has no malice; if there be really a mind, we may rest satisfied that it is the best-natured one in the world. The last case, one would imagine, should be the most comfortable; and the notion of a common parent less frightful than that of forlorn Nature and a fatherless world. Though, as religion stands amongst us, there are many good people who would have less fear in being thus exposed, and would be easier, perhaps, in their minds, if they were assured they had only mere Chance to trust to. For nobody trembles to think there should be no God; but rather that there should be one. This however would be otherwise, if Deity were thought as kindly of as Humanity; and we could be persuaded to believe, that if there really was a God, the highest goodness must of necessity belong to him, without any of those defects of passion,[1] those meannesses and imperfections which we acknowledge such in ourselves, which as good men we endeavour all we can to be superior to, and which we find we every day conquer as we grow better.

Methinks, my lord, it would be well for us if, before we ascended into the higher regions of divinity, we would vouchsafe to descend a little into ourselves, and bestow some poor thoughts upon plain honest morals. When we had once looked into ourselves, and distinguished well the nature of our own affections, we should probably be fitter judges of the divineness

---

[1] For my own part, says honest Plutarch, I had rather men should say of me, "That there neither is nor ever was such a one as Plutarch; than they should say, There was a Plutarch, an unsteady, changeable, easily provokable, and revengeful man, ἄνθρωπος ἀβέβαιος, εὐμετάβολος, εὐχερὴς πρὸς ὀργήν, μικρόλυπος," etc. Plutarch, *de Superstitione* [Compare *Misc.* ii. ch. iii.]

of a character, and discern better what affections were suitable or unsuitable to a perfect being. We might then understand how to love and praise, when we had acquired some consistent notion of what was laudable or lovely. Otherwise we might chance to do God little honour, when we intended him the most. For 'tis hard to imagine what honour can arise to the Deity from the praises of creatures who are unable to discern what is praiseworthy or excellent in their own kind.

If a musician were cried up to the skies by a certain set of people who had no ear in music, he would surely be put to the blush, and could hardly, with a good countenance, accept the benevolence of his auditors, till they had acquired a more competent apprehension of him, and could by their own senses find out something really good in his performance. Till this were brought about, there would be little glory in the case, and the musician, though ever so vain, would have little reason to be contented.

They who affect praise the most, had rather not be taken notice of than be impertinently applauded. I know not how it comes about that he who is ever said to do good the most disinterestedly should be thought desirous of being praised so lavishly, and be supposed to set so high a rate upon so cheap and low a thing as ignorant commendation and forced applause.

'Tis not the same with goodness as with other qualities, which we may understand very well and yet not possess. We may have an excellent ear in music, without being able to perform in any kind. We may judge well of poetry, without being poets or possessing the least of a poetic vein: but we can have no tolerable notion of goodness, without being tolerably good. So that if the praise of a divine being be so great a part of his worship, we should, methinks, learn goodness, were it for nothing else than that we might learn, in some tolerable manner, how to praise. For the praise of goodness from an unsound hollow heart must certainly make the greatest dissonance in the world.

ENTHUSIASM

Section VI

OTHER reasons, my lord, there are, why this plain home-spun philosophy, of looking into ourselves, may do us wondrous service, in rectifying our errors in religion. For there is a sort of enthusiasm of second hand. And when men find no original commotions in themselves, no prepossessing panic which bewitches them, they are apt still, by the testimony of others, to be imposed on, and led credulously into the belief of many false miracles. And this habit may make them variable, and of a very inconstant faith, easy to be carried away with every wind of doctrine, and addicted to every upstart sect or superstition. But the knowledge of our passions in their very seeds, the measuring well the growth and progress of enthusiasm, and the judging rightly of its natural force, and what command it has over our very senses, may teach us to oppose more successfully those delusions which come armed with the specious pretext of moral certainty and matter of fact.

The new prophesying sect I made mention of above, pretend, it seems, among many other miracles, to have had a most signal one, acted premeditately, and with warning, before many hundreds of people, who actually give testimony to the truth of it. But I would only ask, whether there were present, among those hundreds, any one person, who having never been of their sect, or addicted to their way, will give the same testimony with them? I must not be contented to ask, whether such a one had been wholly free of that particular enthusiasm? but, whether, before that time, he was esteemed of so sound a judgment, and clear a head, as to be wholly free of melancholy, and in all likelihood incapable of all enthusiasm besides? For otherwise, the panic may have been caught; the evidence of the senses lost, as in a dream; and the imagination so inflamed, as in a moment to have burnt up every particle of judgment and reason. The combustible matters lic prepared within, and ready to take fire at a spark; but chiefly in a multitude seized with the same spirit.[1] No wonder if the blaze rises so of a sudden; when innumerable eyes glow with the passion, and heaving breasts are labouring with inspiration; when not the aspect only, but the very breath and exhalations of men are infectious, and the inspiring disease imparts itself by insensible transpiration. I am not a divine good enough to resolve what spirit that was which proved so catching among the ancient prophets, that even the profane Saul was taken by it. But I learn from Holy Scripture, that there was the evil as well as the good spirit of prophecy.[2] And I find by present experience, as well as by all histories, sacred and profane, that the operation of this spirit is everywhere the same as to the bodily organs.

A gentleman who has writ lately in defence of revived prophecy, and has since fallen himself into the prophetic ecstasies, tells us "That the ancient prophets had the spirit of God upon them under ecstasy, with divers strange gestures of body denominating them madmen (or enthusiasts), as appears evidently (says he) in the instances of Balaam, Saul, David, Ezekiel, Daniel, etc." And he proceeds to justify this by the practice of the apostolic times, and by the regulation which the Apostle himself applies to these seemingly irregular gifts,[3] so frequent and ordinary (as our author pretends) in the primitive church, on the first rise and spreading of Christianity. But I leave it to him to make the resemblance as well as he can between his own and the apostolic way. I only know that the symptoms he describes, and which himself (poor gentleman!) labours under, are as heathenish as he can possibly pretend them to be Christian. And when I saw him lately under an agitation (as they call it) uttering prophecy in a pompous Latin style, of which, out of his ecstasy, it seems, he is wholly

---

[1] See *Misc.* ii. ch. ii. [hereinafter].

[2] See 1 Kings xxii. 20, etc.; 2 Chron. xviii. 19, etc.; and [hereinafter] *Misc.* ii. ch. iii.   [3] 1 Cor. xiv.

ENTHUSIASM

incapable, it brought into my mind the Latin poet's description of the Sibyl, whose agonies were so perfectly like these—

> Subito non vultus, non color unus,
> Non comptae mansere comae, sed pectus anhelum,
> Et rabie fera corda tument; majorque videri
> Nec mortale sonans: afflata est numine quando
> Jam propiore dei. . . .[1]

And again presently after·—

> Immanis in antro
> Bacchatur vates, magnum si pectore possit
> Excussisse deum; tanto magis ille fatigat
> Os rabidum, fera corda domans, *fingitque premendo*.[2]

Which is the very style of our experienced author. "For the inspired (says he) undergo a probation, wherein the spirit, by frequent agitations, forms the organs, ordinarily for a month or two before utterance."

The Roman historian, speaking of a most horrible enthusiasm which broke out in Rome long before his days, describes this spirit of prophecy: Viros, velut mente capta, cum jactatione fanatica corporis vaticinari.[3] The detestable things which are further related of these enthusiasts, I would not willingly transcribe; but the Senate's mild decree in so execrable a case, I cannot omit copying; being satisfied, that though your lordship has read it before now, you can read it again and again with admiration. In reliquum deinde (says Livy) S. C. cautum est, etc. Si quis tale sacrum solenne et necessarium duceret, nec

---

[1] ["Immediately her face changes, her colour flies, her hair falls in disorder, her breast heaves and her heart swells with mad passion; greater her stature seems, and her voice not mortal, for she is breathed upon by the god now imminent."—Virgil, *Aeneid*, vi. 47-51.]

[2] ["The prophetess rages monstrously in the cave, seeking to cast from her breast the mighty God; so much the more he compels the rabid mouth, ruling the wild heart, and moulds her by his force."—*Ib.* 77-80.]

[3] ["Men vaticinate as if out of their minds, with fanatical convulsions of the body."—Livy, xxxix. 13.]

sine religione et piaculo se id omittere posse; apud praetorem urbanum profiteretur: praetor senatum consuleret. Si ei permissum esset, cum in senatu centum non minus essent, ita id sacrum faceret; dum ne plus quinque sacrificio interessent, neu qua pecunia communis, neu quis magister sacrorum aut sacerdos esset.[1]

So necessary it is to give way to this distemper of enthusiasm, that even that philosopher who bent the whole force of his philosophy against superstition, appears to have left room for visionary fancy, and to have indirectly tolerated enthusiasm. For it is hard to imagine, that one who had so little religious faith as Epicurus, should have so vulgar a credulity as to believe those accounts of armies and castles in the air, and such visionary phenomena. Yet he allows them; and then thinks to solve them by his effluvia, and aerial looking-glasses, and I know not what other stuff; which his Latin poet, however, sets off beautifully, as he does all—

> Rerum simulacra vagari
> Multa modis multis in cunctas undique parteis
> Tenuia, quae facile inter se junguntur in auris,
> Obvia cum veniunt, ut aranea bracteaque auri.
>
> * * * * *
>
> Centauros itaque et Scyllarum membra videmus
> Cerbereasque canum facies simulacraque eorum
> Quorum morte obita tellus amplectitur ossa:
> Omne genus quoniam passim simulacra feruntur,

---

[1] ["As to the future, the Senate enacted that if any one should believe that such a cult was religiously necessary to him, and that he could not without irreligion and impiety forego it, he should inform the praetor of the city, who should consult the Senate. If, with not less than a hundred present, the Senate should give permission, the rites might be performed; but there should not be more than five assisting at the sacrifice, nor should there be any common fund, nor any master of the rites, nor any priest."—Livy, xxxix. 18.]

ENTHUSIASM

Partim sponte sua quae fiunt aere in ipso,
Partim quae variis ab rebus cumque recedunt.[1]

'Twas a sign this philosopher believed there was a good stock of visionary spirit originally in human nature. He was so satisfied that men were inclined to see visions, that rather than they should go without, he chose to make them to their hand. Notwithstanding he denied the principles of religion to be natural,[2] he was forced tacitly to allow there was a wondrous disposition in mankind towards supernatural objects; and that if these ideas were vain, they were yet in a manner innate, or such as men were really born to, and could hardly by any means avoid. From which concession, a divine, methinks, might raise a good argument against him, for the truth as well as the usefulness of religion. But so it is: whether the matter of apparition be true or false, the symptoms are the same, and the passion of equal force in the person who is vision-struck. The *lymphatici* of the Latins were the *nympholepti* of the Greeks. They were persons said to have seen some species of divinity, as either some rural deity, or nymph, which threw them into such transports as overcame their reason. The ecstasies expressed themselves outwardly in quakings, tremblings, tossings of the head and limbs, agitations, and (as Livy calls them) fanatical throws or convulsions, extemporary prayer, prophecy, singing, and the like. All nations have their lymphatics of some kind or another; and all churches, heathen as well as Christian, have had their complaints against fanaticism.

One would think the ancients imagined this disease had

[1] ["Many simulacra of things, thin, manifold in number and form, wander about in all manner of ways, which when in the air they meet, easily conjoin, like cobwebs or gold-leaf. . . . Thus we see Centaurs and limbs of Scylla, and shapes of dogs like Cerberus, and the phantasms of those passed away whose bones the earth enfolds; since everywhere float simulacra of every kind, partly those spontaneously shaped by the air within itself, partly those thrown off by various things."—Lucretius, iv. 724-737.]

[2] *Infra*, Treatise II. part iii. § 3.

some relation to that which they called hydrophoby. Whether the ancient lymphatics had any way like that of biting, to communicate the rage of their distemper, I cannot so positively determine. But certain fanatics there have been since the time of the ancients, who have had a most prosperous faculty of communicating the appetite of the teeth. For since first the snappish spirit got up in religion, all sects have been at it, as the saying is, tooth and nail; and are never better pleased than in worrying one another without mercy.

So far indeed the innocent kind of fanaticism extends itself, that when the party is struck by the apparition, there follows always an itch of imparting it, and kindling the same fire in other breasts. For thus poets are fanatics too. And thus Horace either is or feigns himself *lymphatic,* and shows what an effect the vision of the nymphs and Bacchus had on him—

> Bacchum[1] in remotis carmina rupibus
> Vidi docentem, credite posteri,
>   Nymphasque discentes. . . .
> Evoe! recenti mens trepidat metu,
> Plenoque Bacchi pectore turbidum
>   Lymphatur[2] . . . .

as Heinsius reads.

No poet (as I ventured to say at first to your lordship) can do anything great in his own way without the imagination or supposition of a divine presence, which may raise him to some degree of this passion we are speaking of. Even the cold

[1] ["Bacchus have I seen in far-off stony places teaching his songs (aftercomers, believe me!) and the nymphs conning them. . . . Evoe! my heart trembles with the still-felt fear, and wildly maddens (*lymphatur*) in a breast filled with Bacchus."—Horace, *Odes,* II. xix. The accepted reading is *laetatur,* "exults."]

[2] So again, *Sat.* I. v. 97, Gnatia lymphis iratis exstructa, where Horace wittily treats the people of Gnatia as lymphatics and enthusiasts, for believing a miracle of their priests: Credat Judaeus Apella, Hor. *ibid.* See Heinsius and Torrentius; and the quotation in the following notes, ὑπὸ τῶν Νυμφῶν, etc.

ENTHUSIASM

Lucretius makes use of inspiration, when he writes against it, and is forced to raise an apparition of Nature, in a divine form, to animate and conduct him in his very work of degrading Nature, and despoiling her of all her seeming wisdom and divinity—

> Alma Venus, caeli subter labentia signa
> Quae mare navigerum, quae terras frugiferenteis
> Concelebras. . . .
> Quae quoniam rerum naturam sola gubernas
> Nec sine te quidquam dias in luminis oras
> Exoritur neque fit laetum neque amabile quidquam:
> Te sociam studeo scribundis versibus esse
> Quos ego de rerum natura pangere conor
> Memmiadae nostro.[1]

Section VII

The only thing, my lord, I would infer from all this is, that enthusiasm is wonderfully powerful and extensive; that it is a matter of nice judgment, and the hardest thing in the world to know fully and distinctly; since even atheism[2] is not exempt from it. For, as some have well remarked, there have been enthusiastical atheists. Nor can divine inspiration, by its outward marks, be easily distinguished from it. For inspiration is a real feeling of the Divine Presence, and enthusiasm a false one. But the passion they raise is much alike. For when the mind is taken up in vision, and fixes its view either on any real object, or mere spectre of divinity; when it sees, or thinks it

---

[1] ["Nutrient Venus, who under the gliding signs of heaven fillest with life the ship-bearing sea and the fruitful lands. . . . Since thou alone rulest the nature of things, nor without thee ariseth aught to the holy frontiers of light, nor groweth anything joyous or meet for love, thee would I have for helper in framing the song I seek to build for this our son of the Memmian line."—Lucretius, i. 2-4, 22-26.]

[2] See [hereinafter] *Misc.* ii. ch. ii. in the beginning.

sees, anything prodigious, and more than human; its horror, delight, confusion, fear, admiration, or whatever passion belongs to it, or is uppermost on this occasion, will have something vast, *immane*, and (as painters say) beyond life. And this is what gave occasion to the name of fanaticism, as it was used by the ancients in its original sense, for an apparition transporting the mind.

Something there will be of extravagance and fury, when the ideas or images received are too big for the narrow human vessel to contain. So that inspiration may be justly called divine enthusiasm; for the word itself signifies divine presence, and was made use of by the philosopher whom the earliest Christian Fathers called divine, to express whatever was sublime in human passions.[1] This was the spirit he allotted to heroes, statesmen, poets, orators, musicians, and even philosophers them-

---

[1] ἆρ' οἶσθ' ὅτι ὑπὸ τῶν Νυμφῶν ἐκ προνοίας σαφῶς ἐνθουσιάσω . . . τοσαῦτα μέν σοι καὶ ἔτι πλείω ἔχω μανίας γιγνομένης ἀπὸ θεῶν λέγειν καλὰ ἔργα, etc.—*Phaedr.* καὶ τοὺς πολιτικοὺς οὐχ ἥκιστα τούτων φαῖμεν ἂν θείους τε εἶναι καὶ ἐνθουσιάζειν.—*Meno.* ἔγνων οὖν ἂν καὶ περὶ τῶν ποιητῶν ἐν ὀλίγῳ τοῦτο, ὅτι οὐ σοφίᾳ ποιοῖεν, ἀλλὰ φύσει τινὶ καὶ ἐνθουσιάζοντες, ὥσπερ οἱ θεομάντεις καὶ χρησμῳδοί.—*Apol.* In particular as to philosophers, Plutarch tells us, 'twas the complaint of some of the sour old Romans, when learning first came to them from Greece, that their youth grew enthusiastic with philosophy. For speaking of one of the philosophers of the Athenian Embassy, he says, ἔρωτα δεινὸν ἐμβέβληκε τοῖς νέοις ὑφ' οὗ τῶν ἄλλων ἡδονῶν καὶ διατριβῶν ἐκπεσόντες ἐνθουσιῶσι περὶ φιλοσοφίαν.—Plut. *Cato Major.*

[Plato, *Phaedrus*, 241 E, seems here misquoted. The accepted text means: "I suppose you know that I shall be quite possessed (ἐνθουσιάσω) by the nymphs, to whom you have designedly exposed me."

Plato, *Menon*, 99 D: "And, among them, we should say that the politicians were specially rapt and inspired" (ἐνθουσιάζειν).

Plato, *Apol.* 22 B (slightly misquoted). The right version would give: "So I observed also about poets in a short time that they did not compose out of wisdom, but from an instinct and an inspiration (ἐνθουσιάζοντες) like seers and prophets."

Plutarch, *Cato Major*, 22: "He put a spell upon young men, under which they give up other pleasures and amusements, and are possessed by philosophy" (ἐνθουσιῶσι).]

ENTHUSIASM

selves. Nor can we, of our own accord, forbear ascribing to a noble enthusiasm[1] whatever is greatly performed by any of these. So that almost all of us know something of this principle. But to know it as we should do, and discern it in its several kinds, both in ourselves and others; this is the great work, and by this means alone we can hope to avoid delusion. For to judge the spirits whether they are of God, we must antecedently judge our own spirit, whether it be of reason and sound sense; whether it be fit to judge at all, by being sedate, cool, and impartial, free of every biassing passion, every giddy vapour, or melancholy fume.[2] This is the first knowledge and previous judgment: "To understand ourselves, and know what spirit we are of." Afterwards we may judge the spirit in others, consider what their personal merit is, and prove the validity of their testimony by the solidity of their brain. By this means we may prepare ourselves with some antidote against enthusiasm. And this is what I have dared affirm is best performed by keeping to good-humour. For otherwise the remedy itself may turn to the disease.

And now, my lord, having, after all, in some measure justified enthusiasm, and owned the word, if I appear extravagant in addressing to you after the manner I have done, you must allow me to plead an impulse. You must suppose me (as with truth you may) most passionately yours; and with that kindness which is natural to you on other occasions, you must tolerate your enthusiastic friend, who, excepting only in the case of this overforward zeal, must ever appear, with the highest respect, my lord,   Your Lordship's, etc.

---

[1] Of this passion, in the nobler and higher sense, see more [hereinafter] in the *Inquiry Concerning Virtue*, bk. i. part iii. § 3, end; *Moralists*, part iii. § 2; *Miscellaneous Reflections*, Misc. ii. ch. i.

[2] [Compare the more extended argument of Locke, *Essay*, bk. iv. ch. xix., which is here condensed.]

TREATISE II

SENSUS COMMUNIS;

AN ESSAY ON THE FREEDOM

OF

WIT AND HUMOUR

IN A LETTER TO A FRIEND

---

hac urget lupus, hac canis. . . .
Hor *Sat.* ii. ii.

Printed first in the year MDCCIX.

AN ESSAY ON THE FREEDOM OF WIT AND HUMOUR

PART I

Section I

I HAVE been considering, my friend, what your fancy was, to express such a surprise as you did the other day, when I happened to speak to you in commendation of *raillery*. Was it possible you should suppose me so grave a man as to dislike *all* conversation of this kind? or were you afraid I should not stand the trial, if you put me to it, by making the experiment in my own case?

I must confess you had reason enough for your caution if you could imagine me at the bottom so true a zealot as not to bear the least raillery on my own opinions. 'Tis the case, I know, with many. Whatever they think grave or solemn, they suppose must never be treated out of a grave and solemn way, though what another thinks so, they can be contented to treat otherwise; and are forward to try the edge of ridicule against any opinions besides their own.

The question is, whether this be fair or no? and, whether it be not just and reasonable to make as free with our own opinions as with those of other people? For to be sparing in this case may be looked upon as a piece of selfishness. We may be charged perhaps with wilful ignorance and blind idolatry for having taken opinions upon trust, and consecrated in ourselves certain idol-notions, which we will never suffer to be unveiled or seen in open light. They may perhaps be monsters, and not divinities, or sacred truths, which are kept thus choicely in some dark corner of our minds. The spectres may impose on us, whilst we refuse to turn them every way, and view their shapes and complexions in every light. For that which can be shown only in a certain light is questionable. Truth, 'tis supposed, may bear all lights; and one of those principal lights, or natural mediums, by which things are to be viewed, in order to a thorough recognition, is ridicule itself, or that manner of proof by which we discern whatever is liable to just raillery in any subject. So much, at least, is allowed by all who at any time appeal to this criterion. The gravest gentlemen, even in the gravest subjects, are supposed to acknowledge this, and can have no right, 'tis thought, to deny others the freedom of this appeal; whilst they are free to censure like other men, and in their gravest arguments make no scruple to ask, Is it not ridiculous?

Of this affair, therefore, I design you should know fully what my sentiments are. And by this means you will be able to judge of me, whether I was sincere the other day in the defence of raillery, and can continue still to plead for those ingenious friends of ours, who are often censured for their humour of this kind, and for the freedom they take in such an airy way of conversation and writing.

SECTION II

In good earnest, when one considers what use is sometimes made of this species of wit, and to what an excess it has risen of late in some characters of the age, one may be startled a little, and in doubt what to think of the practice, or whither this rallying humour will at length carry us. It has passed from the men of pleasure to the men of business. Politicians have been infected with it; and the grave affairs of State have been treated with an air of irony and banter. The ablest negotiators

FREEDOM OF WIT AND HUMOUR

have been known the notablest buffoons; the most celebrated authors, the greatest masters of burlesque.

There is indeed a kind of defensive raillery (if I may so call it) which I am willing enough to allow in affairs of whatever kind; when the spirit of curiosity would force a discovery of more truth than can conveniently be told. For we can never do more injury to truth than by discovering too much of it on some occasions. 'Tis the same with understandings as with eyes: to such a certain size and make just so much light is necessary, and no more. Whatever is beyond, brings darkness and confusion.

'Tis real humanity and kindness to hide strong truths from tender eyes. And to do this by a pleasant amusement is easier and civiller than by a harsh denial or remarkable reserve. But to go about industriously to confound men, in a mysterious manner, and to make advantage or draw pleasure from that perplexity they are thrown into by such uncertain talk, is as unhandsome in a way of raillery as when done with the greatest seriousness, or in the most solemn way of deceit. It may be necessary, as well now as heretofore, for wise men to speak in parables, and with a double meaning, that the enemy may be amused, and they only who have ears to hear may hear. But 'tis certainly a mean, impotent, and dull sort of wit which amuses all alike, and leaves the most sensible man, and even a friend, equally in doubt, and at a loss to understand what one's real mind is, upon any subject.

This is that gross sort of raillery which is so offensive in good company. And indeed there is as much difference between one sort and another as between fair-dealing and hypocrisy, or between the genteelest wit and the most scurrilous buffoonery. But by freedom of conversation this illiberal kind of wit will lose its credit. For wit is its own remedy. Liberty and commerce bring it to its true standard. The only danger is, the laying an embargo. The same thing happens here, as in the case of trade. Impositions and restrictions reduce it to a low ebb. Nothing is so advantageous to it as a free port.[1]

We have seen in our own time the decline and ruin of a false sort of wit, which so much delighted our ancestors, that their poems and plays, as well as sermons, were full of it. All humour had something of the quibble. The very language of the Court was punning. But 'tis now banished the town, and all good company: there are only some few footsteps of it in the country; and it seems at last confined to the nurseries of youth, as the chief entertainment of pedants and their pupils. And thus in other respects wit will mend upon our hands, and humour will refine itself, if we take care not to tamper with it, and bring it under constraint, by severe usage and rigorous prescriptions. All politeness is owing to liberty. We polish one another, and rub off our corners and rough sides by a sort of amicable collision. To restrain this, is inevitably to bring a rust upon men's understandings. 'Tis a destroying of civility, good breeding, and even charity itself, under pretence of maintaining it.

SECTION III

To describe true raillery would be as hard a matter, and perhaps as little to the purpose, as to define good breeding. None can understand the speculation, beside those who have the practice. Yet every one thinks himself well-bred; and the formallest pedant imagines he can rally with a good grace and humour. I have known some of those grave gentlemen undertake to correct an author for defending the use of raillery, who at the same

[1] [This is one of a number of passages in the literature of two or more centuries ago showing a belief in Free Trade before it became a legislative principle. Shaftesbury had doubtless profited by the teaching of Dudley North, who in his economics was closely followed by Locke. Two generations earlier, Pepys (under date 1664, Feb. 29) cites Sir Philip Warwick as ingeniously expounding the "paradox" that it does not impoverish the nation to export less than it imports.]

time have upon every turn made use of that weapon, though they were naturally so very awkward at it. And this I believe may be observed in the case of many zealots, who have taken upon them to answer our modern free-writers. The tragical gentlemen, with the grim aspect and mien of true inquisitors, have but an ill grace when they vouchsafe to quit their austerity, and be jocose and pleasant with an adversary, whom they would choose to treat in a very different manner. For to do them justice, had they their wills, I doubt not but their conduct and mien would be pretty much of a piece. They would in all probability soon quit their farce, and make a thorough tragedy. But at present there is nothing so ridiculous as this Janus-face of writers, who with one countenance force a smile, and with another show nothing beside rage and fury. Having entered the lists, and agreed to the fair laws of combat by wit and argument, they have no sooner proved their weapon, than you hear them crying aloud for help, and delivering over to the secular arm.

There cannot be a more preposterous sight than an executioner and a merry-Andrew acting their part upon the same stage. Yet I am persuaded any one will find this to be the real picture of certain modern zealots in their controversial writings. They are no more masters of gravity than they are of good-humour. The first always runs into harsh severity, and the latter into an awkward buffoonery. And thus between anger and pleasure, zeal and drollery, their writing has much such a grace as the play of humorsome children, who, at the same instant, are both peevish and wanton, and can laugh and cry almost in one and the same breath.

How agreeable such writings are like to prove, and of what effect towards the winning over or convincing those who are supposed to be in error, I need not go about to explain. Nor can I wonder, on this account, to hear those public lamentations of zealots, that whilst the books of their adversaries are so current, their answers to them can hardly make their way into the world, or be taken the least notice of. Pedantry and bigotry are mill-stones able to sink the best book which carries the least part of their dead weight. The temper of the pedagogue suits not with the age. And the world, however it may be taught, will not be tutored. If a philosopher speaks, men hear him willingly while he keeps to his philosophy. So is a Christian heard while he keeps to his professed charity and meekness. In a gentleman we allow of pleasantry and raillery as being managed always with good breeding, and never gross or clownish. But if a mere scholastic, intrenching upon all these characters, and writing as it were by starts and rebounds from one of these to another, appears upon the whole as little able to keep the temper of Christianity as to use the reason of a philosopher or the raillery of a man of breeding, what wonder is it, if the monstrous product of such a jumbled brain be ridiculous to the world?

If you think, my friend, that by this description I have done wrong to these zealot-writers in religious controversy, read only a few pages in any one of them (even where the contest is not abroad, but within their own pale) and then pronounce.

Section IV

But now that I have said thus much concerning authors and writings, you shall hear my thoughts, as you have desired, upon the subject of conversation, and particularly a late one of a free kind, which you remember I was present at, with some friends of yours, whom you fancied I should in great gravity have condemned.

'Twas, I must own, a very diverting one, and perhaps not the less so for ending as abruptly as it did, and in such a sort of confusion as almost brought to nothing whatever had been advanced in the discourse before. Some particulars of this conversation may not perhaps be so proper to commit to paper. 'Tis enough that I put you in mind of the conversation in general. A great many fine schemes, 'tis true, were destroyed;

FREEDOM OF WIT AND HUMOUR

many grave reasonings overturned; but this being done without offence to the parties concerned, and with improvement to the good-humour of the company, it set the appetite the keener to such conversations. And I am persuaded, that had Reason herself been to judge of her own interest, she would have thought she received more advantage in the main from that easy and familiar way, than from the usual stiff adherence to a particular opinion.

But perhaps you may still be in the same humour of not believing me in earnest. You may continue to tell me I affect to be paradoxical in commending a conversation as advantageous to reason, which ended in such a total uncertainty of what reason had seemingly so well established.

To this I answer, that according to the notion I have of reason, neither the written treatises of the learned, nor the set discourses of the eloquent, are able of themselves to teach the use of it. 'Tis the habit alone of reasoning which can make a reasoner. And men can never be better invited to the habit than when they find pleasure in it. A freedom of raillery, a liberty in decent language to question everything, and an allowance of unravelling or refuting any argument, without offence to the arguer, are the only terms which can render such speculative conversations any way agreeable. For, to say truth, they have been rendered burdensome to mankind by the strictness of the laws prescribed to them, and by the prevailing pedantry and bigotry of those who reign in them, and assume to themselves to be dictators in these provinces.

Semper ego auditor tantum?[1] is as natural a case of complaint in divinity, in morals, and in philosophy, as it was of old the satirist's in poetry. Vicissitude is a mighty law of discourse, and mightily longed for by mankind. In matter of reason, more is done in a minute or two, by way of question and reply, than by a continued discourse of whole hours. Orations are fit only to move the passions; and the power of declamation is to terrify, exalt, ravish, or delight, rather than satisfy or instruct.

---

[1] ["Must I always be a listener only?"—Juvenal, *Sat.* i. 1.]

SHAFTESBURY'S CHARACTERISTICS

A free conference is a close fight. The other way, in comparison to it, is merely a brandishing or beating the air. To be obstructed therefore and manacled in conferences, and to be confined to hear orations on certain subjects, must needs give us a distaste, and render the subjects so managed as disagreeable as the managers. Men had rather reason upon trifles, so they may reason freely, and without the imposition of authority, than on the usefullest and best subjects in the world, where they are held under a restraint and fear.

Nor is it a wonder that men are generally such faint reasoners, and care so little to argue strictly on any trivial subject in company, when they dare so little exert their reason in greater matters, and are forced to argue lamely where they have need of the greatest activity and strength. The same thing therefore happens here as in strong and healthy bodies which are debarred their natural exercise and confined in a narrow space. They are forced to use odd gestures and contortions. They have a sort of action, and move still, though with the worst grace imaginable. For the animal spirits in such sound and active limbs cannot lie dead or without employment. And thus the natural free spirits of ingenious men, if imprisoned and controlled, will find out other ways of motion to relieve themselves in their constraint; and whether it be in burlesque, mimicry, or buffoonery, they will be glad at any rate to vent themselves, and be revenged on their constrainers.

If men are forbid to speak their minds seriously on certain subjects, they will do it ironically. If they are forbid to speak at all upon such subjects, or if they find it really dangerous to do so, they will then redouble their disguise, involve themselves in mysteriousness, and talk so as hardly to be understood, or at least not plainly interpreted, by those who are disposed to do them a mischief. And thus raillery is brought more in fashion, and runs into an extreme. 'Tis the persecuting spirit has raised the bantering one; and want of liberty may account

FREEDOM OF WIT AND HUMOUR

for want of a true politeness, and for the corruption or wrong use of pleasantry and humour.

If in this respect we strain the just measure of what we call urbanity, and are apt sometimes to take a buffooning rustic air, we may thank the ridiculous solemnity and sour humour of our pedagogues; or rather, they may thank themselves, if they in particular meet with the heaviest of this kind of treatment. For it will naturally fall heaviest where the constraint has been the severest. The greater the weight is, the bitterer will be the satire. The higher the slavery, the more exquisite the buffoonery.

That this is really so, may appear by looking on those countries where the spiritual tyranny is highest. For the greatest of buffoons are the Italians; and in their writings, in their freer sort of conversations, on their theatres, and in their streets, buffoonery and burlesque are in the highest vogue. 'Tis the only manner in which the poor cramped wretches can discharge a free thought. We must yield to them the superiority in this sort of wit. For what wonder is it if we, who have more of liberty, have less dexterity in that egregious way of raillery and ridicule?

Section V

'Tis for this reason, I verily believe, that the ancients discover so little of this spirit, and that there is hardly such a thing found as mere burlesque in any authors of the politer ages. The manner indeed in which they treated the very gravest subjects was somewhat different from that of our days. Their treatises were generally in a free and familiar style. They chose to give us the representation of real discourse and converse, by treating their subjects in the way of dialogue[1] and free debate. The scene was commonly laid at table, or in the public walks or meeting-places; and the usual wit and

---

[1] See the following treatise, viz. *Soliloquy*, part i. § 3.

humour of their real discourses appeared in those of their own composing. And this was fair. For without wit and humour, reason can hardly have its proof or be distinguished. The magisterial voice and high strain of the pedagogue commands reverence and awe. 'Tis of admirable use to keep understandings at a distance and out of reach. The other manner, on the contrary, gives the fairest hold, and suffers an antagonist to use his full strength hand to hand upon even ground.

'Tis not to be imagined what advantage the reader has when he can thus cope with his author, who is willing to come on a fair stage with him, and exchange the tragic buskin for an easier and more natural gait and habit. Grimace and tone are mighty helps to imposture. And many a formal piece of sophistry holds proof under a severe brow, which would not pass under an easy one. 'Twas the saying of an ancient sage,[1] "that humour was the only test of gravity; and gravity of humour. For a subject which would not bear raillery was suspicious; and a jest which would not bear a serious examination was certainly false wit."

But some gentlemen there are so full of the spirit of bigotry and false zeal, that when they hear principles examined, sciences and arts inquired into, and matters of importance treated with this frankness of humour, they imagine presently that all professions must fall to the ground, all establishments come to ruin, and nothing orderly or decent be left standing in the world. They fear, or pretend to fear, that religion itself will be endangered by this free way, and are therefore as much alarmed at this liberty in private conversation,

[1] Gorgias Leontinus apud Arist. *Rhetor.* iii. 18, τὴν μὲν σπουδὴν διαφθείρειν γέλωτι τὸν δὲ γέλωτα σπουδῇ, which the translator renders, *seria risu, risum seriis discutere*. [As is complained by Brown in his *Essays on the Characteristics* (i. § 9), Shaftesbury here perverts the passage he cites. The saying of Gorgias, endorsed by Aristotle, was simply that in argument one should meet serious pleading with humour, and humour with serious pleading. The second sentence put by Shaftesbury in quotation marks is his own addendum.]

FREEDOM OF WIT AND HUMOUR

and under prudent management, as if it were grossly used in public company, or before the solemnest assembly. But the case, as I apprehend it, is far different. For you are to remember, my friend, that I am writing to you in defence only of the liberty of *the club*, and of that sort of freedom which is taken amongst gentlemen and friends who know one another perfectly well. And that 'tis natural for me to defend liberty with this restriction, you may infer from the very notion I have of liberty itself.

'Tis surely a violation of the freedom of public assemblies for any one to take the chair who is neither called nor invited to it. To start questions, or manage debates, which offend the public ear, is to be wanting in that respect which is due to common society. Such subjects should either not be treated at all in public, or in such a manner as to occasion no scandal or disturbance. The public is not, on any account, to be laughed at to its face; or so reprehended for its follies as to make it think itself contemned. And what is contrary to good breeding is in this respect as contrary to liberty. It belongs to men of slavish principles to affect a superiority over the vulgar, and to despise the multitude. The lovers of mankind respect and honour conventions and societies of men. And in mixed company, and places where men are met promiscuously on account of diversion or affairs, 'tis an imposition and hardship to force them to hear what they dislike, and to treat of matters in a dialect which many who are present have perhaps been never used to. 'Tis a breach of the harmony of public conversation to take things in such a key as is above the common reach, puts others to silence, and robs them of their privilege of turn. But as to private society, and what passes in select companies, where friends meet knowingly, and with that very design of exercising their wit, and looking freely into all subjects, I see no pretence for any one to be offended at the way of raillery and humour, which is the very life of such conversations; the only thing which makes good company, and frees it from the formality of business, and the tutorage and dogmaticalness of the schools.

Section VI

To return therefore to our argument. If the best of our modern conversations are apt to run chiefly upon trifles; if rational discourses (especially those of a deeper speculation) have lost their credit, and are in disgrace because of their formality; there is reason for more allowance in the way of humour and gaiety. An easier method of treating these subjects will make them more agreeable and familiar. To dispute about them, will be the same as about other matters. They need not spoil good company, or take from the ease or pleasure of a polite conversation. And the oftener these conversations are renewed, the better will be their effect. We shall grow better reasoners, by reasoning pleasantly, and at our ease; taking up or laying down these subjects as we fancy. So that, upon the whole, I must own to you, I cannot be scandalised at the raillery you took notice of, nor at the effect it had upon our company. The humour was agreeable, and the pleasant confusion which the conversation ended in, is at this time as pleasant to me upon reflection, when I consider that instead of being discouraged from resuming the debate, we were so much the readier to meet again at any time, and dispute upon the same subjects, even with more ease and satisfaction than before.

We had been a long while entertained, you know, upon the subject of morality and religion. And amidst the different opinions started and maintained by several of the parties, with great life and ingenuity, one or other would every now and then take the liberty to appeal to common sense. Every one allowed the appeal, and was willing to stand the trial. No one but was assured common sense would justify him. But when issue was joined, and the cause examined at the bar, there could be no judgment given. The parties however were not less forward in renewing their appeal on the very next occasion which presented. No one would offer to call the authority of the court in question, till a gentleman, whose good understanding was never yet brought in doubt, desired the company, very gravely, that they would tell him what common sense was.

"If by the word sense we were to understand opinion and judgment, and by the word common the generality or any considerable part of mankind, 'twould be hard, he said, to discover where the subject of common sense could lie. For that which was according to the sense of one part of mankind, was against the sense of another. And if the majority were to determine common sense, it would change as often as men changed. That which was according to common sense to-day, would be the contrary to-morrow, or soon after."

But notwithstanding the different judgments of mankind in most subjects, there were some however in which 'twas supposed they all agreed, and had the same thoughts in common.—The question was asked still, *Where?* "For whatever was of any moment, 'twas supposed, might be reduced under the head of religion, policy, or morals.

"Of the differences in religion there was no occasion to speak; the case was so fully known to all, and so feelingly understood by Christians, in particular, among themselves. They had made sound experiment upon one another; each party in their turn. No endeavours had been wanting on the side of any particular sect. Whichever chanced to have the power, failed not of putting all means in execution, to make their private sense the public one. But all in vain. *Common sense* was as hard still to determine as *catholic* or *orthodox*. What with one was inconceivable mystery, to another was of easy comprehension. What to one was absurdity, to another was demonstration.

"As for policy; what sense or whose could be called common, was equally a question. If plain British or Dutch sense were right, Turkish and French sense must certainly be very wrong. And as mere nonsense as passive obedience seemed, we found it to be the common sense of a great party amongst ourselves, a greater party in Europe, and perhaps the greatest part of all the world besides.

"As for morals; the difference, if possible, was still wider. For without considering the opinions and customs of the many barbarous and illiterate nations, we saw that even the few who had attained to riper letters, and to philosophy, could never as yet agree on one and the same system, or acknowledge the same moral principles. And some even of our most admired modern philosophers had fairly told us, that virtue and vice had, after all, no other law or measure than mere fashion and vogue."

It might have appeared perhaps unfair in our friends had they treated only the graver subjects in this manner, and suffered the lighter to escape. For in the gayer part of life, our follies are as solemn as in the most serious. The fault is, we carry the laugh but half-way. The false earnest is ridiculed, but the false jest passes secure, and becomes as errant deceit as the other. Our diversions, our plays, our amusements become solemn. We dream of happiness and possessions, and enjoyments in which we have no understanding, no certainty; and yet we pursue these as the best known and most certain things in the world. There is nothing so foolish and deluding as a partial scepticism.[1] For whilst the doubt is cast only on one side, the certainty grows so much stronger on the other. Whilst only one face of folly appears ridiculous, the other grows more solemn and deceiving.

But 'twas not thus with our friends. They seemed better critics, and more ingenious and fair in their way of questioning received opinions, and exposing the ridicule of things. And if you will allow me to carry on their humour, I will venture to make the experiment throughout; and try what certain knowledge or assurance of things may be recovered, in that very way,

[1] *Moralists,* part ii. § 1.

FREEDOM OF WIT AND HUMOUR

by which all certainty, you thought, was lost, and an endless scepticism introduced.

PART II

Section I

If a native of Ethiopia were on a sudden transported into Europe, and placed either at Paris or Venice at a time of carnival, when the general face of mankind was disguised, and almost every creature wore a mask, 'tis probable he would for some time be at a stand, before he discovered the cheat; not imagining that a whole people could be so fantastical as upon agreement, at an appointed time, to transform themselves by a variety of habits, and make it a solemn practice to impose on one another, by this universal confusion of characters and persons. Though he might at first perhaps have looked on this with a serious eye, it would be hardly possible for him to hold his countenance when he had perceived what was carrying on. The Europeans, on their side, might laugh perhaps at this simplicity. But our Ethiopian would certainly laugh with better reason. 'Tis easy to see which of the two would be ridiculous. For he who laughs and is himself ridiculous, bears a double share of ridicule. However, should it so happen that in the transport of ridicule, our Ethiopian, having his head still running upon masks, and knowing nothing of the fair complexion and common dress of the Europeans, should upon the sight of a natural face and habit, laugh just as heartily as before, would not he in his turn become ridiculous, by carrying the jest too far; when by a silly presumption he took nature for mere art, and mistook perhaps a man of sobriety and sense for one of those ridiculous mummers?

There was a time when men were accountable only for their actions and behaviour. Their opinions were left to themselves.

SHAFTESBURY'S CHARACTERISTICS

They had liberty to differ in these as in their faces. Every one took the air and look which was natural to him. But in process of time it was thought decent to mend men's countenances, and render their intellectual complexions uniform and of a sort. Thus the magistrate became a dresser, and in his turn was dressed too, as he deserved, when he had given up his power to a new order of tire-men. But though in this extraordinary conjuncture 'twas agreed that there was only one certain and true dress, one single peculiar air, to which it was necessary all people should conform, yet the misery was, that neither the magistrate nor the tire-men themselves could resolve which of the various modes was the exact true one. Imagine, now, what the effect of this must needs be; when men became persecuted thus on every side about their air and feature, and were put to their shifts how to adjust and compose their mien, according to the right mode; when a thousand models, a thousand patterns of dress were current, and altered every now and then, upon occasion, according to fashion and the humour of the times. Judge whether men's countenances were not like to grow constrained, and the natural visage of mankind, by this habit, distorted, convulsed, and rendered hardly knowable.

But as unnatural or artificial as the general face of things may have been rendered by this unhappy care of dress, and over-tenderness for the safety of complexions, we must not therefore imagine that all faces are alike besmeared or plastered. All is not fucus or mere varnish. Nor is the face of Truth less fair and beautiful, for all the counterfeit vizards which have been put upon her. We must remember the Carnival, and what the occasion has been of this wild concourse and medley; who were the institutors of it; and to what purpose men were thus set awork and amused. We may laugh sufficiently at the original cheat; and, if pity will suffer us, may make ourselves diversion enough with the folly and madness of those who are thus caught and practised on by these impostures; but we must remember withal our Ethiopian, and beware lest by

FREEDOM OF WIT AND HUMOUR

taking plain Nature for a vizard, we become more ridiculous than the people whom we ridicule. Now if a jest or ridicule thus strained be capable of leading the judgment so far astray, 'tis probable that an excess of fear or horror may work the same effect.

Had it been your fortune, my friend, to have lived in Asia at the time when the Magi[1] by an egregious imposture got possession of the empire, no doubt you would have had a detestation of the act; and perhaps the very persons of the men might have grown so odious to you that after all the cheats and abuses they had committed, you might have seen them dispatched with as relentless an eye as our later European ancestors saw the destruction of a like politic body of conjurers, the Knights Templars, who were almost become an over-match for the civil sovereign. Your indignation perhaps might have carried you to propose the razing all monuments and memorials of these magicians. You might have resolved not to leave so much as their houses standing. But if it had happened that these magicians, in the time of their dominion, had made any collection of books, or compiled any themselves, in which they had treated of philosophy, or morals, or any other science, or part of learning, would you have carried your resentment so far as to have extirpated these also, and condemned every opinion or doctrine they had espoused, for no other reason than merely because they had espoused it? Hardly a Scythian, a Tartar, or a Goth, would act or reason so absurdly. Much less would you, my friend, have carried on this magophony, or priest-massacre, with such a barbarous zeal. For, in good earnest, to destroy a philosophy in hatred to a man, implies as errant a Tartar-notion as to destroy or murder a man in order to plunder him of his wit, and get the inheritance of his understanding.

I must confess indeed that had all the institutions, statutes, and regulations of this ancient hierarchy resembled the funda-

[1] *Misc.* ii. ch. 1.

mental one of the Order itself,[1] they might with a great deal of justice have been suppressed; for one cannot, without some abhorrence, read that law of theirs:—

Nam magus ex matre et gnato gignatur oportet.[2]

But the conjurers (as we'll rather suppose) having considered that they ought in their principle to appear as fair as possible to the world, the better to conceal their practice, found it highly for their interest to espouse some excellent moral rules, and establish the very best maxims of this kind. They thought it for their advantage perhaps, on their first setting out, to recommend the greatest purity of religion, the greatest integrity of life and manners. They may perhaps, too, in general, have preached up charity and good-will. They may have set to view the fairest face of human nature; and together with their byelaws and political institutions have interwove the honestest morals and best doctrine in the world.

How therefore should we have behaved ourselves in this affair? How should we have carried ourselves towards this order of men, at the time of the discovery of their cheat, and ruin of their empire? Should we have fallen to work instantly with their systems, struck at their opinions and doctrines without distinction, and erected a contrary philosophy in their teeth? Should we have flown at every religious and moral principle, denied every natural and social affection, and rendered men as much wolves[3] as was possible to one another, whilst we described them such; and endeavoured to make them see themselves by far more monstrous and corrupt than with the worst intentions it was ever possible for the worst of them to become?—This,

[1] Πέρσαι δὲ καὶ μάλιστα αὐτῶν οἱ σοφίαν ἀσκεῖν δοκοῦντες, οἱ Μάγοι, γαμοῦσι τὰς μητέρας.—Sext. Empir. *Pyrrh.* iii. 24.
["The Persians, and especially their Wise Men, the Magi, marry their mothers."]

[2] ["For a Magus must be born of a mother and her son."—Catullus, 87 (90).]

[3] *Infra*, part iii. § 3, and *Moralists*, part ii. § 5, at the end.

you'll say, doubtless would have been a very preposterous part, and could never have been acted by other than mean spirits, such as had been held in awe and over-frighted by the Magi.[1]

And yet an able and witty philosopher[2] of our nation was, we know, of late years, so possessed with a horror of this kind, that both with respect to politics and morals he directly acted in this spirit of massacre. The fright he took upon the sight of the then governing powers who unjustly assumed the authority of the people, gave him such an abhorrence of all popular government, and of the very notion of liberty itself, that to extinguish it for ever, he recommends the very extinguishing of Letters, and exhorts princes not to spare so much as an ancient Roman or Greek historian. . . . Is not this in truth somewhat Gothic? And has not our philosopher, in appearance, something of the savage, that he should use philosophy and learning as the Scythians are said to have used Anacharsis and others, for having visited the wise of Greece, and learnt the manners of a polite people?

His quarrel with religion was the same as with liberty. The same times gave him the same terror in this other kind. He had nothing before his eyes beside the ravage of enthusiasm, and the artifice of those who raised and conducted that spirit. And the good sociable man, as savage and unsociable as he would make himself and all mankind appear by his philosophy, exposed himself during his life, and took the utmost pains that after his death we might be delivered from the occasion of these

---

[1] *Misc.* ii. ch. ii in the notes.

[2] Mr. Hobbes, who thus expresses himself: "By reading of these Greek and Latin authors, men from their childhood have gotten a habit (under a false show of liberty) of favouring tumults, and of licentious controlling the actions of their sovereigns."—*Leviathan*, part ii. ch. xxi. p. 111. By this reasoning of Mr. Hobbes it should follow that there can never be any tumults or deposing of sovereigns at Constantinople or in Mogol. See again, pp. 171 and 377, and what he intimates to his prince (p. 193) concerning this extirpation of ancient literature, in favour of his *Leviathan* thesis and new philosophy.

terrors. He did his utmost to show us "that both in religion and morals we were imposed on by our governors; that there was nothing which by nature inclined us either way; nothing which naturally drew us to the love of what was without or beyond ourselves."[1] Though the love of such great truths and sovereign maxims, as he imagined these to be, made him the most laborious of all men in composing systems of this kind for our use; and forced him, notwithstanding his natural fear, to run continually the highest risk of being a martyr for our deliverance.

Give me leave therefore, my friend, on this occasion, to prevent your seriousness, and assure you that there is no such mighty danger as we are apt to imagine from these fierce prosecutors of superstition, who are so jealous of every religious or moral principle. Whatever savages they may appear in philosophy, they are in their common capacity as civil persons as one can wish. Their free communicating of their principles may witness for them. 'Tis the height of sociableness to be thus friendly and communicative.

If the principles, indeed, were concealed from us, and made a mystery, they might become considerable. Things are often made so by being kept as secrets of a sect or party; and nothing helps this more than the antipathy and shyness of a contrary party. If we fall presently into horrors and consternation upon the hearing maxims which are thought poisonous, we are in no disposition to use that familiar and easy part of reason which is the best antidote. The only poison to reason is passion. For false reasoning is soon redressed where passion is removed. But if the very hearing certain propositions of philosophy be sufficient to move our passion, 'tis plain the poison has already gained on us, and we are effectually prevented in the use of our reasoning faculty.

Were it not for the prejudices of this kind, what should hinder us from diverting ourselves with the fancy of one of

[1] *Inquiry Concerning Virtue*, bk. ii. part i. § 1, at the end.

FREEDOM OF WIT AND HUMOUR

these modern reformers we have been speaking of? What should we say to one of these anti-zealots, who, in the zeal of such a cool philosophy, should assure us faithfully "that we were the most mistaken men in the world to imagine there was any such thing as natural faith or justice? For that it was only force and power which constituted right. That there was no such thing in reality as virtue; no principle of order in things above or below; no secret charm or force of nature by which every one was made to operate willingly or unwillingly towards public good, and punished and tormented if he did otherwise." . . . Is not this the very charm itself? Is not the gentleman at this instant under the power of it? . . . "Sir! the philosophy you have condescended to reveal to us is most extraordinary. We are beholden to you for your instruction. But, pray, whence is this zeal in our behalf? What are we to you? Are you our father? Or if you were, why this concern for us? Is there then such a thing as natural affection? If not, why all this pains, why all this danger on our account? Why not keep this secret to yourself? Of what advantage is it to you to deliver us from the cheat? The more are taken in it the better. 'Tis directly against your interest to undeceive us and let us know that only private interest governs you, and that nothing nobler, or of a larger kind, should govern us whom you converse with. Leave us to ourselves, and to that notable art by which we are happily tamed, and rendered thus mild and sheepish. 'Tis not fit we should know that by nature we are all wolves. Is it possible that one who has really discovered himself such, should take pains to communicate such a discovery?"

Section II

In reality, my friend, a severe brow may well be spared on this occasion, when we are put thus upon the defence of common honesty by such fair honest gentlemen, who are in practice so different from what they would appear in speculation. Knaves

SHAFTESBURY'S CHARACTERISTICS

I know there are in notion and principle, as well as in practice, who think all honesty as well as religion a mere cheat, and by a very consistent reasoning have resolved deliberately to do whatever by power or art they are able for their private advantage; but such as these never open themselves in friendship to others. They have no such passion for truth, or love for mankind. They have no quarrel with religion or morals; but know what use to make of both upon occasion. If they ever discover their principles, 'tis only at unawares. They are sure to preach honesty and go to church.

On the other side, the gentlemen for whom I am apologising cannot however be called hypocrites. They speak as ill of themselves as they possibly can. If they have hard thoughts of human nature, 'tis a proof still of their humanity that they give such warning to the world. If they represent men by nature treacherous and wild, 'tis out of care for mankind, lest by being too tame and trusting, they should easily be caught.

Impostors naturally speak the best of human nature, that they may the easier abuse it. These gentlemen, on the contrary, speak the worst; and had rather they themselves should be censured with the rest, than that a few should by imposture prevail over the many. For 'tis opinion of goodness which creates easiness of trust, and by trust we are betrayed to power; our very reason being thus captivated by those in whom we come insensibly to have an implicit faith. But supposing one another to be by nature such very savages, we shall take care to come less in one another's power; and apprehending power to be insatiably coveted by all, we shall the better fence against the evil; not by giving all into one hand (as the champion of this cause would have us), but, on the contrary, by a right division and balance of power, and by the restraint of good laws and limitations, which may secure the public liberty.

Should you therefore ask me, whether I really thought these gentlemen were fully persuaded of the principles they so often advance in company? I should tell you, that though I would

FREEDOM OF WIT AND HUMOUR

not absolutely arraign the gentlemen's sincerity, yet there was something of mystery in the case, more than was imagined. The reason, perhaps, why men of wit delight so much to espouse these paradoxical systems, is not in truth that they are so fully satisfied with them, but in a view the better to oppose some other systems, which by their fair appearance have helped, they think, to bring mankind under subjection. They imagine that by this general scepticism, which they would introduce, they shall better deal with the dogmatical spirit which prevails in some particular subjects. And when they have accustomed men to bear contradiction in the main, and hear the nature of things disputed at large, it may be safer (they conclude) to argue separately upon certain nice points in which they are not altogether so well satisfied. So that from hence, perhaps, you may still better apprehend why, in conversation, the spirit of raillery prevails so much, and notions are taken up for no reason besides their being odd and out of the way.

Section III

But let who will condemn the humour thus described, for my part I am in no such apprehension from this sceptical kind of wit. Men indeed may, in a serious way, be so wrought on and confounded, by different modes of opinion, different systems and schemes imposed by authority, that they may wholly lose all notion or comprehension of truth. I can easily apprehend what effect awe has over men's understandings. I can very well suppose men may be frighted out of their wits, but I have no apprehension they should be laughed out of them. I can hardly imagine that in a pleasant way they should ever be talked out of their love for society, or reasoned out of humanity and common sense. A mannerly wit can hurt no cause or interest for which I am in the least concerned; and philosophical speculations, politely managed, can never surely render mankind more unsociable or uncivilised. This is not the quarter from whence

SHAFTESBURY'S CHARACTERISTICS

I can possibly expect an inroad of savageness and barbarity. And by the best of my observation I have learnt that virtue is never such a sufferer, by being contested, as by being betrayed. My fear is not so much from its witty antagonists, who give it exercise, and put it on its defence, as from its tender nurses, who are apt to overlay it, and kill it with excess of care and cherishing.

I have known a building, which by the officiousness of the workmen has been so shored and screwed up on the side where they pretended it had a leaning, that it has at last been turned the contrary way and overthrown. There has something, perhaps, of this kind happened in morals. Men have not been contented to show the natural advantages of honesty and virtue. They have rather lessened these, the better, as they thought, to advance another foundation. They have made virtue so mercenary a thing, and have talked so much of its rewards, that one can hardly tell what there is in it, after all, which can be worth rewarding. For to be bribed only or terrified into an honest practice, bespeaks little of real honesty or worth. We may make, 'tis true, whatever bargain we think fit; and may bestow in favour what overplus we please; but there can be no excellence or wisdom in voluntarily rewarding what is neither estimable nor deserving. And if virtue be not really estimable in itself, I can see nothing estimable in following it for the sake of a bargain.

If the love of doing good be not, of itself, a good and right inclination, I know not how there can possibly be such a thing as goodness or virtue. If the inclination be right, 'tis a perverting of it, to apply it solely to the reward, and make us conceive such wonders of the grace and favour which is to attend virtue, when there is so little shown of the intrinsic worth or value of the thing itself.

I could be almost tempted to think that the true reason why some of the most heroic virtues have so little notice taken of them in our holy religion, is because there would have been

FREEDOM OF WIT AND HUMOUR

no room left for disinterestedness had they been entitled to a share of that infinite reward which Providence has by revelation assigned to other duties. Private friendship,[1] and zeal for the public and our country, are virtues purely voluntary in a Christian. They are no essential parts of his charity. He is not so tied to the affairs of this life, nor is he obliged to enter into such engagements with this lower world, as are of no help to him in acquiring a better. His conversation is in heaven: Nor has he occasion for such supernumerary cares, or embarrassments here on earth, as may obstruct his way thither, or retard him in the careful task of working out his own salvation. If nevertheless any portion of reward be reserved hereafter for the generous part of a patriot, or that of a thorough friend, this is

[1] By private friendship no fair reader can here suppose is meant that common benevolence and charity which every Christian is obliged to show towards all men, and in particular towards his fellow-Christians, his neighbour, brother, and kindred, of whatever degree; but that peculiar relation which is formed by a consent and harmony of minds, by mutual esteem, and reciprocal tenderness and affection; and which we emphatically call a friendship. Such was that between the two Jewish heroes after mentioned, whose love and tenderness was surpassing that of women (2 Sam. i.). Such were those friendships described so frequently by poets, between Pylades and Orestes, Theseus and Pirithous, with many others. Such were those between philosophers, heroes, and the greatest of men; between Socrates and Antisthenes, Plato and Dion, Epaminondas and Pelopidas, Scipio and Laelius, Cato and Brutus, Thrasea and Helvidius. And such there may have lately been, and are still perhaps in our own age, though envy suffers not the few examples of this kind to be remarked in public. The author's meaning is indeed so plain of itself, that it needs no explanatory apology to satisfy an impartial reader. As for others who object the singularity of the assertion, as differing (they suppose) from what our reverend doctors in religion commonly maintain, they may read what the learned and pious Bishop Taylor says in his Treatise of Friendship. "You inquire," says he, "how far a dear and a perfect friendship is authorised by the principles of Christianity? To this I answer, that the word friendship in the sense we commonly mean by it, is not so much as named in the New Testament, and our religion takes no notice of it. You think it strange; but read on, before you spend so much as the beginning of a passion or a wonder upon it. There is mention of friendship of the world;

still behind the curtain, and happily concealed from us; that we may be the more deserving of it when it comes.

It appears indeed under the Jewish dispensation that each of these virtues had their illustrious examples, and were in some manner recommended to us as honourable, and worthy our imitation. Even Saul himself, as ill a prince as he is represented, appears both living and dying to have been respected and praised for the love he bore his native country. And the love which was so remarkable between his son and his successor, gives us a noble view of a disinterested friendship, at least on one side. But the heroic virtue of these persons had only the common reward of praise attributed to it, and could not claim a future recompense under a religion which taught no future state, nor exhibited any rewards or punishments, besides such as were temporal, and had respect to the written law.

and it is said to be enmity with God; but the word is nowhere else named, or to any other purpose, in all the New Testament. It speaks of friends often; but by friends are meant our acquaintance, or our kindred, the relatives of our family, or our fortune, or our sect, etc.—And I think I have reason to be confident, that the word friend (speaking of human intercourse) is no other ways used in the Gospels, or Epistles, or Acts of the Apostles." And afterwards, "Christian charity," says he, "is friendship to all the world; and when friendships were the noblest things in the world, charity was little, like the sun drawn in at a chink, or his beams drawn into the centre of a burning-glass. But Christian charity is friendship expanded like the face of the sun, when it mounts above the eastern hills." In reality the good Bishop draws all his notions as well as examples of private friendship from the heathen world, or from the times preceding Christianity. And after citing a Greek author, he immediately adds: "Of such immortal, abstracted, pure friendships, indeed, there is no great plenty; but they who are the same to their friend ἀπόπροθεν, when he is in another country, or in another world, are fit to preserve the sacred fire for eternal sacrifices, and to perpetuate the memory of those exemplary friendships of the best men, which have filled the world with history and wonder; for in no other sense but this can it be true that friendships are pure loves, regarding to do good more than to receive it. He that is a friend after death, hopes not for a recompense from his friend, and makes no bargain either for fame or love; but is rewarded with the conscience and satisfaction of doing bravely."

FREEDOM OF WIT AND HUMOUR

And thus the Jews as well as heathens were left to their philosophy, to be instructed in the sublime part of virtue, and induced by reason to that which was never enjoined them by command. No premium or penalty being enforced in these cases, the disinterested part subsisted, the virtue was a free choice, and the magnanimity of the act was left entire. He who would be generous had the means. He who would frankly serve his friend, or country, at the expense even of his life,[1] might do it on fair terms. *Dulce et decorum est*[2] was his sole reason. 'Twas inviting and becoming. 'Twas good and honest. And that this is still a good reason, and according to common sense, I will endeavour to satisfy you. For I should think myself very ridiculous to be angry with any one for thinking me dishonest, if I could give no account of my honesty, nor show upon what principle I differed from a knave.[3]

PART III

SECTION I

THE Roman satirist may be thought more than ordinarily satirical, when speaking of the nobility and court; he is so far from allowing them to be the standard of politeness and good sense, that he makes them in a manner the reverse—

> Rarus enim ferme sensus communis in illa
> Fortuna. . . .[4]

---

[1] "Peradventure," says the holy Apostle, "for a good man some would even dare to die," τάχα τὶς καὶ τολμᾷ, etc., Rom. v. 7. This the Apostle judiciously supposes to belong to human nature; though he is so far from founding any precept on it, that he ushers his private opinion with a very dubious peradventure.

[2] Hor. *Od.* iii. 2.

[3] *Infra*, part iv. § 1. *Advice to an Author*, part i. § 2.

[4] Juv. viii. 73. [Shaftesbury here takes it to mean " rare is common sense in men of that rank."]

Some of the most ingenious commentators,[1] however, interpret this very differently from what is generally apprehended. They make this common sense of the poet, by a Greek derivation, to signify sense of public weal, and of the common interest; love of the community or society, natural affection, humanity, obligingness, or that sort of civility which rises from a just sense of the common rights of mankind, and the natural equality there is among those of the same species.

And indeed if we consider the thing nicely, it must seem somewhat hard in the poet to have denied wit or ability to a court such as that of Rome, even under a Tiberius or a Nero. But for humanity or sense of public good, and the common interest of mankind, 'twas no such deep satire to question whether this was properly the spirit of a court. 'Twas difficult to apprehend what community subsisted among courtiers, or

[1] Viz. the two Casaubons, Is. and Mer., Salmasius, and our English Gataker: see the first in Capitolinus, *Vit. M. Ant.* sub finem; the second in his Comment on M. Ant. i. §§ 13, 16; Gataker on the same place, and Salmasius in the same Life of Capitolinus, at the end of his annotations. The Greek word is κοινονοημοσύνη, which Salmasius interprets, "moderatam, usitatam et ordinariam hominis mentem quae in commune quodammodo consulit, nec omnia ad commodum suum refert, respectumque etiam habet eorum cum quibus versatur, modeste, modiceque de se sentiens. At contra inflati et superbi omnes se sibi tantum suisque commodis natos arbitrantur, et prae se caeteros contemnunt et negligunt; et hi sunt qui *sensum communem* non habere recte dici possunt. Nam ita *sensum communem* accipit Juvenalis Sat. viii., Rarus enim ferme sensus communis, etc. φιλανθρωπίαν et χρηστότητα Galenus vocat, quam Marcus de se loquens κοινονοημοσύνην; et alibi, ubi de eadem re loquitur, μετριότητα καὶ εὐγνωμοσύνην, qua gratiam illi fecerit Marcus simul eundi ad Germanicum bellum ac sequendi se." In the same manner Isaac Casaubon: Herodianus, says he, calls this the τὸ μέτριον καὶ ἰσόμετρον. "Subjicit vero Antoninus quasi hanc vocem interpretans, καὶ τὸ ἐφεῖσθαι τοῖς φίλοις μήτε συνδειπνεῖν αὐτῷ πάντως, μήτε συναποδημεῖν ἐπάναγκες." This, I am persuaded, is the *sensus communis* of Horace (1 *Sat.* iii.) which has been unobserved, as far as I can learn, by any of his commentators; it being remarkable withal, that in this early Satire of Horace, before his latter days, and when his philosophy as yet inclined to the less rigid assertors of virtue, he puts this expression (as may

FREEDOM OF WIT AND HUMOUR

what public between an absolute prince and his slave-subjects. And for real society, there could be none between such as had no other sense than that of private good.

Our poet therefore seems not so immoderate in his censure, if we consider it is the heart, rather than the head, he takes to task, when, reflecting on a court education, he thinks it unapt to raise any affection towards a country, and looks upon young princes and lords as the young masters of the world; who being indulged in all their passions, and trained up in all manner of licentiousness, have that thorough contempt and disregard of

---

be seen by the whole Satire taken together) into the mouth of a Crispinus, or some ridiculous mimic of that severe philosophy, to which the coinage of the word κοινονοημοσύνη properly belonged. For so the poet again (*Sat.* iv. 77) uses the word *sensus*, speaking of those who without sense of manners, or common society, without the least respect or deference to others, press rudely upon their friends, and upon all company in general, without regard to time or place, or anything besides their selfish and brutish humour :—

       Haud illud quaerentes num sine sensu,
    Tempore num faciant alieno.

ἀναισθητῶς, as old Lambin interprets it, though without any other explanation, referring only to the *sensus communis* of Horace in that other Satire. Thus Seneca (*Epist.* 105), Odium autem ex offensa sic vitabis, neminem lacessendo gratuito : a quo te *sensus communis* tuebitur. And Cicero accordingly, Justitiae partes sunt, non violare homines: verecundiae, non offendere. —i. *De Off.* It may be objected possibly by some, particularly versed in the philosophy above-mentioned, that the κανὸς νοῦς, to which the κοινονοημοσύνη seems to have relation, is of a different meaning. But they will consider withal how small the distinction was in that philosophy between the ὑπόληψις and the vulgar αἴσθησις; how generally passion was by those philosophers brought under the head of opinion. And when they consider, besides this, the very formation of the word κοινονοημοσύνη upon the model of the other femalised virtues, the εὐγνωμοσύνη, σωφροσύνη, δικαιοσύνη, etc., they will no longer hesitate on this interpretation.—The reader may perhaps by this note see better why the Latin title of *sensus communis* has been given to this second treatise. He may observe, withal, how the same poet Juvenal uses the word *sensus* in *Sat.* xv., Haec nostri pars optima sensus.

mankind, which mankind in a manner deserves, where arbitrary power is permitted and a tyranny adored—

> Haec satis ad juvenem, quem nobis fama superbum
> Tradit et inflatum, plenumque Nerone propinquo.[1]

A public spirit can come only from a social feeling or sense of partnership with human kind. Now there are none so far from being partners in this sense, or sharers in this common affection, as they who scarcely know an equal, nor consider themselves as subject to any law of fellowship or community. And thus morality and good government go together. There is no real love of virtue, without the knowledge of public good. And where absolute power is, there is no public.

They who live under a tyranny, and have learnt to admire its power as sacred and divine, are debauched as much in their religion as in their morals. Public good, according to their apprehension, is as little the measure or rule of government in the universe as in the State. They have scarce a notion of what is good or just, other than as mere will and power have determined. Omnipotence, they think, would hardly be itself, were it not at liberty to dispense with the laws of equity,[2] and change at pleasure the standard of moral rectitude.

But notwithstanding the prejudices and corruptions of this kind, 'tis plain there is something still of a public principle, even where it is most perverted and depressed. The worst of magistracies, the mere despotic kind, can show sufficient instances of zeal and affection towards it. Where no other government is known, it seldom fails of having that allegiance and duty paid it which is owing to a better form. The Eastern countries, and many barbarous nations, have been and still are examples of this kind. The personal love they bear their prince, however severe towards them, may show how natural an affection there

---

[1] ["So much for the young man whom fame gives out as proud and puffed-up, and full of his relationship to Nero."—Juvenal, viii. 71, 72.]

[2] Infra, *Advice to an Author*, part iii. § 1.

FREEDOM OF WIT AND HUMOUR

is towards government and order among mankind. If men have really no public parent, no magistrate in common to cherish and protect them, they will still imagine they have such a one; and, like new-born creatures who have never seen their dam, will fancy one for themselves, and apply (as by Nature prompted) to some like form, for favour and protection. In the room of a true foster-father and chief, they will take after a false one; and in the room of a legal government and just prince, obey even a tyrant, and endure a whole lineage and succession of such.

As for us Britons, thank Heaven, we have a better sense of government delivered to us from our ancestors. We have the notion of a public, and a constitution; how a legislative and how an executive is modelled. We understand weight and measure in this kind, and can reason justly on the balance of power and property. The maxims we draw from hence, are as evident as those in mathematics. Our increasing knowledge shows us every day, more and more, what common sense is in politics; and this must of necessity lead us to understand a like sense in morals, which is the foundation.

'Tis ridiculous to say there is any obligation on man to act sociably or honestly in a formed government, and not in that which is commonly called the state of nature.[1] For, to speak in the fashionable language of our modern philosophy: "Society being founded on a compact, the surrender made of every man's private unlimited right, into the hands of the majority, or such as the majority should appoint, was of free choice, and by a promise." Now the promise itself was made in the state of nature; and that which could make a promise obligatory in the state of nature, must make all other acts of humanity as much our real duty and natural part. Thus faith, justice, honesty, and virtue, must have been as early as the state of nature, or they could never have been at all. The civil union, or confederacy, could never make right or wrong, if they subsisted not

[1] *Moralists,* part ii. § 4, latter end.

before. He who was free to any villainy before his contract, will and ought to make as free with his contract when he thinks fit. The natural knave has the same reason to be a civil one, and may dispense with his politic capacity as oft as he sees occasion. 'Tis only his word stands in his way. . . . A man is obliged to keep his word. Why? Because he has given his word to keep it. . . . Is not this a notable account of the original of moral justice, and the rise of civil government and allegiance!

Section II

But to pass by these cavils of a philosophy which speaks so much of nature with so little meaning, we may with justice surely place it as a principle, " That if anything be natural, in any creature, or any kind, 'tis that which is preservative of the kind itself, and conducing to its welfare and support." If in original and pure nature it be wrong to break a promise, or be treacherous, 'tis as truly wrong to be in any respect inhuman, or any way wanting in our natural part towards human kind. If eating and drinking be natural, herding is so too. If any appetite or sense be natural, the sense of fellowship is the same. If there be anything of nature in that affection which is between the sexes, the affection is certainly as natural towards the consequent offspring; and so again between the offspring themselves, as kindred and companions, bred under the same discipline and economy. And thus a clan or tribe is gradually formed; a public is recognised; and besides the pleasure found in social entertainment, language, and discourse, there is so apparent a necessity for continuing this good correspondency and union, that to have no sense or feeling of this kind, no love of country, community, or anything in common, would be the same as to be insensible even of the plainest means of self-preservation, and most necessary condition of self-enjoyment.

How the wit of man should so puzzle this cause as to make civil government and society appear a kind of invention and creature of art, I know not. For my own part, methinks, this herding principle, and associating inclination, is seen so natural and strong in most men, that one might readily affirm 'twas even from the violence of this passion that so much disorder arose in the general society of mankind.

Universal good, or the interest of the world in general, is a kind of remote philosophical object. That greater community falls not easily under the eye. Nor is a national interest, or that of a whole people, or body politic, so readily apprehended. In less parties, men may be intimately conversant and acquainted with one another. They can there better taste society, and enjoy the common good and interest of a more contracted public. They view the whole compass and extent of their community, and see and know particularly whom they serve, and to what end they associate and conspire. All men have naturally their share of this combining principle; and they who are of the sprightliest and most active faculties have so large a share of it, that unless it be happily directed by right reason, it can never find exercise for itself in so remote a sphere as that of the body politic at large. For here perhaps the thousandth part of those whose interests are concerned are scarce so much as known by sight. No visible band is formed, no strict alliance; but the conjunction is made with different persons, orders, and ranks of men; not sensibly, but in idea, according to that general view or notion of a state or commonwealth.

Thus the social aim is disturbed for want of certain scope. The close sympathy and conspiring virtue is apt to lose itself, for want of direction, in so wide a field. Nor is the passion anywhere so strongly felt or vigorously exerted as in actual conspiracy or war; in which the highest geniuses are often known the forwardest to employ themselves. For the most generous spirits are the most combining. They delight most to move in concert, and feel (if I may so say) in the strongest manner the force of the confederating charm.

'Tis strange to imagine that war, which of all things appears the most savage, should be the passion of the most heroic spirits. But 'tis in war that the knot of fellowship is closest drawn. 'Tis in war that mutual succour is most given, mutual danger run, and common affection most exerted and employed. For heroism and philanthropy are almost one and the same. Yet by a small misguidance of the affection, a lover of mankind becomes a ravager; a hero and deliverer becomes an oppressor and destroyer.

Hence other divisions amongst men. Hence, in the way of peace and civil government, that love of party and subdivision by cabal. For sedition is a kind of *cantonising* already begun within the State. To *cantonise*[1] is natural; when the society grows vast and bulky; and powerful States have found other advantages in sending colonies abroad than merely that of having elbow-room at home, or extending their dominion into distant countries. Vast empires are in many respects unnatural; but particularly in this, that be they ever so well constituted, the affairs of many must, in such governments, turn upon a very few, and the relation be less sensible, and in a manner lost, between the magistrate and people, in a body so unwieldy in its limbs, and whose members lie so remote from one another and distant from the head.

'Tis in such bodies as these that strong factions are aptest to engender. The associating spirits, for want of exercise, form new movements, and seek a narrower sphere of activity, when they want action in a greater. Thus we have wheels within wheels. And in some national constitutions (notwithstanding the absurdity in politics) we have one empire within another. Nothing is so delightful as to incorporate. Distinctions of many kinds are invented. Religious societies are formed. Orders are erected, and their interests espoused and served with the utmost zeal and passion. Founders and patrons of this sort are never

[1] [This use of the term, and a general application of the substantive, were common in the seventeenth century. *E.g.* Locke: "They canton out to themselves a little Goshen in the intellectual world."—*Conduct of the Understanding.*]

wanting. Wonders are performed, in this wrong social spirit, by those members of separate societies. And the associating genius of man is never better proved than in those very societies, which are formed in opposition to the general one of mankind, and to the real interest of the State.

In short, the very spirit of faction, for the greatest part, seems to be no other than the abuse or irregularity of that social love and common affection which is natural to mankind. For the opposite of sociableness is selfishness. And of all characters, the thorough selfish one is the least forward in taking party. The men of this sort are, in this respect, true men of moderation. They are secure of their temper, and possess themselves too well to be in danger of entering warmly into any cause, or engaging deeply with any side or faction.

Section III

You have heard it, my friend, as a common saying, that interest governs the world. But, I believe, whoever looks narrowly into the affairs of it will find that passion, humour, caprice, zeal, faction, and a thousand other springs, which are counter to self-interest, have as considerable a part in the movements of this machine. There are more wheels and counterpoises in this engine than are easily imagined. 'Tis of too complex a kind to fall under one simple view, or be explained thus briefly in a word or two. The studiers of this mechanism must have a very partial eye to overlook all other motions besides those of the lowest and narrowest compass. 'Tis hard that in the plan or description of this clock-work no wheel or balance should be allowed on the side of the better and more enlarged affections; that nothing should be understood to be done in kindness or generosity, nothing in pure good-nature or friendship, or through any social or natural affection of any kind; when, perhaps, the mainsprings of this machine will be found to be either these very natural affections themselves, or a compound kind derived from them, and retaining more than one half of their nature.

But here, my friend, you must not expect that I should draw you up a formal scheme of the passions,[1] or pretend to show you their genealogy and relation: how they are interwoven with one another, or interfere with our happiness and interest. 'Twould be out of the genius and compass of such a letter as this, to frame a just plan or model by which you might, with an accurate view, observe what proportion the friendly and natural affections seem to bear in this order of architecture.

Modern projectors, I know, would willingly rid their hands of these natural materials, and would fain build after a more uniform way. They would new-frame the human heart, and have a mighty fancy to reduce all its motions, balances, and weights, to that one principle and foundation of a cool and deliberate selfishness. Men, it seems, are unwilling to think they can be so outwitted and imposed on by Nature, as to be made to serve her purposes rather than their own. They are ashamed to be drawn thus out of themselves, and forced from what they esteem their true interest.

There has been in all times a sort of narrow-minded philosophers, who have thought to set this difference to rights by conquering Nature in themselves. A primitive father and founder among these, saw well this power of Nature,[2] and understood it so far, that he earnestly exhorted his followers neither to beget children nor serve their country. There was no dealing with Nature, it seems, while these alluring objects stood in the way. Relations, friends, countrymen, laws, politic constitutions, the beauty of order and government, and the interest of society and mankind, were objects which, he well saw, would naturally raise a stronger affection than any which was grounded upon the narrow bottom of mere self.

---

[1] See the fourth Treatise, viz. *Inquiry Concerning Virtue.*
[2] Treatise I. 6; Treatise IV. ii. 1; and Treatise VI. ii. 1.

FREEDOM OF WIT AND HUMOUR

His advice, therefore, not to marry, nor engage at all in the public, was wise, and suitable to his design. There was no way to be truly a disciple of this philosophy, but to leave family, friends, country, and society, to cleave to it. . . . And, in good earnest, who would not, if it were happiness to do so?—The philosopher, however, was kind in telling us his thought. 'Twas a token of his fatherly love of mankind—

> Tu pater, et rerum inventor! Tu patria nobis
> Suppeditas praecepta![1]

But the revivers of this philosophy in latter days appear to be of a lower genius. They seem to have understood less of this force of Nature, and thought to alter the thing by shifting a name. They would so explain all the social passions and natural affections as to denominate them of the selfish kind. Thus civility, hospitality, humanity towards strangers or people in distress, is only a more deliberate selfishness. An honest heart is only a more cunning one; and honesty and good-nature, a more deliberate or better-regulated self-love. The love of kindred, children and posterity, is purely love of self and of one's own immediate blood; as if, by this reckoning, all mankind were not included: all being of one blood, and joined by inter-marriages and alliances, as they have been transplanted in colonies and mixed one with another. And thus love of one's country and love of mankind must also be self-love. Magnanimity and courage, no doubt, are modifications of this universal self-love! For courage,[2] says our modern philosopher, is constant anger; and all men, says a witty poet,[3] would be cowards if they durst.

That the poet and the philosopher both were cowards,

---

[1] ["Thou, Father, art (*es* is the revised reading) discoverer of things; thou givest us fatherly precepts."—Lucretius, iii. 9.]

[2] Sudden courage (says Mr. Hobbes, *Lev.* vi.) is anger. Therefore courage considered as constant, and belonging to a character, must, in his account, be defined constant anger, or anger constantly returning.

[3] Lord Rochester, *Satire against Man*.

may be yielded perhaps without dispute. They may have spoken the best of their knowledge. But for true courage, it has so little to do with anger, that there lies always the strongest suspicion against it where this passion is highest. The true courage is the cool and calm. The bravest of men have the least of a brutal bullying insolence; and in the very time of danger are found the most serene, pleasant, and free. Rage, we know, can make a coward forget himself and fight. But what is done in fury or anger can never be placed to the account of courage. Were it otherwise, womankind might claim to be the stoutest sex; for their hatred and anger have ever been allowed the strongest and most lasting.

Other authors there have been of a yet inferior kind: a sort of distributors and petty retailers of this wit,[1] who have run changes, and divisions without end, upon this article of self-love. You have the very same thought spun out a hundred ways, and drawn into mottoes and devices to set forth this riddle, that "act as disinterestedly or generously as you please, self still is at the bottom, and nothing else." Now if these gentlemen who delight so much in the play of words, but are cautious how they grapple closely with definitions, would tell us only what self-interest was,[2] and determine happiness and good, there would be an end of this enigmatical wit. For in this we should all agree, that happiness was to be pursued, and in fact was always sought after; but whether found in following Nature, and giving way to common affection, or in suppressing it, and turning every passion towards private advantage, a narrow self-end, or the preservation of mere life,

---

[1] The French translator supposes with good reason that our author, in this passage, had an eye to those sentences or maxims which pass under the name of the Duke de la Rochefoucault. He has added, withal, the censure of this kind of wit, and of these maxims in particular, by some authors of the same nation. The passages are too long to insert here, though they are otherwise very just and entertaining. That which he has cited of old Montaigne is from the first chapter of his second Essay.

[2] *Inquiry*, bk. i. part ii. § 2; bk. ii. part i. §§ 1, 3, part ii. § 2.

this would be the matter in debate between us. The question would not be, "who loved himself, or who not," but "who loved and served himself the rightest, and after the truest manner."

'Tis the height of wisdom, no doubt, to be rightly selfish. And to value life, as far as life is good, belongs as much to courage as to discretion; but a wretched life is no wise man's wish. To be without honesty is, in effect, to be without natural affection or sociableness of any kind. And a life without natural affection, friendship, or sociableness would be found a wretched one were it to be tried. 'Tis as these feelings and affections are intrinsically valuable and worthy that self-interest is to be rated and esteemed. A man is by nothing so much himself as by his temper and the character of his passions and affections. If he loses what is manly and worthy in these, he is as much lost to himself as when he loses his memory and understanding. The least step into villainy or baseness changes the character and value of a life. He who would preserve life at any rate must abuse himself more than any one can abuse him. And if life be not a dear thing indeed, he who has refused to live a villain and has preferred death to a base action has been a gainer by the bargain.

Section IV

'Tis well for you, my friend, that in your education you have had little to do with the philosophy[1] or philosophers of our days. A good poet and an honest historian may afford learning enough for a gentleman; and such a one, whilst he reads these authors as his diversion, will have a truer relish of their sense, and understand them better than a pedant with all his labours and the assistance of his volumes of com-

---

[1] Our author, it seems, writes at present as to a young gentleman chiefly of a court breeding. See, however, his further sentiments more particularly in Treatise III. (viz. *Soliloquy*) *infra*, part iii. § 3, etc., in the notes.

mentators. I am sensible that of old 'twas the custom to send the youth of highest quality to philosophers to be formed. 'Twas in their schools, in their company, and by their precepts and example that the illustrious pupils were inured to hardship and exercised in the severest courses of temperance and self-denial. By such an early discipline they were fitted for the command of others; to maintain their country's honour in war, rule wisely in the State, and fight against luxury and corruption in times of prosperity and peace. If any of these arts are comprehended in university learning, 'tis well. But as some universities in the world are now modelled, they seem not so very effectual to these purposes, nor so fortunate in preparing for a right practice of the world, or a just knowledge of men and things. Had you been thorough-paced in the ethics or politics of the schools, I should never have thought of writing a word to you upon common sense or the love of mankind. I should not have cited the poet's *dulce et decorum*; nor, if I had made a character for you, as he for his noble friend, should I have crowned it with his

> Non ille pro caris amicis
> Aut patria timidus perire.[1]

Our philosophy nowadays runs after the manner of that able sophister who said, "Skin for skin: all that a man hath will he give for his life."[2] 'Tis orthodox divinity, as well as sound philosophy, with some men to rate life by the number and exquisiteness of the pleasing sensations. These they constantly set in opposition to dry virtue and honesty; and upon this foot they think it proper to call all men fools who would hazard a life or part with any of these pleasing sensations except on the condition of being repaid in the same coin and with good interest into the bargain. Thus, it seems, we are

[1] ["He fears not to die for his dear friends and fatherland."—Horace, *Odes*, IV. ix. 51, 52.]   [2] Job ii. 4.

FREEDOM OF WIT AND HUMOUR

to learn virtue by usury, and enhance the value of life, and of the pleasures of sense, in order to be wise and to live well.

But you, my friend, are stubborn in this point; and instead of being brought to think mournfully of death, or to repine at the loss of what you may sometimes hazard by your honesty, you can laugh at such maxims as these, and divert yourself with the improved selfishness and philosophical cowardice of these fashionable moralists. You will not be taught to value life at their rate, or degrade honesty as they do, who make it only a name. You are persuaded there is something more in the thing than fashion or applause; that worth and merit are substantial, and no way variable by fancy or will; and that honour is as much itself when acting by itself and unseen, as when seen and applauded by all the world.

Should one who had the countenance of a gentleman ask me "Why I would avoid being nasty, when nobody was present?" In the first place I should be fully satisfied that he himself was a very nasty gentleman who could ask this question, and that it would be a hard matter for me to make him ever conceive what true cleanliness was. However, I might, notwithstanding this, be contented to give him a slight answer, and say "'twas because I had a nose." Should he trouble me further and ask again, "what if I had a cold? or what if naturally I had no such nice smell?" I might answer perhaps, "that I cared as little to see myself nasty as that others should see me in that condition." But what if it were in the dark? Why even then, though I had neither nose nor eyes, my sense of the matter would still be the same: my nature would rise at the thought of what was sordid; or if it did not, I should have a wretched nature indeed, and hate myself for a beast. Honour myself I never could whilst I had no better a sense of what in reality I owed myself, and what became me as a human creature.

Much in the same manner have I heard it asked, Why should a man be honest in the dark? What a man must be to ask this question I will not say. But for those who have no better a reason for being honest than the fear of a gibbet or a jail, I should not, I confess, much covet their company or acquaintance. And if any guardian of mine who had kept his trust, and given me back my estate when I came of age, had been discovered to have acted thus through fear only of what might happen to him, I should, for my own part, undoubtedly continue civil and respectful to him; but for my opinion of his worth, it would be such as the Pythian God had of his votary, who devoutly feared him, and therefore restored to a friend what had been deposited in his hands—

> Reddidit ergo metu, non moribus; et tamen omnem
> Vocem adyti dignam templo, veramque probavit,
> Extinctus tota pariter cum prole domoque.[1]

I know very well that many services to the public are done merely for the sake of a gratuity; and that informers in particular are to be taken care of and sometimes made pensioners of State. But I must beg pardon for the particular thoughts I may have of these gentlemen's merit; and shall never bestow my esteem on any other than the voluntary discoverers of villainy and hearty prosecutors of their country's interest. And in this respect, I know nothing greater or nobler than the undertaking and managing some important accusation, by which some high criminal of State, or some formed body of conspirators against the public, may be arraigned and brought to punishment through the honest zeal and public affection of a private man.

I know, too, that the mere vulgar of mankind often stand in need of such a rectifying object as the gallows before their eyes. Yet I have no belief that any man of a liberal education, or common honesty, ever needed to have recourse to this idea in

---

[1] ["So he paid it back, from fear, not from principle. Yet still he proved the oracle true and fit to be God's voice, for he and his house perished root and branch."—Juv. xiii. 204-206.]

his mind, the better to restrain him from playing the knave. And if a saint had no other virtue than what was raised in him by the same objects of reward and punishment, in a more distant state, I know not whose love or esteem he might gain besides, but for my own part I should never think him worthy of mine.

" Nec furtum feci nec fugi," si mihi dicat
Servus: " habes pretium, loris non urens," aio.
" Non hominem occidi."   " Non pasces in cruce corvos."
" Sum bonus et frugi."   Renuit negitatque Sabellus.[1]

PART IV

SECTION I

BY this time, my friend, you may possibly, I hope, be satisfied that as I am in earnest in defending raillery, so I can be sober too in the use of it. 'Tis in reality a serious study to learn to temper and regulate that humour which nature has given us as a more lenitive remedy against vice, and a kind of specific against superstition and melancholy delusion. There is a great difference between seeking how to raise a laugh from everything, and seeking in everything what justly may be laughed at. For nothing is ridiculous except what is deformed; nor is anything proof against raillery except what is handsome and just. And therefore 'tis the hardest thing in the world to deny fair honesty the use of this weapon, which can never bear an edge against herself, and bears against everything contrary.

If the very Italian buffoons were to give us the rule in these cases, we should learn by them that in their lowest and most

[1] ["If my slave tells me, 'I have not stolen, nor run away,' I answer, 'You have your reward, you are not flogged.' 'I have not killed a man!' 'The crows do not devour you on the cross.' 'I am good and honest!' My Sabine bailiff shakes his head and denies it."—Horace, *Epist.* I. xvi. 46-49.]

scurrilous way of wit, there was nothing so successfully to be played upon as the passions of cowardice and avarice. One may defy the world to turn real bravery or generosity into ridicule. A glutton or mere sensualist is as ridiculous as the other two characters. Nor can an unaffected temperance be made the subject of contempt to any besides the grossest and most contemptible of mankind. Now these three ingredients make up a virtuous character, as the contrary three a vicious one. How therefore can we possibly make a jest of honesty? To laugh both ways is nonsensical. And if the ridicule lie against sottishness, avarice, and cowardice, you see the consequence. A man must be soundly ridiculous who, with all the wit imaginable, would go about to ridicule wisdom, or laugh at honesty, or good manners.

A man of thorough good breeding,[1] whatever else he be, is incapable of doing a rude or brutal action. He never deliberates in this case, or considers of the matter by prudential rules of self-interest and advantage. He acts from his nature, in a manner necessarily, and without reflection; and if he did not, it were impossible for him to answer his character, or be found that truly well-bred man on every occasion. 'Tis the same with the honest man. He cannot deliberate in the case of a plain villainy. A "plum" is no temptation to him. He likes and loves himself too well to change hearts with one of those corrupt miscreants, who amongst them gave that name to a round sum of money gained by rapine and plunder of the commonwealth. He who would enjoy a freedom of mind, and be truly possessor of himself, must be above the thought of stooping to what is villainous or base. He, on the other side, who has a heart to stoop, must necessarily quit the thought of manliness, resolution, friendship, merit, and a character with himself and others. But to affect these enjoyments and advantages, together with the privileges of a licentious principle; to pretend to enjoy society and a free mind in company with a knavish heart, is as ridiculous

---

[1] *Miscellaneous Reflections*, Misc. iii. ch. i.

as the way of children, who eat their cake and afterwards cry for it. When men begin to deliberate about dishonesty, and finding it go less against their stomach, ask slily, "Why they should stick at a good piece of knavery for a good sum?" they should be told, as children, that they cannot eat their cake and have it.

When men indeed are become accomplished knaves they are past crying for their cake. They know themselves, and are known by mankind. 'Tis not these who are so much envied or admired. The moderate kind are the more taking with us. Yet had we sense we should consider 'tis in reality the thorough profligate knave, the very complete unnatural villain alone, who can any way bid for happiness with the honest man. True interest is wholly on one side or the other. All between is inconsistency,[1] irresolution, remorse, vexation, and an ague fit: from hot to cold; from one passion to another quite contrary; a perpetual discord of life; and an alternate disquiet and self-dislike. The only rest or repose must be through one determined, considerate resolution, which when once taken must be courageously kept; and the passions and affections brought under obedience to it; the temper steeled and hardened to the mind; the disposition to the judgment. Both must agree, else all must be disturbance and confusion. So that to think with one's self in good earnest, "why may not one do this little villainy, or commit this one treachery, and but for once," is the most ridiculous imagination in the world, and contrary to common sense. For a common honest man, whilst left to himself, and undisturbed by philosophy and subtle reasonings about

---

[1] Our author's French translator cites, on this occasion, very aptly those verses of Horace, *Sat.* ii. vii. 18-20 :—

> Quanto constantior idem
> In vitiis, tanto levius miser ac prior ille
> Qui jam contento, jam laxo fune laborat.

["At any rate he was so much the more consistent in vice, and so far less miserable than that other, who pulls now on a loose and now on a tight cord."]

his interest, gives no other answer to the thought of villainy than that he cannot possibly find in his heart to set about it, or conquer the natural aversion he has to it. And this is natural and just.

The truth is, as notions stand now in the world with respect to morals, honesty is like to gain little by philosophy, or deep speculations of any kind. In the main, 'tis best to stick to common sense and go no farther. Men's first thoughts in this matter are generally better than their second: their natural notions better than those refined by study or consultation with casuists. According to common speech, as well as common sense, honesty is the best policy; but according to refined sense, the only well-advised persons, as to this world, are errant knaves; and they alone are thought to serve themselves who serve their passions, and indulge their loosest appetites and desires. Such, it seems, are the wise, and such the wisdom of this world!

An ordinary man talking of a vile action, in a way of common sense, says naturally and heartily, " he would not be guilty of such a thing for the whole world." But speculative men find great modifications in the case; many ways of evasion; many remedies; many alleviations. A good gift rightly applied; a right method of suing out a pardon; good alms-houses, and charitable foundations erected for right worshippers, and a good zeal shown for the right belief, may sufficiently atone for one wrong practice, especially when it is such as raises a man to a considerable power (as they say) of doing good, and serving the true cause.

Many a good estate, many a high station has been gained upon such a bottom as this. Some crowns too may have been purchased on these terms; and some great emperors (if I mistake not) there have been of old, who were much assisted by these or the like principles; and in return were not ungrateful to the cause and party which had assisted them. The forgers of such morals have been amply endowed, and the world has paid roundly for its philosophy, since the original plain principles of

FREEDOM OF WIT AND HUMOUR

humanity, and the simple honest precepts of peace and mutual love, have, by a sort of spiritual chemists, been so sublimated as to become the highest corrosives, and passing through their limbecks, have yielded the strongest spirit of mutual hatred and malignant persecution.

Section II

But our humours, my friend, incline us not to melancholy reflections. Let the solemn reprovers of vice proceed in the manner most suitable to their genius and character. I am ready to congratulate with them on the success of their labours, in that authoritative way which is allowed them. I know not, in the meanwhile, why others may not be allowed to ridicule folly, and recommend wisdom and virtue (if possibly they can) in a way of pleasantry and mirth. I know not why poets, or such as write chiefly for the entertainment of themselves and others, may not be allowed this privilege. And if it be the complaint of our standing reformers that they are not heard so well by the gentlemen of fashion; if they exclaim against those airy wits who fly to ridicule as a protection, and make successful sallies from that quarter; why should it be denied one, who is only a volunteer in this cause, to engage the adversary on his own terms, and expose himself willingly to such attacks, on the single condition of being allowed fair play in the same kind?

By gentlemen of fashion, I understand those to whom a natural good genius, or the force of good education, has given a sense of what is naturally graceful and becoming. Some by mere nature, others by art and practice, are masters of an ear in music, an eye in painting, a fancy in the ordinary things of ornament and grace, a judgment in proportions of all kinds, and a general good taste in most of those subjects which make the amusement and delight of the ingenious people of the world. Let such gentlemen as these be as extravagant as they please, or as irregular in their morals, they must at the same time discover their inconsistency, live at variance with themselves, and in contradiction to that principle on which they ground their highest pleasure and entertainment.

Of all other beauties which virtuosos pursue, poets celebrate, musicians sing, and architects or artists, of whatever kind, describe or form, the most delightful, the most engaging and pathetic, is that which is drawn from real life, and from the passions. Nothing affects the heart like that which is purely from itself, and of its own nature; such as the beauty of sentiments, the grace of actions, the turn of characters, and the proportions and features of a human mind. This lesson of philosophy, even a romance, a poem, or a play may teach us; whilst the fabulous author leads us with such pleasure through the labyrinth of the affections, and interests us, whether we will or no, in the passions of his heroes and heroines:—

> Angit,
> Irritat, mulcet, falsis terroribus implet,
> Ut magus.[1]

Let poets, or the men of harmony, deny, if they can, this force of Nature, or withstand this moral magic. They, for their parts, carry a double portion of this charm about them. For in the first place, the very passion which inspires them is itself the love of numbers, decency and proportion; and this too, not in a narrow sense, or after a selfish way (for who of them composes for himself?), but in a friendly social view, for the pleasure and good of others, even down to posterity and future ages. And in the next place, 'tis evident in these performers that their chief theme and subject, that which raises their genius the most, and by which they so effectually move others, is purely manners and the moral part. For this is the effect, and this the beauty of their art; "in vocal measures of syllables

---

[1] ["Like a Mage, he tortures, enrages, soothes, fills us with false terrors."—Hor. *Epist.* II. i. 211-213.]

and sounds to express the harmony and numbers of an inward kind, and represent the beauties of a human soul by proper foils and contrarieties, which serve as graces in this limning, and render this music of the passions more powerful and enchanting."

The admirers of beauty in the fair sex would laugh, perhaps, to hear of a moral part in their amours. Yet what a stir is made about a heart! What curious search of sentiments and tender thoughts! What praises of a humour, a sense, a *je ne sçai quoi* of wit, and all those graces of a mind which these virtuoso-lovers delight to celebrate! Let them settle this matter among themselves, and regulate, as they think fit, the proportions which these different beauties hold one to another. They must allow still, there is a beauty of the mind, and such as is essential in the case. Why else is the very air of foolishness enough to cloy a lover at first sight? Why does an idiot-look and manner destroy the effect of all those outward charms, and rob the fair one of her power, though regularly armed in all the exactness of features and complexion? We may imagine what we please of a substantial solid part of beauty; but were the subject to be well criticised we should find, perhaps, that what we most admired, even in the turn of outward features, was only a mysterious expression, and a kind of shadow of something inward in the temper; and that when we were struck with a majestic air, a sprightly look, an Amazon bold grace, or a contrary soft and gentle one, 'twas chiefly the fancy of these characters or qualities which wrought on us: our imagination being busied in forming beauteous shapes and images of this rational kind, which entertained the mind and held it in admiration, whilst other passions of a lower species were employed another way. The preliminary addresses, the declarations, the explanations, confidences, clearings, the dependence on something mutual, something felt by way of return, the *spes animi credula mutui*—all these become necessary ingredients in the affair of love, and are authentically established by the men of elegance and art in this way of passion.

SHAFTESBURY'S CHARACTERISTICS

Nor can the men of cooler passions and more deliberate pursuits withstand the force of beauty in other subjects. Every one is a virtuoso of a higher or lower degree. Every one pursues a Grace and courts a Venus of one kind or another. The *venustum*, the *honestum*, the *decorum* of things will force its way. They who refuse to give it scope in the nobler subjects of a rational and moral kind will find its prevalency elsewhere in an inferior order of things. They who overlook the main springs of action, and despise the thought of numbers and proportion in a life at large, will, in the mean particulars of it, be no less taken up and engaged, as either in the study of common arts, or in the care and culture of mere mechanic beauties. The models of houses, buildings, and their accompanying ornaments; the plans of gardens, and their compartments; the ordering of walks, plantations, avenues; and a thousand other symmetries, will succeed in the room of that happier and higher symmetry and order of a mind. The species[1] of fair, noble, handsome, will discover itself on a thousand occasions, and in a thousand subjects. The spectre still will haunt us in some shape or other; and when driven from our cool thoughts, and frighted from the closet, will meet us even at court, and fill our heads with dreams of grandeur, titles, honours, and a false magnificence and beauty, to which we are ready to sacrifice our highest pleasure and ease, and for the sake of which we become the merest drudges and most abject slaves.

The men of pleasure, who seem the greatest contemners of this philosophical beauty, are forced often to confess her charms. They can as heartily as others commend honesty; and are as much struck with the beauty of a generous part. They admire the thing itself, though not the means. And, if possible, they would so order it, as to make probity and luxury agree. But the rules of harmony will not permit it. The dissonances are too strong. However, the attempts of this kind are not unpleasant to observe. For though some of the voluptuous are

---

[1] *Misc.* iii. ch. ii.

found sordid pleaders for baseness and corruption of every sort, yet others, more generous, endeavour to keep measures with honesty; and understanding pleasure better, are for bringing it under some rule. They condemn *this* manner; they praise *the other.* "So far was right; but further, wrong. Such a case was allowable; but such a one not to be admitted." They introduce a justice and an order in their pleasures. They would bring reason to be of their party, account in some manner for their lives, and form themselves to some kind of consonancy and agreement. Or should they find this impracticable on certain terms, they would choose to sacrifice their other pleasures to those which arise from a generous behaviour, a regularity of conduct, and a consistency of life and manners :—

Et verae numerosque modosque ediscere vitae.[1]

Other occasions will put us upon this thought; but chiefly a strong view of merit, in a generous character, opposed to some detestably vile one. Hence it is that among poets, the satirists seldom fail in doing justice to virtue. Nor are any of the nobler poets false to this cause. Even modern wits, whose turn is all towards gallantry and pleasure, when bare-faced villainy stands in their way, and brings the contrary species in view, can sing in passionate strains the praises of plain honesty.

When we are highly friends with the world, successful with the fair, and prosperous in the possession of other beauties, we may perchance, as is usual, despise this sober mistress. But when we see, in the issue, what riot and excess naturally produce in the world; when we find that by luxury's means, and for the service of vile interests, knaves are advanced above us, and the vilest of men preferred before the honestest; we then behold virtue in a new light, and by the assistance of such a foil, can discern the beauty of honesty, and the reality of those charms which before we understood not to be either natural or powerful.

[1] ["To learn the measures and rules of the true life."—Hor. *Epist.* II. ii. 144.]

SHAFTESBURY'S CHARACTERISTICS

Section III

AND thus, after all, the most natural beauty in the world is honesty and moral truth. For all beauty is truth. True features make the beauty of a face; and true proportions the beauty of architecture; as true measures that of harmony and music. In poetry, which is all fable, truth still is the perfection. And whoever is scholar enough to read the ancient philosopher, or his modern copyists,[1] upon the nature of a dramatic and epic poem, will easily understand this account of truth.[2]

A painter, if he has any genius, understands the truth and unity of design; and knows he is even then unnatural when he follows Nature too close, and strictly copies Life. For his art allows him not to bring all nature into his piece, but a part only. However, his piece, if it be beautiful, and carries truth, must be a whole, by itself, complete, independent, and withal as great and comprehensive as he can make it. So that particulars, on this occasion, must yield to the general design, and all things be subservient to that which is principal; in order to form a certain easiness of sight, a simple, clear, and united view,[3]

---

[1] The French translator, no doubt, has justly hit our author's thought, by naming in his margin the excellent Bossu *Du poème épique*; who in that admirable comment and explanation of Aristotle, has perhaps not only shown himself the greatest of the French critics, but presented the world with a view of ancient literature and just writing beyond any other modern of whatever nation.

[2] *Misc.* iii. ch. ii. and v. ch. i.

[3] The τὸ εὐσύνοπτον, as the great Master of arts calls it in his *Poetics*, ch. xxiii. but particularly ch. vii., where he shows "that the τὸ καλόν, the beautiful, or the sublime, in these above-mentioned arts, is from the expression of greatness with order: that is to say, exhibiting the principal or main of what is designed, in the very largest proportions in which it is capable of being viewed. For when it is gigantic, 'tis in a manner out of sight, and can be no way comprehended in that simple and united view. As, on the contrary, when a piece is of the miniature kind; when it runs into the detail and nice delineation of every little particular; 'tis as it

which would be broken and disturbed by the expression of any thing peculiar or distinct.

Now the variety of Nature is such, as to distinguish everything she forms, by a peculiar original character, which, if strictly observed, will make the subject appear unlike to any-

were invisible, for the same reason; because the summary beauty, the whole itself, cannot be comprehended in that one united view; which is broken and lost by the necessary attraction of the eye to every small and subordinate part. In a poetic system, the same regard must be had to the memory as in painting to the eye. The dramatic kind is confined within the convenient and proper time of a spectacle. The epic is left more at large. Each work, however, must aim at vastness, and be as great, and of as long duration as possible; but so as to be comprehended (as to the main of it) by one easy glance or retrospect of memory. And this the philosopher calls, accordingly, the τὸ εὐμνημόνευτον." I cannot better translate the passage than as I have done in these explanatory lines. For besides what relates to mere art, the philosophical sense of the original is so majestic, and the whole treatise so masterly, that when I find even the Latin interpreters come so short, I should be vain to attempt anything in our language. I would only add a small remark of my own, which may perhaps be noticed by the studiers of statuary and painting: that the greatest of the ancient as well as modern artists, were ever inclined to follow this rule of the philosopher; and when they erred in their designs, or draughts, it was on the side of greatness, by running into the unsizable and gigantic, rather than into the minute and delicate. Of this, Mich. Angelo, the great beginner and founder among the moderns, and Zeuxis the same among the ancients, may serve as instances. See Pliny, xxxv. 9, concerning Zeuxis, and the notes of Father Hardouin in his edition *in usum Delphini*, p. 200, on the words, deprehenditur tamen Zeuxis, etc. And again Pliny himself upon Euphranor, in the same book, ch 11, p. 226, docilis ac laboriosus ante omnes, et in quocumque genere excellens, ac sibi aequalis. Hic primus videtur expressisse dignitates heroum, et usurpasse symmetriam. Sed fuit universitate corporum exilior, capitibus articulisque grandior. Volumina quoque composuit de symmetria et coloribus, etc. ["A good learner and painstaking, uniformly excellent in every branch. He is thought to have first done justice to the majesty of heroes and first mastered proportion, but his bodies were over-slender, his heads and limbs over-large. He wrote too on proportion and colouring." Pliny, *H. N.* xxxv. 128.] Vide infra, *Advice to an Author*, part iii. § 3, in the notes.

thing extant in the world besides. But this effect the good poet and painter seek industriously to prevent. They hate minuteness, and are afraid of singularity; which would make their images, or characters, appear capricious and fantastical. The mere face-painter, indeed, has little in common with the poet; but, like the mere historian, copies what he sees, and minutely traces every feature and odd mark. 'Tis otherwise with the men of invention and design. 'Tis from the many objects of nature, and not from a particular one, that those geniuses form the idea of their work. Thus the best artists are said to have been indefatigable in studying the best statues: as esteeming them a better rule than the perfectest human bodies could afford. And thus some considerable wits[1] have recommended the best poems as preferable to the best of histories; and better teaching the truth of characters and nature of mankind.

Nor can this criticism be thought high-strained. Though few confine themselves to these rules, few are insensible of them. Whatever quarter we may give to our vicious poets, or other composers of irregular and short-lived works, we know very well that the standing pieces of good artists must be formed after a more uniform way. Every just work of theirs comes under those natural rules of proportion and truth. The creature of their brain must be like one of Nature's formation. It must have a body and parts proportionable; or the very vulgar will not fail to criticise the work when it has neither head nor tail. For so common sense (according to just philosophy) judges of those works which want the justness of a whole, and show their author, however curious and exact in particulars, to be in the main a very bungler—

---

[1] Thus the great Master himself in his *Poetics* above cited, viii., διὸ καὶ φιλοσοφώτερον καὶ σπουδαιότερον ποίησις ἱστορίας ἐστιν· ἡ μὲν γὰρ ποίησις μᾶλλον τὰ καθόλου, ἡ δ' ἱστορία τὰ καθ' ἕκαστον λέγει. ["Poetry is both a more philosophic and a more real thing than history; for poetry tells rather the universal, history the particular."—Arist. *Poet.* xcvi.]

FREEDOM OF WIT AND HUMOUR

Infelix operis summa, quia ponere totum
Nesciet.[1]

Such is poetical and such (if I may so call it) graphical or plastic truth. Narrative or historical truth must needs be highly estimable; especially when we consider how mankind, who are become so deeply interested in the subject, have suffered by the want of clearness in it. 'Tis itself a part of moral truth. To be a judge in one, requires a judgment in the other. The morals, the character, and genius of an author must be thoroughly considered; and the historian or relator of things important to mankind must, whoever he be, approve himself many ways to us, both in respect of his judgment, candour, and disinterestedness, ere we are bound to take anything on his authority. And as for critical truth,[2] or the judgment and determination of what commentators, translators, paraphrasts, grammarians and others have, on this occasion, delivered to us; in the midst of such variety of style, such different readings, such interpolations and corruptions in the originals; such mistakes of copyists, transcribers, editors, and a hundred such accidents to which ancient books are subject; it becomes, upon the whole, a matter of nice speculation, considering withal that the reader, though an able linguist, must be supported by so many other helps from chronology, natural philosophy, geography, and other sciences.

And thus many previous truths are to be examined and understood in order to judge rightly of historical truth, and of the past actions and circumstances of mankind, as delivered to us by ancient authors of different nations, ages, times, and different in their characters and interests. Some moral and philosophical truths there are withal so evident in themselves, that 'twould be easier to imagine half mankind to have run mad, and joined precisely in one and the same species of folly, than to admit anything as truth which should be advanced against such natural knowledge, fundamental reason, and common sense.

---

[1] Hor. *De Arte Poet.* 34. [2] *Misc.* v. ch. iii.

SHAFTESBURY'S CHARACTERISTICS

This I have mentioned, the rather because some modern zealots appear to have no better knowledge of truth, nor better manner of judging it, than by counting noses. By this rule, if they can poll an indifferent number out of a mob; if they can produce a set of Lancashire noddles, remote provincial headpieces, or visionary assemblers, to attest a story of a witch upon a broomstick, and a flight in the air, they triumph in the solid proof of their new prodigy, and cry, *magna est veritas et praevalebit!*

Religion, no doubt, is much indebted to these men of prodigy, who, in such a discerning age, would set her on the foot of popular tradition, and venture her on the same bottom with parish tales, and gossiping stories of imps, goblins, and demoniacal pranks, invented to fright children, or make practice for common exorcists and "cunning men"! For by that name, you know, country people are used to call those dealers in mystery who are thought to conjure in an honest way, and foil the devil at his own weapon.

And now, my friend, I can perceive 'tis time to put an end to these reflections, lest by endeavouring to expound things any further, I should be drawn from my way of humour to harangue profoundly on these subjects. But should you find I had moralised in any tolerable manner, according to common sense, and without canting, I could be satisfied with my performance, such as it is, without fearing what disturbance I might possibly give to some formal censors of the age, whose discourses and writings are of another strain. I have taken the liberty, you see, to laugh upon some occasions; and if I have either laughed wrong, or been impertinently serious, I can be content to be laughed at in my turn. If contrariwise I am railed at, I can laugh still, as before, and with fresh advantage to my cause. For though, in reality, there could be nothing less a laughing matter than the provoked rage, ill-will, and fury of certain zealous gentlemen, were they armed as lately they have been known; yet as the magistrate has since taken

FREEDOM OF WIT AND HUMOUR

care to pare their talons, there is nothing very terrible in their encounter. On the contrary, there is something comical in the case. It brings to one's mind the fancy of those grotesque figures and dragon-faces, which are seen often in the frontispiece and on the corner-stones of old buildings. They seem placed there as the defenders and supporters of the edifice; but with all their grimace, are as harmless to people without, as they are useless to the building within. Great efforts of anger to little purpose, serve for pleasantry and farce. Exceeding fierceness, with perfect inability and impotence, make the highest ridicule.—I am, dear friend, affectionately yours, etc.

TREATISE III

SOLILOQUY

OR

ADVICE TO AN AUTHOR

Nec te quaesiveris extra.
Pers. *Sat.* i.

Printed first in the year MDCCX.

ADVICE TO AN AUTHOR

PART I

SECTION I

I HAVE often thought how ill-natured a maxim it was, which on many occasions I have heard from people of good understanding, "that, as to what related to private conduct, no one was ever the better for advice." But upon farther examination I have resolved with myself that the maxim might be admitted without any violent prejudice to mankind. For in the manner advice was generally given, there was no reason, I thought, to wonder it should be so ill received. Something there was which strangely inverted the case, and made the giver to be the only gainer. For by what I could observe in many occurrences of our lives, that which we called giving advice was, properly, taking an occasion to show our own wisdom at another's expense. On the other side, to be instructed, or to receive advice on the terms usually prescribed to us, was little better than tamely to afford another the occasion of raising himself a character from our defects.

In reality, however able or willing a man may be to advise, 'tis no easy matter to make advice a free gift. For to make a gift free indeed, there must be nothing in it which takes from another to add to ourself. In all other respects, to give and to dispense is generosity and good-will; but to bestow wisdom, is to gain a mastery which cannot so easily be allowed us. Men willingly learn whatever else is taught them. They can bear a master in mathematics, in music, or in any other science, but not in understanding and good sense.

'Tis the hardest thing imaginable for an author not to appear assuming in this respect. For all authors at large are, in a manner, professed masters of understanding to the age. And for this reason, in early days, poets were looked upon as authentic sages, for dictating rules of life, and teaching manners and good sense. How they may have lost their pretension, I cannot say. 'Tis their peculiar happiness and advantage not to be obliged to lay their claim openly. And if whilst they profess only to please, they secretly advise and give instruction, they may now perhaps, as well as formerly, be esteemed with justice the best and most honourable among authors.

Meanwhile, "if dictating and prescribing be of so dangerous a nature in other authors, what must his case be who dictates to authors themselves?"

To this I answer: that my pretension is not so much to give advice, as to consider of the way and manner of advising. My science, if it be any, is no better than that of a language-master, or a logician. For I have taken it strongly into my head, that there is a certain knack or legerdemain in argument, by which we may safely proceed to the dangerous part of advising, and make sure of the good fortune to have our advice accepted if it be anything worth.

My proposal is to consider of this affair as a case of surgery. 'Tis practice, we all allow, which makes a hand. "But who, on this occasion, will be practised on? Who will willingly be the first to try our hand, and afford us the requisite experience?" Here lies the difficulty. For supposing we had hospitals for this sort of surgery, and there were always in readiness certain meek patients who would bear any incisions, and be probed or tented at our pleasure, the advantage no doubt would be considerable in this way of practice. Some insight must needs be obtained. In time a hand too might be acquired; but in all likelihood a very rough one, which would by no means serve the purpose of this latter surgery. For here, a tenderness of hand is principally requisite. No surgeon will be called who has not feeling and compassion. And where to find a subject in which the operator is likely to preserve the highest tenderness, and yet act with the greatest resolution and boldness, is certainly a matter of no slight consideration.

I am sensible there is in all considerable projects, at first appearance, a certain air of chimerical fancy and conceit, which is apt to render the projectors somewhat liable to ridicule. I would therefore prepare my reader against this prejudice, by assuring him that in the operation proposed there is nothing which can justly excite his laughter; or if there be, the laugh perhaps may turn against him by his own consent and with his own concurrence, which is a specimen of that very art or science we are about to illustrate.

Accordingly, if it be objected against the above-mentioned practice and art of surgery, "that we can nowhere find such a meek patient, with whom we can in reality make bold, and for whom nevertheless we are sure to preserve the greatest tenderness and regard," I assert the contrary; and say, for instance, that we have each of us ourselves to practise on. "Mere quibble!" you will say; "for who can thus multiply himself into two persons and be his own subject? Who can properly laugh at himself, or find in his heart to be either merry or severe on such an occasion?" Go to the poets, and they will present you with many instances. Nothing is more common with them, than this sort of soliloquy. A person of profound parts, or perhaps of ordinary capacity, happens on some occasion to commit a fault. He is concerned for it. He comes alone upon the stage; looks about him to see if anybody be near; then takes himself to task, without sparing himself in the least. You would wonder to hear how close he pushes matters, and how thoroughly he carries on the business of self-dissection. By virtue of this soliloquy he becomes two distinct persons. He is pupil and preceptor. He teaches, and he learns. And in good earnest, had I nothing else to plead in behalf of the morals of our modern dramatic poets, I should defend them still against their accusers for the sake of this very practice, which they have taken care to keep up in its full force. For whether the practice be natural or no, in respect of common custom and usage, I take upon me to assert, that it is an honest and laudable practice; and that if already it be not natural to us, we ought however to make it so, by study and application.

"Are we to go therefore to the stage for edification? Must we learn our catechism from the poets? And, like the players, speak aloud what we debate at any time with ourselves alone?" Not absolutely so, perhaps. Though where the harm would be, of spending some discourse, and bestowing a little breath and clear voice purely upon ourselves, I cannot see. We might peradventure be less noisy and more profitable in company, if at convenient times we discharged some of our articulate sound, and spoke to ourselves *viva voce* when alone. For company is an extreme provocative to fancy, and, like a hot bed in gardening, is apt to make our imaginations sprout too fast. But by this anticipating remedy of soliloquy, we may effectually provide against the inconvenience.

We have an account in history of a certain nation who seem to have been extremely apprehensive of the effects of this frothiness or ventosity in speech, and were accordingly resolved to provide thoroughly against the evil. They carried this remedy of ours so far, that it was not only their custom, but their religion and law, to speak, laugh, use action, gesticulate, and do all in the same manner when by themselves as when they were in company. If you had stolen upon them unawares at any time when they had been alone, you might have found them in high dispute, arguing with themselves, reproving, counselling, haranguing themselves, and in the most florid manner accosting their own persons. In all likelihood they had been once a people remarkably fluent in expression, much pestered with orators and preachers, and mightily subject to that disease which has been since called the leprosy of eloquence, till some sage legislator arose amongst them, who, when he could not oppose the torrent of words and stop the flux of speech by any immediate application, found means to give a vent to the loquacious humour, and broke the force of the distemper by eluding it.

Our present manners, I must own, are not so well calculated for this method of soliloquy as to suffer it to become a national practice. 'Tis but a small portion of this regimen which I would willingly borrow and apply to private use, especially in the case of authors. I am sensible how fatal it might prove to many honourable persons, should they acquire such a habit as this, or offer to practise such an art within reach of any mortal ear. For 'tis well known we are not many of us like that Roman who wished for windows to his breast, that all might be as conspicuous there as in his house, which for that very reason he had built as open as was possible. I would therefore advise our probationer upon his first exercise to retire into some thick wood, or rather take the point of some high hill, where, besides the advantage of looking about him for security, he would find the air perhaps more rarefied and suitable to the perspiration required, especially in the case of a poetical genius—

Scriptorum chorus omnis amat nemus et fugit urbes.[1]

'Tis remarkable in all great wits, that they have owned this practice of ours, and generally described themselves as a people liable to sufficient ridicule for their great loquacity by themselves, and their profound taciturnity in company. Not only the poet and philosopher, but the orator himself was wont to have recourse to our method. And the prince of this latter tribe may be proved to have been a great frequenter of the woods and river-banks, where he consumed abundance of his

[1] ["The whole band of authors loves a wood and shuns a city."—Hor. *Epist.* II. ii. 77.]

breath, suffered his fancy to evaporate, and reduced the vehemence both of his spirit and voice. If other authors find nothing which invites them to these recesses, 'tis because their genius is not of force enough; or though it be, their character, they may imagine, will hardly bear them out. For to be surprised in the odd actions, gestures, or tones, which are proper to such ascetics, I must own would be an ill adventure for a man of the world. But with poets and philosophers 'tis a known case:—

Aut insanit homo, aut versus facit.[1]

Composing and raving must necessarily, we see, bear a resemblance. And for those composers who deal in systems and airy speculations, they have vulgarly passed for a sort of prose poets. Their secret practice and habit has been as frequently noted:—

Murmura cum secum et rabiosa silentia rodunt.[2]

Both these sorts are happily indulged in this method of evacuation. They are thought to act naturally and in their proper way when they assume these odd manners. But of other authors 'tis expected they should be better bred. They are obliged to preserve a more conversible habit, which is no small misfortune to them. For if their meditation and reverie be obstructed by the fear of a nonconforming mien in conversation, they may happen to be so much the worse authors for being finer gentlemen. Their fervency of imagination may possibly be as strong as either the philosopher's or the poet's. But being denied an equal benefit of discharge, and withheld from the wholesome manner of relief in private, 'tis no wonder if they appear with so much froth and scum in public.

'Tis observable that the writers of memoirs and essays are chiefly subject to this frothy distemper. Nor can it be doubted that this is the true reason why these gentlemen entertain the

[1] ["The man is either raving or composing."—Hor. *Sat.* II. vii. 118.]
[2] Pers. *Sat.* iii.

world so lavishly with what relates to themselves. For having had no opportunity of privately conversing with themselves, or exercising their own genius so as to make acquaintance with it or prove its strength, they immediately fall to work in a wrong place, and exhibit on the stage of the world that practice which they should have kept to themselves, if they designed that either they or the world should be the better for their moralities. Who indeed can endure to hear an empiric talk of his own constitution, how he governs and manages it, what diet agrees best with it, and what his practice is with himself? The proverb, no doubt, is very just, Physician cure thyself. Yet methinks one should have but an ill time to be present at these bodily operations. Nor is the reader in truth any better entertained when he is obliged to assist at the experimental discussions of his practising author, who all the while is in reality doing no better than taking his physic in public.

For this reason I hold it very indecent for any one to publish his meditations, occasional reflections, solitary thoughts, or other such exercises as come under the notion of this self-discoursing practice. And the modestest title I can conceive for such works would be that of a certain author who called them his crudities. 'Tis the unhappiness of those wits who conceive suddenly, but without being able to go out their full time, that after many miscarriages and abortions, they can bring nothing well-shapen or perfect into the world. They are not, however, the less fond of their offspring, which in a manner they beget in public. For so public-spirited they are, that they can never afford themselves the least time to think in private for their own particular benefit and use. For this reason, though they are often retired, they are never by themselves. The world is ever of the party. They have their author-character in view, and are always considering how this or that thought would serve to complete some set of contemplations, or furnish out the commonplace book from whence these treasured riches are to flow in plenty on the necessitous world.

SHAFTESBURY'S CHARACTERISTICS

But if our candidates for authorship happen to be of the sanctified kind, 'tis not to be imagined how much farther still their charity is apt to extend. So exceeding great is their indulgence and tenderness for mankind, that they are unwilling the least sample of their devout exercise should be lost. Though there are already so many formularies and rituals appointed for this species of soliloquy, they can allow nothing to lie concealed which passes in this religious commerce and way of dialogue between them and their soul.

These may be termed a sort of pseudo-ascetics, who can have no real converse either with themselves, or with heaven, whilst they look thus asquint upon the world, and carry titles and editions along with them in their meditations. And although the books of this sort, by a common idiom, are called good books, the authors, for certain, are a sorry race; for religious crudities are undoubtedly the worst of any. A saint-author of all men least values politeness.[1] He scorns to confine that spirit in which he writes to rules of criticism and profane learning. Nor is he inclined in any respect to play the critic on himself, or regulate his style or language by the standard of good company, and people of the better sort. He is above the consideration of that which in a narrow sense we call manners. Nor is he apt to examine any other faults than those which he calls sins; though a sinner against good-breeding and the laws of decency will no more be esteemed a good author, than will a sinner against grammar, good argument, or good sense. And if moderation and temper are not of the party with a writer, let his cause be ever so good, I doubt whether he will be able to recommend it with great advantage to the world.

On this account, I would principally recommend our exercise of self-converse to all such persons as are addicted to write after the manner of holy advisers, especially if they lie under an indispensable necessity of being talkers or haranguers in the same kind. For to discharge frequently and vehemently in

[1] *Misc.* v. ch. i. in the notes.

public, is a great hindrance to the way of private exercise, which consists chiefly in control. But where, instead of control, debate, or argument, the chief exercise of the wit consists in uncontrollable harangues and reasonings, which must neither be questioned nor contradicted, there is great danger lest the party, through this habit, should suffer much by crudities, indigestions, choler, bile, and particularly by a certain tumour or flatulency, which renders him of all men the least able to apply the wholesome regimen of self-practice. 'Tis no wonder if such quaint practitioners grow to an enormous size of absurdity, whilst they continue in the reverse of that practice by which alone we correct the redundancy of humours, and chasten the exuberance of conceit and fancy.

A remarkable instance of the want of this sovereign remedy may be drawn from our common great talkers, who engross the greatest part of the conversations of the world, and are the forwardest to speak in public assemblies. Many of these have a sprightly genius, attended with a mighty heat and ebullition of fancy. But 'tis a certain observation in our science, that they who are great talkers in company have never been any talkers by themselves, nor used to these private discussions of our home regimen. For which reason their froth abounds. Nor can they discharge anything without some mixture of it. But when they carry their attempts beyond ordinary discourse, and would rise to the capacity of authors, the case grows worse with them. Their page can carry none of the advantages of their person. They can no way bring into paper those airs they give themselves in discourse. The turns of voice and action, with which they help out many a lame thought and incoherent sentence, must here be laid aside, and the speech taken to pieces, compared together, and examined from head to foot. So that unless the party has been used to play the critic thoroughly upon himself, he will hardly be found proof against the criticisms of others. His thoughts can never appear very correct, unless they have been used to sound correction by themselves, and been well formed and disciplined before they are brought into the field. 'Tis the hardest thing in the world to be a good thinker without being a strong self-examiner and thorough-paced dialogist in this solitary way.

Section II

But to bring our case a little closer still to morals. I might perhaps very justifiably take occasion here to enter into a spacious field of learning, to show the antiquity of that opinion: "That we have each of us a daemon, genius, angel, or guardian-spirit, to whom we were strictly joined and committed from our earliest dawn of reason, or moment of our birth." This opinion, were it literally true, might be highly serviceable, no doubt, towards the establishment of our system and doctrine. For it would infallibly be proved a kind of sacrilege or impiety to slight the company of so divine a guest, and in a manner banish him our breast, by refusing to enter with him into those secret conferences by which alone he could be enabled to become our adviser and guide. But I should esteem it unfair to proceed upon such an hypothesis as this, when the very utmost the wise ancients ever meant by this daemon companion I conceive to have been no more than enigmatically to declare, "that we had each of us a patient in ourself; that we were properly our own subjects of practice; and that we then became due practitioners, when by virtue of an intimate recess we could discover a certain duplicity of soul, and divide ourselves into two parties." One of these, as they supposed, would immediately approve himself a venerable sage; and with an air of authority erect himself our counsellor and governor, whilst the other party, who had nothing in him besides what was base and servile, would be contented to follow and obey.

According therefore as this recess was deep and intimate, and the dual number practically formed in us, we were supposed to advance in morals and true wisdom. This, they thought, was the only way of composing matters in our breast, and establishing that subordinacy which alone could make us agree with ourselves and be of a piece within. - They esteemed this a more religious work than any prayers, or other duty in the temple. And this they advised us to carry thither, as the best offering which could be made—

> Compositum jus, fasque animi, sanctosque recessus
> Mentis. . . .[1]

This was, among the ancients, that celebrated Delphic inscription, Recognise yourself; which was as much as to say, divide yourself, or be two. For if the division were rightly made, all within would of course, they thought, be rightly understood and prudently managed. Such confidence they had in this home-dialect of soliloquy. For it was accounted the peculiar of philosophers and wise men, to be able to hold themselves in talk. And it was their boast on this account, "that they were never less alone than when by themselves." A knave, they thought, could never be by himself. Not that his conscience was always sure of giving him disturbance; but he had not, they supposed, so much interest with himself as to exert this generous faculty, and raise himself a companion, who being fairly admitted into partnership, would quickly mend his partner, and set his affairs on a right foot.

One would think there was nothing easier for us than to know our own minds, and understand what our main scope was; what we plainly drove at, and what we proposed to ourselves, as our end, in every occurrence of our lives. But our thoughts have generally such an obscure implicit language, that 'tis the hardest thing in the world to make them speak out distinctly. For this reason, the right method is to give them voice and accent. And this, in our default, is what the moralists or philosophers endeavour to do to our hand, when,

---

[1] ["Duty to God and man well blended in the mind, purity in the shrine of the heart."—Persius, *Sat.* ii. 73: Conington's translation.]

as is usual, they hold us out a kind of vocal looking-glass, draw sound out of our breast, and instruct us to personate ourselves in the plainest manner.

> Illa sibi introrsum, et sub lingua immurmurat; o si
> Ebullit patrui praeclarum funus![1]

A certain air of pleasantry and humour, which prevails nowadays in the fashionable world, gives a son the assurance to tell a father he has lived too long; and a husband the privilege of talking of his second wife before his first. But let the airy gentleman, who makes thus bold with others, retire awhile out of company, and he scarce dares tell himself his wishes. Much less can he endure to carry on his thought, as he necessarily must, if he enters once thoroughly into himself, and proceeds by interrogatories to form the home acquaintance and familiarity required. For thus, after some struggle, we may suppose him to accost himself: "Tell me now, my honest heart! am I really honest, and of some worth? or do I only make a fair show, and am intrinsically no better than a rascal? As good a friend, a countryman, or a relation, as I appear outwardly to the world, or as I would willingly perhaps think myself to be, should I not in reality be glad they were hanged, any of them, or broke their necks, who happened to stand between me and the least portion of an estate? Why not? since 'tis my interest. Should I not be glad therefore to help this matter forwards, and promote my interest, if it lay fairly in my power? No doubt; provided I were sure not to be punished for it. And what reason has the greatest rogue in nature for not doing thus? The same reason, and no other. Am I not then, at the bottom, the same as he? The same: an arrant villain, though perhaps more a coward, and not so perfect in my kind. If interest therefore points me out this

[1] [This passage is from Persius, *Sat.* ii. 10, but the reading which Shaftesbury followed is not now generally accepted. It might mean that the prayer which a man utters within and secretly, when he has prayed aloud for sound mind and credit, is for the speedy death of a rich uncle.]

road, whither would humanity and compassion lead me? Quite contrary. Why therefore do I cherish such weaknesses? Why do I sympathise with others? Why please myself in the conceit of worth and honour? a character, a memory, an issue, or a name? What else are these but scruples in my way? Wherefore do I thus belie my own interest, and by keeping myself half-knave, approve myself a thorough fool?"

This is a language we can by no means endure to hold with ourselves, whatever raillery we may use with others. We may defend villainy, or cry up folly, before the world; but to appear fools, madmen, or varlets to ourselves, and prove it to our own faces that we are really such, is insupportable. For so true a reverence has every one for himself when he comes clearly to appear before his close companion, that he had rather profess the vilest things of himself in open company than hear his character privately from his own mouth. So that we may readily from hence conclude that the chief interest of ambition, avarice, corruption, and every sly insinuating vice is to prevent this interview and familiarity of discourse which is consequent upon close retirement and inward recess. 'Tis the grand artifice of villainy and lewdness, as well as of superstition and bigotry, to put us upon terms of greater distance and formality with ourselves, and evade our proving method of soliloquy. And for this reason, how specious soever may be the instruction and doctrine of formalists, their very manner itself is a sufficient blind or *remora* in the way of honesty and good sense.

I am sensible that should my reader be peradventure a lover, after the more profound and solemn way of love, he would be apt to conclude that he was no stranger to our proposed method of practice; being conscious to himself of having often made vigorous excursions into those solitary regions above-mentioned, where soliloquy is upheld with most advantage. He may chance to remember how he has many times addressed the woods and rocks in audible articulate sounds, and seemingly expostulated with himself in such a manner as if he had really formed the requisite distinction, and had the power to entertain himself in due form. But it is very apparent, that though all were true we have here supposed, it can no way reach the case before us. For a passionate lover, whatever solitude he may affect, can never be truly by himself. His case is like the author's who has begun his courtship to the public, and is embarked in an intrigue which sufficiently amuses and takes him out of himself. Whatever he meditates alone, is interrupted still by the imagined presence of the mistress he pursues. Not a thought, not an expression, not a sigh, which is purely for himself. All is appropriated, and all devoutly tendered to the object of his passion. Insomuch that there is nothing ever so trivial or accidental of this kind, which he is not desirous should be witnessed by the party whose grace and favour he solicits.

'Tis the same reason which keeps the imaginary saint, or mystic, from being capable of this entertainment. Instead of looking narrowly into his own nature and mind, that he may be no longer a mystery to himself, he is taken up with the contemplation of other mysterious natures, which he can never explain or comprehend. He has the spectres of his zeal before his eyes, and is as familiar with his modes, essences, personages, and exhibitions of deity, as the conjuror with his different forms, species, and orders of genii or daemons. So that we make no doubt to assert that not so much as a recluse religionist, a votary, or hermit, was ever truly by himself. And thus since neither lover, author, mystic, nor conjuror (who are the only claimants) can truly or justly be entitled to a share in this self-entertainment, it remains that the only person entitled is the man of sense, the sage, or philosopher. However, since of all other characters we are generally the most inclined to favour that of a lover, it may not, we hope, be impertinent, on this occasion, to recite the story of an amour.

A virtuous young prince of a heroic soul, capable of love and friendship, made war upon a tyrant, who was in every respect his reverse. 'Twas the happiness of our prince to be as great a conqueror by his clemency and bounty as by his arms and military virtue. Already he had won over to his party several potentates and princes, who before had been subject to the tyrant. Among those who adhered still to the enemy, there was a prince who, having all the advantage of person and merit, had lately been made happy in the possession and mutual love of the most beautiful princess in the world. It happened that the occasions of the war called the new-married prince to a distance from his beloved princess. He left her secure, as he thought, in a strong castle, far within the country; but in his absence the place was taken by surprise, and the princess brought a captive to the quarters of our heroic prince.

There was in the camp a young nobleman, favourite of the prince; one who had been educated with him, and was still treated by him with perfect familiarity. Him he immediately sent for, and with strict injunctions committed the captive princess to his charge; resolving she should be treated with that respect which was due to her high rank and merit. 'Twas the same young lord who had discovered her disguised among the prisoners, and learnt her story; the particulars of which he now related to the prince. He spoke in ecstasy on this occasion; telling the prince how beautiful she appeared, even in the midst of sorrow; and though disguised under the meanest habit, yet how distinguishable, by her air and manner, from every other beauty of her sex. But what appeared strange to our young nobleman was that the prince, during this whole relation, discovered not the least intention of seeing the lady, or satisfying that curiosity which seemed so natural on such an occasion. He pressed him; but without success. "Not see her, sir!" said he, wondering, "when she is so handsome, beyond what you have ever seen!"

"For that very reason," replied the prince, "I would the rather decline the interview. For should I, upon the bare report of her beauty, be so charmed as to make the first visit at this urgent time of business, I may upon sight, with better reason, be induced perhaps to visit her when I am more at leisure; and so again and again, till at last I may have no leisure left for my affairs."

"Would you, sir, persuade me then," said the young nobleman, smiling, "that a fair face can have such power as to force the will itself, and constrain a man in any respect to act contrary to what he thinks becoming him? Are we to hearken to the poets in what they tell us of that incendiary love, and his irresistible flames? A real flame, we see, burns all alike. But that imaginary one of beauty hurts only those who are consenting. It affects no otherwise than as we ourselves are pleased to allow it. In many cases we absolutely command it: as where relation and consanguinity are in the nearest degree. Authority and law, we see, can master it. But 'twould be vain as well as unjust for any law to intermeddle or prescribe, were not the case voluntary and our will entirely free."

"How comes it then," replied the prince, "that if we are thus masters of our choice, and free at first to admire and love where we approve, we cannot afterwards as well cease to love whenever we see cause? This latter liberty you will hardly defend. For I doubt not you have heard of many who, though they were used to set the highest value upon liberty before they loved, yet afterwards were necessitated to serve in the most abject manner, finding themselves constrained and bound by a stronger chain than any of iron or adamant."

"Such wretches," replied the youth, "I have often heard complain; who, if you will believe them, are wretched indeed, without means or power to help themselves. You may hear them in the same manner complain grievously of life itself. But though there are doors enough to go out of life, they find it convenient to keep still where they are. They are the very same pretenders, who through this plea of irresistible necessity make bold with what is another's, and attempt unlawful beds. But the law, I perceive, makes bold with them in its turn, as with other invaders of property. Neither is it your custom, sir, to pardon such offences. So that beauty itself, you must allow, is innocent and harmless, and can compel no one to do anything amiss. The debauched compel themselves, and unjustly charge their guilt on love. They who are honest and just, can admire and love whatever is beautiful, without offering at anything beyond what is allowed. How then is it possible, sir, that one of your virtue should be in pain on any such account, or fear such a temptation? You see, sir, I am sound and whole, after having beheld the princess. I have conversed with her; I have admired her in the highest degree; yet am myself still, and in my duty; and shall be ever in the same manner at your command."

"'Tis well," replied the prince; "keep yourself so. Be ever the same man; and look to your charge carefully, as becomes you. For it may so happen in the present posture of the war that this fair captive may stand us in good stead."

With this the young nobleman departed to execute his commission; and immediately took such care of the captive princess and her household, that she seemed as perfectly obeyed, and had everything which belonged to her in as great splendour now, as in her principality, and in the height of fortune. He found her in every respect deserving, and saw in her a generosity of soul which was beyond her other charms. His study to oblige her, and soften her distress, made her in return desirous to express a gratitude, which he easily perceived. She showed on every occasion a real concern for his interest; and when he happened to fall ill, she took such tender care of him herself, and by her servants, that he seemed to owe his recovery to her friendship.

From these beginnings, insensibly, and by natural degrees (as may easily be conceived) the youth fell desperately in love. At first he offered not to make the least mention of his passion to the princess; for he scarce dared tell it to himself But afterwards he grew bolder. She received his declaration with an unaffected trouble and concern, spoke to him as a friend, to dissuade him as much as possible from such an extravagant attempt. But when he talked to her of force, she immediately sent away one of her faithful domestics to the prince to implore his protection. The prince received the message with the appearance of more than ordinary concern; sent instantly for one of his first Ministers; and bid him go with that domestic to the young nobleman, and let him understand "that force was not to be offered to such a lady; persuasion he might use, if he thought fit."

The Minister, who was no friend to the young nobleman, failed not to aggravate the message, inveighed publicly against him on this occasion, and to his face reproached him as a traitor and dishonourer of his prince and nation, with all else which could be said against him, as guilty of the highest sacrilege, perfidiousness, and breach of trust. So that in reality the youth looked upon his case as desperate, fell into the deepest melancholy, and prepared himself for that fate which he thought he well deserved.

In this condition the prince sent to speak with him alone; and when he saw him in the utmost confusion, "I find," said he, "my friend, I am now become dreadful to you indeed; since you can neither see me without shame, nor imagine me to be without resentment. But away with all those thoughts from this time forwards. I know how much you have suffered on this occasion. I know the power of love, and am no otherwise safe myself, than by keeping out of the way of beauty. 'Twas I who was in fault; 'twas I who unhappily matched you with that unequal adversary, and gave you that impracticable task and hard adventure, which no one yet was ever strong enough to accomplish."

"In this, sir," replied the youth, "as in all else, you express that goodness which is so natural to you. You have compassion, and can allow for human frailty; but the rest of mankind will never cease to upbraid me. Nor shall I ever be forgiven, were I able ever to forgive myself. I am reproached by my nearest friends. I must be odious to all mankind wherever I am known. The least punishment I can think due to me, is banishment for ever from your presence."

"Think not of such a thing for ever," said the prince, "but trust me; if you retire only for a while, I shall so order it, that you shall soon return again with the applause even of those who are now your enemies, when they find what a considerable service you shall have rendered both to them and me."

Such a hint was sufficient to revive the spirits of our despairing youth. He was transported to think that his misfortunes could be turned any way to the advantage of his prince: he entered with joy into the scheme the prince had laid for him, and appeared eager to depart and execute what was appointed him. "Can you, then," said the prince, "resolve to quit the charming princess?"

"Oh sir!" replied the youth, "well am I now satisfied that I have in reality within me two distinct separate souls. This lesson of philosophy I have learnt from that villainous sophister Love. For 'tis impossible to believe that, having one and the same soul, it should be actually both good and bad, passionate for virtue and vice, desirous of contraries. No. There must of necessity be two: and when the good prevails, 'tis then we act handsomely; when the ill, then basely and villainously. Such was my case. For lately the ill soul was wholly master. But now the good prevails by your assistance, and I am plainly a new creature, with quite another apprehension, another reason, another will."

Thus it may appear how far a lover by his own natural strength may reach the chief principle of philosophy, and understand our doctrine of two persons in one individual self. Not that our courtier, we suppose, was able of himself to form this distinction justly and according to art. For could he have effected this, he would have been able to cure himself without the assistance of his prince. However, he was wise enough to see in the issue that his independency and freedom were mere glosses, and resolution a nose of wax. For let Will be ever so free, Humour and Fancy, we see, govern it. And these, as free as we suppose them, are often changed we know not how, without asking our consent, or giving us any account. If opinion be that which governs and makes the change, 'tis itself as liable to be governed and varied in its turn. And by what I can observe of the world, fancy and opinion stand pretty much upon the same bottom. So that if there be no certain inspector or auditor established within us to take account of these opinions and fancies in due form, and minutely to animadvert upon their several growths and habits, we are as little like to continue a day in the same will as a tree, during a summer, in the same shape, without the gardener's assistance, and the vigorous application of the shears and pruning-knife.

As cruel a court as the Inquisition appears, there must, it seems, be full as formidable a one erected in ourselves, if we would pretend to that uniformity of opinion which is necessary to hold us to one will, and preserve us in the same mind from one day to another. Philosophy, at this rate, will be thought perhaps little better than persecution; and a supreme judge in matters of inclination and appetite must needs go exceedingly against the heart. Every pretty fancy is disturbed by it; every pleasure interrupted by it. The course of good-humour will hardly allow it, and the pleasantry of wit almost absolutely rejects it. It appears, besides, like a kind of pedantry to be thus magisterial with ourselves, thus strict over our imaginations, and with all the airs of a real pedagogue to be solicitously taken up in the sour care and tutorage of so many boyish fancies, unlucky appetites and desires, which are perpetually playing truant and need correction.

We hope, however, that by our method of practice and the help of the grand *arcanum* which we have professed to reveal, this regimen or discipline of the fancies may not in the end prove so severe or mortifying as is imagined. We hope also that our patient (for such we naturally suppose our reader) will consider duly with himself that what he endures in this operation is for no inconsiderable end, since 'tis to gain him a Will, and ensure him a certain resolution, by which he shall know where to find himself; be sure of his own meaning and design; and as to all his desires, opinions, and inclinations, be warranted one and the same person to-day as yesterday, and to-morrow as to-day.

This, perhaps, will be thought a miracle by one who well considers the nature of mankind, and the growth, variation, and inflection of Appetite and Humour. For Appetite, which is elder brother to Reason, being the lad of stronger growth, is sure, on every contest, to take the advantage of drawing all to his own side. And Will, so highly boasted, is at best merely a top or football between these youngsters, who prove very unfortunately matched; till the youngest, instead of now and then a kick or lash bestowed to little purpose, forsakes the ball or top itself, and begins to lay about his elder brother. 'Tis then that the scene changes. For the elder, like an arrant coward, upon this treatment, presently grows civil, and affords the younger as fair play afterwards as he can desire.

And here it is that our sovereign remedy and gymnastic method of soliloquy takes its rise; when by a certain powerful figure of inward rhetoric the mind apostrophises its own fancies, raises them in their proper shapes and personages, and addresses them familiarly, without the least ceremony or respect. By this means it will soon happen that two formed parties will erect themselves within. For the imaginations or fancies being thus roundly treated are forced to declare themselves and take party. Those on the side of the elder brother Appetite are strangely subtle and insinuating. They have always the faculty to speak by nods and winks. By this practice they conceal half their meaning, and, like modern politicians, pass for deeply wise, and adorn themselves with the finest pretexts and most specious glosses imaginable; till, being confronted with their fellows of a plainer language and expression, they are forced to quit their mysterious manner, and discover themselves mere sophisters and impostors who have not the least to do with the party of reason and good sense.

Accordingly we might now proceed to exhibit distinctly, and in due method, the form and manner of this probation or exercise as it regards all men in general. But the case of authors in particular being, as we apprehend, the most urgent, we shall apply our rule in the first place to these gentlemen, whom it so highly imports to know themselves, and understand the natural strength and powers as well as the weaknesses of a human mind. For without this understanding, the historian's judgment will be very defective; the politician's views very narrow and chimerical, and the poet's brain, however stocked with fiction, will be but poorly furnished, as in the sequel we shall make appear. He who deals in characters must of necessity know his own, or he will know nothing. And he who would give the world a profitable entertainment of this sort, should be sure to profit, first, by himself. For in this sense, Wisdom as well as Charity may be honestly said to begin at home. There is no way of estimating manners, or apprising the different humours, fancies, passions, and apprehensions of others, without first taking an inventory of the same kind of goods within ourselves, and surveying our domestic fund. A little of this home practice will serve to make great discoveries—

Tecum habita et noris quam sit tibi curta suppellex.[1]

Section III

Whoever has been an observer of action and grace in human bodies must of necessity have discovered the great difference in this respect between such persons as have been taught by nature

[1] ["Live at home and learn how slenderly furnished your apartments are."—Persius, *Sat.* iv. 52: Conington's translation.]

ADVICE TO AN AUTHOR

only, and such as by reflection and the assistance of art have learnt to form those motions which on experience are found the easiest and most natural. Of the former kind are either those good rustics who have been bred remote from the formed societies of men, or those plain artisans and people of lower rank who, living in cities and places of resort, have been necessitated however to follow mean employments, and wanted the opportunity and means to form themselves after the better models. There are some persons indeed so happily formed by Nature herself, that with the greatest simplicity or rudeness of education they have still something of a natural grace and comeliness in their action; and there are others of a better education who, by a wrong aim and injudicious affectation of grace, are of all people the farthest removed from it. 'Tis undeniable, however, that the perfection of grace and comeliness in action and behaviour can be found only among the people of a liberal education. And even among the graceful of this kind, those still are found the gracefullest who early in their youth have learnt their exercises, and formed their motions under the best masters.

Now such as these masters and their lessons are to a fine gentleman, such are philosophers and philosophy to an author. The case is the same in the fashionable and in the literate world. In the former of these it is remarked that by the help of good company, and the force of example merely, a decent carriage is acquired, with such apt motions and such a freedom of limbs as on all ordinary occasions may enable the party to demean himself like a gentleman. But when, upon further occasion, trial is made in an extraordinary way—when exercises of the genteeler kind are to be performed in public—'twill easily appear who of the pretenders have been formed by rudiments, and had masters in private, and who, on the other side, have contented themselves with bare imitation, and learnt their part casually and by rote. The parallel is easily made on the side of writers. They have at least as much need of learning the several motions, counterpoises and balances of the mind and passions, as the other students those of the body and limbs—

> Scribendi recte sapere est et principium et fons;
> Rem tibi Socraticae poterunt ostendere chartae.[1]

The gallant, no doubt, may pen a letter to his mistress, as the courtier may a compliment to the Minister, or the Minister to the favourite above him, without going such vast depths into learning or philosophy. But for these privileged gentlemen,

---

[1] Hor. *de Arte Poet.* See even the dissolute Petronius's judgment of a writer:—

> Artis severae si quis amat effectus,
> Mentemque magnis applicat; prius more
> Frugalitatis lege polleat exacta;
> Nec curet alto regiam trucem vultu.
> * * * * *
> neve plausor in scaena
> Sedeat redemptus, histrioniae addictus.
> * * * * *
> Mox et Socratico plenus grege, mutet habenas
> Liber, et ingentis quatiat Demosthenis arma.
> * * * * *
> His animum succinge bonis, sic flumine largo
> Plenus, Pierio defundes pectore verba.

[1] [(i) "Sound knowledge is the first requisite for writing well; the books of Socrates' school will yield you the matter."—Hor. *Ars Poet.* 309, 310.]

[(ii) Petron. c. v. The readings followed by Shaftesbury are not very good. The general sense is given thus by Wilson (translation of the *Satyricon* of Petronius Arbiter, 1708: reprinted for private circulation, 1899):—

> By liberal arts would you acquire renown,
> And rise to power by honours of the gown?
> Strict in your life, of conversation chaste,
> Far from the court with just precaution haste,
> The haughty great but very rare attend,
> * * * * *
> And fly the luscious accents of the stage,
> * * * * *
> Next let philosophy employ your thought,
> And maxims learn the wise Athenian taught, etc.]

though they set fashions and prescribe rules in other cases, they are no controllers in the commonwealth of Letters. Nor are they presumed to write to the age, or for remote posterity. Their works are not of a nature to entitle them to hold the rank of authors, or be styled writers by way of excellence in the kind. Should their ambition lead them into such a field, they would be obliged to come otherwise equipped. They who enter the public lists must come duly trained and exercised, like well-appointed cavaliers expert in arms, and well instructed in the use of their weapon and management of their steed. For to be well accoutred and well mounted is not sufficient. The horse alone can never make the horseman, nor limbs the wrestler or the dancer. No more can a genius alone make a poet, or good parts a writer in any considerable kind. The skill and grace of writing is founded, as our wise poet tells us, in knowledge and good sense; and not barely in that knowledge which is to be learnt from common authors, or the general conversation of the world; but from those particular rules of art which philosophy alone exhibits.

The philosophical writings to which our poet in his *Art of Poetry* refers, were in themselves a kind of poetry, like the mimes,[1] or personated pieces of early times, before philosophy was in vogue, and when as yet dramatical imitation was scarce formed; or at least, in many parts, not brought to due perfection. They were pieces which, besides their force of style and hidden numbers, carried a sort of action and imitation, the same as the epic and dramatic kinds. They were either real dialogues, or recitals of such personated discourses; where the persons themselves had their characters preserved throughout, their manners, humours, and distinct turns of temper and understanding maintained, according to the most exact poetical truth. 'Twas not enough that these pieces treated fundamentally of morals, and in consequence pointed out real characters and manners: they exhibited them alive, and set the

[1] *Infra,* part ii § 2, in the notes.

countenances and complexions of men plainly in view. And by this means they not only taught us to know others, but, what was principal and of highest virtue in them, they taught us to know ourselves.

The philosophical hero of these poems, whose name they carried both in their body and front, and whose genius and manner they were made to represent, was in himself a perfect character; yet in some respects so veiled and in a cloud, that to the unattentive surveyor he seemed often to be very different from what he really was; and this chiefly by reason of a certain exquisite and refined raillery which belonged to his manner, and by virtue of which he could treat the highest subjects and those of the commonest capacity both together, and render them explanatory of each other. So that in this genius of writing there appeared both the heroic and the simple, the tragic and the comic vein. However, it was so ordered that, notwithstanding the oddness or mysteriousness of the principal character, the under-parts or second characters showed human nature more distinctly and to the life. We might here, therefore, as in a looking-glass, discover ourselves, and see our minutest features nicely delineated, and suited to our own apprehension and cognizance. No one who was ever so little a while an inspector, could fail of becoming acquainted with his own heart. And, what was of singular note in these magical glasses, it would happen that, by constant and long inspection, the parties accustomed to the practice would acquire a peculiar speculative habit, so as virtually to carry about with them a sort of pocket-mirror, always ready and in use. In this, there were two faces which would naturally present themselves to our view: one of them, like the commanding genius, the leader and chief above-mentioned; the other like that rude, undisciplined, and headstrong creature whom we ourselves in our natural capacity most exactly resembled. Whatever we were employed in, whatever we set about, if once we had acquired the habit of this mirror we should, by virtue of the double reflection, distinguish ourselves into two different parties. And in this dramatic method, the work of self-inspection would proceed with admirable success.

'Tis no wonder that the primitive poets were esteemed such sages in their times, since it appears they were such well-practised dialogists, and accustomed to this improving method, before ever philosophy had adopted it. Their mimes or characterised discourses were as much relished as their most regular poems; and were the occasion perhaps that so many of these latter were formed in such perfection. For poetry itself was defined an imitation chiefly of men and manners; and was that in an exalted and noble degree which in a low one we call mimicry. 'Tis in this that the great mimographer,[1] the father and prince of poets, excels so highly; his characters being wrought to a likeness beyond what any succeeding masters were ever able to describe. Nor are his works, which are so full of action, any other than an artful series or chain of dialogues, which turn upon one remarkable catastrophe or event. He describes no qualities or virtues; censures no manners; makes no encomiums, nor gives characters himself; but brings his actors still in view. 'Tis they who show themselves. 'Tis they who speak in such a manner as distinguishes them in all things from all others, and makes them ever like themselves. Their different compositions and allays so justly made, and equally carried on through every particle of the action, give more instruction than all the comments or glosses in the world. The poet, instead of

---

[1] "Ὅμηρος δὲ ἄλλα τε πολλὰ ἄξιος ἐπαινεῖσθαι, καὶ δὴ καὶ ὅτι μόνος τῶν ποιητῶν, οὐκ ἀγνοεῖ ὃ δεῖ ποιεῖν αὐτόν. αὐτὸν γὰρ δεῖ τὸν ποιητὴν ἐλάχιστα λέγειν· οὐ γάρ ἐστι κατὰ ταῦτα μιμητής· οἱ μὲν οὖν ἄλλοι αὐτοὶ μὲν δι' ὅλου ἀγωνίζονται, μιμοῦνται δὲ ὀλίγα καὶ ὀλιγάκις.

["Homer, excellent in many other respects, is specially so because he is the only poet who knows what part to take himself. For the poet in his own person should speak as little as may be, for it is not his speaking which makes him an imitator. Now, other poets are on the stage themselves all the time, but their imitations are short and few."—Arist. *Poet.* xxiv.]

giving himself those dictating and masterly airs of wisdom, makes hardly any figure at all, and is scarce discoverable in his poem. This is being truly a master. He paints so as to need no inscription over his figures to tell us what they are or what he intends by them. A few words let fall on any slight occasion, from any of the parties he introduces, are sufficient to denote their manners and distinct character. From a finger or a toe he can represent to our thoughts the frame and fashion of a whole body. He wants no other help of art to personate his heroes and make them living. There was no more left for tragedy to do after him than to erect a stage and draw his dialogues and characters into scenes; turning, in the same manner, upon one principal action or event, with that regard to place and time which was suitable to a real spectacle. Even comedy itself was adjudged to this great master;[1] it being derived from those parodies or mock-humours of which he had given the specimen[2] in a concealed sort of raillery intermixed with the sublime. . . . A dangerous stroke of art! and which required a masterly hand, like that of the philosophical hero whose character was represented in the dialogue writings above mentioned.

From hence possibly we may form a notion of that resemblance which on so many occasions was heretofore remarked between the prince of poets and the divine philosopher who was said to rival him, and who, together with his contemporaries of the same school, writ wholly in that manner of dialogue above described. From hence too we may comprehend perhaps why the study of dialogue was heretofore thought so advantageous to writers, and why this manner of writing was judged so difficult, which at first sight, it must be owned, appears the easiest of any.

I have formerly wondered indeed why a manner, which was familiarly used in treatises upon most subjects with so much

[1] *Infra*, part ii. § 2, in the notes.
[2] Not only in his *Margites*, but even in his *Iliad* and *Odyssey*.

success among the ancients, should be so insipid and of little esteem with us moderns. But I afterwards perceived that, besides the difficulty of the manner itself, and that mirror faculty which we have observed it to carry in respect of ourselves, it proves also of necessity a kind of mirror or looking-glass to the age. If so, it should of consequence (you will say) be the more agreeable and entertaining.

True, if the real view of ourselves be not perhaps displeasing to us. But why more displeasing to us than to the ancients? Because perhaps they could with just reason bear to see their natural countenances represented. And why not we the same? What should discourage us? For are we not as handsome, at least in our own eyes? Perhaps not, as we shall see when we have considered a little further what the force is of this mirror-writing, and how it differs from that more complacent modish way in which an author, instead of presenting us with other natural characters, sets off his own with the utmost art, and purchases his reader's favour by all imaginable compliances and condescensions.

An author who writes in his own person has the advantage of being who or what he pleases. He is no certain man, nor has any certain or genuine character; but suits himself on every occasion to the fancy of his reader, whom, as the fashion is nowadays, he constantly caresses and cajoles. All turns upon their two persons. And as in an amour or commerce of love-letters, so here the author has the privilege of talking eternally of himself, dressing and sprucing himself up, whilst he is making diligent court, and working upon the humour of the party to whom he addresses. This is the coquetry of a modern author, whose epistles dedicatory, prefaces, and addresses to the reader are so many affected graces, designed to draw the attention from the subject towards himself, and make it be generally observed, not so much what he says, as what he appears, or is, and what figure he already makes, or hopes to make, in the fashionable world.

SHAFTESBURY'S CHARACTERISTICS

These are the airs which a neighbouring nation give themselves, more particularly in what they call their memoirs. Their very essays on politics, their philosophical and critical works, their comments upon ancient and modern authors, all their treatises are memoirs. The whole writing of this age is become indeed a sort of memoir-writing. Though in the real memoirs of the ancients, even when they writ at any time concerning themselves, there was neither the *I* nor *thou* throughout the whole work. So that all this pretty amour and intercourse of caresses between the author and reader was thus entirely taken away.

Much more is this the case in dialogue. For here the author is annihilated, and the reader, being no way applied to, stands for nobody. The self-interesting parties both vanish at once. The scene presents itself as by chance and undesigned. You are not only left to judge coolly and with indifference of the sense delivered, but of the character, genius, elocution, and manner of the persons who deliver it. These two are mere strangers, in whose favour you are no way engaged. Nor is it enough that the persons introduced speak pertinent and good sense at every turn. It must be seen from what bottom they speak; from what principle, what stock or fund of knowledge they draw; and what kind or species of understanding they possess. For the understanding here must have its mark, its characteristic note, by which it may be distinguished. It must be such and such an understanding; as when we say, for instance, such or such a face; since Nature has characterised tempers and minds as peculiarly as faces. And for an artist who draws naturally, 'tis not enough to show us merely faces which may be called men's: every face must be a certain man's.

Now as a painter who draws battles or other actions of Christians, Turks, Indians, or any distinct and peculiar people, must of necessity draw the several figures of his piece in their proper and real proportions, gestures, habits, arms, or at least with as fair resemblance as possible, so in the same manner that writer, whoever he be, among us moderns, who shall venture to bring his fellow-moderns into dialogue, must introduce them in their proper manners, genius, behaviour and humour. And this is the mirror or looking-glass above described.

For instance, a dialogue, we will suppose, is framed after the manner of our ancient authors. In it a poor philosopher, of a mean figure, accosts one of the powerfullest, wittiest, handsomest, and richest noblemen of the time as he is walking leisurely towards the temple. "You are going then," says he (calling him by his plain name) " to pay your devotions yonder at the temple? I am so. But with an air methinks, as if some thought perplexed you.

"What is there in the case which should perplex one? The thought perhaps of your petitions, and the consideration what vows you had best offer to the Deity. Is that so difficult? Can any one be so foolish as to ask of Heaven what is not for his good? Not if he understands what his good is.

"Who can mistake it, if he has common sense, and knows the difference between prosperity and adversity? 'Tis prosperity therefore you would pray for?

"Undoubtedly. For instance, that absolute sovereign, who commands all things by virtue of his immense treasures, and governs by his sole will and pleasure, him you think prosperous and his state happy."

Whilst I am copying this (for 'tis no more indeed than a borrowed sketch from one of those originals before mentioned) I see a thousand ridicules arising from the manner, the circumstances and action itself, compared with modern breeding and civility.—Let us therefore mend the matter if possible, and introduce the same philosopher, addressing himself in a more obsequious manner, to *his Grace, his Excellency,* or *his Honour,* without failing in the least tittle of the ceremonial. Or let us put the case more favourably still for our man of letters. Let us suppose him to be *incognito,* without the least appearance of a character, which in our age is so little recommending. Let his garb and action be of the more modish sort, in order to introduce him better and gain him audience. And with these advantages and precautions, imagine still in what manner he must accost this pageant of state, if at any time he finds him at leisure, walking in the fields alone, and without his equipage. Consider how many bows and simpering faces! how many preludes, excuses, compliments!—Now put compliments, put ceremony into a dialogue, and see what will be the effect!

This is the plain dilemma against that ancient manner of writing which we can neither well imitate nor translate, whatever pleasure or profit we may find in reading those originals. For what shall we do in such a circumstance? What if the fancy takes us, and we resolve to try the experiment in modern subjects? See the consequence!—If we avoid ceremony we are unnatural; if we use it, and appear as we naturally are, as we salute, and meet, and treat one another, we hate the sight. . . . What's this but hating our own faces? Is it the painter's fault? Should he paint falsely or affectedly; mix modern with ancient, join shapes preposterously, and betray his art? If not, what medium is there? What remains for him but to throw away the pencil? . . . No more designing after the life; no more mirror-writing or personal representation of any kind whatever.

Thus dialogue is at an end. The ancients could see their own faces, but we cannot. And why this? Why, but because we have less beauty; for so our looking-glass can inform us. . . . Ugly instrument! And for this reason to be hated. . . . Our commerce and manner of conversation, which we think the politest imaginable, is such, it seems, as we ourselves cannot endure to see represented to the life. 'Tis here, as in our real portraitures, particularly those at full length, where the poor pencil-man is put to a thousand shifts, whilst he strives to dress us in affected habits, such as we never wore; because should he paint us in those we really wear, they would of necessity make the piece to be so much more ridiculous as it was more natural and resembling.

Thus much for antiquity and those rules of art, those philosophical sea-cards, by which the adventurous geniuses of the times were wont to steer their courses and govern their impetuous muse. These were the *chartae* of our Roman master-poet, and these the pieces of art, the mirrors, the exemplars he bids us place before our eyes—

> Vos exemplaria Graeca
> Nocturna versate manu, versate diurna [1]

And thus poetry and the writer's art, as in many respects it resembles the statuary's and the painter's, so in this more particularly, that it has its original draughts and models for study and practice; not for ostentation, to be shown abroad or copied for public view. These are the ancient busts, the trunks of statues, the pieces of anatomy, the masterly rough drawings which are kept within, as the secret learning, the mystery, and fundamental knowledge of the art. There is this essential difference however between the artists of each kind: that they who design merely after bodies, and form the graces of this sort, can never, with all their accuracy or correctness of design, be able to reform themselves, or grow a jot more shapely in their persons. But for those artists who copy from another life, who study the graces and perfections of minds, and are real masters of those rules which constitute this latter science, 'tis impossible they should fail of being themselves improved, and amended in their better part.

I must confess there is hardly anywhere to be found a more insipid race of mortals than those whom we moderns are contented to call poets, for having attained the chiming faculty of a language, with an injudicious random use of wit and fancy. But for the man who truly and in a just sense deserves the

---

[1] ["Thumb your Greek patterns by night and by day."—Hor. *de Arte Poet.* 268.]

name of poet, and who as a real master, or architect in the kind, can describe both men and manners, and give to an action its just body and proportions, he will be found, if I mistake not, a very different creature. Such a poet is indeed a second *Maker*; a just Prometheus under Jove. Like that sovereign artist or universal plastic nature, he forms a whole, coherent and proportioned in itself, with due subjection and subordinacy of constituent parts. He notes the boundaries of the passions, and knows their exact tones and measures; by which he justly represents them, marks the sublime of sentiments and action, and distinguishes the beautiful from the deformed, the amiable from the odious. The moral artist who can thus imitate the Creator, and is thus knowing in the inward form and structure of his fellow-creature, will hardly, I presume, be found unknowing in himself, or at a loss in those numbers which make the harmony of a mind. For knavery is mere dissonance and disproportion. And though villains may have strong tones and natural capacities of action, 'tis impossible that true judgment and ingenuity should reside where harmony and honesty have no being.[1]

But having entered thus seriously into the concerns of authors, and shown their chief foundation and strength, their preparatory discipline and qualifying method of self-examination, 'tis fit, ere we disclose this mystery any farther, we should consider the advantages or disadvantages our authors may

---

[1] The maxim will hardly be disproved by fact or history, either in respect of philosophers themselves or others who were the great geniuses or masters in the liberal arts. The characters of the two best Roman poets are well known. Those of the ancient tragedians no less. And the great epic master, though of an obscurer and remoter age, was ever presumed to be far enough from a vile or knavish character. The Roman as well as the Grecian orator was true to his country, and died in like manner a martyr for its liberty. And those historians who are of highest value were either in a private life approved good men, or noted such by their actions in the public. As for poets in particular (says the learned and wise Strabo), "Can we possibly imagine that the genius, power, and excellence of a real poet consists in aught else than the just imitation of

possibly meet with from abroad, and how far their genius may be depressed or raised by any external causes arising from the humour or judgment of the world.

Whatever it be which influences in this respect must proceed either from the grandees and men in power, the critics and men of art, or the people themselves, the common audience, and mere vulgar. We shall begin therefore with the grandees and pretended masters of the world, taking the liberty, in favour of authors, to bestow some advice also on these high persons, if possibly they are disposed to receive it in such a familiar way as this.

PART II

Section I

As usual as it is with mankind to act absolutely by will and pleasure, without regard to counsel or the rigid method of rule and precept, it must be acknowledged nevertheless that the good and laudable custom of asking advice is still upheld and kept in fashion as a matter of fair repute and honourable appearance, insomuch that even monarchs, and absolute princes

---

life in formed discourse and numbers? But how should he be that just imitator of life whilst he himself knows not its measures, nor how to guide himself by judgment and understanding? For we have not surely the same notion of the poet's excellence as of the ordinary craftsman's, the subject of whose art is senseless stone or timber, without life, dignity, or beauty; whilst the poet's art turning principally on men and manners, he has his virtue and excellence as poet naturally annexed to human excellence, and to the worth and dignity of man. Insomuch that 'tis impossible he should be a great and worthy poet who is not first a worthy and good man." οὐ γὰρ οὕτω φαμὲν τὴν τῶν ποιητῶν ἀρετὴν ὡς ἢ τεκτόνων ἢ χαλκέων, etc., ἡ δὲ ποιητοῦ συνέζευκται τῇ τοῦ ἀνθρώπου· καὶ οὐχ οἷόν τε ἀγαθὸν γενέσθαι ποιητήν, μὴ πρότερον γενηθέντα ἄνδρα ἀγαθόν.—I. i. See below, part ii. § 3, at the end, and part iii § 3, in the notes, and *Misc.* v. ch. i. ii.

themselves, disdain not, we see, to make profession of the practice.

'Tis, I presume, on this account that the royal persons are pleased on public occasions to make use of the noted style of *we* and *us*. Not that they are supposed to have any converse with themselves, as being endowed with the privilege of becoming plural and enlarging their capacity in the manner above described. Single and absolute persons in government, I am sensible, can hardly be considered as any other than single and absolute in morals. They have no inmate-controller to cavil with them or dispute their pleasure. Nor have they, from any practice abroad, been able at any time to learn the way of being free and familiar with themselves at home. Inclination and will in such as these admit as little restraint or check in private meditation as in public company. The world, which serves as a tutor to persons of an inferior rank, is submissive to these royal pupils, who from their earliest days are used to see even their instructors bend before them, and to hear everything applauded which they themselves perform.

For fear therefore lest their humour merely, or the caprice of some favourite, should be presumed to influence them when they come to years of princely discretion and are advanced to the helm of government, it has been esteemed a necessary decency to summon certain advisers by profession to assist as attendants to the single person, and be joined with him in his written edicts, proclamations, letters-patent, and other instruments of regal power. For this use privy-counsellors have been erected, who, being persons of considerable figure and wise aspect, cannot be supposed to stand as statues or mere ciphers in the government, and leave the royal acts erroneously and falsely described to us in the plural number, when at the bottom a single will or fancy was the sole spring and motive.

Foreign princes indeed have most of them that unhappy prerogative of acting unadvisedly and wilfully in their national affairs. But 'tis known to be far otherwise with the legal and just princes of our Island. They are surrounded with the best of counsellors, the laws. They administer civil affairs by legal officers who have the direction of their public will and conscience; and they annually receive advice and aid in the most effectual manner from their good people. To this wise genius of our Constitution we may be justly said to owe our wisest and best princes, whose high birth or royal education could not alone be supposed to have given them that happy turn, since by experience we find that those very princes, from whose conduct the world abroad as well as we at home have reaped the greatest advantages, were such as had the most controverted titles, and in their youth had stood in the remoter prospects of regal power, and lived the nearest to a private life.

Other princes we have had, who, though difficult perhaps in receiving counsel, have been eminent in the practice of applying it to others. They have listed themselves advisers in form, and by publishing their admonitory works have added to the number of those whom in this treatise we have presumed to criticise. But our criticism being withal an apology for authors and a defence of the literate tribe, it cannot be thought amiss in us to join the royal with the plebeian penmen in this common cause.

'Twould be a hard case indeed should the princes of our nation refuse to countenance the industrious race of authors, since their royal ancestors and predecessors have had such honour derived to them from this profession. 'Tis to this they owe that bright jewel of their crown, purchased by a warlike prince, who having assumed the author, and essayed his strength in the polemic writings of the school-divines, thought it an honour on this account to retain the title of DEFENDER OF THE FAITH.

Another prince, of a more pacific nature and fluent thought, submitting arms and martial discipline to the gown, and confiding in his princely science and profound learning, made his style and speech the nerve and sinew of his government. He gave us his works full of wise exhortation and advice to his royal son, as well as of instruction to his good people, who could not without admiration observe their author-sovereign thus studious and contemplative in their behalf. 'Twas then one might have seen our nation growing young and docile, with that simplicity of heart which qualified them to profit like a scholar-people under their royal preceptor. For with abundant eloquence he graciously gave lessons to his parliament, tutored his ministers, and edified the greatest churchmen and divines themselves, by whose suffrage he obtained the highest appellations which could be merited by the acutest wit and truest understanding. From hence the British nations were taught to own in common a Solomon for their joint sovereign, the founder of their late completed union. Nor can it be doubted that the pious treatise of self-discourse ascribed to the succeeding monarch contributed in a great measure to his glorious and never-fading titles of Saint and Martyr.

However it be, I would not willingly take upon me to recommend this author-character to our future princes. Whatever crowns or laurels their renowned predecessors may have gathered in this field of honour, I should think that for the future the speculative province might more properly be committed to private heads. 'Twould be a sufficient encouragement to the learned world, and a sure earnest of the increase and flourishing of Letters in our nation, if its sovereigns would be contented to be the patrons of wit, and vouchsafe to look graciously on the ingenious pupils of art. Or were it the custom of their prime ministers to have any such regard, it would of itself be sufficient to change the face of affairs. A small degree of favour would ensure the fortunes of a distressed and ruinous tribe, whose forlorn condition has helped to draw disgrace upon arts and sciences, and kept them far off from that politeness and beauty in which they would soon appear if the aspiring genius of our nation were forwarded by the least care or culture.

ADVICE TO AN AUTHOR

There should not, one would think, be any need of courtship or persuasion to engage our grandees in the patronage of Arts and Letters. For in our nation, upon the foot things stand, and as they are likely to continue, 'tis not difficult to foresee that improvements will be made in every art and science. The Muses will have their turn, and with or without their Maecenases will grow in credit and esteem as they arrive to greater perfection and excel in every kind. There will arise such spirits as would have credited their court patrons had they found any so wise as to have sought them out betimes, and contributed to their rising greatness.

'Tis scarce a quarter of an age since such a happy balance of power was settled between our prince and people as has firmly secured our hitherto precarious liberties, and removed from us the fear of civil commotions, wars and violence, either on account of religion and worship, the property of the subject, or the contending titles of the Crown. But as the greatest advantages of this world are not to be bought at easy prices, we are still at this moment expending both our blood and treasure to secure to ourselves this inestimable purchase of our free government and national constitution. And as happy as we are in this establishment at home, we are still held in a perpetual alarm by the aspect of affairs abroad, and by the terror of that Power which, ere mankind had well recovered the misery of those barbarous ages consequent to the Roman yoke, has again threatened the world with a universal monarchy and a new abyss of ignorance and superstition.

The British Muses, in this din of arms, may well lie abject and obscure, especially being as yet in their mere infant state. They have hitherto scarce arrived to anything of shapeliness or person. They lisp as in their cradles; and their stammering tongues, which nothing besides their youth and rawness can excuse, have hitherto spoken in wretched pun and quibble. Our dramatic Shakspere, our Fletcher, Jonson, and our epic Milton preserve this style. And even a latter race, scarce free of this infirmity, and aiming at a false sublime, with crowded simile and mixed metaphor (the hobby-horse and rattle of the Muses), entertain our raw fancy and unpractised ear, which has not as yet had leisure to form itself and become truly musical.[1]

But those reverend bards, rude as they were, according to their time and age, have provided us however with the richest ore. To their eternal honour they have withal been the first of Europeans who, since the Gothic model of poetry, attempted to throw off the horrid discord of jingling rhyme.[2] They have asserted ancient poetic liberty, and have happily broken the ice for those who are to follow them, and who, treading in their footsteps, may at leisure polish our language, lead our ear to finer pleasure, and find out the true rhythmus and harmonious numbers, which alone can satisfy a just judgment and muse-like apprehension.

'Tis evident our natural genius shines above that airy neighbouring nation, of whom, however, it must be confessed that with truer pains and industry they have sought politeness, and studied to give the Muses their due body and proportion, as well as the natural ornaments of correctness, chastity, and grace of style. From the plain model of the ancients they have raised a noble satirist.[3] In the epic kind their attempts have been less successful. In the dramatic they have been so happy as to raise their stage to as great perfection as the genius of their nation will permit.[4] But the high spirit of

---

[1] See *Misc.* v. ch. i. towards the end, and in the notes.

[2] [Dryden, who gave so much higher praise to Shakspere, had declined with Rymer to praise Milton for his preference of blank verse to rhyme. But Shaftesbury's less unlucky position seems to have been reached rather by way of classicist prejudice than of superiority in taste. See his estimate of Shakspere's style in § iii. hereinafter. Addison's defence of Milton in the *Spectator* began (Jan. 1712) within a year of the issue of the *Characteristics*.]   [3] Boileau.

[4] [Dryden is at this point the luckier critic. Compare his preface to *All for Love*. Shaftesbury's further explanation, however, is suggestive, apart from his unhappy definition of the genius of tragedy.]

tragedy can ill subsist where the spirit of liberty is wanting. The genius of this poetry consists in the lively representation of the disorders and misery of the great; to the end that the people and those of a lower condition may be taught the better to content themselves with privacy, enjoy their safer state, and prize the equality and justice of their guardian laws. If this be found agreeable to the just tragic model, which the ancients have delivered to us, 'twill easily be conceived how little such a model is proportioned to the capacity or taste of those who in a long series of degrees, from the lowest peasant to the high slave of royal blood, are taught to idolise the next in power above them, and think nothing so adorable as that unlimited greatness and tyrannic power, which is raised at their own expense and exercised over themselves.

'Tis easy, on the other hand, to apprehend the advantages of our Britain in this particular, and what effect its established liberty will produce in everything which relates to art, when peace returns to us on these happy conditions. 'Twas the fate of Rome to have scarce an intermediate age, or single period of time, between the rise of arts and fall of liberty. No sooner had that nation begun to lose the roughness and barbarity of their manners, and learn of Greece to form their heroes, their orators and poets on a right model, than by their unjust attempt upon the liberty of the world they justly lost their own. With their liberty they lost not only their force of eloquence, but even their style and language itself. The poets who afterwards arose among them were mere unnatural and forced plants. Their two most accomplished, who came last, and closed the scene, were plainly such as had seen the days of liberty, and felt the sad effects of its departure. Nor had these been ever brought in play, otherwise than through the friendship of the famed Maecenas, who turned a prince[1] naturally cruel and barbarous to the love and courtship of the Muses. These tutoresses formed in their royal pupil a new nature.

---

[1] *Infra*, § iii. in the notes.

SHAFTESBURY'S CHARACTERISTICS

They taught him how to charm mankind. They were more to him than his arms or military virtue, and, more than Fortune herself, assisted him in his greatness, and made his usurped dominion so enchanting to the world, that it could see without regret its chains of bondage firmly riveted. The corrupting sweets of such a poisonous government were not indeed long-lived. The bitter soon succeeded; and in the issue the world was forced to bear with patience those natural and genuine tyrants who succeeded to this specious machine of arbitrary and universal power.

And now that I am fallen unawares into such profound reflections on the periods of government, and the flourishing and decay of Liberty and Letters, I cannot be contented to consider merely of the enchantment which wrought so powerfully upon mankind when first this universal monarchy was established. I must wonder still more when I consider how after the extinction of this Caesarean and Claudian family, and a short interval of princes raised and destroyed with much disorder and public ruin, the Romans should regain their perishing dominion, and retrieve their sinking state, by an after-race of wise and able princes successively adopted, and taken from a private state to rule the empire of the world. They were men who not only possessed the military virtues and supported that sort of discipline in the highest degree; but as they sought the interest of the world, they did what was in their power to restore liberty, and raise again the perishing arts and decayed virtue of mankind. But the season was now past! The fatal form of government was become too natural; and the world, which had bent under it, and was become slavish and dependent, had neither power nor will to help itself. The only deliverance it could expect was from the merciless hands of the barbarians, and a total dissolution of that enormous empire and despotic power, which the best hands could not preserve from being destructive to human nature. For even barbarity and Gothicism were already entered into arts ere the savages had made any impression on the empire. All the advantage which a fortuitous and almost miraculous succession of good princes could procure their highly favoured arts and sciences, was no more than to preserve during their own time those perishing remains,[1] which had for awhile with difficulty subsisted after the decline of Liberty. Not a statue, not a medal, not a tolerable piece of architecture could show itself afterwards. Philosophy, wit and learning, in which some of those good princes had themselves been so renowned, fell with them; and ignorance and darkness overspread the world, and fitted it for the chaos and ruin which ensued.

We are now in an age when Liberty is once again in its ascendant. And we are ourselves the happy nation who not only enjoy it at home, but by our greatness and power give life and vigour to it abroad; and are the head and chief of the European League,[2] founded on this common cause. Nor can it, I presume, be justly feared that we should lose this noble ardour, or faint under the glorious toil, though, like ancient Greece, we should for succeeding ages be contending with a foreign power, and endeavouring to reduce the exorbitancy of a *Grand Monarch*. 'Tis with us at present as with the Roman people in those early days,[3] when they wanted only repose from arms to apply themselves to the improvement of arts and studies. We should in this case need no ambitious monarch to be allured, by hope of fame or secret views of power, to give pensions abroad as well as at home, and purchase flattery from every profession and science. We should find a

---

[1] *Infra*, § 2, and part iii. § 3, in the notes.
[2] [Against Louis XIV.]
[3]   Serus enim Graecis admovit acumina chartis;
    Et post Punica bella quietus, quaerere coepit,
    Quid Sophocles et Thespis et Aeschylus utile ferrent.

["Not till late did the Roman apply his shrewdness to the books of Greece; and it was when resting after the Punic Wars that he began to inquire what useful thing Sophocles and Thespis and Aeschylus offered."
—Hor. *Ep.* II. i. 161-163.]

better fund within ourselves, and might, without such assistance, be able to excel by our own virtue and emulation.

Well it would be, indeed, and much to the honour of our nobles and princes, would they freely help in this affair, and by a judicious application of their bounty facilitate this happy birth, of which I have ventured to speak in a prophetic style. Twould be of no small advantage to them during their life, and would, more than all their other labours, procure them an immortal memory. For they must remember that their fame is in the hands of penmen; and that the greatest actions lose their force and perish in the custody of unable and mean writers.

Let a nation remain ever so rude or barbarous, it must have its poets, rhapsoders, historiographers, antiquaries of some kind or other, whose business it will be to recount its remarkable transactions, and record the achievements of its civil and military heroes. And though the military kind may happen to be the farthest removed from any acquaintance with Letters or the Muses, they are yet, in reality, the most interested in the cause and party of these remembrancers. The greatest share of fame and admiration falls naturally on the armed worthies. The great in council are second in the Muses' favour. But if worthy poetic geniuses are not found, nor able penmen raised, to rehearse the lives and celebrate the high actions of great men, they must be traduced by such recorders as chance presents. We have few modern heroes who, like Xenophon or Caesar, can write their own *Commentaries*. And the raw memoir-writings and unformed pieces of modern statesmen, full of their interested and private views, will in another age be of little service to support their memory or name, since already the world begins to sicken with the kind. 'Tis the learned, the able and disinterested historian, who takes place at last. And when the signal poet or herald of fame is once heard, the inferior trumpets sink in silence and oblivion.

ADVICE TO AN AUTHOR

But supposing it were possible for the hero or statesman to be absolutely unconcerned for his memory, or what came after him, yet for the present merely, and during his own time, it must be of importance to him to stand fair with the men of letters and ingenuity, and to have the character and repute of being favourable to their art. Be the illustrious person ever so high or awful in his station, he must have descriptions made of him in verse and prose, under feigned or real appellations. If he be omitted in sounding ode or lofty epic, he must be sung at least in doggerel and plain ballad. The people will needs have his effigies, though they see his person ever so rarely; and if he refuses to sit to the good painter, there are others who, to oblige the public, will take the design in hand. We shall take up with what presents, and rather than be without the illustrious physiognomy of our great man, shall be contented to see him portraitured by the artist who serves to illustrate prodigies in fairs and adorn heroic sign-posts. The ill paint of this kind cannot, it is true, disgrace his excellency, whose privilege it is, in common with the royal issue, to be raised to this degree of honour, and to invite the passenger or traveller by his signal representative. 'Tis supposed in this case that there are better pictures current of the hero, and that such as these are no true or favourable representations. But in another sort of limning there is great danger lest the hand should disgrace the subject. Vile encomiums and wretched panegyrics are the worst of satires; and when sordid and low geniuses make their court successfully in one way, the generous and able are aptest to revenge it in another.

All things considered as to the interest of our potentates and grandees, they appear to have only this choice left them: either wholly, if possible, to suppress Letters, or give a helping hand towards their support. Wherever the author-practice and liberty of the pen has in the least prevailed, the governors of the State must be either considerable gainers or sufferers by its means. So that 'twould become them either by a right Turkish policy to strike directly at the profession, and overthrow the very art and mystery itself, or with alacrity to support and encourage it in the right manner, by a generous and impartial regard to merit. To act narrowly, or by halves; or with indifference and coolness; or fantastically, and by humour merely, will scarce be found to turn to their account. They must do justice, that justice may be done them in return. 'Twill be in vain for our Alexanders to give orders that none besides a Lysippus should make their statue, nor any besides an Apelles should draw their picture. Insolent intruders will do themselves the honour to practise on the features of these heroes. And a vile Chaerilus after all shall, with their own consent perhaps, supply the room of a deserving and noble artist.

In a government where the people are sharers in power, but no distributers or dispensers of rewards, they expect it of their princes and great men that they should supply the generous part, and bestow honour and advantages on those from whom the nation itself may receive honour and advantage. 'Tis expected that they who are high and eminent in the State should not only provide for its necessary safety and subsistence, but omit nothing which may contribute to its dignity and honour. The Arts and Sciences must not be left patronless. The public itself will join with the good wits and judges in the resentment of such a neglect. 'Tis no small advantage, even in an absolute government, for a ministry to have wit on their side, and engage the men of merit in this kind to be their well-wishers and friends. And in those states where ambitious leaders often contend for the supreme authority, 'tis a considerable advantage to the ill cause of such pretenders when they can obtain a name and interest with the men of letters. The good emperor Trajan, though himself no mighty scholar, had his due as well as an Augustus; and was as highly celebrated for his munificence and just encouragement of every art and virtue. And Caesar, who could write so well himself, and maintained his cause by wit as well as arms, knew experimentally what it was to have even a Catullus his enemy; and though lashed so often in his lampoons, continued to forgive and court him. The traitor knew the importance of this mildness. May none who have the same designs, understand so well the advantages of such a conduct! I would have required only this one defect in Caesar's generosity to have been secure of his never rising to greatness, or enslaving his native country. Let him have shown a ruggedness and austerity towards free geniuses, or a neglect or contempt towards men of wit; let him have trusted to his arms, and declared against Arts and Letters; and he would have proved a second Marius, or a Catiline of meaner fame and character.

'Tis, I know, the imagination of some who are called great men that in regard of their high stations they may be esteemed to pay a sufficient tribute to Letters, and discharge themselves as to their own part in particular; if they choose indifferently any subject for their bounty, and are pleased to confer their favour either on some one pretender to art, or promiscuously to such of the tribe of writers whose chief ability has lain in making their court well, and obtaining to be introduced to their acquaintance. This they think sufficient to instal them patrons of wit, and masters of the literate order. But this method will of any other the least serve their interest or design. The ill placing of rewards is a double injury to merit; and in every cause or interest passes for worse than mere indifference or neutrality. There can be no excuse for making an ill choice. Merit in every kind is easily discovered when sought. The public itself fails not to give sufficient indication, and points out those geniuses who want only countenance and encouragement to become considerable. An ingenious man never starves unknown; and great men must wink hard or 'twould be impossible for them to miss such advantageous opportunities of showing their generosity and acquiring the universal esteem, acknowledgments, and good wishes of the ingenious and learned part of mankind.

Section II

WHAT judgment therefore we are to form concerning the influence of our grandees in matters of Art and Letters, will easily be gathered from the reflections already made. It may appear from the very freedom we have taken in censuring these men of power, what little reason authors have to plead them as their excuse for any failure in the improvement of their art and talent. For in a free country such as ours there is not any order or rank of men more free than that of writers; who if they have real ability and merit, can fully right themselves when injured, and are ready furnished with means sufficient to make themselves considered by the men in highest power.

Nor should I suspect the genius of our writers, or charge them with meanness and insufficiency on the account of this low-spiritedness which they discover, were it not for another sort of fear by which they more plainly betray themselves, and seem conscious of their own defect. The critics, it seems, are formidable to them. The critics are the dreadful spectres, the giants, the enchanters, who traverse and disturb them in their works. These are the persecutors, for whose sake they are ready to hide their heads; begging rescue and protection of all good people; and flying in particular to the great, by whose favour they hope to be defended from this merciless examining race. "For what can be more cruel than to be forced to submit to the rigorous laws of wit, and write under such severe judges as are deaf to all courtship, and can be wrought upon by no insinuation or flattery to pass by faults and pardon any transgression of art?"

To judge indeed of the circumstances of a modern author by the pattern of his prefaces,[1] dedications, and introductions,

---

[1] *Infra*, part iii. § 3; and *Misc.* v. ch. ii. the former part, in the notes.

one would think that at the moment when a piece of his was in hand, some conjuration was forming against him, some diabolical powers drawing together to blast his work and cross his generous design. He therefore rouses his indignation, hardens his forehead, and with many furious defiances and " Avaunt-Satans!" enters on his business; not with the least regard to what may justly be objected to him in a way of criticism, but with an absolute contempt of the manner and art itself.

Odi profanum vulgus et arceo[1] was in its time, no doubt, a generous defiance. The "Avaunt!" was natural and proper in its place, especially where religion and virtue were the poet's theme. But with our moderns the case is generally the very reverse. And accordingly the defiance or "avaunt" should run much after this manner: "As for you vulgar souls, mere naturals, who know no art, were never admitted into the temple of wisdom, nor ever visited the sanctuaries of wit or learning, gather yourselves together from all parts, and hearken to the song or tale I am about to utter. But for you men of science and understanding, who have ears and judgment, and can weigh sense, scan syllables, and measure sounds; you who by a certain art distinguish false thought from true, correctness from rudeness, and bombast and chaos from order and the sublime; away hence! or stand aloof! whilst I practise upon the easiness of those mean capacities and apprehensions, who make the most numerous audience, and are the only competent judges of my labours."

'Tis strange to see how differently the vanity of mankind runs in different times and seasons. 'Tis at present the boast of almost every enterpriser in the Muses' art, "That by his genius alone, and a natural rapidity of style and thought, he is able to carry all before him; that he plays with his business, does things in passing, at a venture, and in the quickest period of time." In the days of Attic elegance, as works were then truly of another form and turn, so workmen were of another humour, and had their vanity of a quite contrary kind. They became

[1] ["Avaunt, ye uninitiated crowd"—Hor. *Odes*, I iii. 1.]

rather affected in endeavouring to discover the pains they had taken to be correct. They were glad to insinuate how laboriously and with what expense of time they had brought the smallest work of theirs (as perhaps a single ode or satire, an oration or panegyric) to its perfection. When they had so polished their piece, and rendered it so natural and easy, that it seemed only a lucky flight, a hit of thought, or flowing vein of humour, they were then chiefly concerned lest it should in reality pass for such, and their artifice remain undiscovered. They were willing it should be known how serious their play was, and how elaborate their freedom and facility; that they might say as the agreeable and polite poet, glancing on himself,

Ludentis speciem dabit et torquebitur. . . .[1]

And,

Ut sibi quivis
Speret idem, sudet multum, frustraque laboret
Ausus idem, tantum series juncturaque pollet.[2]

Such accuracy of workmanship requires a critic's eye. 'Tis lost upon a vulgar judgment. Nothing grieves a real artist more than that indifference of the public which suffers work to pass uncriticised. Nothing, on the other side, rejoices him more than the nice view and inspection of the accurate examiner and judge of work. 'Tis the mean genius, the slovenly performer, who knowing nothing of true workmanship, endeavours by the best outward gloss and dazzling show to turn the eye from a direct and steady survey of his piece.

What is there which an expert musician more earnestly desires than to perform his part in the presence of those who are knowing in his art? 'Tis to the ear alone he applies himself; the critical, the nice ear. Let his hearers be of what

---

[1] ["He will seem in sport, yet really be toiling."—Hor. *Epist.* II. ii. 124.]

[2] ["So that any man may hope the same success, toil greatly, and work in vain at the same task,—so great is the might of the sequence and connection in writing."—Hor. *De Arte Poet.* 240-242.]

character they please: be they naturally austere, morose, or rigid; no matter, so they are critics; able to censure, remark and sound every accord and symphony. What is there mortifies the good painter more than when amidst his admiring spectators there is not one present who has been used to compare the hands of different masters, or has an eye to distinguish the advantages or defects of every style? Through all the inferior orders of mechanics, the rule is found to hold the same. In every science, every art, the real masters or proficients rejoice in nothing more than in the thorough search and examination of their performances, by all the rules of art and nicest criticism. Why therefore (in the Muses' name!) is it not the same with our pretenders to the writing art, our poets, and prose authors in every kind? Why in this profession are we found such critic-haters, and indulged in this unlearned aversion, unless it be taken for granted that as wit and learning stand at present in our nation, we are still upon the foot of empirics and mountebanks?

From these considerations I take upon me absolutely to condemn the fashionable and prevailing custom of inveighing against critics as the common enemies, the pests and incendiaries of the commonwealth of Wit and Letters. I assert, on the contrary, that they are the props and pillars of this building; and that without the encouragement and propagation of such a race, we should remain as Gothic architects as ever.

In the weaker and more imperfect societies of mankind,[1] such as those composed of federate tribes, or mixed colonies, scarce settled in their new seats, it might pass for sufficient good-fortune if the people proved only so far masters of language as to be able to understand one another, in order to confer about their wants, and provide for their common necessities. Their exposed and indigent state could not be presumed to afford them either that full leisure or easy disposition which was requisite to raise them to any curiosity of speculation. They

[1] As to this, and what remains of the section, see *Misc.* iii. ch. i.

who were neither safe from violence, nor secure of plenty, were unlikely to engage in unnecessary arts. Nor could it be expected they should turn their attention towards the numbers of their language, and the harmonious sounds which they accidentally emitted. But when, in process of time, the affairs of the society were settled on an easy and secure foundation; when debates and discourses on these subjects of common interest and public good were grown familiar; and the speeches of prime men and leaders were considered and compared together, there would naturally be observed not only a more agreeable measure of sound, but a happier and more easy rangement of thoughts, in one speaker than in another.

It may be easily perceived from hence that the goddess PERSUASION must have been in a manner the mother of poetry, rhetoric, music, and the other kindred arts. For 'tis apparent that where chief men and leaders had the strongest interest to persuade, they used the highest endeavours to please. So that in such a state or polity as has been described, not only the best order of thought and turn of fancy, but the most soft and inviting numbers, must have been employed to charm the public ear, and to incline the heart by the agreeableness of expression.

Almost all the ancient masters of this sort were said to have been musicians. And tradition, which soon grew fabulous, could not better represent the first founders or establishers of these larger societies than as real songsters, who, by the power of their voice and lyre, could charm the wildest beasts, and draw the rude forests and rocks into the form of fairest cities. Nor can it be doubted that the same artists, who so industriously applied themselves to study the numbers of speech, must have made proportionable improvements in the study of mere sounds and natural harmony, which of itself must have considerably contributed towards the softening the rude manners and harsh temper of their new people.

If therefore it so happened in these free communities, made by consent and voluntary association, that after awhile the power of one or of a few grew prevalent over the rest; if force took place, and the affairs of the society were administered without their concurrence by the influence of awe and terror; it followed that these pathetic sciences and arts of speech were little cultivated since they were of little use. But where persuasion was the chief means of guiding the society; where the people were to be convinced before they acted; there elocution became considerable, there orators and bards were heard, and the chief geniuses and sages of the nation betook themselves to the study of those arts by which the people were rendered more treatable in a way of reason and understanding, and more subject to be led by men of science and erudition. The more these artists courted the public, the more they instructed it. In such constitutions as these 'twas the interest of the wise and able that the community should be judges of ability and wisdom. The high esteem of ingenuity was what advanced the ingenious to the greatest honours. And they who rose by science and politeness in the higher arts could not fail to promote that taste and relish to which they owed their personal distinction and pre-eminence.

Hence it is that those arts have been delivered to us in such perfection by free nations, who from the nature of their government, as from a proper soil, produced the generous plants; whilst the mightiest bodies and vastest empires, governed by force and a despotic power, could, after ages of peace and leisure, produce no other than what was deformed and barbarous of the kind.

When the persuasive arts were grown thus into repute, and the power of moving the affections become the study and emulation of the forward wits and aspiring geniuses of the times, it would necessarily happen that many geniuses of equal size and strength, though less covetous of public applause, of power, or of influence over mankind, would content themselves with the contemplation merely of these enchanting arts. These they would the better enjoy the more they refined their taste and cultivated their ear. For to all music there must be an ear proportionable. There must be an art of hearing found ere the performing arts can have their due effect, or anything exquisite in the kind be felt or comprehended. The just performers therefore in each art would naturally be the most desirous of improving and refining the public ear, which they could no way so well effect as by the help of those latter geniuses, who were in a manner their interpreters to the people, and who by their example taught the public to discover what was just and excellent in each performance.

Hence was the origin of critics, who, as arts and sciences advanced, would necessarily come withal into repute, and being heard with satisfaction in their turn, were at length tempted to become authors and appear in public. These were honoured with the name of *Sophists*: a character which in early times was highly respected. Nor did the gravest philosophers, who were censors of manners and critics of a higher degree, disdain to exert their criticism in the inferior arts, especially in those relating to speech and the power of argument and persuasion.

When such a race as this was once risen, 'twas no longer possible to impose on mankind by what was specious and pretending. The public would be paid in no false wit or jingling eloquence. Where the learned critics were so well received, and philosophers themselves disdained not to be of the number, there could not fail to arise critics of an inferior order who would subdivide the several provinces of this empire. Etymologists, philologists, grammarians, rhetoricians, and others of considerable note and eminent in their degree, would everywhere appear, and vindicate the truth and justice of their art by revealing the hidden beauties which lay in the works of just performers, and by exposing the weak sides, false ornaments, and affected graces of mere pretenders. Nothing of what we call sophistry in argument or bombast in style, nothing of the effeminate kind or of the false tender, the pointed witticism, the disjointed thought, the crowded simile, or the mixed metaphor, could pass even on the common ear; whilst the notaries, the expositors and prompters above mentioned, were everywhere at hand and ready to explode the unnatural manner.

'Tis easy to imagine that, amidst the several styles and manners of discourse or writing, the easiest attained and earliest practised was the miraculous, the pompous, or what we generally call the sublime. Astonishment is of all other passions the easiest raised in raw and unexperienced mankind. Children in their earliest infancy are entertained in this manner; and the known way of pleasing such as these is to make them wonder, and lead the way for them in this passion by a feigned surprise at the miraculous objects we set before them. The best music of barbarians is hideous and astonishing sounds. And the fine sights of Indians are enormous figures, various odd and glaring colours, and whatever of that sort is amazingly beheld with a kind of horror and consternation.

In poetry and studied prose the astonishing part, or what commonly passes for sublime, is formed by the variety of figures, the multiplicity of metaphors,[1] and by quitting as much as

[1] λέξεως δὲ ἀρετὴ σαφῆ καὶ μὴ ταπεινὴν εἶναι· σαφεστάτη μὲν οὖν ἐστιν ἡ ἐκ τῶν κυρίων ὀνομάτων, ἀλλὰ ταπεινή . . . σεμνὴ δὲ καὶ ἐξαλλάττουσα τὸ ἰδιωτικὸν, ἡ τοῖς ξενικοῖς κεχρημένη. ξενικὸν δὲ λέγω, γλῶτταν, καὶ μεταφορὰν, καὶ ἐπέκτασιν, καὶ πᾶν τὸ παρὰ τὸ κύριον. ἀλλ' ἄν τις ἅμα ἅπαντα τοιαῦτα ποιήσῃ, ἢ αἴνιγμα ἔσται, ἢ βαρβαρισμός. ἂν μὲν οὖν ἐκ μεταφορῶν, αἴνιγμα, ἐὰν δὲ ἐκ γλωττῶν, βαρβαρισμός. ["The excellence of diction is to be clear without being mean. Clearest is the diction which is made up of usual words, but it is mean. . . . That is majestic and free from commonplace which uses strange words. By *strange* I mean out-of-the-way words, or metaphorical, or extended in usage; in fact all which are unusual. But if a man compose in such words only, his composition will be either a riddle or gibberish: if he compose in metaphors, a riddle; if in out-of-the-way words, gibberish too."—Arist. *Poet.* xxii.] This the same master-critic explains further in his *Rhetorics*, III. i., where he refers to these passages of his *Poetics*. ἐπεὶ δ' οἱ ποιηταὶ λέγοντες εὐήθη διὰ τὴν λέξιν ἐδόκουν πορίσασθαι τήνδε τὴν δόξαν, διὰ τοῦτο ποιητικὴ πρώτη ἐγένετο λέξις, . . . καὶ νῦν ἔτι οἱ πολλοὶ τῶν ἀπαιδεύτων τοὺς τοιούτους οἴονται διαλέγεσθαι κάλλιστα. τοῦτο δ' οὐκ ἔστιν. . . . οὐδὲ γὰρ οἱ τὰς τραγῳδίας ποιοῦντες ἔτι χρῶνται τὸν αὐτὸν τρόπον ἀλλ' ὥσπερ καὶ ἐκ τῶν τετραμέτρων εἰς τὸ ἰαμβεῖον μετέβησαν διὰ τὸ τῷ λόγῳ τοῦτο τῶν μέτρων ὁμοιότατον εἶναι τῶν ἄλλων,

possible the natural and easy way of expression for that which is most unlike to humanity or ordinary use. This the prince of critics assures us to have been the manner of the earliest poets, before the age of Homer, or till such time as this father-poet came into repute, who deposed that spurious race and gave rise to a legitimate and genuine kind. He retained only what was decent of the figurative or metaphoric style, introduced the natural and simple, and turned his thoughts towards the real beauty of composition, the unity of design, the truth of characters, and the just imitation of Nature in each particular.

The manner of this father-poet was afterwards variously imitated, and divided into several shares; especially when it came to be copied in dramatic. Tragedy came first, and took what was most solemn and sublime. In this part the poets succeeded sooner than in Comedy or the facetious kind; as was natural indeed to suppose, since this was in reality the easiest manner of the two, and capable of being brought the soonest to perfection. For so the same prince of critics[1] sufficiently informs

οὕτω καὶ τῶν ὀνομάτων ἀφείκασιν, ὅσα παρὰ τὴν διάλεκτόν ἐστιν. . . . καὶ ἔτι νῦν οἱ τὰ ἐξάμετρα ποιοῦντες ἀφήκασι, διὸ γελοῖον μιμεῖσθαι τούτους οἱ αὐτοὶ οὐκ ἔτι χρῶνται ἐκείνῳ τῷ τρόπῳ. ["But as the poets, while uttering simple things, were thought to have acquired a reputation through their style, the first (rhetorical) style was poetic in character . . .; and even now most uneducated men think that speakers of that sort speak best. But this is not so. . . . For not even writers of tragedy use it any longer in the same way, but, just as they changed from tetrameter to iambic metre because the latter is the metre most like prose, so too they have abandoned such terms as are alien to the style of conversation . . . and even the writers of hexameters have abandoned them. So it is absurd to copy men who themselves no longer follow this fashion."] That among the early reformers of this bombastic manner he places Homer as the chief, we may see easily in his *Poetics*. As particularly in that passage, ἔτι τὰς διανοίας καὶ τὴν λέξιν ἔχειν καλῶς, οἷς ἅπασιν Ὅμηρος κέχρηται, καὶ πρῶτος καὶ ἱκανῶς. . . . πρὸς δὲ τούτοις λέξει καὶ διανοίᾳ πάντας ὑπερβέβληκε. ["Further, the thoughts and the diction must be well chosen. In all these points Homer set, and well set, the example. . . . Moreover he exceeds all in diction and thought."—Arist. *Poet.* xxiv.]

[1] γενομένης οὖν ἀπ' ἀρχῆς αὐτοσχεδιαστικῆς, καὶ αὐτὴ καὶ ἡ κωμῳδία, etc.—*De*

us. And 'tis highly worth remarking, what this mighty genius and judge of art declares concerning Tragedy: that whatever idea might be formed of the utmost perfection of this kind of poem, it could in practice rise no higher than it had been already carried in his time;[1] "having at length," says he, "attained its ends, and being apparently consummate in itself." But for Comedy, it seems, 'twas still in hand. It had been

Poet. iv When he has compared both this and Tragedy together, he recapitulates in his next chapter, αἱ μὲν οὖν τῆς τραγῳδίας μεταβάσεις, καὶ δι' ὧν ἐγένοντο, οὐ λελήθασιν. ἡ δὲ κωμῳδία διὰ τὸ μὴ σπουδάζεσθαι ἐξ ἀρχῆς ἔλαθεν. καὶ γὰρ χορὸν κωμῳδῶν ὀψέ ποτε ὁ ἄρχων ἔδωκεν, etc., see *Misc.* iii. ch. i. in the notes. [(i.) "Both Tragedy and Comedy were at first improvisations merely."—Arist. *Poet.* iv. (ii.) "The changes which passed over Tragedy, and the authors of them, are known; but Comedy, because it was not at first taken seriously, passed unnoticed. For only late did the Archon grant a comic chorus," etc.—Arist. *Poet.* v.]

[1] καὶ πολλὰς μεταβολὰς μεταβαλοῦσα ἡ τραγῳδία ἐπαύσατο, ἐπεὶ ἔσχε τὴν αὑτῆς φύσιν, iv. So true a prophet as well as critic was this great man. For by the event it appeared that Tragedy being raised to its height by Sophocles and Euripides, and no room left for further excellence or emulation, there were no more tragic poets besides these endured after the author's time. Whilst Comedy went on improving still to the second and third degree, Tragedy finished its course under Euripides; whom though our great author criticises with the utmost severity in his *Poetics,* yet he plainly enough confesses to have carried the style of Tragedy to its full height and dignity. For as to the reformation which that poet made in the use of the sublime and figurative speech in general, see what our discerning author says in his *Rhetorics;* where he strives to show the impertinence and nauseousness of the florid speakers, and such as understood not the use of the simple and natural manner. "The just masters and right managers of the poetic or high style should learn," says he, "how to conceal the manner as much as possible." διὸ δεῖ λανθάνειν ποιοῦντας, καὶ μὴ δοκεῖν λέγειν πεπλασμένως, ἀλλὰ πεφυκότως. τοῦτο γὰρ πιθανόν, ἐκεῖνο δὲ τοὐναντίον, ὡς γὰρ πρὸς ἐπιβουλεύοντα διαβάλλονται, καθάπερ πρὸς τοὺς οἴνους τοὺς μεμιγμένους, καὶ οἷον ἡ Θεοδώρου φωνὴ πέπονθε πρὸς τὴν τῶν ἄλλων ὑποκριτῶν· ἡ μὲν γὰρ τοῦ λέγοντος ἔοικεν εἶναι, αἱ δ' ἀλλότριαι. κλέπτεται δ' εὖ, ἐάν τις ἐκ τῆς εἰωθυίας διαλέκτου ἐκλέγων συντιθῇ· ὅ περ Εὐριπίδης ποιεῖ. καὶ ὑπέδειξε πρῶτος. ["So we must do it unobserved and have the appearance of speaking not in an affected, but in a natural way; for the one carries conviction, the other the reverse. For (with the latter) men are on their guard, suspecting deceit, as they would be against

already in some manner reduced; but, as he plainly insinuates, it lay yet unfinished, notwithstanding the witty labours of an Aristophanes, and the other comic poets of the first manner, who had flourished a whole age before this critic. As perfect as were those wits in style and language, and as fertile in all the varieties and turns of humour, yet the truth of characters, the beauty of order, and the simple imitation of Nature were in a manner wholly unknown to them, or through petulancy or debauch of humour were, it seems, neglected and set aside. A Menander had not as yet appeared; who arose soon after, to accomplish the prophecy of our grand master of art and consummate philologist.

Comedy[1] had at this time done little more than what the ancient parodies[2] had done before it. 'Twas of admirable use to explode the false sublime of early poets, and such as in its own age were on every occasion ready to relapse into that vicious manner. The good tragedians themselves could hardly escape its lashes. The pompous orators were its never-failing subjects.

adulterated wines. Your style should be like the voice of Theodorus as compared with that of other actors; for his seemed the very voice of the character, theirs foreign to it. The trick is successfully performed if a man make up his diction by choosing from ordinary conversation. Euripides does this, and first gave the suggestion."—Arist. *Rhet.* III. ii. 4, 5.]

[1] ὥσπερ δὲ καὶ τὰ σπουδαῖα μάλιστα ποιητὴς Ὅμηρος ἦν (μόνος γὰρ οὐχ ὅτι εὖ, ἀλλ' ὅτι καὶ μιμήσεις δραματικὰς ἐποίησεν) οὕτω καὶ τὰ τῆς κωμῳδίας σχήματα πρῶτος ὑπέδειξεν. ["And, just as Homer is especially a poet in the serious vein (for he composed his imitations not only well, but also in dramatic form), so too he first sketched the outline of Comedy."—Arist. *Poet.* iv.] No wonder if, in this descent, Comedy came late. See below, p. 166, in the notes, and above, p. 130.

[2] The parodies were very ancient, but they were in reality no other than mere burlesque or farce. Comedy, which borrowed something from those humours, as well as from the Phallica below mentioned, was not, however, raised to any form or shape of art (as said above) till about the time of Aristophanes, who was the first model, and a beginner of the kind; at the same time that Tragedy had undergone all its changes, and was already come to its last perfection, as the grand critic has shown us, and as our other authorities plainly evince.

ADVICE TO AN AUTHOR

Everything which might be imposing, by a false gravity or solemnity, was forced to endure the trial of this touchstone. Manners and characters, as well as speech and writings, were discussed with the greatest freedom. Nothing could be better fitted than this genius of wit to unmask the face of things, and remove those larvae naturally formed from the tragic manner and pompous style which had preceded.

> Et docuit magnumque loqui, nitique cothurno.
> Successit vetus his comoedia.[1]

'Twas not by chance that this succession happened in Greece after the manner described, but rather through necessity, and from the reason and nature of things.[2] For in healthy bodies Nature dictates remedies of her own, and provides for the cure of what has happened amiss in the growth and progress of a

---

[1] ["(Aeschylus) taught how to use high-flown language and to strut in the buskin. After them (Aeschylus and Thespis) came the Old Comedy."—Hor. *A. P.* 280, 281.] The immediate preceding verses of Horace, after his having spoken of the first tragedy under Thespis, are:—

> Post hunc personae pallaeque repertor honestae
> Aeschylus, et modicis instravit pulpita tignis
> Et docuit, etc.

["After him (Thespis) Aeschylus, inventor of the mask and the becoming robe, laid his stage upon beams of moderate height," etc.—Hor. *A. P.* 278, 279.] Before the time of Thespis, Tragedy indeed was said to be, as Horace calls it here (in a concise way), *ignotum genus*. It lay in a kind of chaos intermixed with other kinds, and hardly distinguishable by its gravity and pomp from the humours which gave rise afterwards to Comedy. But in a strict historical sense, as we find Plato speaking in his *Minos*, Tragedy was of ancienter date, and even of the very ancientest with the Athenians. His words are, ἡ δὲ τραγῳδία ἐστι παλαιὸν ἐνθάδε, οὐχ ὡς οἴονται ἀπὸ Θεσπίδος ἀρξαμένη οὐδ' ἀπὸ Φρυνίχου. ἀλλ' εἰ θέλεις ἐννοῆσαι, πάνυ παλαιὸν αὐτὸ εὑρήσεις ὃν τῆσδε τῆς πόλεως εὕρημα. ["But Tragedy is quite old here and did not, as people think, begin with Thespis or Phrynichus. But if you choose to consider, you will find it a very old invention of this city."—Plato(?), *Minos*, 320 E.]

[2] Of this subject see more in *Misc.* iii. ch. i.

constitution. The affairs of this free people being in the increase, and their ability and judgment every day improving as Letters and Arts advanced, they would of course find in themselves a strength of nature, which by the help of good ferments and a wholesome opposition of humours would correct in one way whatever was excessive or peccant (as physicians say) in another. Thus the florid and over-sanguine humour of the high style was allayed by something of a contrary nature. The comic genius was applied as a kind of caustic to those exuberances and funguses of the swoln dialect and magnificent manner of speech. But after awhile even this remedy itself was found to turn into a disease, as medicines, we know, grow corrosive when the fouler matters on which they wrought are sufficiently purged and the obstructions removed.

> In vitium libertas excidit, et vim
> Dignam lege regi.[1]

'Tis a great error to suppose, as some have done, that the restraining this licentious manner of wit by law was a violation of the liberty of the Athenian state, or an effect merely of the power of foreigners, whom it little concerned after what manner those citizens treated one another in their comedies, or what sort of wit or humour they made choice of for their ordinary diversions. If upon a change of government, as during the usurpation of the Thirty, or when that nation was humbled at any time either by a Philip, an Alexander, or an Antipater, they had been forced against their wills to enact such laws as these, 'tis certain they would have soon repealed them when those terrors were removed (as they soon were) and the people

---

[1] It follows—

> Lex est accepta, chorusque
> Turpiter obticuit, sublato jure nocendi.

["Freedom slipped into License and a violence which called for legal restraint. The law was submitted to, and the chorus fell scandalously silent, because it might not sting."—Hor. *A. P.* 282-284.]

restored to their former liberties. For notwithstanding what this nation suffered outwardly, by several shocks received from foreign states, notwithstanding the dominion and power they lost abroad, they preserved the same government at home. And how passionately interested they were in what concerned their diversions and public spectacles; how jealous and full of emulation in what related to their poetry, wit, music, and other arts, in which they excelled all other nations; is well known to persons who have any comprehension of ancient manners, or been the least conversant in history.

Nothing therefore could have been the cause of these public decrees, and of this gradual reform in the commonwealth of wit, beside the real reform of taste and humour in the commonwealth or government itself. Instead of any abridgment, 'twas in reality an increase of liberty, an enlargement of the security of property, and an advancement of private ease and personal safety, to provide against what was injurious to the good name and reputation of every citizen. As this intelligence in life and manners grew greater in that experienced people, so the relish of wit and humour would naturally in proportion be more refined. Thus Greece in general grew more and more polite, and as it advanced in this respect, was more averse to the obscene buffooning manner. The Athenians still went before the rest, and led the way in elegance of every kind. For even their first comedy was a refinement upon some irregular attempts which had been made in that dramatic way. And the grand critic[1] shows us that in his own time the Phallica, or scurrilous and obscene farce, prevailed still, and had the countenance of the magistrate in some cities of Greece who were behind the rest in this reform of taste and manners.

[1] καὶ ἡ μὲν ἀπὸ τῶν ἐξαρχόντων τὸν διθύραμβον, ἡ δὲ ἀπὸ τῶν τὰ φαλλικὰ ἃ ἔτι καὶ νῦν ἐν πολλαῖς τῶν πόλεων διαμένει νομιζόμενα, κατὰ μικρὸν ηὐξήθη, etc. ["Tragedy began with the leaders of the dithyrambic songs; Comedy with the leaders of the Phallic songs which are still customary in many cities."—Arist. *Poet.* iv.]

SHAFTESBURY'S CHARACTERISTICS

But what is yet a more undeniable evidence of this natural and gradual refinement of styles and manners among the ancients, particularly in what concerned their stage, is, that this very case of prohibition and restraint happened among the Romans themselves, where no effects of foreign power or of a home tyranny can be pretended. Their Fescennine and Atellan way of wit was in early days prohibited, and laws made against it for the public's sake and in regard to the welfare of the community; such licentiousness having been found in reality contrary to the just liberty of the people.

> Doluere cruento
> Dente lacessiti; fuit intactis quoque cura
> Conditione super communi. Quin etiam lex
> Poenaque lata malo quae nollet carmine quemquam
> Describi.[1]

In defence of what I have here advanced, I could, besides the authority of grave historians and chronologists,[2] produce

---

[1] ["Men were vexed when bitten by its bloody teeth; the unbitten too were anxious for the common weal; and even a law and penalty were enacted against libelling any one in verse."—Hor. *Ep.* II. i. 150-154.]

[2] To confirm what is said of this natural succession of wit and style, according to the several authorities above cited in the immediate preceding notes, see Strabo. ὡς δ' εἰπεῖν, ὁ πεζὸς λόγος, ὅ γε κατεσκευασμένος, μίμημα τοῦ ποιητικοῦ ἐστι πρώτιστα γὰρ ἡ ποιητικὴ κατασκευὴ παρῆλθεν εἰς τὸ μέσον καὶ εὐδοκίμησεν· εἶτα ἐκείνην μιμούμενοι, λύσαντες τὸ μέτρον, τἆλλα δὲ φυλάξαντες τὰ ποιητικά, συνέγραψαν οἱ περὶ Κάδμον, καὶ Φερεκύδην, καὶ Ἑκαταῖον εἶτα οἱ ὕστερον, ἀφαιροῦντες ἀεί τι τῶν τοιούτων, εἰς τὸ νῦν εἶδος κατήγαγον, ὡς ἂν ἀπὸ ὕψους τινός. καθάπερ ἂν τις καὶ τὴν κωμῳδίαν φαίη λαβεῖν τὴν σύστασιν ἀπὸ τῆς τραγῳδίας καὶ τοῦ κατ' αὐτὴν ὕψους καταβιβασθεῖσαν εἰς τὸ λογοειδὲς νυνὶ καλούμενον. ["In fact, prose speech when carefully wrought is an imitation of poetic. For in the first instance poetic style came forward and gained a name, and then Cadmus, Pherecydes, or Hecataeus wrote in imitation thereof, giving up the metre, but keeping other poetic features. Later writers afterwards, dropping these point by point, brought the style down as if from a height to the present form, just as we might say that Comedy sprang from Tragedy by being brought down from Tragedy and its elevation to what is now called prosaic."—Strabo, i. p. 18.]

ADVICE TO AN AUTHOR

the testimony of one of the wisest and most serious of ancient authors, whose single authority would be acknowledged to have equal force with that of many concurring writers. He shows us that this first-formed comedy and scheme of ludicrous wit was introduced upon the neck of *the Sublime*.[1] The familiar airy muse was privileged as a sort of counter-pedagogue against the pomp and formality of the more solemn writers. And what is highly remarkable, our author shows us that in philosophy itself there happened, almost at the very same time, a like succession of wit and humour; when in opposition to the sublime philosopher, and afterwards to his grave disciple and successor in the Academy,[2] there arose a comic philosophy in the person of another master and other disciples, who personally, as well as in their writings, were set in direct opposition to the

---

[1] πρῶτον αἱ τραγῳδίαι παρήχθησαν ὑπομνηστικαὶ τῶν συμβαινόντων, καὶ ὅτι ταῦτα οὕτω πέφυκε γίνεσθαι, καὶ ὅτι οἷς ἐπὶ τῆς σκηνῆς ψυχαγωγεῖσθε, τούτοις μὴ ἄχθεσθε ἐπὶ τῆς μείζονος σκηνῆς. . . . μετὰ δὲ τὴν τραγῳδίαν ἡ ἀρχαία κωμῳδία παρήχθη, παιδαγωγικὴν παρρησίαν ἔχουσα, καὶ τῆς ἀτυφίας οὐκ ἀχρήστως δι' αὐτῆς τῆς εὐθυρρημοσύνης ὑπομιμνήσκουσα· πρὸς οἷόν τι καὶ Διογένης ταυτὶ παρελάμβανε. μετὰ ταῦτα τίς ἡ μέση κωμῳδία, καὶ λοιπὸν ἡ νέα, etc. ["First, tragedies were brought out to remind you of what happens, and to remind you that events naturally happen thus, and that when a thing has amused you on the stage, you must not be shocked at it on the larger stage. . . . And after Tragedy the Old Comedy was brought out, using the freedom of a teacher, and usefully warning us by its plain speech against pride. (For some such purpose used Diogenes to borrow these points) After this, observe what was the Middle Comedy and the New," etc.—Marcus Aurelius, xi. 6.]

οὕτως δεῖ παρ' ὅλον τὸν βίον ποιεῖν, καὶ ὅπου λίαν ἀξιόπιστα τὰ πράγματα φαντάζεται, ἀπογυμνοῦν αὐτά, καὶ τὴν εὐτέλειαν αὐτῶν καθορᾶν, καὶ τὴν ἱστορίαν, ἐφ' ᾗ σεμνύνεται, περιαιρεῖν. δεινὸς γὰρ ὁ τῦφος παραλογιστής καὶ ὅτε δοκεῖς μάλιστα περὶ τὰ σπουδαῖα καταγίνεσθαι, τότε μάλιστα καταγοητεύει ὅρα γοῦν ὁ Κράτης. τί περὶ αὐτοῦ τοῦ Ξενοκράτους λέγει. ["In this way we must act all through life, and where things seem most worthy of trust we must strip them and see their poorness, and get rid of the claptrap of which they are so proud. For pride is a great deceiver, and when you think you are most occupied with serious things, then it takes you in most. See at all events what Crates says even of Xenocrates."—Mar. Aur. vi. 13.]

[2] See the citations immediately preceding.

former; not as differing in opinions or maxims,[1] but in their style and manner; in the turn of humour and method of instruction.

'Tis pleasant enough to consider how exact the resemblance was between the lineage of Philosophy and that of Poetry as derived from their two chief founders or patriarchs, in whose loins the several races lay as it were enclosed. For as the grand poetic sire[2] was, by the consent of all antiquity, allowed to have furnished subject both to the tragic, the comic, and every other kind of genuine poetry, so the philosophical patriarch in the same manner, containing within himself the several geniuses of Philosophy, gave rise to all those several manners in which that science was delivered.

His disciple of noble birth and lofty genius, who aspired to poetry and rhetoric,[3] took the *Sublime* part, and shone above his other condisciples. He of mean birth and poorest circumstances, whose constitution as well as condition inclined him

---

[1] Tunica distantia. ["The difference being one of dress only."—Juv. xiii. 122.]

[2] See above, p. 160, in the notes. According to this Homerical lineage of Poetry, Comedy would naturally prove the Drama of latest birth. For though Aristotle in the same place cites Homer's *Margites* as analogous to Comedy, yet the *Iliad* and *Odyssey*, in which the heroic style prevails, having been ever highest in esteem, were likeliest to be first wrought and cultivated.

[3] His *Dialogues* were real poems (as has been shown above, p. 127, etc.) This may easily be collected from the *Poetics* of the grand master. We may add what is cited by Athenaeus from another treatise of that author, ὁ τοὺς ἄλλους ἁπαξαπλῶς κακολογήσας, ἐν μὲν τῇ Πολιτείᾳ Ὅμηρον ἐκβάλλων καὶ τὴν μιμητικὴν ποίησιν, αὐτὸς δὲ [Πλάτων] τοὺς διαλόγους μιμητικῶς γράψας, ὧν τῆς ἰδέας οὐδ' αὐτὸς εὑρετής ἐστιν. πρὸ γὰρ αὐτοῦ τοῦθ' εὗρε τὸ εἶδος τῶν λόγων ὁ Τήϊος Ἀλεξαμενός, ὡς Νικίας ὁ Νικαεὺς ἱστορεῖ καὶ Σωτίων. Ἀριστοτέλης δὲ ἐν τῷ περὶ Ποιητῶν οὕτως γράφει· "οὐκοῦν οὐδὲ ἐμμέτρους τοὺς καλουμένους Σώφρονος Μίμους μὴ φῶμεν εἶναι λόγους καὶ μιμήσεις, ἢ τοὺς Ἀλεξαμενοῦ τοῦ Τηΐου τοὺς πρώτους γραφέντας τῶν Σωκρατικῶν διαλόγων;" ἄντικρυς φάσκων ὁ πολυμαθέστατος Ἀριστοτέλης πρὸ Πλάτωνος διαλόγους γεγραφέναι τὸν Ἀλεξαμενόν. ["(Plato) the man who vilified others in general, who while in his *Republic* he rejected Homer and imitative poetry, himself wrote dialogues in imitative style. Yet he did not

most to the way we call satiric, took the reproving part, which in his better-humoured and more agreeable successor turned into the comic kind, and went upon the model of that ancient comedy which was then prevalent.[1] But another noble disciple, whose genius was towards action, and who proved afterwards the greatest hero of his time, took the genteeler part and softer manner. He joined what was deepest and most solid in philosophy with what was easiest and most refined in breeding, and in the character and manner of a gentleman. Nothing could be remoter than his genius was from the scholastic, the rhetorical, or mere poetic kind. He was as distant on one hand from the sonorous, high, and pompous strain, as on the other hand from the ludicrous, mimical, or satiric.

This was that natural and simple genius of antiquity,[2] comprehended by so few and so little relished by the vulgar. This was that philosophical Menander of earlier time, whose works one may wonder to see preserved from the same fate, since in the darker ages through which they passed they might probably be alike neglected, on the account of their like simplicity of style and composition.

There is, besides the several manners of writing above described, another of considerable authority and weight, which had its rise chiefly from the critical art itself, and from the more accurate inspection into the works of preceding masters. The grand critic of whom we have already spoken was a chief and leader in this order of penmen. For though the Sophists of elder time had treated many subjects methodically and in form, yet this writer was the first who gained repute in the

invent that style For Alexamenos of Teos thought of it before him, as Nicias of Nicaea and Sotion say. Aristotle too writes thus in his book on *Poets*: 'Therefore we must not say that the so-called mimes of Sophron are metrical dialogues or imitations, or the dialogues of Alexamenos of Teos, which were the earliest written of the Socratic dialogues.' "—Athenaeus, 505.]

[1] According to the two citations, p. 165.
[2] Xenophon. See *Misc.* v. ch. 1.

methodic kind. As the talent of this great man was more towards polite learning and the arts than towards the deep and solid parts of philosophy, it happened that in his school there was more care taken of other sciences than of ethics, dialect, or logic, which provinces were chiefly cultivated by the successors of the Academy and Porch.

It has been observed of this methodic or scholastic manner that it naturally befitted an author who, though endowed with a comprehensive and strong genius, was not in himself of a refined temper, blessed by the Graces, or favoured by any Muse; one who was not of a fruitful imagination, but rather dry and rigid, yet withal acute and piercing, accurate and distinct. For the chief nerve and sinew of this style consists in the clear division and partition of the subjects. Though there is nothing exalting in the manner, 'tis naturally powerful and commanding, and, more than any other, subdues the mind and strengthens its determinations. 'Tis from this genius that firm conclusions and steady maxims are best formed, which if solidly built, and on sure ground, are the shortest and best guides towards wisdom and ability in every kind; but if defective or unsound in the least part, must of necessity lead us to the grossest absurdities and stiffest pedantry and conceit.

Now though every other style and genuine manner of composition has its order and method as well as this which, in a peculiar sense, we call the methodic, yet it is this manner alone which professes method, dissects itself in parts, and makes its own anatomy. The sublime can no way condescend thus, or bear to be suspended in its impetuous course. The comic or derisory manner is farther still from making show of method. 'Tis then, if ever, that it presumes to give itself this wise air, when its design is to expose the thing itself, and ridicule the formality and sophistry so often sheltered beneath it. The simple manner, which being the strictest imitation of Nature should of right be the completest in the distribution of its parts and symmetry of its whole, is yet so far from making

ADVICE TO AN AUTHOR

any ostentation of method, that it conceals the artifice as much as possible, endeavouring only to express the effect of art under the appearance of the greatest ease and negligence. And even when it assumes the censuring or reproving part, it does it in the most concealed and gentle way.

The authors indeed of our age are as little capable of receiving as of giving advice in such a way as this; so little is the general palate formed as yet to a taste of real simplicity. As for the Sublime, though it be often the subject of criticism, it can never be the manner or afford the means. The way of form and method, the didactive or perceptive manner, as it has been usually practised amongst us, and as our ears have been long accustomed, has so little force towards the winning our attention, that it is apter to tire us than the metre of an old ballad. We no sooner hear the theme propounded, the subject divided and subdivided (with first of the first and so forth, as order requires), than instantly we begin a strife with Nature, who otherwise might surprise us in the soft fetters of sleep, to the great disgrace of the orator and scandal of the audience. The only manner left in which criticism can have its just force amongst us is the ancient comic; of which kind were the first Roman miscellanies or satiric pieces; a sort of original writing of their own, refined afterwards by the best genius and politest poet of that nation, who, notwithstanding, owns the manner to have been taken from the Greek comedy above mentioned. And if our home wits would refine upon this pattern, they might perhaps meet with considerable success.

In effect we may observe that in our own nation the most successful criticism or method of refutation is that which borders most on the manner of the earliest Greek comedy. The highly-rated burlesque poem,[1] written on the subject of our religious controversies in the last age, is a sufficient token of this kind. And that justly admired piece of comic wit[2]

[1] *Hudibras.*
[2] *The Rehearsal.* See *Misc.* v. ch. ii. in the notes.

given us some time after by an author of the highest quality, has furnished our best wits in all their controversies, even in religion and politics, as well as in the affairs of wit and learning, with the most effectual and entertaining method of exposing folly, pedantry, false reason and ill writing. And without some such tolerated manner of criticism as this, how grossly we might have been imposed on, and should continue to be for the future, by many pieces of dogmatical rhetoric and pedantic wit, may easily be apprehended by those who know anything of the state of Letters in our nation, or are in the least fitted to judge of the manner of the common poets or formal authors of the times.

In what form or manner soever criticism may appear amongst us, or critics choose to exert their talent, it can become none besides the grossly superstitious or ignorant to be alarmed at this spirit. For if it be ill-managed, and with little wit, it will be destroyed by something wittier in the kind. If it be witty itself, it must of necessity advance wit.

And thus from the consideration of ancient as well as modern time, it appears that the cause and interest of critics is the same with that of wit, learning, and good sense.

Section III

Thus we have surveyed the state of authors as they are influenced from without, either by the frowns or favour of the great, or by the applause or censure of the critics. It remains only to consider how the people, or world in general, stand affected towards our modern penmen, and what occasion these adventurers may have of complaint or boast from their encounter with the public.

There is nothing more certain than that a real genius and thorough artist in whatever kind can never, without the greatest unwillingness and shame, be induced to act below his character, and for mere interest be prevailed with to prostitute his art or science by performing contrary to its known rules. Whoever has heard anything of the lives of famous statuaries, architects, or painters, will call to mind many instances of this nature. Or whoever has made any acquaintance with the better sort of mechanics, such as are real lovers of their art and masters in it, must have observed their natural fidelity in this respect. Be they ever so idle, dissolute, or debauched, how regardless soever of other rules, they abhor any transgression in their art, and would choose to lose customers and starve rather than by a base compliance with the world to act contrary to what they call the justness and truth of work.

"Sir," says a poor fellow of this kind to his rich customer, "you are mistaken in coming to me for such a piece of workmanship. Let who will make it for you as you fancy, I know it to be wrong. Whatever I have made hitherto has been true work. And neither for your sake or any body's else shall I put my hand to any other."

This is virtue! real virtue and love of truth; independent of opinion and above the world. This disposition transferred to the whole of life, perfects a character and makes that probity and worth which the learned are often at such a loss to explain. For is there not a workmanship and a truth in actions? Or is the workmanship of this kind less becoming, or less worthy our notice, that we should not in this case be as surly at least as the honest artisan, who has no other philosophy than what nature and his trade have taught him?

When one considers this zeal and honesty of inferior artists, one would wonder to see those who pretend to skill and science in a higher kind have so little regard to truth and the perfection of their art. One would expect it of our writers that if they had real ability they should draw the world to them, and not meanly suit themselves to the world in its weak state. We may justly indeed make allowances for the simplicity of those early geniuses of our nation who after so many barbarous ages, when Letters lay yet in their ruins, made bold excursions into a vacant field to seize the posts of honour and attain the stations which were yet unpossessed by the wits of their own country. But since the age is now so far advanced, learning established, the rules of writing stated, and the truth of art so well apprehended and everywhere confessed and owned, 'tis strange to see our writers as unshapen still and monstrous in their works as heretofore. There can be nothing more ridiculous than to hear our poets in their prefaces talk of Art and Structure, whilst in their pieces they perform as ill as ever, and with as little regard to those professed rules of art as the honest bards their predecessors, who had never heard of any such rules, or at least had never owned their justice or validity.

Had the early poets of Greece thus complimented their nation by complying with its first relish and appetite, they had not done their countrymen such service nor themselves such honour as we find they did by conforming to truth and nature. The generous spirits who first essayed the way had not always the world on their side, but soon drew after them the best judgments, and soon afterwards the world itself. They forced their way into it, and by weight of merit turned its judgment on their side. They formed their audience, polished the age, refined the public ear and framed it right, that in return they might be rightly and lastingly applauded. Nor were they disappointed in their hope. The applause soon came and was lasting, for it was sound. They have justice done them at this day. They have survived their nation and live, though in a dead language. The more the age is enlightened, the more they shine. Their fame must necessarily last as long as Letters, and posterity will ever own their merit.

Our modern authors, on the contrary, are turned and modelled (as themselves confess) by the public relish and current humour of the times. They regulate themselves by the irregular fancy of the world, and frankly own they are preposterous and absurd, in order to accommodate themselves to the genius of the age. In our days the audience makes the poet, and the bookseller the author, with what profit to the public, or what prospect of lasting fame and honour to the writer, let any one who has judgment imagine.

But though our writers charge their faults thus freely on the public, it will, I doubt, appear from many instances that this practice is mere imposture, since those absurdities, which they are the aptest to commit, are far from being delightful or entertaining. We are glad to take up with what our language can afford us, and by a sort of emulation with other nations are forced to cry up such writers of our own as may best serve us for comparison. But when we are out of this spirit it must be owned we are not apt to discover any great fondness or admiration of our authors. Nor have we any whom by mutual consent we make to be our standard. We go to plays or to other shows, and frequent the theatre as the booth. We read epics and dramatics as we do satires and lampoons; for we must of necessity know what wit as well as what scandal is stirring. Read we must; let writers be ever so indifferent. And this perhaps may be some occasion of the laziness and negligence of our authors, who observing this need which our curiosity brings on us, and making an exact calculation in the way of trade, to know justly the quality and quantity of the public demand, feed us thus from hand to mouth; resolving not to over-stock the market, or be at the pains of more correctness or wit than is absolutely necessary to carry on the traffic.

Our satire therefore is scurrilous, buffooning, and without morals or instruction, which is the majesty and life of this kind of writing. Our encomium or panegyric is as fulsome and displeasing by its prostitute and abandoned manner of praise. The worthy persons who are the subjects of it may well be esteemed sufferers by the manner. And the public, whether it will or no, is forced to make untoward reflections when led to it by such satirising panegyrists. For in reality the nerve and sinew of modern panegyric lies in a dull kind of satire, which the author, it is true, intends should turn to the advantage of his subject, but which, if I mistake not, will appear to have a very contrary effect.

The usual method which our authors take when they would commend either a brother-author, a wit, a hero, a philosopher, or a statesman, is to look abroad to find within the narrow compass of their learning some eminent names of persons who answered to these characters in a former time. These they are sure to lash, as they imagine, with some sharp stroke of satire. And when they have stripped these reverend personages of all their share of merit, they think to clothe their hero with the spoils. Such is the sterility of these encomiasts! They know not how to praise but by detraction. If a fair one is to be celebrated, Helen must in comparison be deformed, Venus herself degraded. That a modern may be honoured, some ancient must be sacrificed. If a poet is to be extolled, down with a Homer or a Pindar. If an orator or philosopher, down with Demosthenes, Tully, Plato. If a general of our army, down with any hero whatever of time past. "The Romans knew no discipline! The Grecians never learnt the art of war!"

Were there an art of writing to be formed upon the modern practice, this method we have described might perhaps be styled the *Rule of Dispatch*, or the Herculean law, by which encomiasts, with no other weapon than their single club, may silence all other fame, and place their hero in the vacant throne of honour. I would willingly however advise these celebrators to be a little more moderate in the use of this club-method. Not that I pretend to ask quarter for the ancients; but for the sake merely of those moderns whom our panegyrists undertake to praise, I would wish them to be a little cautious of comparing characters. There is no need to call up a Publicola or a Scipio, an Aristides or a Cato, to serve as foils. These were patriots and good generals in their time, and did their country honest service. No offence to any who at present do the same. The Fabriciuses, the Aemiliuses, the Cincinnatuses (poor men!) may be suffered to rest quietly; or if their ghosts should by this unlucky kind of enchantment be raised in mockery and contempt, they may perhaps prove troublesome in earnest, and cast such reflections on our panegyrists and their modern patrons as may be no-way for the advantage of either. The well-deserving ancients will have always a strong party among the wise and learned of every age; and the memory of foreign worthies, as well as those of our own nation, will with gratitude be cherished by the nobler spirits of mankind. The interest of the dead is not so disregarded but that in case of violence offered them through partiality to the living, there are hands ready prepared to make sufficient reprisals.

'Twas in times when flattery grew much in fashion that the title of *panegyric* was appropriated to such pieces as contained only a profuse and unlimited praise of some single person. The ancient panegyrics were no other than merely such writings as authors of every kind recited at the solemn assemblies of the people. They were the exercises of the wits and men of letters, who as well as the men of bodily dexterity bore their part at the Olympic and other national and panegyric games.

The British nation, though they have nothing of this kind ordained or established by their laws, are yet by nature wonderfully inclined to the same panegyric exercises. At their fairs, and during the time of public festivals, they perform their rude Olympics and show an activity and address beyond any other modern people whatever. Their trials of skill, it is true, are wholly of the body, not of the brain. Nor is it to be wondered at, if being left to themselves, and no way assisted by the laws or magistrate, their bodily exercises retain something of the barbarian character, or at least show their manners[1] to hold

[1] Whoever has a thorough taste of the wit and manner of Horace, if he only compares his Epistle to Augustus (ii.) with the secret character of that prince from Suetonius and other authors, will easily find what judgment that poet made of the Roman taste, even in the person of his sovereign and admired Roman prince, whose natural love of amphitheatrical spectacles and other entertainments (little accommodated to the interest of the Muses) is there sufficiently insinuated. The prince indeed was (as 'tis said above,

more of Rome than Greece.¹ The gladiatorian and other sanguinary sports which we allow our people, discover sufficiently our national taste. And the baitings and slaughter of so many sorts of creatures, tame as well as wild, for diversion merely, may witness the extraordinary inclination we have for amphitheatrical spectacles.

I know not whether it be from this killing disposition remarked in us that our satirists prove such very slaughter-men, and even our panegyric authors or encomiasts delight so much in the dispatching method above described; but sure I am that our dramatic poets² stand violently affected this way, and delight to make havoc and destruction of every kind.

'Tis alleged indeed by our stage-poets, in excuse for vile ribaldry and other gross irregularities, both in the fable and language of their pieces, that their success, which depends chiefly on the ladies, is never so fortunate as when this havoc is made on virtue and good sense, and their pieces are exhibited

p. 143) obliged in the highest degree to his poetical and witty friends for guiding his taste and forming his manners, as they really did, with good effect, and great advantage to his interest. Witness what even that flattering court historian, Dion, relates of the frank treatment which that prince received from his friend Maecenas, who was forced to draw him from his bloody tribunal and murderous delight with the reproach of Surge vero tandem, Carnifex! But Horace, according to his character and circumstances, was obliged to take a finer and more concealed manner both with the prince and favourite.

    Omne vafer vitium ridenti Flaccus amico
    Tangit, et admissus circum praecordia ludit.

["Roguish Horace makes his friend laugh, yet probes every fault, and, never refused admission, plays about his inmost feelings."—Pers. i. 116, 117.] See *Misc.* v. ch. i. in the notes.

¹ We may add to this note what Tacitus or Quintilian remarks on the subject of the Roman taste: Jam vero propria et peculiaria hujus urbis vitia poene in utero matris concipi mihi videntur, histrionalis favor, et gladiatorum equorumque studia; quibus occupatus et obsessus animus quantulum loci bonis artibus relinquit?—*Dial. de Oratoribus*, xxix.

² See *Misc.* v. ch. i. towards the end.

publicly in this monstrous form. I know not how they can answer it to the fair sex to speak (as they pretend) experimentally, and with such nice distinction of their audience. How far this excuse may serve them in relation to common amours and love adventures I will not take upon me to pronounce; but I must own, I have often wondered to see our fighting plays become so much the entertainment of that tender sex.[1]

They who have no help from learning to observe the wider periods or revolutions of human kind, the alterations which happen in manners, and the flux and reflux of politeness, wit, and art, are apt at every turn to make the present age their standard, and imagine nothing barbarous or savage but what is contrary to the manners of their own time. The same pretended judges, had they flourished in our Britain at the time when Caesar made his first descent, would have condemned as a whimsical critic the man who should have made bold to censure our deficiency of clothing, and laugh at the blue cheeks and party-coloured skins which were then in fashion with our ancestors. Such must of necessity be the judgment of those who are only critics by fashion. But to a just Naturalist or Humanist, who knows the creature Man and judges of his growth and improvement in society, it appears evidently that we British men were as barbarous and uncivilised in respect of the Romans under a Caesar, as the Romans themselves were in respect of the Grecians when they invaded that nation under a Mummius.

The noble wits of a court education, who can go no farther back into antiquity than their pedigree will carry them, are able however to call to mind the different state of manners in some few reigns past, when Chivalry was in such repute. The ladies were then spectators not only of feigned combats and martial exercises, but of real duels and bloody feats of arms. They sat as umpires and judges of the doughty frays. These were the saint-protectrices to whom the champions chiefly paid their vows, and to whom they recommended themselves by these

[1] See *Misc.* v. ch. i. towards the end.

gallant quarrels and elegant decisions of right and justice. Nor is this spirit so entirely lost amongst us but that even at this hour the fair sex inspire us still with the fancy of like gallantries. They are the chief subject of many such civil turmoils, and remain still the secret influencing constellation by which we are engaged to give and ask that satisfaction which is peculiar to the fine gentlemen of the age. For thus a certain gallant of our court expressed the case very naturally, when being asked by his friends, why one of his established character for courage and good sense would answer the challenge of a coxcomb, he confessed, "That for his own sex, he could safely trust their judgment; but how should he appear at night before the maids of honour?"

Such is the different genius of nations, and of the same nation in different times and seasons. For so among the ancients some have been known tender of the sex[1] to such a

[1] Contra ea, pleraque nostris moribus sunt decora, quae apud illos turpia putantur. Quem enim Romanorum pudet uxorem ducere in convivium? Aut cujus materfamilias non primum locum tenet aedium, atque in celebritate versatur? quod multo fit aliter in Graecia. Nam neque in convivium adhibetur, nisi propinquorum, neque sedet, nisi in interiore parte aedium, quae gynaeconitis appellatur: quo nemo accedit, nisi propinqua cognatione conjunctus. ["Whereas many things are respectable according to our customs which the Greeks think disreputable. For what Roman is ashamed to take his wife to a dinner-party? or who is there whose wife does not occupy the first place in the house and go into society? Things are very different in Greece. For a lady does not appear at a dinner-party except at a dinner of relations, nor does she sit anywhere but in the back of the house, in what is called the *gynaeconitis*, to which none but relations have admission."—Corn. Nepos, Praef] See also Ælian, i. 10, and the law in Pausanias, v. 6, and the story of Ælian better related as to the circumstances. Hinc de saxo foeminas dejicere Eleorum lex jubet, quae ad Olympicos ludos penetrasse deprehensae fuerint, vel quae omnino Alphaeum transmiserint, quibus est eis interdictum diebus: Non tamen deprehensam esse ullam perhibent praeter unam Callipatiram, quam alii Pherenicen nominant. Haec viro mortuo cum virili ornatu exercitationum se magistrum simulans, Pisidorum filium in certamen deduxit; jamque eo vincente sepimentum in quo magistros seclusos habent, transiluit veste

degree as not to suffer them to expose their modesty by the view of masculine games, or theatrical representations of any kind whatever. Others, on the contrary, have introduced them into their amphitheatres, and made them sharers in the cruellest spectacles.

But let our authors or poets complain ever so much of the genius of our people, 'tis evident we are not altogether so barbarous or Gothic as they pretend. We are naturally no ill soil, and have musical parts which might be cultivated with great advantage if these gentlemen would use the art of masters in their composition. They have power to work upon our better inclinations, and may know by certain tokens that their audience is disposed to receive nobler subjects, and taste a better manner, than that which, through indulgence to themselves more than to the world, they are generally pleased to make their choice.

Besides some laudable attempts which have been made with tolerable success of late years towards a just manner of writing, both in the heroic and familiar style, we have older proofs of a right disposition in our people towards the moral and instructive way. Our old dramatic poet[1] may witness for

---

amissa. Inde foeminam agnitam omni crimine liberarunt. Datum hoc ex judicum aequitate, patris, fratrum, et filii gloriae; qui omnes ex Olympicis ludis victores abierant. Ex eo lege sancitum, ut nudati adessent ludis ipsi etiam magistri. ["Therefore the Elean law bids hurl from a rock women who are caught at the Olympic Games, or who have even crossed the river Alphaeus on the forbidden days. Yet they say no one was ever caught except a certain Callipatira or Pherenice. She, after the death of her husband, took her son Pisidorus to the games, dressed as a man and pretending to be his trainer; and when he won, she jumped the rope which shuts off trainers and dropped her cloak. Then when she was seen to be a woman, she was acquitted by the indulgence of the stewards in honour of her father, her brothers, and her son, all of whom had won prizes at the Olympic Games. But after that a law was passed that trainers too must attend the games uncloaked."—Shaftesbury has chosen to quote Pausanias in a Latin version.]

[1] Shakspere.

our good ear and manly relish. Notwithstanding his natural rudeness, his unpolished style, and antiquated phrase and wit, his want of method and coherence, and his deficiency in almost all the graces and ornaments of this kind of writings, yet by the justness of his moral, the aptness of many of his descriptions, and the plain and natural turn of several of his characters, he pleases his audience, and often gains their ear without a single bribe from Luxury or Vice. That piece [1] of his which appears to have most affected English hearts, and has perhaps been oftenest acted of any which have come upon our stage, is almost one continued moral: a series of deep reflections drawn from one mouth, upon the subject of one single accident and calamity, naturally fitted to move horror and compassion. It may be properly said of this play, if I mistake not, that it has only one character or principal part. It contains no adoration or flattery of the sex; no ranting at the gods; no blustering heroism; nor anything of that curious mixture of the fierce and tender which makes the hinge of modern tragedy, and nicely varies it between the points of Love and Honour.

Upon the whole, since in the two great poetic stations, the epic and dramatic, we may observe the moral genius so naturally prevalent; since our most approved heroic poem [2] has neither the softness of language nor the fashionable turn of wit, but merely solid thought, strong reasoning, noble passion, and a continued thread of moral doctrine, piety, and virtue to recommend it; we may justly infer that it is not so much the public ear as the ill hand and vicious manner of our poets which needs redress.

And thus at last we are returned to our old article of advice: that main preliminary of self-study and inward converse which we have found so much wanting in the authors of our time. They should add the wisdom of the heart to the task and exercise of the brain, in order to bring proportion and beauty into their works. That their composition and vein of

---

[1] The tragedy of *Hamlet*.   [2] Milton's *Paradise Lost*.

ADVICE TO AN AUTHOR

writing may be natural and free, they should settle matters in the first place with themselves. And having gained a mastery here, they may easily, with the help of their genius and a right use of art, command their audience and establish a good taste.

'Tis on themselves that all depends. We have considered their other subjects of excuse. We have acquitted the great men, their presumptive patrons, whom we have left to their own discretion. We have proved the critics not only an inoffensive but a highly useful race. And for the audience, we have found it not so bad as might perhaps at first be apprehended.

It remains that we pass sentence on our authors after having precluded them their last refuge. Nor do we condemn them on their want of wit or fancy, but of judgment and correctness, which can only be attained by thorough diligence, study, and impartial censure of themselves. 'Tis manners which is wanting.[1] 'Tis a due sentiment of morals which alone can make us knowing in order and proportion, and give us the just tone and measure of human passion.

So much the poet must necessarily borrow of the philosopher as to be master of the common topics of morality. He must at least be speciously honest, and in all appearance a friend to Virtue throughout his poem. The good and wise will abate him nothing in this kind; and the people, though corrupt, are in the main best satisfied with this conduct.

> [1] Speciosa locis, morataque recte
> Fabula, nullius veneris, sine pondere et arte,
> Valdius oblectat populum, meliusque moratur,
> Quam versus inopes rerum, nugaeque canorae.[2]

---

[1] *Supra*, p. 136, and *infra*, part iii. § 3, in the notes; and *Misc.* v. chs. i. ii.
[2] ["Sometimes a play if it is embellished with sentiments and well-drawn as to its characters, though it has no grace, no weight of language, no art, delights the people more and keeps their attention better than verses with little in them and well-rounded trifles."—Hor. *A. P.* 319-322.]

SHAFTESBURY'S CHARACTERISTICS

PART III

Section I

'Tis esteemed the highest compliment which can be paid a writer, on the occasion of some new work he has made public, to tell him "that he has undoubtedly surpassed himself." And indeed when one observes how well this compliment is received, one would imagine it to contain some wonderful hyperbole of praise. For according to the strain of modern politeness, 'tis not an ordinary violation of truth which can afford a tribute sufficient to answer any common degree of merit. Now 'tis well known that the gentlemen whose merit lies towards authorship are unwilling to make the least abatement on the foot of this ceremonial. One would wonder therefore to find them so entirely satisfied with a form of praise which in plain sense amounts to no more than a bare affirmative "that they have in some manner differed from themselves, and are become somewhat worse or better than their common rate." For if the vilest writer grows viler than ordinary, or exceeds his natural pitch on either side, he is justly said to exceed or go beyond himself.

We find in the same manner that there is no expression more generally used in a way of compliment to great men and princes than that plain one which is so often verified, and may be safely pronounced for truth on most occasions: "That they have acted like themselves, and suitably to their own genius and character." The compliment, it must be owned, sounds well. No one suspects it. For what person is there who in his imagination joins not something worthy and deserving with his true and native self, as oft as he is referred to it, and made to consider who he is? Such is the natural affection of all mankind towards moral beauty and perfection that they never fail in making this presumption in behalf of themselves: "That by nature they have something estimable and worthy in respect of others of their kind; and that their genuine, true, and natural self is, as it ought to be, of real value in society, and justly honourable for the sake of its merit and good qualities." They conclude therefore they have the height of praise allotted them when they are assured by any one that they have done nothing below themselves, or that in some particular action they have exceeded the ordinary tenor of their character.

Thus is every one convinced of the reality of a better self, and of the cult or homage which is due to it. The misfortune is, we are seldom taught to comprehend this self by placing it in a distinct view from its representative or counterfeit. In our holy religion, which for the greatest part is adapted to the very meanest capacities, 'tis not to be expected that a speculation of this kind should be openly advanced. 'Tis enough that we have hints given us of a nobler self than that which is commonly supposed the basis and foundation of our actions. Self-interest is there taken as it is vulgarly conceived. Though on the other side there are, in the most sacred characters,[1] examples given us of the highest contempt of all such interested views, of a willingness to suffer without recompense for the sake of others, and of a desire to part even with life and being itself on account of what is generous and worthy. But in the same manner as the celestial phænomena are in the sacred volumes generally treated according to common imagination and the then current system of Astronomy and Natural Science, so the moral appearances are in many places preserved without alteration, according to vulgar prejudice and the general conception of interest and self-good. Our real and genuine self is sometimes supposed that ambitious one which is fond of power and glory, sometimes that childish one which is taken with vain show, and is to be invited to obedience by promise of finer habitations, precious stones and metals, shining garments, crowns, and other such

[1] Exod. xxxii. 31, 32, etc., and Rom. ix. 1, 2, 3, etc.

dazzling beauties, by which another earth or material city is represented.

It must be owned that even at that time when a greater and purer Light disclosed itself in the chosen nation, their natural gloominess appeared still,[1] by the great difficulty they had to know themselves, or learn their real interest, after such long tutorage and instruction from above. The simplicity of that people must certainly have been very great, when the best doctrine could not go down without a treat, and the best disciples had their heads so running upon their loaves, that they were apt to construe every divine saying in a belly-sense,[2] and thought nothing more self-constituent than that inferior receptacle. Their taste in morals could not fail of being suitable to this extraordinary estimation of themselves. No wonder if the better and nobler self was left as a mystery to a people who of all human kind were the most grossly selfish, crooked, and perverse. So that it must necessarily be confessed in honour of their divine legislators, patriots, and instructors, that they exceeded all others in goodness and generosity, since they could so truly love their nation and brethren such as they were, and could have so generous and disinterested regards for those who were in themselves so sordidly interested and undeserving.

But whatever may be the proper effect or operation of religion, 'tis the known province of philosophy to teach us ourselves, keep us the self-same persons, and so regulate our governing fancies, passions, and humours, as to make us comprehensible to ourselves, and knowable by other features than those of a bare countenance. For 'tis not certainly by virtue of our face merely that we are ourselves. 'Tis not we who change when our complexion or shape changes. But there is that, which being wholly metamorphosed and converted, we are thereby in reality transformed and lost.

Should an intimate friend of ours, who had endured many sicknesses and run many ill adventures while he travelled

---

[1] *Supra*, p. 22, and *Misc.* ii. chs. i. iii.   [2] Matt. xvi. 6, 7, 8, etc.

through the remotest parts of the East, and hottest countries of the South, return to us so altered in his whole outward figure, that till we had for a time conversed with him we could not know him again to be the same person, the matter would not seem so very strange, nor would our concern on this account be very great. But should a like face and figure of a friend return to us with thoughts and humours of a strange and foreign turn, with passions, affections, and opinions wholly different from anything we had formerly known, we should say in earnest, and with the greatest amazement and concern, that this was another creature, and not the friend whom we once knew familiarly. Nor should we in reality attempt any renewal of acquaintance or correspondence with such a person, though perhaps he might preserve in his memory the faint marks or tokens of former transactions which had passed between us.

When a revolution of this kind, though not so total, happens at any time in a character; when the passion or humour of a known person changes remarkably from what it once was; 'tis to philosophy we then appeal. 'Tis either the want or weakness of this principle which is charged on the delinquent. And on this bottom it is that we often challenge ourselves when we find such variation in our manners, and observe that it is not always the same self nor the same interest we have in view, but often a direct contrary one, which we serve still with the same passion and ardour. When from a noted liberality we change perhaps to as remarkable a parsimony; when from indolence and love of rest we plunge into business, or from a busy and severe character, abhorrent from the tender converse of the fair sex, we turn on a sudden to a contrary passion, and become amorous or uxorious; we acknowledge the weakness, and charging our defect on the general want of philosophy we say (sighing) "that, indeed, we none of us truly know ourselves." And thus we recognise the authority and proper object of philosophy; so far at least, that though we pretend not to be complete philosophers, we confess "that as we have more or less of this intelligence or comprehension of ourselves we are accordingly more or less truly men, and either more or less to be depended on in friendship, society, and the commerce of life."

The fruits of this science are indeed the fairest imaginable, and upon due trial are found to be as well relished and of as good favour with mankind. But when invited to the speculation, we turn our eyes on that which we suppose the tree, 'tis no wonder if we slight the gardenership and think the manner of culture a very contemptible mystery. "Grapes," 'tis said, "are not gathered from thorns, nor figs from thistles." Now if in the literate world there be any choking weed, anything purely thorn or thistle, 'tis in all likelihood that very kind of plant which stands for philosophy in some famous schools.[1] There can be nothing more ridiculous than to expect that manners or understanding should sprout from such a stock. It pretends indeed some relation to manners as being definitive of the natures, essences, and properties of spirits, and some relation to reason as describing the shapes and forms of certain instruments employed in the reasoning art. But had the craftiest of men, for many ages together, been employed in finding out a method to confound reason and degrade the understanding of mankind, they could not, perhaps, have succeeded better than by the establishment of such a mock-science.

I knew once a notable enthusiast[2] of the itinerant kind, who being upon a high spiritual adventure in a country where prophetic missions are treated as no jest, was, as he told me, committed a close prisoner, and kept for several

---

[1] *Infra,* part iii. § 3, and *Misc.* iii. ch. ii.

[2] [Leibnitz appears to be right in supposing this to refer to the younger Van Helmont (1618-1699), who was thrown into the prison of the Inquisition at Rome in 1662. He published his *Alphabeti vere naturalis hebraici brevissima delineatio* at Sulzbach in 1667. For some time he sojourned in England, where he composed for the Countess of Conway his *Two Hundred*

months where he saw no manner of light. In this banishment from letters and discourse the man very wittily invented an amusement much to his purpose, and highly preservative both of health and humour. It may be thought, perhaps, that of all seasons or circumstances here was one the most suitable to our oft-mentioned practice of soliloquy; especially since the prisoner was one of those whom in this age we usually call philosophers, a successor of Paracelsus, and a master in the occult sciences. But as to moral science or anything relating to self-converse, he was a mere novice. To work therefore he went after a different method. He tuned his natural pipes, not after the manner of a musician, to practise what was melodious and agreeable in sounds, but to fashion and form all sorts of articulate voices the most distinctly that was possible. This he performed by strenuously exalting his voice, and essaying it in all the several dispositions and configurations of his throat and mouth. And thus bellowing, roaring, snarling, and otherwise variously exerting his organs of sound, he endeavoured to discover what letters of the alphabet could best design each species, or what new letters were to be invented to mark the undiscovered modifications. He found, for instance, the letter *a* to be a most genuine character, an original and pure vowel, and justly placed as principal in the front of the alphabetic order. For having duly extended his under jaw to its utmost distance from the upper, and by a proper insertion of his fingers provided against the contraction of either corner of his mouth, he experimentally discovered it impossible for human tongue under these circumstances to emit any other modification of sound than that which was described by this primitive character. The vowel *o* was formed

Problems concerning the Revolutions of the Soul; but Shaftesbury doubtless made his acquaintance in Holland, where he latterly resided Leibnitz, who esteemed him and wrote his epitaph, denies that he was a mere novice in moral science, and highly praises his moral character, remarking that his works show his least admirable side.]

by an orbicular disposition of the mouth, as was aptly delineated in the character itself. The vowel *u* by a parallel protrusion of the lips. The other vowels and consonants by other various collisions of the mouth, and operations of the active tongue upon the passive gum or palate. The result of this profound speculation and long exercise of our prisoner was a philosophical treatise, which he composed when he was set at liberty. He esteemed himself the only master of voice and language on the account of this his radical science and fundamental knowledge of sounds. But whoever had taken him to improve their voice, or teach them an agreeable or just manner of accent or delivery, would, I believe, have found themselves considerably deluded.

'Tis not that I would condemn as useless this speculative science of articulation. It has its place no doubt among the other sciences, and may serve to grammar as grammar serves to rhetoric and to other arts of speech and writing. The solidity of mathematics and its advantage to mankind is proved by many effects in those beneficial arts and sciences which depend on it, though astrologers, horoscopers, and other such are pleased to honour themselves with the title of mathematicians. As for metaphysics,[1] and that which in the schools is taught for logic or for ethics, I shall willingly allow it to pass for philosophy when by any real effects it is proved capable to refine our spirits, improve our understandings, or mend our manners. But if the defining material and immaterial substances, and distinguishing their properties and modes, is recommended to us as the right manner of proceeding in the discovery of our own natures, I shall be apt to suspect such a study as the more delusive and infatuating on account of its magnificent pretension.

The study of triangles and circles interferes not with the study of minds; nor does the student in the meanwhile suppose himself advancing in wisdom or the knowledge of himself or

[1] [Shaftesbury uses the term in its old application to a body of scholastic definitions, not to philosophy commonly so called.]

mankind. All he desires is to keep his head sound as it was before. And well, he thinks indeed, he has come off if by good fortune there be no crack made in it. As for other ability or improvement in the knowledge of human nature or the world, he refers himself to other studies and practice. Such is the mathematician's modesty and good sense. But for the philosopher who pretends to be wholly taken up in considering his higher faculties, and examining the powers and principles of his understanding, if in reality his philosophy be foreign to the matter professed, if it goes beside the mark and reaches nothing we can truly call our interest or concern, it must be somewhat worse than mere ignorance or idiotism. The most ingenious way of becoming foolish is by a system. And the surest method to prevent good sense is to set up something in the room of it. The liker anything is to wisdom, if it be not plainly the thing itself, the more directly it becomes its opposite.

One would expect it of these physiologists and searchers of modes and substances that being so exalted in their understandings and enriched with science above other men, they should be as much above them in their passions and sentiments. The consciousness of being admitted into the secret recesses of nature and the inward resources of a human heart should, one would think, create in these gentlemen a sort of magnanimity which might distinguish them from the ordinary race of mortals. But if their pretended knowledge of the machine of this world, and of their own frame, is able to produce nothing beneficial either to the one or to the other, I know not to what purpose such a philosophy can serve, except only to shut the door against better knowledge, and introduce impertinence and conceit with the best countenance of authority.

'Tis hardly possible for a student, but more especially an author, who has dealt in ideas and treated formally of the passions in a way of Natural Philosophy, not to imagine himself more wise on this account and more knowing in his own character and the genius of mankind. But that he is mistaken in his calculation, experience generally convinces us, none being found more impotent in themselves, of less command over their passions, less free from superstition and vain fears, or less safe from common imposture and delusion, than the noted headpieces of this stamp. Nor is this a wonder. The speculation in a manner bespeaks the practice. There needs no formal deduction to make this evident. A small help from our familiar method of soliloquy may serve turn, and we may perhaps decide this matter in a more diverting way by confronting this super-speculative philosophy with a more practical sort, which relates chiefly to our acquaintance, friendship, and good correspondence with ourselves.

On this account it may not be to my reader's disadvantage if, forgetting him for awhile, I apply chiefly to myself, and as occasion offers assume that self-conversant practice which I have pretended to disclose. 'Tis hoped therefore he will not esteem it as ill-breeding if I lose the usual regard to his presence. And should I fall insensibly into one of the paroxysms described, and as in a sort of frenzy enter into high expostulation with myself, he will not surely be offended with the free language or even with the reproaches he hears from a person who only makes bold with whom he may.

If a passenger should turn by chance into a watchmaker's shop, and thinking to inform himself concerning watches, should inquire of what metal, or what matter, each part was composed; what gave the colours, or what made the sounds; without examining what the real use was of such an instrument, or by what movements its end was best attained, and its perfection acquired; 'tis plain that such an examiner as this would come short of any understanding in the real nature of the instrument. Should a philosopher, after the same manner, employing himself in the study of human nature, discover only what effects each passion wrought upon the body; what change of aspect or feature they produced; and in what different manner they affected the limbs and muscles, this might possibly qualify him to give advice to an anatomist or a limner, but not to mankind or to himself; since according to this survey he considered not the real operation or energy of his subject, nor contemplated the man, as real man, and as a human agent, but as a watch or common machine.

"The passion of Fear," as a modern philosopher[1] informs me, "determines the spirits to the muscles of the knees, which are instantly ready to perform their motion, by taking up the legs with incomparable celerity in order to remove the body out of harm's way." Excellent mechanism! But whether the knocking together of the knees be any more the cowardly symptom of flight, than the chattering of the teeth is the stout symptom of resistance, I shall not take upon me to determine. In this whole subject of inquiry I shall find nothing of the least self-concernment. And I may depend upon it, that by the most refined speculation of this kind I shall neither learn to diminish my fears or raise my courage. This, however, I may be assured of, that 'tis the nature of fear, as well as of other passions, to have its increase and decrease, as it is fed by opinion and influenced by custom and practice.

These passions, according as they have the ascendency in me, and differ in proportion with one another, affect my character, and make me different with respect to myself and others. I must, therefore, of necessity find redress and improvement in this case, by reflecting justly on the manner of my own motion, as guided by affections which depend so much on apprehension and conceit. By examining the various turns, inflections, declensions, and inward revolutions of the passions, I must undoubtedly come the better to understand a human breast, and judge the better both of others and myself. 'Tis impossible to make the least advancement in such a study without acquiring some advantage from the regulation and government of those passions on which the conduct of a life depends.

[1] Monsieur des Cartes, in his *Treatise of the Passions*.

For instance, if superstition be the sort of fear which most oppresses, 'tis not very material to inquire, on this occasion, to what parts or districts the blood or spirits are immediately detached, or where they are made to rendezvous. For this no more imports me to understand, than it depends on me to regulate or change. But when the grounds of this superstitious fear are considered to be from opinion, and the subjects of it come to be thoroughly searched and examined, the passion itself must necessarily diminish, as I discover more and more the imposture which belongs to it.

In the same manner, if vanity be from opinion, and I consider how vanity is conceived, from what imaginary advantages and inconsiderable grounds; if I view it in its excessive height, as well as in its contrary depression; 'tis impossible I should not in some measure be relieved of this distemper.

> Laudis amore tumes? Sunt certa piacula. . . .
> Sunt verba et voces quibus hunc lenire dolorem
> Possis, et magnam morbi deponere partem.[1]

The same must happen in respect of anger, ambition, love, desire, and the other passions from whence I frame the different notion I have of interest. For as these passions veer, my interest veers, my steerage varies; and I make alternately, now this, now that, to be my course and harbour. The man in anger has a different happiness from the man in love. And the man lately become covetous has a different notion of satisfaction from what he had before, when he was liberal. Even the man in humour has another thought of interest and advantage than the man out of humour, or in the least disturbed. The examination, therefore, of my humours, and the inquiry[2]

---

[1] ["Are you swollen up with the love of praise? There are sure remedies. . . . There are spells and charms by which you may ease this pain and throw off a great part of your complaint."—Shaftesbury quotes these lines from Horace, *Ep.* I. i. 34-36, in the wrong order.]

[2] See *Inquiry*, viz. Treatise IV. of these volumes.

after my passions, must necessarily draw along with it the search and scrutiny of my opinions, and the sincere consideration of my scope and end. And thus the study of human affection cannot fail of leading me towards the knowledge of human nature and of myself.

This is the philosophy which by Nature has the pre-eminence above all other science or knowledge. Nor can this surely be of the sort called vain or deceitful,[1] since it is the only means by which I can discover vanity and deceit. This is not of that kind which depends on genealogies or traditions,[2] and ministers questions and vain jangling.[3] It has not its name, as other philosophies, from the mere subtlety and nicety of the speculation, but by way of excellence, from its being superior to all other speculations, from its presiding over all other sciences and occupations, teaching the measure of each, and assigning the just value of everything in life. By this science religion itself is judged, spirits are searched, prophecies proved, miracles distinguished: the sole measure and standard being taken from moral rectitude, and from the discernment of what is sound and just in the affections. For if the tree is known only by its fruits,[4] my first endeavour must be to distinguish the true taste of fruits, refine my palate, and establish a just relish in the kind. So that to bid me judge authority by morals, whilst the rule of morals is supposed dependent on mere authority and will,[5] is the same in reality as to bid me see with my eyes shut, measure without a standard, and count without arithmetic.

And thus Philosophy, which judges both of herself and of everything besides, discovers her own province and chief command, teaches me to distinguish between her person and her likeness, and shows me her immediate and real self, by that sole privilege of teaching me to know myself and what belongs

---

[1] Col. ii. 8.   [2] Tit. iii. 9.   [3] 1 Tim. i. 4, 6; vi. 20.
[4] Luke vi. 43, 44; Matt. vii. 16. See Treatise v. part ii. § 5.
[5] *Supra*, p. 72. [The allusion is presumably to Locke. See his *Essay*, bk. i. ch. iii. § 6.]

to me. She gives to every inferior science its just rank; leaves some to measure sounds, others to scan syllables, others to weigh vacuums, and define spaces and extensions; but reserves to herself her due authority and majesty, keeps her state and ancient title of vitae dux, virtutis indagatrix,[1] and the rest of those just appellations which of old belonged to her when she merited to be apostrophised, as she was, by the orator: "Tu inventrix legum, tu magistra morum et disciplinae. . . . Est autem unus dies bene et ex praeceptis tuis actus, peccanti immortalitati anteponendus."[2] Excellent mistress! but easy to be mistaken! whilst so many handmaids wear as illustrious apparel, and some are made to outshine her far in dress and ornament.

In reality, how specious a study, how solemn an amusement is raised from what we call philosophical speculations, the formation of ideas, their compositions, comparisons, agreement, and disagreement! What can have a better appearance, or bid fairer for genuine and true philosophy? Come on then. Let me philosophise in this manner, if this be indeed the way I am to grow wise. Let me examine my ideas of space and substance; let me look well into matter and its modes; if this be looking into myself, if this be to improve my understanding and enlarge my mind. For of this I may soon be satisfied. Let me observe therefore, with diligence, what passes here; what connection and consistency, what agreement or disagreement I find within; "whether, according to my present ideas, that which I approve this hour, I am like to approve as well the next; and in case it be otherwise with me, how or after what manner I shall relieve myself; how ascertain my ideas, and keep my opinion, liking, and esteem of things the same." If this remains unsolved, if I am still the same mystery

---

[1] ["Guide of life, investigator of virtue."]

[2] ["Thou didst find out laws, thou wast the teacher of character and method. . . . One day spent well and under thy rules is better than an eternity of error."—Cic. *Tusc. Disp.* v. 5.]

to myself as ever, to what purpose is all this reasoning and acuteness? wherefore do I admire my philosopher, or study to become such a one myself?

To-day things have succeeded well with me, consequently my ideas are raised. "'Tis a fine world! All is glorious! Everything delightful and entertaining! Mankind, conversation, company, society; what can be more desirable?" To-morrow comes disappointment, crosses, disgrace. And what follows? "O miserable mankind! Wretched state! Who would live out of solitude? Who would write or act for such a world?" Philosopher! where are thy ideas? Where is truth, certainty, evidence, so much talked of? 'Tis here surely they are to be maintained if anywhere. 'Tis here I am to preserve some just distinctions and adequate ideas, which if I cannot do a jot the more by what such a philosophy can teach me, the philosophy is in this respect imposing and delusive. For whatever its other virtues are, it relates not to me myself, it concerns not the man, nor any other wise affects the mind than by the conceit of knowledge and the false assurance raised from a supposed improvement.

Again, what are my ideas of the world, of pleasure, riches, fame, life? What judgment am I to make of mankind and human affairs? What sentiments am I to frame? What opinions? What maxims? If none at all, why do I concern myself in speculations about my ideas? What is it to me, for instance, to know what kind of idea I can form of space? "Divide a solid body of whatever dimension," says a renowned modern philosopher, "and 'twill be impossible for the parts to move within the bounds of its superficies, if there be not left in it a void space, as big as the least part into which the said body is divided."[1]

Thus the atomist, or Epicurean, pleading for a vacuum. The plenitudinarian, on the other side, brings his fluid in play,

[1] These are the words of the particular author cited. [The citation is from Locke, *Essay*, bk. ii. ch. xiii. § 23, but it is *not* verbatim.]

and joins the idea of body and extension. Of this, says one, I have clear ideas. Of this, says the other, I can be certain. And what say I if in the whole matter there be no certainty at all? For mathematicians are divided, and mechanics proceed as well on one hypothesis as on the other. My mind, I am satisfied, will proceed either way alike, for it is concerned on neither side. . . . "Philosopher, let me hear concerning what is of some moment to me. Let me hear concerning life what the right notion is, and what I am to stand to upon occasion; that I may not when life seems retiring, or has run itself out to the very dregs, cry Vanity; condemn the world and at the same time complain that life is short and passing." For why so short indeed if not found sweet? Why do I complain both ways? Is vanity, mere vanity, a happiness? Or can misery pass away too soon?

This is of moment to me to examine. This is worth my while. If, on the other side, I cannot find the agreement or disagreement of my ideas in this place, if I can come to nothing certain here, what is all the rest to me? What signifies it how I come by my ideas, or how compound them; which are simple, and which complex? If I have a right idea of life, now when perhaps I think slightly of it, and resolve with myself "that it may easily be laid down on any honourable occasion of service to my friends or country," teach me how I may preserve this idea, or at least how I may get safely rid of it; that it may trouble me no more nor lead me into ill adventures. Teach me how I came by such an opinion of worth and virtue; what it is which at one time raises it so high, and at another time reduces it to nothing; how these disturbances and fluctuations happen, "By what innovation, what composition, what intervention of other ideas." If this be the subject of the philosophical art, I readily apply to it and embrace the study. If there be nothing of this in the case, I have no occasion for this sort of learning, and am no more desirous of knowing how I form or compound those ideas which are marked by words, than I am of knowing how, and by what motions of my tongue or palate, I form those articulate sounds, which I can full as well pronounce without any such science or speculation.

Section II

But here it may be convenient for me to quit myself awhile in favour of my reader, lest if he prove one of the uncourteous sort, he should raise a considerable objection in this place. He may ask perhaps "why a writer for self-entertainment should not keep his writings to himself, without appearing in public or before the world."

In answer to this I shall only say that for appearing in public or before the world, I do not readily conceive what our worthy objector may understand by it. I can call to mind, indeed, among my acquaintance, certain merchant-adventurers in the letter-trade, who in correspondence with their factor-bookseller are entered into a notable commerce with the world. They have directly, and in due form of preface and epistle dedicatory, solicited the public, and made interest with friends for favour and protection on this account. They have ventured, perhaps, to join some great man's reputation with their own; having obtained his permission to address a work to him on presumption of its passing for something considerable in the eyes of mankind. One may easily imagine that such patronised and avowed authors as these would be shrewdly disappointed if the public took no notice of their labours. But for my own part, 'tis of no concern to me what regard the public bestows on my amusements, or after what manner it comes acquainted with what I write for my private entertainment, or by way of advice to such of my acquaintance as are thus desperately embarked.

'Tis requisite that my friends who peruse these advices should read them in better characters than those of my own hand-writing; and by good luck I have a very fair hand offered, which may save me the trouble of re-copying, and can readily furnish me with as many handsome copies as I would desire for my own and friends' service. I have not indeed forbid my amanuensis the making as many as he pleases for his own benefit. What I write is not worth being made a mystery. And if it be worth any one's purchasing, much good may it do the purchaser. 'Tis a traffic I have no share in, though I accidentally furnish the subject-matter.

And thus am I nowise more an author for being in print. I am conscious of no additional virtue or dangerous quality from having lain at any time under the weight of that alphabetic engine called the Press. I know no conjuration in it, either with respect to Church or State. Nor can I imagine why the machine should appear so formidable to scholars and renowned clerks, whose very mystery and foundation depends on the letter-manufacture. To allow benefit of clergy and to restrain the press seems to me to have something of cross-purpose in it. I can hardly think that the quality of what is written can be altered by the manner of writing, or that there can be any harm in a quick way of copying fair and keeping copies alike. Why a man may not be permitted to write with iron as well as quill, I cannot conceive; or how a writer changes his capacity by this new dress, any more than by the wear of wove-stockings, after having worn no other manufacture than the knit.

So much for my reader, if perchance I have any besides the friend or two above mentioned. For being engaged in morals, and induced to treat so rigorous a subject as that of self-examination, I naturally call to mind the extreme delicacy and tenderness of modern appetites in respect of the philosophy of this kind. What distaste possibly may have arisen from some medicinal doses of a like nature administered to raw stomachs at a very early age, I will not pretend to examine. But whatever manner in philosophy happens to bear the least resemblance to that of Catechism, cannot, I am persuaded, of itself prove very inviting. Such a smart way of questioning ourselves in our youth has made our manhood more averse to the expostulatory discipline. And though the metaphysical points of our belief are by this method, with admirable care and caution, instilled into tender minds, yet the manner of this anticipating philosophy may make the after-work of reason, and the inward exercise of the mind at a riper age, proceed the more heavily and with greater reluctance.

It must needs be a hard case with us, after having passed so learned a childhood, and been instructed in our own and other higher natures, essences, incorporeal substances, personalities, and the like, to condescend at riper years to ruminate and con over this lesson a second time. 'Tis hard after having, by so many pertinent interrogatories and decisive sentences, declared who and what we are, to come leisurely, in another view, to inquire concerning our real self and end, the judgment we are to make of interest, and the opinion we should have of advantage and good, which is what must necessarily determine us in our conduct and prove the leading principle of our lives.

Can we bear looking anew into these mysteries? Can we endure a new schooling after having once learnt our lesson from the world? Hardly, I presume. For by the lesson of this latter school, and according to the sense I acquire in converse with prime men, should I at any time ask myself what governed me? I should answer readily, My interest "But what is interest? and how governed? By opinion and fancy. Is everything therefore my interest which I fancy such? or may my fancy possibly be wrong? It may. If my fancy of interest therefore be wrong, can my pursuit or aim be right? Hardly so. Can I then be supposed to hit, when I know not, in reality, so much as how to aim?"

My chief interest it seems, therefore, must be to get an aim, and know certainly where my happiness and advantage lies. "Where else can it lie than in my pleasure, since my advantage and good must ever be pleasing, and what is pleasing can never be other than my advantage and good? Excellent! Let fancy therefore govern, and interest be what we please. For if that which pleases us be our good[1] because it pleases us, anything may be our interest or good. Nothing can come amiss. That which we fondly make our happiness at one time, we may as readily unmake at another. No one can learn what real good is. Nor can any one upon this foot be said to understand his interest."

Here, we see, are strange embroils! ... But let us try to deal more candidly with ourselves, and frankly own that pleasure is no rule of good,[2] since when we follow pleasure merely, we are disgusted, and change from one sort to another; condemning that at one time which at another we earnestly approve, and never judging equally of happiness whilst we follow passion and mere humour.

A lover, for instance, when struck with the idea or fancy of his enjoyment, promises himself the highest felicity if he succeeds in his new amour.... He succeeds in it, finds not the felicity he expected, but promises himself the same again in some other.... The same thing happens; he is disappointed as before, but still has faith.... Wearied with this game, he quits the chace, renounces the way of courtship and intrigue, and detests the ceremony and difficulty of the pleasure.... A new species of amours invites him. Here too he meets the same inquietude and inconstancy.... Scorning to grow sottish and plunge in the lowest sink of vice, he shakes off his intemperance, despises gluttony and riot, and hearkens to Ambition. He grows a man of business and seeks authority and fame....

Quo teneam vultus mutantem Protea nodo?[3]

Lest this therefore should be my own case, let me see whether I can control my fancy and fix it, if possible, on something

---

[1] *Moralists,* part ii. § 1; *Misc.* iv. ch. i.
[2] *Infra,* p. 218.
[3] ["With what chain can I bind the ever-changing figure of Proteus?"—Hor. *Ep.* 1. i. 90.]

which may hold good. . . . When I exercise my reason in moral subjects, when I employ my affection in <u>friendly and social actions</u>, I find I can sincerely enjoy myself. If there be a pleasure therefore of this kind, why not indulge it? Or what harm would there be, supposing it should grow greater by indulgence? If I am lazy and indulge myself in the languid pleasure, I know the harm and can foresee the drone. If I am luxurious, I know the harm of this also, and have the plain prospect of the sot. If avarice be my pleasure, the end I know is being a miser. But if honesty be my delight, I know no other consequence from indulging such a passion than that of growing better natured, and enjoying more and more the pleasures of society. On the other hand, if this honest pleasure be lost by knavish indulgence and immorality, there can hardly be a satisfaction left of any kind, since good-nature and social affection are so essential even to the pleasures of a debauch.[1]

If therefore the only pleasure I can freely and without reserve indulge, be that of the honest and moral kind; if the rational and social enjoyment be so constant in itself and so essential to happiness; why should I not bring my other pleasures to correspond and be friends with it, rather than raise myself other pleasures which are destructive of this foundation, and have no manner of correspondency with one another?

Upon this bottom let me try how I can bear the assault of Fancy, and maintain myself in my moral fortress against the attacks which are raised on the side of corrupt interest and a wrong self. When the idea of pleasure strikes I ask myself, "Before I was thus struck by the idea, was anything amiss with me? No. Therefore remove the idea and I am well. But having this idea such as I now have, I cannot want the thing without regret. See therefore which is best: either to suffer under this want till the idea be removed; or by satisfying the want, confirm not only this idea but all of the same stamp!"

In reality has not every fancy a like privilege of passing, if

---

[1] *Inquiry*, bk. ii. part ii. § 1, 2.

any single one be admitted upon its own authority? And what must be the issue of such an economy if the whole fantastic crew be introduced, and the door refused to none? What else is it than this management which leads to the most dissolute and profligate of characters? What is it, on the contrary, which raises us to any degree of worth or steadiness, besides a direct contrary practice and conduct? Can there be strength of mind, can there be command over oneself, if the ideas of pleasure, the suggestions of fancy, and the strong pleadings of appetite and desire are not often withstood, and the imaginations soundly reprimanded and brought under subjection?

Thus it appears that the method of examining our ideas is no pedantic practice. Nor is there anything ungallant in the manner of thus questioning the lady fancies, which present themselves as charmingly dressed as possible to solicit their cause and obtain a judgment by favour of that worse part and corrupt self to whom they make their application.

It may be justly said of these, that they are very powerful solicitresses. They never seem to importune us, though they are ever in our eye, and meet us whichever way we turn. They understand better how to manage their appearance than by always throwing up their veil and showing their faces openly in a broad light, to run the danger of cloying our sight, or exposing their features to a strict examination. So far are they from such forwardness, that they often stand as at a distance, suffering us to make the first advance, and contenting themselves with discovering a side-face, or bestowing now and then a glance in a mysterious manner, as if they endeavoured to conceal their persons.

One of the most dangerous of these enchantresses appears in a sort of dismal weed, with the most mournful countenance imaginable; often casting up her eyes, and wringing her hands, so that 'tis impossible not to be moved by her, till her meaning be considered and her imposture fully known. The airs she borrows are from the tragic muse Melpomene. Nor is she in her own person any way amiable or attractive. Far from it. Her art is to render herself as forbidding as possible, that her sisters may by her means be the more alluring. And if by her tragic aspect and melancholy looks she can persuade us that Death (whom she represents) is such a hideous form, she conquers in behalf of the whole fantastic tribe of wanton, gay, and fond desires. Effeminacy and cowardice instantly prevail. The poorest means of life grow in repute when the ends and just conditions of it are so little known, and the dread of parting with it raised to so high a degree. The more eagerly we grasp at Life, the more impotent we are in the enjoyment of it. By this avidity its very lees and dregs are swallowed. The ideas of sordid pleasure are advanced. Worth, manhood, generosity, and all the nobler opinions and sentiments of honest, good, and virtuous pleasure disappear and fly before this Queen of Terrors.

'Tis a mighty delight which a sort of counter-philosophers take in seconding this phantom, and playing her upon our understandings whenever they would take occasion to confound them. The vicious poets employ this spectre too on their side, though after a different manner. By the help of this tragic actress they gain a fairer audience for the luxurious fancies, and give their Eratos and other playsome Muses a fuller scope in the support of riot and debauch. The gloomy prospect of death becomes the incentive to pleasures of the lowest order. Ashes and shade, the tomb and cypress, are made to serve as foils to luxury. The abhorrence of an insensible state makes mere vitality and animal sensation highly cherished.

> Indulge genio; carpamus dulcia; nostrum est
> Quod vivis; cinis, et manes, et fabula fies.[1]

'Tis no wonder if Luxury profits by the deformity of this spectre-opinion. She supports her interest by this childish bug-bear; and, like a mother by her infant, is hugged so much the closer

[1] ["Give your genius play; let us take our pleasures; your life (alone) is ours; you will (soon) be but dust, a ghost, a name."—Pers. v. 151, 152.]

by her votary as the fear presses him and grows importunate. She invites him to live fast, according to her best measure of life. And well she may. Who would not willingly make life pass away as quickly as was possible, when the nobler pleasures of it were already lost or corrupted by a wretched fear of death? The intense selfishness and meanness which accompanies this fear, must reduce us to a low ebb of enjoyment, and in a manner bring to nothing that main sum of satisfactory sensation by which we vulgarly rate the happiness of our private condition and fortune.

But see! A lovely form advances to our assistance, introduced by the prime Muse, the beauteous Calliope! She shows us what real beauty is, and what those numbers are which make life perfect and bestow the chief enjoyment. She sets virtue before our eyes, and teaches us how to rate life from the experience of the most heroic spirits. She brings her sisters Clio and Urania to support her. From the former she borrows whatever is memorable in history and ancient time to confront the tragic spectre, and show the fixed contempt which the happiest and freest nations, as well as single heroes and private men worthy of any note, have ever expressed for that impostress. From the latter she borrows what is sublimest in philosophy to explain the laws of nature, the order of the universe, and represent to us the justice of accompanying this amiable administration. She shows us that by this just compliance we are made happiest; and that the measure of a happy life is not from the fewer or more suns we behold, the fewer or more breaths we draw, or meals we repeat, but from the having once lived well, acted our part handsomely, and made our exit cheerfully, and as became us.

Thus we retain on virtue's side the noblest party of the Muses. Whatever is august among those sisters, appears readily in our behalf. Nor are the more jocund ladies wanting in their assistance when they act in the perfection of their art, and inspire some better geniuses in this kind of poetry. Such were the nobler lyrics, and those of the latter and more refined comedy of the ancients. The Thalias, the Polyhymnias, the Terpsychores, the Euterpes willingly join their parts, and being alike interested in the cause of numbers, are with regret employed another way, in favour of disorder. Instead of being made sirens to serve the purposes of vice, they would with more delight accompany their elder sisters, and add their graces and attractive charms to what is most harmonious, muse-like, and divine in human life. There is this difference only between these and the more heroic dames: that they can more easily be perverted and take the vicious form. For what person of any genius or masterly command in the poetic art could think of bringing the epic or tragic muse to act the pander, or be subservient to effeminacy and cowardice? 'Tis not against death, hazards, or toils, that tragedy and the heroic fable are pointed. 'Tis not mere life which is here exalted, or has its price enhanced. On the contrary, its calamities are exposed; the disorders of the passions set to view; fortitude recommended; honour advanced; the contempt of death placed as the peculiar note of every generous and happy soul; and the tenacious love of life as the truest character of an abject wretch.

> Usque adeone mori miserum est?[1]

'Tis not to be imagined how easily we deal with the deluding apparitions and false ideas of happiness and good, when this frightful spectre of misery and ill is after this manner well laid, and by honest magic conjured down, so as not to give the least assistance to the other tempting forms. This is that occult science, or sort of counter-necromancy, which instead of ghastliness and horror, inspires only what is gentle and humane, and dispels the imposing phantoms of every kind. He may pass undoubtedly for no mean conjurer who can deal with spirits of this sort. . . . But hold! . . . Let us try the experiment in

[1] ["Is it so hard to die?"—Virg. *Aeneid*, xii. 646]

due form, and draw the magic circle. Let us observe how the inferior imps appear when the head goblin is securely laid. . . .

See! The enchantress Indolence presents herself in all the pomp of ease and lazy luxury. She promises the sweetest life, and invites us to her pillow; enjoins us to expose ourselves to no adventurous attempt, and forbids us any engagement which may bring us into action. "Where, then, are the pleasures which Ambition promises and Love affords? How is the gay world enjoyed? Or are those to be esteemed no pleasures which are lost by dulness and inaction? But indolence is the highest pleasure. To live, and not to feel! To feel no trouble. What good then? Life itself. And is this properly to live? Is sleeping, life? Is this what I should study to prolong? . . ." Here the fantastic tribe itself seems scandalised. A civil war begins. The major part of the capricious dames range themselves on Reason's side, and declare against the languid siren. Ambition blushes at the offered sweet. Conceit and Vanity take superior airs. Even Luxury herself, in her polite and elegant humour, reproves the apostate sister, and marks her as an alien to true pleasure. . . . "Away, thou drowsy phantom! Haunt me no more. For I have learned from better than thy sisterhood that life and happiness consist in action and employment."

But here a busy form solicits us: active, industrious, watchful, and despising pains and labour. She wears the serious countenance of virtue, but with features of anxiety and disquiet. What is it she mutters? What looks she on with such admiration and astonishment? Bags! coffers! heaps of shining metal! "What! for the service of Luxury? for her these preparations? Art thou then her friend, grave fancy! is it for her thou toilest? No, but for provision against want. But, luxury apart, tell me now, hast thou not already a competence? 'Tis good to be secure against the fear of starving. Is there then no death beside this? No other passage out of life? Are other doors secured if this be barred? Say, Avarice, thou emptiest of phantoms, is it not vile cowardice thou servest? What further have I then to do with thee, thou doubly vile dependent, when once I have dismissed thy patroness and despised her threats?"

Thus I contend with fancy and opinion,[1] and search the mint and foundery of imagination. For here the appetites and desires are fabricated; hence they derive their privilege and currency. If I can stop the mischief here and prevent false coinage, I am safe. "Idea! wait awhile till I have examined thee, whence thou art and to whom thou retainest. Art thou of Ambition's train? or dost thou promise only pleasure? Say, what am I to sacrifice for thy sake? What honour? What truth? What manhood? What bribe is it thou bringest along with thee? Describe the flattering object, but without flattery; plain as the thing is, without addition, without sparing or reserve. Is it wealth? is it a report? a title? or a female? Come not in a troop, ye fancies! bring not your objects crowding to confound the sight, but let me examine your worth and weight distinctly. Think not to raise accumulative happiness. For if separately you contribute nothing, in conjunction you can only amuse."

Whilst I am thus penning a soliloquy in form, I cannot forbear reflecting on my work. And when I view the manner of it with a familiar eye, I am readier, I find, to make myself diversion on this occasion than to suppose I am in good earnest about a work of consequence. "What! am I to be thus fantastical? Must I busy myself with phantoms? fight with apparitions and chimeras? For certain, or the chimeras will be beforehand with me, and busy themselves so as to get the better of my understanding. What! talk to myself like some madman, in different persons, and under different characters! Undoubtedly, or 'twill be soon seen who is a real madman, and changes character in earnest without knowing how to help it."

This indeed is but too certain: that as long as we enjoy a mind, as long as we have appetites and sense, the fancies of all kinds will be hard at work; and whether we are in company

[1] *Misc.* iv. ch. i. middle part.

or alone they must range still and be active. They must have their field. The question is, whether they shall have it wholly to themselves, or whether they shall acknowledge some controller or manager. If none, 'tis this, I fear, which leads to madness. 'Tis this, and nothing else, which can be called madness or loss of reason. For if Fancy be left judge of anything, she must be judge of all. Everything is right, if anything be so, because I fancy it. "The house turns round. The prospect turns. No, but my head turns indeed: I have a giddiness; that is all. Fancy would persuade me thus and thus, but I know better." 'Tis by means therefore of a controller and correcter of fancy that I am saved from being mad. Otherwise, 'tis the house turns when I am giddy. 'Tis things which change (for so I must suppose) when my passion merely or temper changes. "But I was out of order. I dreamt. Who tells me this? Who besides the correctrice by whose means I am in my wits, and without whom I am no longer myself."

Every man indeed who is not absolutely beside himself, must of necessity hold his fancies under some kind of discipline and management. The stricter this discipline is, the more the man is rational and in his wits. The looser it is, the more fantastical he must be, and the nearer to the madman's state. This is a business which can never stand still. I must always be winner or loser at the game. Either I work upon my fancies, or they on me. If I give quarter, they will not. There can be no truce, no suspension of arms between us. The one or the other must be superior and have the command. For if the fancies are left to themselves, the government must of course be theirs. And then, what difference between such a state and madness?

The question therefore is the same here as in a family or household when 'tis asked, "Who rules? or who is master?"

Learn by the voices. Observe who speaks aloud in a commanding tone; who talks, who questions, or who is talked

ADVICE TO AN AUTHOR

with, and who questioned. For if the servants take the former part, they are the masters, and the government of the house will be found such as naturally may be expected in these circumstances.

How stands it therefore in my own economy, my principal province and command? How stand my fancies? How deal they with me? Or do I take upon me rather to deal with them? Do I talk, question, arraign? Or am I talked with, arraigned, and contented to hear without giving a reply? If I vote with Fancy, resign my opinion to her command,[1] and judge of happiness and misery as she judges, how am I myself?

He who in a plain imagines precipices at his feet, impending rocks over his head; fears bursting clouds in a clear sky; cries fire! deluge! earthquake, or thunder! when all is quiet, does he not rave? But one whose eyes seemingly strike fire by a blow, one whose head is giddy from the motion of a ship after having been newly set ashore, or one who from a distemper in his ear hears thundering noises, can readily redress these several apprehensions, and is by this means saved from madness.

A distemper in my eye may make me see the strangest kind of figures. And when cataracts and other impurities are gathering in that organ, flies, insects, and other various forms seem playing in the air before me. But let my senses err ever so widely, I am not on this account beside myself; nor am I out of my own possession whilst there is a person left within who has power to dispute the appearances and redress the imagination.

I am accosted by ideas and striking apprehensions, but I take nothing on their report. I hear their story and return them answer as they deserve. Fancy and I are not all one. The disagreement makes me my own. When, on the contrary, I have no debate with her, no controversy, but take for happiness and misery, for good and ill, whatever she presents as such,

---
[1] *Misc.* iv. ch. i. middle part.

SHAFTESBURY'S CHARACTERISTICS

I must then join voices with her and cry precipice! fire! Cerberus! Elysium! . . .

> Sandy deserts, flowery fields,
> Seas of milk, and ships of amber!

A Grecian prince, who had the same madness as Alexander, and was deeply struck with the fancy of conquering worlds, was ingeniously shown the method of expostulating with his lady governess, when by a discreet friend, and at an easy hour, he was asked little by little concerning his design, and the final purpose and promised good which the flattering dame proposed to him. The story is sufficiently noted. All the artifice employed against the prince was a well-managed interrogatory of what next? Lady Fancy was not aware of the design upon her; but let herself be wormed out by degrees. At first she said the prince's design was only upon a tract of land, which stood out like a promontory before him and seemed to eclipse his glory. A fair rich island, which was close by, presented itself next, and as it were naturally invited conquest. The opposite coast came next in view. Then the continent on each side the larger sea. And then (what was easiest of all, and would follow of course) the dominion both of sea and land. "And what next?" replied the friend. "What shall we do when we are become thus happy and have obtained our highest wish? Why then we will sit down peaceably, and be good company over a bottle. Alas, sir, what hinders us from doing the same where we now are? Will our humour or our wine grow better? Shall we be more secure or at heart's ease? What you may possibly lose by these attempts is easy to conceive. But which way you will be a gainer, your own fancy, you see, cannot so much as suggest." Fancy in the meanwhile carried her point; for she was absolute over the monarch, and had been too little talked to by herself to bear being reproved in company. The prince grew sullen, turned the discourse, abhorred the profanation offered to his sovereign-empress,

ADVICE TO AN AUTHOR

delivered up his thoughts to her again with deep devotion, and fell to conquering with all his might. The sound of victory rung in his ears. Laurels and crowns played before his eyes. . . . What was this beside giddiness and dream? Appearances uncorrected? " Worlds dancing? Phantoms playing?

Seas of milk, and ships of amber!"

'Tis easy to bring the hero's case home to ourselves, and see, in the ordinary circumstances of life, how love, ambition, and the gayer tribe of fancies, as well as the gloomy and dark spectres of another sort, prevail over our mind. 'Tis easy to observe how they work on us when we refuse to be beforehand with them, and bestow repeated lessons on the encroaching sorceresses. On this it is that our offered advice and method of soliloquy depends. And whether this be of any use towards making us either wiser or happier, I am confident it must help to make us wittier and politer. It must, beyond any other science, teach us the turns of humour and passion, the variety of manners, the justness of characters, and truth of things, which when we rightly understand we may naturally describe. And on this depends chiefly the skill and art of a good writer. So that if to write well be a just pretence to merit, 'tis plain that writers who are apt to set no small value on their art must confess there is something valuable in this self-examining practice and method of inward colloquy.

As for the writer of these papers (as modern authors are pleased modestly to style themselves) he is contented, for his part, to take up with this practice, barely for his own proper benefit, without regard to the high function or capacity of author. It may be allowed him in this particular to imitate the best genius and most gentleman-like of Roman poets. And though by an excess of dulness it should be his misfortune to learn nothing of this poet's wit, he is persuaded he may learn something of his honesty and good-humour.

SHAFTESBURY'S CHARACTERISTICS

> Neque enim, cum lectulus, aut me
> Porticus excepit, desum mihi: "Rectius hoc est:
> Hoc faciens, vivam melius: sic dulcis amicis
> Occurram." . . . Haec ego mecum
> Compressis agito labris.[1]

SECTION III

WE are now arrived to that part of our performance where it becomes us to cast our eye back on what has already passed. The observers of Method generally make this the place of *recapitulation*. Other artists have substituted the practice of apology or extenuation. For the anticipating manner of prefatory discourse is too well known to work any surprising effect in the author's behalf, preface being become only another word to signify excuse. Besides that the author is generally the most straitened in that preliminary part which on other accounts is too apt to grow voluminous. He therefore takes the advantage of his corollary or winding-up, and ends pathetic-

---

[1] And again:—

> Quocirca mecum loquor haec, tacitusque recordor:
> Si tibi nulla sitim finiret copia lymphae,
> Narrares medicis: quod quanto plura parasti,
> Tanto plura cupis, nulline faterier audes?
>
> *   *   *   *   *   *   *
>
> Non es avarus: abi. quid? caetera jam simul isto
> Cum vitio fugere? caret tibi pectus inani
> Ambitione? Caret mortis formidine et ira?

[(i) "For I do not fail when my study-couch or a colonnade has received me. 'This is more right; if I do thus, I shall live better; so my friends will be glad to meet me.' . . . These are my silent reflections with myself."—Hor. *Sat.* I. iv. 133-138.]

[(ii) "And so I speak as follows to myself and try to remember in silence:—'If no abundance of water ended your thirst, you would tell the doctors; seeing that the more money you have, the more you want, dare you tell no one? . . . You are not avaricious. Very good. But have other faults gone too? Is your heart free from unsatisfying ambition? from the fear of death? from anger?'"—Hor. *Ep.* II. ii. 145-148, 205-207.]

ally by endeavouring in the softest manner to reconcile his reader to those faults which he chooses rather to excuse than to amend.

General practice has made this a necessary part of elegance, hardly to be passed over by any writer. 'Tis the chief stratagem by which he engages in personal conference with his reader, and can talk immoderately of himself with all the seeming modesty of one who is the furthest from any selfish views or conceited thoughts of his own merit. There appears such a peculiar grace and ingenuity in the method of confessing laziness, precipitancy, carelessness, or whatever other vices have been the occasion of the author's deficiency, that it would seem a pity had the work itself been brought to such perfection as to have left no room for the penitent party to enlarge on his own demerits. For from the multiplicity of these he finds subject to ingratiate himself with his reader, who doubtless is not a little raised by this submission of a confessing author, and is ready, on these terms, to give him absolution and receive him into his good grace and favour.

In the *galante* world, indeed, we easily find how far a humility of this kind prevails. They who hope to rise by merit are likeliest to be disappointed in their pretensions. The confessing lover, who ascribes all to the bounty of the fair one, meets his reward the sooner for having studied less how to deserve it. For merit is generally thought presumptuous, and supposed to carry with it a certain assurance and ease with which a mistress is not so well contented. The claim of well-deserving seems to derogate from the pure grace and favour of the benefactrice, who then appears to herself most sovereign in power, and likeliest to be obeyed without reserve, when she bestows her bounty where there is least title or pretension.

Thus a certain adoration of the sex which passes in our age without the least charge of profaneness or idolatry, may, according to vulgar imagination, serve to justify these *galant* votaries in the imitation of the real religious and devout. The method of self-abasement[1] may perhaps be thought the properest to make approaches to the sacred shrines; and the entire resignation of merit, in each case, may be esteemed the only ground of well-deserving. But what we allow to Heaven or to the fair should not, methinks, be made a precedent in favour of the world. Whatever deference is due to that body of men whom we call readers, we may be supposed to treat them with sufficient honour if with thorough diligence and pains we endeavour to render our works perfect, and leave them to judge of the performance as they are able.

However difficult or desperate it may appear in any artist to endeavour to bring perfection into his work, if he has not at least the idea of perfection to give him aim he will be found very defective and mean in his performance. Though his intention be to please the world, he must nevertheless be, in a manner, above it, and fix his eye upon that consummate grace, that beauty of Nature, and that perfection of numbers which the rest of mankind, feeling only by the effect whilst ignorant of the cause, term the *je ne sçay quoy*, the unintelligible or the I know not what, and suppose to be a kind of charm or enchantment of which the artist himself can give no account.

But here I find I am tempted to do what I have myself condemned. Hardly can I forbear making some apology for my frequent recourse to the rules of common artists, to the masters of exercise, to the academies of painters, statuaries, and to the rest of the *virtuoso* tribe. But in this I am so fully satisfied I have reason on my side, that let custom be ever so strong against me, I had rather repair to these inferior schools to search for Truth and Nature than to some other places where higher arts and sciences are professed.

I am persuaded that to be a *virtuoso* (so far as befits a gentleman) is a higher step towards the becoming a man of virtue and good sense than the being what in this age we call

---

[1] *Supra*, p. 28.

ADVICE TO AN AUTHOR

a scholar.[1] For even rude Nature itself, in its primitive simplicity, is a better guide to judgment than improved sophistry and pedantic learning. The "faciunt, nae, intellegendo, ut nihil intellegant" will be ever applied by men of discernment and free thought to such logic, such principles, such forms and rudiments of knowledge as are established in certain schools of literature and science. The case is sufficiently understood even by those who are unwilling to confess the truth of it. Effects betray their causes. And the known turn and figure of those understandings, which sprout from nurseries of this kind, give a plain idea of what is judged on this occasion. 'Tis no wonder if after so wrong a ground of education there appears to be such need of redress and amendment from that excellent school which we call the world. The mere amusements of gentlemen are found more improving than the profound researches of pedants;

[1] It seems indeed somewhat improbable that according to modern erudition, and as science is now distributed, our ingenious and noble youths should obtain the full advantage of a just and liberal education by uniting the scholar-part with that of the real gentleman and man of breeding. Academies for exercises, so useful to the public, and essential in the formation of a genteel and liberal character, are unfortunately neglected. Letters are indeed banished, I know not where, in distant cloisters and unpractised cells, as our poet has it, confined to the commerce and mean fellowship of bearded boys. The sprightly arts and sciences are severed from philosophy, which consequently must grow dronish, insipid, pedantic, useless, and directly opposite to the real knowledge and practice of the world and mankind. Our youth accordingly seem to have their only chance between two widely different roads: either that of pedantry and school-learning, which lies amidst the dregs and most corrupt part of ancient literature, or that of the fashionable illiterate world, which aims merely at the character of the fine gentleman, and takes up with the foppery of modern languages and foreign wit. The frightful aspect of the former of these roads makes the journey appear desperate and impracticable. Hence that aversion so generally conceived against a learned character, wrong turned, and hideously set out under such difficulties, and in such seeming labyrinths and mysterious forms. As if a Homer or a Xenophon imperfectly learnt, in raw years, might not afterwards, in a riper age, be studied as well in a capital city and amidst the world as at a college or country-town! Or as

and in the management of our youth we are forced to have recourse to the former, as an antidote against the genius peculiar to the latter. If the formalists of this sort were erected into patentees with a sole commission of authorship, we should undoubtedly see such writing in our days as would either wholly wean us from all books in general, or at least from all such as were the product of our own nation under such a subordinate and conforming government.

However this may prove, there can be no kind of writing which relates to men and manners where it is not necessary for the author to understand poetical and moral truth,[1] the beauty of sentiments, the sublime of characters, and carry in his eye the model or exemplar of that natural grace which gives to every action its attractive charm. If he has naturally no eye or ear for these interior numbers, 'tis not likely he should be able to judge better of that exterior proportion and symmetry of composition which constitutes a legitimate piece.

Could we once convince ourselves of what is in itself so evident,[2] "That in the very nature of things there must of necessity be the foundation of a right and wrong taste, as well in respect of inward characters and features as of outward

---

if a Plutarch, a Tully, or a Horace, could not accompany a young man in his travels, at a court, or (if occasion were) even in a camp! The case is not without precedent. Leisure is found sufficient for other reading of numerous modern translations and worse originals, of Italian or French authors, who are read merely for amusement. The French indeed may boast of some legitimate authors of a just relish, correct, and without any mixture of the affected or spurious kinds: the false tender, or the false sublime; the conceited jingle or the ridiculous point. They are such geniuses as have been formed upon the natural model of the ancients, and willingly own their debt to those great masters. But for the rest, who draw from another fountain, as the Italian authors in particular, they may be reckoned no better than the corrupters of true learning and erudition, and can indeed be relished by those alone whose education has unfortunately denied them the familiarity of the noble ancients, and the practice of a better and more natural taste. See above, p. 186, etc., and *Moralists*, part i. § 1.   [1] *Supra*, p. 136.   [2] *Misc.* iii. ch. ii.

person, behaviour, and action," we should be far more ashamed of ignorance and wrong judgment in the former than in the latter of these subjects. Even in the Arts, which are mere imitations of that outward grace and beauty, we not only confess a taste, but make it a part of refined breeding to discover amidst the many false manners and ill styles the true and natural one, which represents the real beauty and Venus of the kind.[1] 'Tis the like moral grace and Venus which, discovering itself in the turns of character and the variety of human affection, is copied by the writing artist. If he knows not this Venus, these graces, nor was ever struck with the beauty, the decorum of this inward kind, he can neither paint advantageously after the life nor in a feigned subject where he has full scope. For never can he, on these terms, represent merit and virtue, or mark deformity and blemish.[2] Never can he with justice and true proportion assign the boundaries of either part, or separate the distant characters. The schemes must be defective and the draughts confused where the standard is weakly established and the measure out of use. Such a designer, who has so little feeling of these proportions, so little consciousness of this excellence or these perfections, will never be found able to describe a perfect character; or, what is more according to art,[3] "express the effect and force of this perfection from the result of various and mixed characters of life."

And thus the sense of inward numbers, the knowledge and practice of the social virtues, and the familiarity and favour of the moral graces, are essential to the character of a deserving artist and just favourite of the Muses. Thus are the Arts and Virtues mutually friends; and thus the science of virtuosi and that of virtue itself become, in a manner, one and the same.

One who aspires to the character of a man of breeding and politeness is careful to form his judgment of arts and sciences upon right models of perfection. If he travels to Rome, he

---

[1] *Supra,* p. 92, etc.; and *Misc.* iii. ch. ii. in the notes.
[2] *Supra,* p. 136. [3] See *Misc.* v. ch. i. in the notes.

inquires which are the truest pieces of architecture, the best remains of statues, the best paintings of a Raphael or a Caraccio. However antiquated, rough, or dismal they may appear to him at first sight, he resolves to view them over and over, till he has brought himself to relish them, and finds their hidden graces and perfections. He takes particular care to turn his eye from everything which is gaudy, luscious, and of a false taste. Nor is he less careful to turn his ear from every sort of music besides that which is of the best manner and truest harmony.

'Twere to be wished we had the same regard to a right taste in life and manners. What mortal being, once convinced of a difference in inward character, and of a preference due to one kind above another, would not be concerned to make his own the best? If civility and humanity be a taste; if brutality, insolence, riot, be in the same manner a taste, who, if he could reflect, would not choose to form himself on the amiable and agreeable rather than the odious and perverse model? Who would not endeavour to force Nature as well in this respect as in what relates to a taste or judgment in other arts and sciences? For in each place the force on Nature is used only for its redress. If a natural good taste be not already formed in us, why should not we endeavour to form it, and cultivate it till it become natural? . . .

"I like! I fancy! I admire! How? By accident, or as I please? No. But I learn to fancy, to admire, to please, as the subjects themselves are deserving, and can bear me out. Otherwise, I like at this hour but dislike the next. I shall be weary of my pursuit, and, upon experience, find little pleasure in the main,[1] if my choice and judgment in it be from no other rule than that single one, because I please. Grotesque and monstrous figures often please. Cruel spectacles and barbarities are also found to please, and, in some tempers, to please beyond all other subjects. But is this pleasure right? And shall I follow it if it presents? not strive with it, or endeavour to

---

[1] *Supra*, p. 200, and *Moralists*, part ii. § 1.

prevent its growth or prevalency in my temper? ... How stands the case in a more soft and flattering kind of pleasure? ... Effeminacy pleases me. The Indian figures, the Japan work, the enamel strikes my eye. The luscious colours and glossy paint gain upon my fancy. A French or Flemish style is highly liked by me at first sight, and I pursue my liking. But what ensues? ... Do I not for ever forfeit my good relish? How is it possible I should thus come to taste the beauties of an Italian master, or of a hand happily formed on nature and the ancients? 'Tis not by wantonness and humour that I shall attain my end and arrive at the enjoyment I propose. The art itself is severe,[1] the rules rigid. And if I expect the knowledge should come to me by accident, or in play, I shall be grossly

[1] Thus Pliny speaking with a masterly judgment of the dignity of the then declining art of painting ("de dignitate artis morientis") shows it to be not only severe in respect of the discipline, style, design, but of the characters and lives of the noble masters; not only in the effect, but even in the very materials of the art, the colours, ornaments, and particular circumstances belonging to the profession. Euphranoris discipulus Antidotus ... diligentior quam numerosior, et in coloribus severus ... Niciae comparatur, et aliquanto praefertur Athenion Maronites, Glaucionis Corinthii discipulus, et austerior colore, et in austeritate jucundior, ut in ipsa pictura eruditio eluceat.... Quod nisi in juventa obiisset, nemo ei compararetur.... Pausiae filius et discipulus Aristolaus e severissimis pictoribus fuit.... Fuit et nuper gravis ac severus pictor Amulius.. . Paucis diei horis pingebat, id quodque cum gravitate, quod semper togatus, quamquam in machinis. ["Antidotus, a pupil of Euphranor, was more painstaking than prolific, and was austere in his colouring.. . Athenion of Maronea is compared with Nicias, but greatly preferred to him. He was a pupil of Glaucion the Corinthian, rather gloomy in colouring, yet pleasant in his gloom, so that his cultivation comes out in his very painting. ... Had he not died young, no one could be compared with him. ... Aristolaus, son and pupil of Pausias, was one of the most austere of painters. ... Lately too we had Amulius, a severe and serious painter. ... He used only to paint a few hours a day, but that very seriously, for he always wore full dress, even on his scaffolding."—Pliny, *H. N.* xxxv. (cc. 37, 40) 119-137.] One of the mortal symptoms upon which Pliny pronounces the sure death of this noble art, not long survivor to him, was what belonged in common to all the other perishing arts after the Fall of Liberty: I mean the luxury of

deluded, and prove myself, at best, a mock-virtuoso or mere pedant of the kind."

Here therefore we have once again exhibited our moral science in the same method and manner of soliloquy as above. To this correction of humour and formation of a taste our reading, if it be of the right sort, must principally contribute. Whatever company we keep, or however polite and agreeable their characters may be with whom we converse or correspond, if the authors we read are of another kind, we shall find our palate strangely turned their way. We are the unhappier in this respect for being scholars if our studies be ill chosen. Nor

---

the Roman Court, and the change of taste and manners naturally consequent to such a change of government and dominion. This excellent, learned, and polite critic represents to us the false taste springing from the Court itself, and from that opulence, splendour, and affectation of magnificence and expense proper to the place. Thus in the statuary and architecture then in vogue nothing could be admired beside what was costly in the mere matter or substance of the work. Precious rock, rich metal, glittering stones, and other luscious ware, poisonous to art, came every day more into request, and were imposed as necessary materials on the best masters. 'Twas in favour of these Court beauties and gaudy appearances that all good drawing, just design, and truth of work began to be despised. Care was taken to procure from distant parts the most gorgeous splendid colours, of the most costly growth or composition; not such as had been used by Apelles and the great masters, who are justly severe, loyal and faithful to their art. This newer colouring our critic calls the florid kind. The materials were too rich to be furnished by the painter, but were bespoke or furnished at the cost of the person who employed him ("quos dominus pingemi praestat"). The other he calls the austere kind. And thus, says he, "Rerum, non animi pretiis excubatur: The cost, and not the life and art is studied." He shows, on the contrary, what care Apelles took to subdue the florid colours by a darkening varnish: "Et eadem res," says he, "nimis floridis coloribus austeritatem occulte daret." And he says just before, of some of the finest pieces of Apelles, "that they were wrought in four colours only." So great and venerable was simplicity held among the ancients, and so certain was the ruin of all true elegance in life or art where this mistress was once quitted or contemned!—See Pliny, xxxv. See also above, p. 95, in the notes; and p. 145.

can I, for this reason, think it proper to call a man well-read who reads many authors, since he must of necessity have more ill models than good, and be more stuffed with bombast, ill fancy, and wry thought than filled with solid sense and just imagination.

But notwithstanding this hazard of our taste from a multiplicity of reading, we are not, it seems, the least scrupulous in our choice of subject. We read whatever comes next us. What was first put into our hand when we were young, serves us afterwards for serious study and wise research when we are old. We are many of us, indeed, so grave as to continue this exercise of youth through our remaining life. The exercising authors of this kind have been above described[1] in the beginning of this treatise. The manner of exercise is called meditation, and is of a sort so solemn and profound, that we dare not so much as thoroughly examine the subject on which we are bid to meditate. This is a sort of task-reading, in which a taste is not permitted. How little soever we take of this diet, 'tis sufficient to give full exercise to our grave humour, and allay the appetite towards further research and solid contemplation. The rest is holiday, diversion, play, and fancy. We reject all rule, as thinking it an injury to our diversions to have regard to truth or nature, without which, however, nothing can be truly agreeable or entertaining, much less instructive or improving. Through a certain surfeit[2] taken in a wrong kind of serious reading, we apply ourselves, with full content, to the most ridiculous. The more remote our pattern is from anything moral or profitable, the more freedom and satisfaction we find in it. We care not how Gothic or barbarous our models are, what ill-designed or monstrous figures we view, or what false proportions we trace or see described in history, romance, or fiction. And thus our eye and ear is lost. Our relish or taste must of necessity grow barbarous, whilst barbarian customs, savage manners, Indian wars, and wonders of

---

[1] Pp. 109, 110, etc.   [2] *Supra*, pp. 50, 51

the terra incognita, employ our leisure hours and are the chief materials to furnish out a library.

These are in our present days what books of chivalry were in those of our forefathers. I know not what faith our valiant ancestors may have had in the stories of their giants, their dragons, and St. Georges. But for our faith indeed, as well as our taste in this other way of reading, I must confess I cannot consider it without astonishment.

It must certainly be something else than incredulity which fashions the taste and judgment of many gentlemen whom we hear censured as atheists, for attempting to philosophise after a newer manner than any known of late. For my own part, I have ever thought this sort of men to be in general more credulous, though after another manner, than the mere vulgar. Besides what I have observed in conversation with the men of this character, I can produce many anathematised authors who, if they want a true Israelitish faith, can make amends by a Chinese or Indian one. If they are short in Syria or the Palestine, they have their full measure in America or Japan. Histories of Incas or Iroquois, written by friars and missionaries, pirates and renegades, sea-captains and trusty travellers, pass for authentic records and are canonical with the virtuosi of this sort. Though Christian miracles may not so well satisfy them, they dwell with the highest contentment on the prodigies of Moorish and Pagan countries. They have far more pleasure in hearing the monstrous accounts of monstrous men and manners than the politest and best narrations of the affairs, the governments, and lives of the wisest and most polished people.

'Tis the same taste which makes us prefer a Turkish history to a Grecian or a Roman, an Ariosto to a Virgil, and a romance or novel to an Iliad. We have no regard to the character or genius of our author, nor are so far curious as to observe how able he is in the judgment of facts, or how ingenious in the texture of his lies. For facts unably related, though with the greatest sincerity and good faith, may prove the worst sort of deceit;[1] and mere lies, judiciously composed, can teach us the truth of things beyond any other manner.[2] But to amuse ourselves with such authors as neither know how to lie nor tell truth, discovers a taste which, methinks, one should not be apt to envy. Yet so enchanted we are with the travelling memoirs of any casual adventurer, that be his character or genius what it will, we have no sooner turned over a page or two, than we begin to interest ourselves highly in his affairs. No sooner has he taken shipping at the mouth of the Thames, or sent his baggage before him to Gravesend or Buoy in the Nore, than straight our attention is earnestly taken up. If in order to his more distant travels, he takes some part of Europe in his way, we can with patience hear of inns and ordinaries, passage-boats and ferries, foul and fair weather, with all the particulars of the author's diet, habit of body, his personal dangers and mischances on land and sea. And thus, full of desire and hope, we accompany him till he enters on his great scene of action, and begins by the description of some enormous fish or beast. From monstrous brutes he proceeds to yet more monstrous men. For in this race of authors he is ever completest and of the first rank who is able to speak of things the most unnatural and monstrous.[3]

This humour our old tragic poet[4] seems to have discovered.

[1] [This criticism, which is followed up later, is held to have been aimed at Locke, whose acceptance of travellers' tales as to the religion of savages (*Essay*, bk. i. ch. iii. § 9; ch. iv. § 8) Shaftesbury derides in one of his *Letters to a Student*, June 3, 1709.]

[2] The greatest of critics says of the greatest poet, when he extols him the highest, "that above all others he understood how to lie: δεδίδαχε δὲ μάλιστα Ὅμηρος, καὶ τοὺς ἄλλους ψευδῆ λέγειν ὡς δεῖ."—Arist. *De Poet.* xxiv.—See *Misc.* v. ch. i. in the notes.

[3] [As this essay antedates by eight years the writing of *Robinson Crusoe*, it is not unlikely to have influenced Defoe towards the artistic restraint which marks his story in comparison with the class of narratives here described, which would seem to have suggested it.]   [4] Shakspere.

SHAFTESBURY'S CHARACTERISTICS

He hit our taste in giving us a Moorish hero, full-fraught with prodigy, a wondrous story-teller! But for the attentive part, the poet chose to give it to womankind. What passionate reader of travels, or student in the prodigious sciences, can refuse to pity that fair lady, who fell in love with the miraculous Moor? especially considering with what suitable grace such a lover could relate the most monstrous adventures, and satisfy the wondering appetite with the most wondrous tales: Wherein, says the hero-traveller,

> Of antres vast and deserts idle,
> . . . . . .
> It was my hint to speak . . .;
> And of the Cannibals that each other eat,
> The Anthropophagi and men whose heads
> Do grow beneath their shoulders. This to hear
> Would Desdemona seriously incline.

Seriously, 'twas a woeful tale! unfit, one would think, to win a tender fair one. It is true, the poet sufficiently condemns her fancy, and makes her (poor lady!) pay dearly for it in the end. But why, amongst his Greek names, he should have chosen one which denoted the lady superstitious, I cannot imagine: unless, as poets are sometimes prophets too, he should figuratively, under this dark type, have represented to us that about a hundred years after his time, the fair sex of this island should, by other monstrous tales, be so seduced as to turn their favour chiefly on the persons of the tale-tellers, and change their natural inclination for fair, candid, and courteous knights, into a passion for a mysterious race of black enchanters, such as of old were said to creep into houses, and lead captive silly women.

'Tis certain there is a very great affinity between the passion of superstition and that of tales. The love of strange narrations, and the ardent appetite towards unnatural objects, has a near alliance with the like appetite towards the supernatural kind, such as are called prodigious and of dire omen. For so the mind forebodes on every such unusual sight or hearing. Fate, destiny, or the anger of Heaven seems denoted, and as it were delineated, by the monstrous birth, the horrid fact, or dire event. For this reason the very persons of such relators or tale-tellers, with a small help of dismal habit, suitable countenance and tone, become sacred and tremendous in the eyes of mortals who are thus addicted from their youth. The tender virgins, losing their natural softness, assume this tragic passion, of which they are highly susceptible, especially when a suitable kind of eloquence and action attends the character of the narrator. A thousand Desdemonas are then ready to present themselves, and would frankly resign fathers, relations, countrymen, and country itself, to follow the fortunes of a hero of the black tribe.

But whatever monstrous zeal or superstitious passion the poet might foretell, either in the gentlemen, ladies, or common people of an after age, 'tis certain that as to books the same Moorish fancy, in its plain and literal sense, prevails strongly at this present time. Monsters and monster-lands were never more in request; and we may often see a philosopher, or a wit, run a tale-gathering in those idle deserts as familiarly as the silliest woman or merest boy.

One would imagine that our philosophical writers,[1] who

[1] Considering what has been so often said on this subject of philosophy, learning, and the sister arts, after that ancient model which has since been so much corrupted, it may not be amiss perhaps to hear the confession of one of the greatest and most learned of moderns upon this head : "Scilicet assensuri isti sunt veteribus sapientibus, poeticam τῆς σεμνοτάτης φιλοσοφίας εἶναι σύνναον, severissimae philosophiae contubernalem esse, quos videmus omni cura morum posthabita, quae vera philosophia est, in nescio quibus argumentatiunculis, in nugis sophisticis, in puerilibus argutiolis, λωβοῖς denique ῥηματίοις τῆς διαλεκτικῆς, quod sua jam aetate Euphrades, Themistius conquerebatur, summam sapientiam ponere ! Scilicet facundiae Persii virile robur, aut recondita illa eruditio eos capiet, quibus pristinam barbariem mordicus retinere, et in antiquitatis totius ignoratione versari, potius videtur esse ac melius, quam possessionem literarum, olim simili socordia extinctarum, memoria vero patrum magno Dei immortalis beneficio

pretend to treat of morals, should far out-do mere poets in recommending virtue, and representing what was fair and amiable in human actions. One would imagine that if they turned their eye towards remote countries (of which they affect so much to speak) they should search for that simplicity of manners and innocence of behaviour which has been often known among mere savages, ere they were corrupted by our

in lucem revocatarum ex alta hominum oblivione, sibi vindicare, et pro sua quemque virili posteris asserere! ... Scribit vero Arrianus, sapientissimum senem illum Epictetum, impietatis in Deum eos insimulasse, qui in philosophiae studiis τὴν ἀπαγγελτικὴν δύναμιν, sive sermonis curam tanquam rem levem aspernarentur: quoniam quidem, aiebat vir divinus, ἀσεβοῦς ἐστιν ἀνθρώπου τὰς παρὰ τοῦ θεοῦ χάριτας ἀτιμάζειν. En Germanum philosophum! En vocem auream! Nec minus memorabile Synesii philosophi praestantissimi vaticinium tristi eventu confirmatum, quod multo ante ab ipso est editum, cum rationem studiorum similiter perverti ab aequalibus suis cerneret. Disputans enim contra eos qui ad sanctissimae theologiae studia infantiam et sophisticen pro solida eruditione afferrent, fatidicam hanc quasi sortem edidit. κίνδυνος, inquit, εἰς ἄβυσσόν τινα φλυαρίας ἐμπεσόντας τούτους διαφθαρῆναι. Periculum est ne ejusmodi homines in abyssum quamdam ineptiarum delapsi penitus corrumpantur. Utinam defuisset huic oraculo fides. Sed profecto, depravationi illi, et hujus scientiarum reginae, et omnium aliarum, quae postea accidit, occasionem quidem Gothorum et Alanorum invasiones praebuerunt: at causa illius propior ac vera est, ratio studiorum perversa, et in liberalibus disciplinis prava institutio, ac linguarum simul et universae literaturae melioris ignoratio. ... Atqui non in eum certe finem viri magni et praecepta et exempla virtutum memoriae commendata ad posteros transmiserunt, ut ad inanem aurium oblectationem, vel jactationem vanam inutilis eruditionis, ea cognosceremus; verum ut suis nos lucubrationibus excitarent ad effodienda et in actum producenda recti honestique semina; quae cum a natura accepissemus, vitiis tamen circumfusa, et tantum non obruta, sic in nostris animis, nisi cultura melior accedat, latent, quasi in altum quendam scrobem penitus defossa. Huc spectant tot illa volumina quae de morali disciplina philosophi confecerunt. Tendit eodem et Graecorum Latinorumque poetarum pleraque manus; sed itineribus diversis. Quot sunt enim poetarum genera (sunt autem quamplurima) tot fere diverticula et viarum ambages eo ducentium."—Is. Casaub. in Praefatione Commentarii ad Pers. See above, pp. 124, 125, etc., and 135, 136, 186, and 193, 194, and 215, etc., and 217, etc. And *Misc.* ii. chs. i. ii., and v. ch. i. in the notes.

commerce, and, by sad example, instructed in all kinds of treachery and inhumanity. 'Twould be of advantage to us to hear the causes of this strange corruption in ourselves, and be made to consider of our deviation from nature, and from that just purity of manners which might be expected, especially from a people so assisted and enlightened by religion. For who would not naturally expect more justice, fidelity, temperance, and honesty from Christians than from Mahometans or mere pagans? But so far are our modern moralists from condemning any unnatural vices or corrupt manners, whether in our own or foreign climates, that they would have vice itself appear as natural as virtue, and from the worst examples would represent to us "that all actions are naturally indifferent; that they have no note or character of good or ill in themselves; but are distinguished by mere fashion, law, or arbitrary decree." Wonderful philosophy! raised from the dregs of an illiterate mean kind, which was ever despised among the great ancients and rejected by all men of action or sound erudition; but in these ages imperfectly copied from the original, and, with much disadvantage, imitated and assumed in common both by devout and indevout attempters in the moral kind.

Should a writer upon music, addressing himself to the students and lovers of the art, declare to them "that the measure or rule of harmony was caprice or will, humour or fashion," 'tis not very likely he should be heard with great attention or treated with real gravity. For harmony is harmony by nature, let men judge ever so ridiculously of music. So is symmetry and proportion founded still in nature, let men's fancy prove ever so barbarous, or their fashions ever so Gothic in their architecture, sculpture, or whatever other designing art. 'Tis the same case where life and manners are concerned. Virtue has the same fixed standard. The same numbers, harmony, and proportion will have place in morals, and are discoverable in the characters and affections of mankind; in which are laid the just foundations of an art and science superior to every other of human practice and comprehension.

This, I suppose therefore, is highly necessary that a writer should comprehend. For things are stubborn and will not be as we fancy them, or as the fashion varies, but as they stand in nature. Now whether the writer be poet, philosopher, or of whatever kind, he is in truth no other than a copyist after nature. His style may be differently suited to the different times he lives in, or to the different humour of his age or nation; his manner, his dress, his colouring may vary; but if his drawing be uncorrect or his design contrary to nature, his piece will be found ridiculous when it comes thoroughly to be examined. For Nature will not be mocked. The prepossession against her can never be very lasting. Her decrees and instincts are powerful and her sentiments inbred. She has a strong party abroad, and as strong a one within ourselves; and when any slight is put upon her, she can soon turn the reproach and make large reprisals on the taste and judgment of her antagonists.

Whatever philosopher, critic, or author is convinced of this prerogative of nature, will easily be persuaded to apply himself to the great work of reforming his taste, which he will have reason to suspect, if he be not such a one as has deliberately endeavoured to frame it by the just standard of nature. Whether this be his case, he will easily discover by appealing to his memory; for custom and fashion are powerful seducers; and he must of necessity have fought hard against these to have attained that justness of taste which is required in one who pretends to follow nature. But if no such conflict can be called to mind, 'tis a certain token that the party has his taste very little different from the vulgar. And on this account he should instantly betake himself to the wholesome practice recommended in this treatise. He should set afoot the powerfullest faculties of his mind, and assemble the best forces of his wit and judgment, in order to make a formal descent on the territories of the heart; resolving to decline no combat, nor hearken to any terms, till he had pierced into its inmost provinces and reached the seat of empire. No treaties should amuse him; no advantages lead him aside. All other speculations should be suspended, all other mysteries resigned, till this necessary campaign was made and these inward conflicts learnt; by which he would be able to gain at least some tolerable insight into himself and knowledge of his own natural principles.

It may here perhaps be thought that notwithstanding the particular advice we have given in relation to the forming of a taste in natural characters and manners, we are still defective in our performance whilst we are silent on supernatural cases, and bring not into our consideration the manners and characters delivered us in Holy Writ. But this objection will soon vanish when we consider that there can be no rules given by human wit to that which was never humanly conceived, but divinely dictated and inspired.

For this reason 'twould be in vain for any poet or ingenious author to form his characters after the models of our sacred penmen.[1] And whatever certain critics may have advanced concerning the structure of a heroic poem of this kind, I will be bold to prophesy that the success will never be answerable to expectation.

It must be owned that in our sacred history we have both leaders, conquerors, founders of nations, deliverers, and patriots who, even in a human sense, are noway behind the chief of those so much celebrated by the ancients. There is nothing in the story of Aeneas which is not equalled or exceeded by a Joshua or a Moses. But as illustrious as are the acts of these sacred chiefs, 'twould be hard to copy them in just heroic. 'Twould be hard to give to many of them that grateful air which is necessary to render them naturally pleasing to mankind, according to the idea men are universally found to have of heroism and generosity.

[1] *Misc.* v. ch. i. in the notes.

SHAFTESBURY'S CHARACTERISTICS

Notwithstanding the pious endeavours which, as devout Christians, we may have used in order to separate ourselves from the interests of mere heathens and infidels, notwithstanding the true pains we may have taken to arm our hearts in behalf of a chosen people against their neighbouring nations of a false religion and worship, there will be still found such a partiality remaining in us towards creatures of the same make and figure with ourselves, as will hinder us from viewing with satisfaction the punishments inflicted by human hands on such aliens and idolators.

In mere poetry, and the pieces of wit and literature, there is a liberty of thought and easiness of humour indulged to us in which, perhaps, we are not so well able to contemplate the divine judgments, and see clearly into the justice of those ways which are declared to be so far from our ways and above our highest thoughts or understandings. In such a situation of mind we can hardly endure to see heathen treated as heathen, and the faithful made the executioners of the divine wrath. There is a certain perverse humanity in us which inwardly resists the divine commission, though ever so plainly revealed. The wit of the best poet is not sufficient to reconcile us to the campaign of a Joshua, or the retreat of a Moses by the assistance of an Egyptian loan. Nor will it be possible, by the Muses' art, to make that royal hero appear amiable in human eyes who found such favour in the eye of Heaven. Such are mere human hearts that they can hardly find the least sympathy with that only one which had the character of being after the pattern of the Almighty's.

'Tis apparent, therefore, that the manners, actions, and characters of sacred writ are in no wise the proper subject of other authors than divines themselves. They are matters incomprehensible in philosophy; they are above the pitch of the mere human historian, the politician, or the moralist, and are too sacred to be submitted to the poet's fancy when inspired by no other spirit than that of his profane mistresses the Muses.

ADVICE TO AN AUTHOR

I should be unwilling to examine rigorously the performance of our great poet,[1] who sung so piously the Fall of Man. The War in Heaven and the catastrophe of that original pair from whom the generations of mankind were propagated are matters so abstrusely revealed, and with such a resemblance of mythology, that they can more easily bear what figurative construction or fantastic turn the poet may think fit to give them. But should he venture farther into the lives and characters of the patriarchs, the holy matrons, heroes and heroines of the chosen seed; should he employ the sacred machine, the exhibitions and interventions of divinity according to Holy Writ to support the action of his piece; he would soon find the weakness of his pretended orthodox Muse, and prove how little those divine patterns were capable of human imitation, or of being raised to any other majesty, or sublime, than that in which they originally appear.

The theology or theogony of the heathens could admit of such different turns and figurative expressions as suited the fancy and judgment of each philosopher or poet. But the purity of our faith will admit of no such variation. The Christian theology, the birth, procedure, generation, and personal distinction of the Divinity, are mysteries only to be determined by the initiated or ordained, to whom the State has assigned the guardianship and promulgation of the divine oracles. It becomes not those who are uninspired from heaven and uncommissioned from earth, to search with curiosity into the original of those holy rites and records by law established. Should we make such an attempt, we should in probability find the less satisfaction the further we presumed to carry our speculations. Having dared once to quit the authority and direction of the law, we should easily be subject to heterodoxy and error when we had no better warrant left us for the authority of our sacred symbols than the integrity, candour, and disinterestedness of their compilers and registers. How

[1] Milton

great that candour and disinterestedness may have been, we have no other histories to inform us than those of their own licensing or composing. But busy persons, who officiously search into these records, are ready even from hence to draw proofs very disadvantageous to the fame and character of this succession of men. And persons moderately read in these histories are apt to judge no otherwise of the temper of ancient councils than by that of later synods and modern convocations.

When we add to this the melancholy consideration of what disturbances have been raised from the disputes of this kind; what effusion of blood, what devastations of provinces, what shock and ruin of empires have been occasioned by controversies founded on the nicest distinction of an article relating to these mysteries, 'twill be judged vain in any poet or polite author to think of rendering himself agreeable or entertaining whilst he makes such subjects as these to be his theme.

But though the explanation of such deep mysteries and religious duties be allotted as the peculiar province of the sacred order, 'tis presumed, nevertheless, that it may be lawful for other authors to retain their ancient privilege of instructing mankind in a way of pleasure and entertainment. Poets may be allowed their fictions and philosophers their systems. 'Twould go hard with mankind should the patentees for religion be commissioned for all instruction and advice relating to manners or conversation. The stage may be allowed to instruct as well as the pulpit. The way of wit and humour may be serviceable as well as that of gravity and seriousness; and the way of plain reason as well as that of exalted revelation. The main matter is to keep these provinces distinct and settle their just boundaries. And on this account it is that we have endeavoured to represent to modern authors the necessity of making this separation justly and in due form.

'Twould be somewhat hard, methinks, if Religion, as by law

ADVICE TO AN AUTHOR

established,[1] were not allowed the same privilege as Heraldry. 'Tis agreed on all hands that particular persons may design or paint, in their private capacity, after what manner they think fit; but they must blazon only as the public directs. Their lion or bear must be figured as the science appoints, and their supporters and crest must be such as their wise and gallant ancestors have procured for them. No matter whether the shapes of these animals hold just proportion with Nature. No matter though different or contrary forms are joined in one. That which is denied to painters or poets is permitted to heralds. Naturalists may, in their separate and distinct capacity, inquire as they think fit into the real existence and natural truth of things; but they must by no means dispute the authorised forms. Mermaids and griffins were the wonder of our forefathers, and, as such, delivered down to us by the authentic traditions and delineations above mentioned. We ought not so much as to criticise the features or dimensions of a Saracen's face, brought by our conquering ancestors from the holy wars; nor pretend to call in question the figure or size of a dragon, on which the history of our national champion and the establishment of a high order and dignity of the realm depends.

But as worshipful as are the persons of the illustrious heralds, *Clarencieux*, *Garter*, and the rest of those eminent sustainers of British honour and antiquity, 'tis to be hoped that in a more civilised age, such as at present we have the good fortune to live in, they will not attempt to strain their privileges to the same height as formerly. Having been reduced by law or settled practice from the power they once enjoyed, they will not, 'tis presumed, in defiance of the magistrate and civil power, erect anew their stages and lists, introduce the manner of civil combat, set us to tilt and tournament, and raise again those defiances and moral frays of which their Order were once the chief managers and promoters.

[1] *Misc.* i. ch. ii; v. ch. i.

SHAFTESBURY'S CHARACTERISTICS

To conclude: the only method which can justly qualify us for this high privilege of giving advice, is in the first place to receive it ourselves with due submission where the public has vouchsafed to give it us by authority. And if in our private capacity we can have resolution enough to criticise ourselves, and call in question our high imaginations, florid desires, and specious sentiments, according to the manner of soliloquy above prescribed, we shall, by the natural course of things, as we grow wiser, prove less conceited, and introduce into our character that modesty, condescension, and just humanity which is essential to the success of all friendly counsel and admonition. And honest home-philosophy must teach us the wholesome practice within ourselves. Polite reading, and converse with mankind of the better sort, will qualify us for what remains.

TREATISE IV

AN INQUIRY CONCERNING VIRTUE OR MERIT

Formerly Printed from an Imperfect Copy: Now Corrected, and Published entire.

―― Amoto quaeramus seria ludo.
Hor. *Sat.* 1.

Printed first in the Year MDCXCIX.

AN INQUIRY CONCERNING VIRTUE OR MERIT

BOOK I

PART I

SECTION I

RELIGION and Virtue appear in many respects so nearly related, that they are generally presumed inseparable companions. And so willing we are to believe well of their union, that we hardly allow it just to speak or even think of them apart. It may however be questioned whether the practice of the world in this respect be answerable to our speculation. 'Tis certain that we sometimes meet with instances which seem to make against this general supposition. We have known people who, having the appearance of great zeal in religion, have yet wanted even the common affections of humanity, and shown themselves extremely degenerate and corrupt. Others again, who have paid little regard to religion, and been considered as mere atheists, have yet been observed to practise the rules of morality, and act in many cases with such good meaning and affection towards mankind as might seem to force an acknowledgment of their being virtuous. And in general, we find mere moral principles of such weight, that in our dealings with men we are seldom satisfied by the fullest assurance given us of their zeal in religion, till we hear something further of their character. If we are told a man is religious, we still ask, "What are his morals?" But if we hear at first that he has honest moral principles, and is a man of natural justice and good temper, we seldom think of the other question, "Whether he be religious and devout?"

This has given occasion to inquire "what honesty or virtue is, considered by itself, and in what manner it is influenced by religion; how far religion necessarily implies virtue; and whether it be a true saying that it is impossible for an atheist to be virtuous, or share any real degree of honesty or merit."

And here it cannot justly be wondered at if the method of explaining things should appear somewhat unusual, since the subject-matter has been so little examined, and is of so nice and dangerous speculation. For so much is the religious part of mankind alarmed by the freedom of some late pens,[1] and so great a jealousy is raised everywhere on this account, that whatever an author may suggest in favour of religion, he will gain little credit in the cause if he allows the least advantage to any other principle. On the other side, the men of wit and raillery, whose pleasantest entertainment is in the exposing the weak sides of religion, are so desperately afraid of being drawn into any serious thoughts of it, that they look upon a man as guilty of foul play who assumes the air of a free writer, and at the same time preserves any regard for the principles of Natural Religion. They are apt to give as little quarter as they receive, and are resolved to think as ill of the morals of their antagonists as their antagonists can possibly think of theirs. Neither of

[1] [The reference is probably to the *Oracles of Reason* of Charles Blount (posthumously collected in 1695), and John Toland's *Christianity not Mysterious*, published in 1696. These were the first openly deistic treatises after those of Lord Herbert of Cherbury and Hobbes; but the anonymous Unitarian treatise of William Freeke was burnt by the hangman in 1693; and the more moderate work of the Rev. Arthur Bury, *The Naked Gospel* (1690), had been similarly treated. The *Account of the Growth of Deism in England* (1696), and Leslie's *Short and Easy Method with the Deists* (1697), show how far matters had gone.]

CONCERNING VIRTUE OR MERIT

them, it seems, will allow the least advantage to the other. 'Tis as hard to persuade one sort that there is any virtue in religion, as the other that there is any virtue out of the verge of their particular community. So that, between both, an author must pass his time ill who dares plead for religion and moral virtue without lessening the force of either, but allowing to each its proper province and due rank, would hinder their being made enemies by detraction.

However it be, if we would pretend to give the least new light, or explain anything effectually within the intended compass of this inquiry, 'tis necessary to take things pretty deep, and endeavour by some short scheme to represent the original of each opinion, whether natural or unnatural, relating to the Deity. And if we can happily get clear of this thorny part of our philosophy, the rest, 'tis hoped, may prove more plain and easy.

Section II

In the whole of things (or in the universe) either all is according to a good order and the most agreeable to a general interest, or there is that which is otherwise, and might possibly have been better constituted, more wisely contrived, and with more advantage to the general interest of beings, or of the whole.

If everything which exists be according to a good order, and for the best, then of necessity there is no such thing as real ill in the universe, nothing ill with respect to the whole.

Whatsoever then is so as that it could not really have been better, or any way better ordered, is perfectly good; whatsoever in the order of the world can be called ill, must imply a possibility in the nature of the thing to have been better contrived or ordered. For if it could not, it is perfect, and as it should be.

Whatsoever is really ill, therefore, must be caused or produced either by design (that is to say, with knowledge and intelligence) or, in defect of this, by hazard and mere chance.

If there be anything ill in the universe from design, then that which disposes all things is no one good designing principle. For either the one designing principle is itself corrupt, or there is some other in being which operates contrarily and is ill.

If there be any ill in the universe from mere chance, then a designing principle or mind, whether good or bad, cannot be the cause of all things. And consequently if there be supposed a designing principle, who is the cause only of good, but cannot prevent the ill which happens from chance, or from a contrary ill design, then there can be supposed in reality no such thing as a superior good design or mind, other than what is impotent and defective; for not to correct or totally exclude that ill of chance or of a contrary ill design, must proceed either from impotency or ill-will.[1]

Whatsoever is superior in any degree over the world, or rules in Nature with discernment and a mind, is what, by universal agreement, men call God. If there are several such superior minds, they are so many Gods; but if that single or those several superiors are not in their nature necessarily good, they rather take the name of Daemon.

To believe therefore that everything is governed, ordered, or regulated for the best, by a designing principle or mind, necessarily good and permanent, is to be a perfect Theist.

To believe nothing of a designing principle or mind, nor any cause, measure, or rule of things, but chance, so that in Nature neither the interest of the whole nor of any particulars can be said to be in the least designed, pursued, or aimed at, is to be a perfect Atheist.

To believe no one supreme designing principle or mind, but

---

[1] [Compare Spinoza, *Ethics*, part i. Prop. xxxiii. Schol. 2 and App.; part iv. Praef. and Prop. lxiv.; also *Principia philos. Cartesianae*, App. part i. ch. vi.; and Spinoza's first letter to Bleyenberg, Jan. 1664.]

CONCERNING VIRTUE OR MERIT

rather two, three, or more (though in their nature good), is to be a Polytheist.

To believe the governing mind, or minds, not absolutely and necessarily good, nor confined to what is best, but capable of acting according to mere will or fancy, is to be a Daemonist.

There are few who think always consistently, or according to one certain hypothesis, upon any subject so abstruse and intricate as the cause of all things, and the economy or government of the universe. For 'tis evident in the case of the most devout people, even by their own confession, that there are times when their faith hardly can support them in the belief of a supreme Wisdom, and that they are often tempted to judge disadvantageously of a providence and just administration in the whole.

That alone, therefore, is to be called a man's opinion, which is of any other the most habitual to him and occurs upon most occasions. So that 'tis hard to pronounce certainly of any man that he is an atheist, because unless his whole thoughts are at all seasons and on all occasions steadily bent against all supposition or imagination of design in things, he is no perfect Atheist. In the same manner, if a man's thoughts are not at all times steady and resolute against all imagination of chance, fortune, or ill design in things, he is no perfect Theist. But if any one believes more of chance and confusion than of design, he is to be esteemed more an Atheist than a Theist, from that which most predominates or has the ascendant. And in case he believes more of the prevalency of an ill designing principle than of a good one, he is rather a Daemonist, and may be justly so called from the side to which the balance of his judgment most inclines.

All these sorts both of Daemonism, Polytheism, Atheism, and Theism may be mixed.[1] Religion excludes only perfect

---

[1] As thus :—
1. Theism with Daemonism; 2. Daemonism with Polytheism; 3. Theism with Atheism; 4. Daemonism with Atheism; 5. Polytheism with Atheism; 6. Theism (as it stands in opposition to Daemonism, and denotes goodness

atheism. Perfect daemonists undoubtedly there are in religion; because we know whole nations who worship a devil or fiend, to whom they sacrifice and offer prayers and supplications, in reality on no other account than because they fear him. And we know very well that, in some religions, there are those who expressly give no other idea of God than of a being arbitrary, violent, causing ill and ordaining to misery; which in effect is the same as to substitute a daemon or devil in his room.

Now since there are these several opinions concerning a superior Power, and since there may be found perhaps some persons who have no formed opinion at all upon this subject; either through scepticism, negligence of thought, or confusion of judgment; the consideration is, how any of these opinions, or this want of any certain opinion, may possibly consist with virtue and merit, or be compatible with an honest or moral character.

in the superior Deity) with Polytheism; 7. The same Theism or Polytheism with Daemonism; 8. Or with Daemonism and Atheism.

1. As when the one chief mind or sovereign being is (in the believer's sense) divided between a good and an ill nature, by being the cause of ill as well as good, or otherwise when two distinct and contrary principles subsist; one the author of all good, the other of all ill.

2. As when there is not one but several corrupt minds who govern; which opinion may be called Polydaemonism.

3. As when chance is not excluded, but God and chance divide.

4. As when an evil daemon and chance divide.

5. As when many minds and chance divide.

6. As when there are more principal minds than one, but agreeing in good, with one and the same will and reason.

7. As when the same system of Deity or corresponding Deity subsists, together with a contrary principle, or with several contrary principles or governing minds.

8. As when the last case is, together with chance.

CONCERNING VIRTUE OR MERIT

PART II

SECTION I

WHEN we reflect on any ordinary frame or constitution either of Art or Nature, and consider how hard it is to give the least account of a particular part without a competent knowledge of the whole, we need not wonder to find ourselves at a loss in many things relating to the constitution and frame of Nature herself. For to what end in Nature many things, even whole species of creatures, refer, or to what purpose they serve, will be hard for any one justly to determine; but to what end the many proportions and various shapes of parts in many creatures actually serve, we are able, by the help of study and observation, to demonstrate with great exactness.

We know that every creature has a private good and interest of his own, which Nature has compelled him to seek, by all the advantages afforded him within the compass of his make.[1] We know that there is in reality a right and a wrong state of every creature, and that his right one is by nature forwarded and by himself affectionately sought. There being therefore in every creature a certain interest or good, there must be also a certain end to which everything in his constitution must naturally refer. To this end if anything, either in his appetites, passions, or affections, be not conducing but the contrary, we must of necessity own it ill to him. And in this manner he is ill with respect to himself, as he certainly is with respect to others of his kind, when any such appetites or passions make him anyway injurious to them. Now, if by the natural constitution of any rational creature, the same irregularities of appetite which make him ill to others, make him ill also to himself, and if the same regularity of affections which causes him to be good in one

[1] [On the ensuing argument compare Spinoza, *Ethics*, part iv. Props. xix.-xxxv.]

sense, causes him to be good also in the other, then is that goodness by which he is thus useful to others a real good and advantage to himself. And thus virtue and interest may be found at last to agree.

Of this we shall consider particularly in the latter part of our inquiry. Our first design is to see if we can clearly determine what that quality is to which we give the name of goodness or virtue.

Should a historian or traveller describe to us a certain creature of a more solitary disposition than ever was yet heard of; one who had neither mate nor fellow of any kind, nothing of his own likeness, towards which he stood well-affected or inclined, nor anything without or beyond himself for which he had the least passion or concern; we might be apt to say perhaps, without much hesitation, "that this was doubtless a very melancholy creature, and that in this unsociable and sullen state he was like to have a very disconsolate kind of life." But if we were assured that, notwithstanding all appearances, the creature enjoyed himself extremely, had a great relish of life, and was in nothing wanting to his own good, we might acknowledge, perhaps, "that the creature was no monster, nor absurdly constituted as to himself." But we should hardly, after all, be induced to say of him "that he was a good creature."

However, should it be urged against us "that such as he was, the creature was still perfect in himself, and therefore to be esteemed good; for what had he to do with others?"—in this sense, indeed, we might be forced to acknowledge "that he was a good creature; if he could be understood to be absolute and complete in himself, without any real relation to anything in the universe besides." For should there be anywhere in nature a system of which this living creature was to be considered as a part, then could he nowise be allowed good; whilst he plainly appeared to be such a part as made rather to the harm than good of that system or whole in which he was included.

CONCERNING VIRTUE OR MERIT

If therefore in the structure of this or any other animal, there be anything which points beyond himself, and by which he is plainly discovered to have relation to some other being or nature besides his own, then will this animal undoubtedly be esteemed a part of some other system. For instance, if an animal has the proportions of a male, it shows he has relation to a female. And the respective proportions both of the male and female will be allowed, doubtless, to have a joint relation to another existence and order of things beyond themselves. So that the creatures are both of them to be considered as parts of another system, which is that of a particular race or species of living creatures, who have some one common nature, or are provided for by some one order or constitution of things subsisting together, and co-operating towards their conservation and support.

In the same manner, if a whole species of animals contribute to the existence or well-being of some other, then is that whole species, in general, a part only of some other system.

For instance, to the existence of the spider that of the fly is absolutely necessary. The heedless flight, weak frame, and tender body of this latter insect, fits and determines him as much a prey as the rough make, watchfulness, and cunning of the former fits him for rapine and the ensnaring part. The web and wing are suited to each other. And in the structure of each of these animals there is as apparent and perfect a relation to the other as in our own bodies there is a relation of limbs and organs; or as in the branches or leaves of a tree we see a relation of each to the other, and all, in common, to one root and trunk.

In the same manner are flies also necessary to the existence of other creatures, both fowls and fish. And thus are other species or kinds subservient to one another, as being parts of a certain system, and included in one and the same order of beings.

So that there is a system of all animals: an animal-order

or economy, according to which the animal affairs are regulated and disposed.

Now, if the whole system of animals, together with that of vegetables, and all other things in this inferior world, be properly comprehended in one system of a globe or earth, and if, again, this globe or earth itself appears to have a real dependence on something still beyond, as, for example, either on its sun, the galaxy, or its fellow-planets, then is it in reality a part only of some other system. And if it be allowed that there is in like manner a system of all things, and a universal nature, there can be no particular being or system which is not either good or ill in that general one of the universe; for if it be insignificant and of no use, it is a fault or imperfection, and consequently ill in the general system.

Therefore if any being be wholly and really ill, it must be ill with respect to the universal system; and then the system of the universe is ill or imperfect. But if the ill of one private system be the good of others; if it makes still to the good of the general system (as when one creature lives by the destruction of another; one thing is generated from the corruption of another; or one planetary system or vortex may swallow up another), then is the ill of that private system no real ill in itself, any more than the pain of breeding teeth is ill in a system or body which is so constituted that, without this occasion of pain, it would suffer worse by being defective.

So that we cannot say of any being that it is wholly and absolutely ill, unless we can positively show and ascertain that what we call ill is nowhere good besides, in any other system, or with respect to any other order or economy whatsoever.

But were there in the world any entire species of animals destructive to every other, it may be justly called an ill species, as being ill in the animal system. And if in any species of animals (as in men, for example) one man is of a nature pernicious to the rest, he is in this respect justly styled an ill man.

CONCERNING VIRTUE OR MERIT

We do not, however, say of any one that he is an ill man because he has the plague-spots upon him, or because he has convulsive fits which make him strike and wound such as approach him. Nor do we say on the other side that he is a good man when, having his hands tied up, he is hindered from doing the mischief he designs; or (which is in a manner the same) when he abstains from executing his ill purpose through a fear of some impending punishment, or through the allurement of some exterior reward.

So that in a sensible creature that which is not done through any affection at all makes neither good nor ill in the nature of that creature, who then only is supposed good when the good or ill of the system to which he has relation is the immediate object of some passion or affection moving him.

Since it is therefore by affection merely that a creature is esteemed good or ill, natural or unnatural, our business will be to examine which are the good and natural, and which the ill and unnatural affections.

Section II

In the first place, then, it may be observed that if there be an affection towards any subject considered as private good, which is not really such,[1] but imaginary, this affection, as being superfluous, and detracting from the force of other requisite and good affections, is in itself vicious and ill, even in respect of the private interest or happiness of the creature.

If there can possibly be supposed in a creature such an affection towards self-good as is actually, in its natural degree, conducing to his private interest, and at the same time inconsistent with the public good, this may indeed be called still a vicious affection; and on this supposition a creature[1] cannot really be good and natural in respect of his society or public, without being ill and unnatural towards himself. But if the

[1] *Infra*, bk. ii. part i. § 1; part ii. § 3.

affection be then only injurious to the society when it is immoderate, and not so when it is moderate, duly tempered, and allayed, then is the immoderate degree of the affection truly vicious, but not the moderate. And thus if there be found in any creature a more than ordinary self-concernment or regard to private good, which is inconsistent with the interest of the species or public, this must in every respect be esteemed an ill and vicious affection. And this is what we commonly call selfishness,[1] and disapprove so much in whatever creature we happen to discover it.

On the other side, if the affection towards private or self-good, however selfish it may be esteemed, is in reality not only consistent with public good, but in some measure contributing to it; if it be such, perhaps, as for the good of the species in general every individual ought to share; 'tis so far from being ill or blamable in any sense, that it must be acknowledged absolutely necessary to constitute a creature good. For if the want of such an affection as that towards self-preservation be injurious to the species, a creature is ill and unnatural as well through this defect as through the want of any other natural affection. And this no one would doubt to pronounce, if he saw a man who minded not any precipices which lay in his way, nor made any distinction of food, diet, clothing, or whatever else related to his health and being. The same would be averred of one who had a disposition which rendered him averse to any commerce with womankind, and of consequence unfitted him through illness of temper (and not merely through a defect of constitution) for the propagation of his species or kind.

Thus the affection towards self-good may be a good affection or an ill one. For if this private affection be too strong (as when the excessive love of life unfits a creature for any generous act) then is it undoubtedly vicious, and if vicious, the creature who is moved by it is viciously moved, and can never be otherwise than vicious in some degree when moved by that affection.

[1] *Essay on Wit and Humour*, part iii. § 3.

CONCERNING VIRTUE OR MERIT

Therefore if through such an earnest and passionate love of life a creature be accidentally induced to do good (as he might be upon the same terms induced to do ill) he is no more a good creature for this good he executes than a man is the more an honest or good man either for pleading a just cause, or fighting in a good one, for the sake merely of his fee or stipend.

Whatsoever therefore is done which happens to be advantageous to the species through an affection merely towards self-good, does not imply any more goodness in the creature than as the affection itself is good. Let him, in any particular, act ever so well, if at the bottom it be that selfish affection alone which moves him, he is in himself still vicious. Nor can any creature be considered otherwise when the passion towards self-good, though ever so moderate, is his real motive in the doing that to which a natural affection for his kind ought by right to have inclined him.

And indeed whatever exterior helps or succours an ill-disposed creature may find to push him on towards the performance of any one good action, there can no goodness arise in him till his temper be so far changed that in the issue he comes in earnest to be led by some immediate affection, directly and not accidentally, to good and against ill.

For instance, if one of those creatures supposed to be by nature tame, gentle, and favourable to mankind, be, contrary to his natural constitution, fierce and savage, we instantly remark the breach of temper, and own the creature to be unnatural and corrupt. If at any time afterwards the same creature, by good fortune or right management, comes to lose his fierceness, and is made tame, gentle, and treatable like other creatures of his kind, 'tis acknowledged that the creature thus restored becomes good and natural. Suppose now that the creature has indeed a tame and gentle carriage, but that it proceeds only from the fear of his keeper, which if set aside, his predominant passion instantly breaks out; then is his gentleness not his real temper, but his true and genuine nature or natural temper remaining just as it was: the creature is still as ill as ever.

Nothing therefore being properly either goodness or illness in a creature, except what is from natural temper, "A good creature is such a one as by the natural temper or bent of his affections is carried primarily and immediately, and not secondarily and accidentally, to good and against ill;" and an ill creature is just the contrary, viz. "One who is wanting in right affections of force enough to carry him directly towards good, and bear him out against ill; or who is carried by other affections directly to ill and against good."

When in general all the affections or passions are suited to the public good, or good of the species, as above mentioned, then is the natural temper entirely good. If, on the contrary, any requisite passion be wanting, or if there be any one supernumerary or weak, or anywise disserviceable or contrary to that main end, then is the natural temper, and consequently the creature himself, in some measure corrupt and ill.

There is no need of mentioning either envy, malice, frowardness or other such hateful passions, to show in what manner they are ill, and constitute an ill creature. But it may be necessary perhaps to remark, that even as to kindness and love of the most natural sort (such as that of any creature for its offspring) if it be immoderate and beyond a certain degree it is undoubtedly vicious.[1] For thus over-great tenderness destroys the effect of love, and excessive pity renders us incapable of giving succour. Hence the excess of motherly love is owned to be a vicious fondness; over-great pity, effeminacy and weakness; over-great concern for self-preservation, meanness and cowardice; too little, rashness; and none at all, or that which is contrary (viz. a passion leading to self-destruction), a mad and desperate depravity.

[1] [Cp. Spinoza, *Ethics*, part IV. Props. xxxix.-xliv.]

CONCERNING VIRTUE OR MERIT

SECTION III

But to proceed from what is esteemed mere goodness, and lies within the reach and capacity of all sensible creatures, to that which is called virtue or merit, and is allowed to man only.

In a creature capable of forming general notions of things, not only the outward beings which offer themselves to the sense are the objects of the affection, but the very actions themselves, and the affections of pity, kindness, gratitude, and their contraries, being brought into the mind by reflection, become objects. So that, by means of this reflected sense, there arises another kind of affection towards those very affections themselves, which have been already felt, and are now become the subject of a new liking or dislike.

The case is the same in the mental or moral subjects as in the ordinary bodies or common subjects of sense. The shapes, motions, colours, and proportions of these latter being presented to our eye, there necessarily results a beauty or deformity,[1] according to the different measure, arrangement, and disposition of their several parts. So in behaviour and actions, when presented to our understanding, there must be found, of necessity, an apparent difference, according to the regularity or irregularity of the subjects.

The mind, which is spectator or auditor of other minds, cannot be without its eye and ear, so as to discern proportion, distinguish sound, and scan each sentiment or thought which comes before it. It can let nothing escape its censure. It feels the soft and harsh, the agreeable and disagreeable in the affections; and finds a foul and fair, a harmonious and a dissonant, as really and truly here as in any musical numbers or in the outward forms or representations of sensible things. Nor can it withhold its admiration and ecstasy, its aversion and scorn, any more in what relates to one than to the other of these subjects. So that to deny the common and natural sense of

---
[1] *The Moralists*, part iii. § 2.

a sublime and beautiful in things, will appear an affectation merely, to any one who considers duly of this affair.[1]

Now as in the sensible kind of objects the species or images of bodies, colours, and sounds are perpetually moving before our eyes, and acting on our senses even when we sleep; so in the moral and intellectual kind, the forms and images of things are no less active and incumbent on the mind, at all seasons, and even when the real objects themselves are absent.

In these vagrant characters or pictures of manners, which the mind of necessity figures to itself and carries still about with it, the heart cannot possibly remain neutral; but constantly takes part one way or other. However false or corrupt it be within itself, it finds the difference, as to beauty and comeliness, between one heart and another, one turn of affection, one behaviour, one sentiment and another; and accordingly, in all disinterested cases, must approve in some measure of what is natural and honest, and disapprove what is dishonest and corrupt.

Thus the several motions, inclinations, passions, dispositions, and consequent carriage and behaviour of creatures in the various parts of life, being in several views or perspectives represented to the mind, which readily discerns the good and ill towards the species or public, there arises a new trial or exercise of the heart, which must either rightly and soundly affect what is just and right, and disaffect what is contrary, or corruptly affect what is ill and disaffect what is worthy and good.

And in this case alone it is we call any creature worthy or virtuous, when it can have the notion of a public interest, and can attain the speculation or science of what is morally good or ill, admirable or blamable, right or wrong. For though we may vulgarly call an ill horse vicious, yet we never say of a good one, nor of any mere beast, idiot, or changeling, though ever so good-natured, that he is worthy or virtuous.

[1] *Essay on Wit and Humour*, part ii. § 2 (end); *Miscellaneous Reflections*, Misc. ii. ch. i.

CONCERNING VIRTUE OR MERIT

So that if a creature be generous, kind, constant, compassionate, yet if he cannot reflect on what he himself does, or sees others do, so as to take notice of what is worthy or honest, and make that notice or conception of worth and honesty to be an object of his affection, he has not the character of being virtuous; for thus, and no otherwise, he is capable of having a sense of right or wrong, a sentiment or judgment of what is done through just, equal, and good affection, or the contrary.

Whatsoever is done through any unequal affection is iniquitous, wicked, and wrong. If the affection be equal, sound, and good, and the subject of the affection such as may with advantage to society be ever in the same manner prosecuted or affected, this must necessarily constitute what we call equity and right in any action. For wrong is not such action as is barely the cause of harm (since at this rate a dutiful son aiming at an enemy, but by mistake or ill chance happening to kill his father, would do a wrong), but when anything is done through insufficient or unequal affection (as when a son shows no concern for the safety of a father; or, where there is need of succour, prefers an indifferent person to him) this is of the nature of wrong.

Neither can any weakness or imperfection in the senses be the occasion of iniquity or wrong; if the object of the mind itself be not at any time absurdly framed, nor any way improper, but suitable, just, and worthy of the opinion and affection applied to it. For if we will suppose a man who, being sound and entire both in his reason and affection, has nevertheless so depraved a constitution or frame of body that the natural objects are, through his organs of sense, as through ill glasses, falsely conveyed and misrepresented, 'twill be soon observed, in such a person's case, that since his failure is not in his principal or leading part, he cannot in himself be esteemed iniquitous or unjust.

'Tis otherwise in what relates to opinion, belief, or speculation. For as the extravagance of judgment or belief is such that in some countries even monkeys, cats, crocodiles, and other vile or destructive animals have been esteemed holy, and worshipped even as deities; should it appear to any one of the religion or belief of those countries that to save such a creature as a cat, preferably to a parent, was right, and that other men who had not the same religious opinion were to be treated as enemies till converted; this would be certainly wrong and wicked in the believer; and every action, grounded on this belief, would be an iniquitous, wicked, and vicious action.

And thus whatsoever causes a misconception or misapprehension of the worth or value of any object, so as to diminish a due, or raise any undue, irregular or unsocial affection, must necessarily be the occasion of wrong. Thus he who affects or loves a man for the sake of something which is reputed honourable, but which is in reality vicious, is himself vicious and ill. The beginnings of this corruption may be noted in many occurrences; as when an ambitious man, by the fame of his high attempts, a conqueror or a pirate by his boasted enterprises, raises in another person an esteem and admiration of that immoral and inhuman character which deserves abhorrence, 'tis then that the hearer becomes corrupt, when he secretly approves the ill he hears. But on the other side, the man who loves and esteems another, as believing him to have that virtue which he has not, but only counterfeits, is not on this account either vicious or corrupt.

A mistake therefore, in fact, being no cause or sign of ill affection, can be no cause of vice. But a mistake of right being the cause of unequal affection, must of necessity be the cause of vicious action in every intelligent or rational being.

But as there are many occasions where the matter of right may even to the most discerning part of mankind appear difficult, and of doubtful decision, 'tis not a slight mistake of this kind which can destroy the character of a virtuous or worthy man. But when, either through superstition or ill custom, there come to be very gross mistakes in the assignment or application of the affection; when the mistakes are either in their nature so gross, or so complicated and frequent, that a creature cannot well live in a natural state, nor with due affections, compatible with human society and civil life; then is the character of virtue forfeited.

And thus we find how far worth and virtue depend on a knowledge of right and wrong, and on a use of reason, sufficient to secure a right application of the affections; that nothing horrid or unnatural, nothing unexemplary, nothing destructive of that natural affection by which the species or society is upheld, may on any account, or through any principle or notion of honour or religion, be at any time affected or prosecuted as a good and proper object of esteem. For such a principle as this must be wholly vicious; and whatsoever is acted upon it can be no other than vice and immorality. And thus if there be anything which teaches men either treachery, ingratitude, or cruelty, by divine warrant or under colour and pretence of any present or future good to mankind; if there be anything which teaches men to persecute their friends through love,[1] or to torment captives of war in sport, or to offer human sacrifice, or to torment, macerate, or mangle themselves in a religious zeal before their God, or to commit any sort of barbarity or brutality as amiable or becoming; be it custom which gives applause, or religion which gives a sanction; this is not, nor ever can be, virtue of any kind, or in any sense, but must remain still horrid depravity, notwithstanding any fashion, law, custom or religion which may be ill and vicious itself, but can never alter the eternal measures and immutable independent nature of worth and virtue.

Section IV

Upon the whole. As to those creatures who are only capable of being moved by sensible objects, they are accordingly good

---

[1] *Letter Concerning Enthusiasm*, § 2; *Misc.* ii. ch. iii.

or vicious as the sensible affections stand with them. 'Tis otherwise in creatures capable of framing rational objects of moral good. For in one of this kind, should the sensible affections stand ever so much amiss, yet if they prevail not, because of those other rational affections spoken of, 'tis evident the temper still holds good in the main, and the person is with justice esteemed virtuous by all men.

More than this. If by temper any one is passionate, angry, fearful, amorous, yet resists these passions, and notwithstanding the force of their impression adheres to virtue, we say commonly in this case that the virtue is the greater; and we say well. Though if that which restrains the person and holds him to a virtuous-like behaviour be no affection towards goodness or virtue itself, but towards private good merely, he is not in reality the more virtuous, as has been shown before. But this still is evident, that if voluntarily and without foreign constraint an angry temper bears, or an amorous one refrains, so that neither any cruel nor immodest action can be forced from such a person, though ever so strongly tempted by his constitution, we applaud his virtue above what we should naturally do if he were free of this temptation and these propensities. At the same time, there is nobody will say that a propensity to vice can be an ingredient in virtue, or any way necessary to complete a virtuous character.

There seems therefore to be some kind of difficulty in the case, but it amounts only to this. If there be any part of the temper in which ill passions or affections are seated, whilst in another part the affections towards moral good are such as absolutely to master those attempts of their antagonists, this is the greatest proof imaginable that a strong principle of virtue lies at the bottom and has possessed itself of the natural temper. Whereas if there be no ill passions stirring, a person may be indeed more cheaply virtuous, that is to say, he may conform himself to the known rules of virtue without sharing so much of a virtuous principle as another. Yet if that other person,

CONCERNING VIRTUE OR MERIT

who has the principle of virtue so strongly implanted, comes at last to lose those contrary impediments supposed in him, he certainly loses nothing in virtue; but on the contrary, losing only what is vicious in his temper, is left more entire to virtue, and possesses it in a higher degree.

Thus is virtue shared in different degrees by rational creatures, such at least as are called rational, but who come short of that sound and well-established reason which alone can constitute a just affection, a uniform and steady will and resolution. And thus vice and virtue are found variously mixed, and alternately prevalent in the several characters of mankind. For it seems evident from our inquiry, that how ill soever the temper or passions may stand with respect either to the sensible or the moral objects; however passionate, furious, lustful or cruel any creature may become; however vicious the mind be, or whatever ill rules or principles it goes by; yet if there be any flexibleness or favourable inclination towards the least moral object, the least appearance of moral good (as if there be any such thing as kindness, gratitude, bounty, or compassion), there is still something of virtue left, and the creature is not wholly vicious and unnatural.

Thus a ruffian who out of a sense of fidelity and honour of any kind refuses to discover his associates, and rather than betray them is content to endure torments and death, has certainly some principle of virtue, however he may misapply it. 'Twas the same case with that malefactor who, rather than do the office of executioner to his companions, chose to keep them company in their execution.

In short, as it seems hard to pronounce of any man "that he is absolutely an atheist," so it appears altogether as hard to pronounce of any man "that he is absolutely corrupt or vicious," there being few, even of the horridest villains, who have not something of virtue in this imperfect sense. Nothing is more just than a known saying, "That it is as hard to find a man wholly ill as wholly good," because wherever there is any good affection left, there is certainly some goodness or virtue still in being.

And having considered thus of virtue, what it is in itself, we may now consider how it stands with respect to the opinions concerning a Deity, as above mentioned.

PART III

Section I

The nature of virtue consisting (as has been explained) in a certain just disposition or proportionable affection of a rational creature towards the moral objects of right and wrong, nothing can possibly in such a creature exclude a principle of virtue, or render it ineffectual, except what

1. Either takes away the natural and just sense of right and wrong;
2. Or creates a wrong sense of it;
3. Or causes the right sense to be opposed by contrary affections.

On the other side, nothing can assist or advance the principle of virtue except what either in some manner nourishes and promotes a sense of right and wrong, or preserves it genuine and uncorrupt, or causes it when such to be obeyed, by subduing and subjecting the other affections to it.

We are to consider, therefore, how any of the above-mentioned opinions on the subject of a Deity may influence in these cases, or produce either of these three effects.

1. As to the first case, the taking away the natural sense of right and wrong.

It will not surely be understood that by this is meant the taking away the notion of what is good or ill in the species or society. For of the reality of such a good and ill, no rational creature can possibly be insensible. Every one discerns and owns a public interest, and is conscious of what affects his fellowship or community. When we say, therefore, of a creature "that he has wholly lost the sense of right and wrong," we suppose that being able to discern the good and ill of his species, he has at the same time no concern for either, nor any sense of excellency or baseness in any moral action relating to one or the other. So that except merely with respect to a private and narrowly confined self-good, 'tis supposed there is in such a creature no liking or dislike of manners; no admiration or love of anything as morally good, nor hatred of anything as morally ill, be it ever so unnatural or deformed.

There is in reality no rational creature whatsoever who knows not that when he voluntarily offends or does harm to any one, he cannot fail to create an apprehension and fear of like harm, and consequently a resentment and animosity in every creature who observes him. So that the offender must needs be conscious of being liable to such treatment from every one as if he had in some degree offended all.

Thus offence and injury are always known as punishable by every one; and equal behaviour (which is therefore called merit) as rewardable and well-deserving from every one. Of this even the wickedest creature living must have a sense. So that if there be any further meaning in this sense of right and wrong; if in reality there be any sense of this kind which an absolute wicked creature has not; it must consist in a real antipathy or aversion to injustice or wrong, and in a real affection or love towards equity and right for its own sake, and on the account of its own natural beauty and worth.

'Tis impossible to suppose a mere sensible creature originally so ill-constituted and unnatural as that, from the moment he comes to be tried by sensible objects, he should have no one good passion towards his kind, no foundation either of pity, love, kindness, or social affection. 'Tis full as impossible to conceive that a rational creature coming first to be tried by rational objects, and receiving into his mind the images or representations of justice, generosity, gratitude, or other virtue, should have no liking of these or dislike of their contraries, but be found absolutely indifferent towards whatsoever is presented to him of this sort. A soul, indeed, may as well be without sense as without admiration in the things of which it has any knowledge. Coming therefore to a capacity of seeing and admiring in this new way, it must needs find a beauty and a deformity as well in actions, minds, and tempers, as in figures, sounds, or colours. If there be no real amiableness or deformity in moral acts, there is at least an imaginary one of full force. Though perhaps the thing itself should not be allowed in Nature, the imagination or fancy of it must be allowed to be from Nature alone. Nor can anything besides art and strong endeavour, with long practice and meditation, overcome such a natural prevention or prepossession of the mind in favour of this moral distinction.[1]

Sense of right and wrong therefore being as natural to us as natural affection itself, and being a first principle in our constitution and make, there is no speculative opinion, persuasion, or belief, which is capable immediately or directly to exclude or destroy it. That which is of original and pure nature, nothing beside contrary habit and custom (a second nature) is able to displace. And this affection being an original one of earliest rise in the soul or affectionate part, nothing beside contrary affection, by frequent check and control, can operate upon it, so as either to diminish it in part or destroy it in the whole.

'Tis evident in what relates to the frame and order of our bodies, that no particular odd mien or gesture, which is either natural to us and consequent to our make, or accidental and by habit acquired, can possibly be overcome by our immediate disapprobation, or the contrary bent of our will ever so strongly set against it. Such a change cannot be effected

[1] *The Moralists,* part iii. § 2.

without extraordinary means, and the intervention of art and method, a strict attention, and repeated check. And even thus, Nature we find is hardly mastered, but lies sullen, and ready to revolt on the first occasion. Much more is this the mind's case in respect of that natural affection and anticipating fancy which makes the sense of right and wrong. 'Tis impossible that this can instantly, or without much force and violence, be effaced, or struck out of the natural temper, even by means of the most extravagant belief or opinion in the world.

Neither Theism therefore, nor Atheism, nor Daemonism, nor any religious or irreligious belief of any kind being able to operate immediately or directly in this case, but indirectly, by the intervention of opposite or of favourable affections casually excited by any such belief, we may consider of this effect in our last case, where we come to examine the agreement or disagreement of other affections with this natural and moral one which relates to right and wrong.

Section II

2. As to the second case, viz. the wrong sense or false imagination of right and wrong.

This can proceed only from the force of custom and education in opposition to Nature, as may be noted in those countries where, according to custom or politic institution, certain actions naturally foul and odious are repeatedly viewed with applause, and honour ascribed to them. For thus 'tis possible that a man, forcing himself, may eat the flesh of his enemies, not only against his stomach, but against his nature, and think it nevertheless both right and honourable, as supposing it to be of considerable service to his community, and capable of advancing the name and spreading the terror of his nation.

But to speak of the opinions relating to a Deity, and what effect they may have in this place. As to atheism, it does not seem that it can directly have any effect at all towards the setting up a false species of right or wrong. For notwithstanding a man may, through custom, or by licentiousness of practice, favoured by atheism, come in time to lose much of his natural moral sense,[1] yet it does not seem that atheism should of itself be the cause of any estimation or valuing of anything as fair, noble, and deserving, which was the contrary. It can never, for instance, make it be thought that the being able to eat man's flesh, or commit bestiality, is good and excellent in itself. But this is certain, that by means of corrupt religion or superstition, many things the most horridly unnatural and inhuman come to be received as excellent, good, and laudable in themselves.

Nor is this a wonder. For wherever anything, in its nature odious and abominable, is by religion advanced, as the supposed will or pleasure of a supreme Deity, if in the eye of the believer it appears not indeed in any respect the less ill or odious on this account, then must the Deity of necessity bear the blame, and be considered as a being naturally ill and odious, however courted and solicited through mistrust and fear. But this is what religion, in the main, forbids us to imagine. It everywhere prescribes esteem and honour in company with worship and adoration. Whensoever therefore it teaches the love and admiration of a Deity who has any apparent character of ill, it teaches at the same time a love and admiration of that ill, and causes that to be taken for good and amiable which is in itself horrid and detestable.

For instance, if Jupiter be he who is adored and reverenced, and if his history represents him amorously inclined, and permitting his desires of this kind to wander in the loosest manner, 'tis certain that his worshippers, believing this history to be literally and strictly true, must of course be taught a greater

[1] [This expression appears to have been first introduced into ethics by Shaftesbury. It occurs several times above in the marginal headings of the *Inquiry*.]

CONCERNING VIRTUE OR MERIT

love of amorous and wanton acts. If there be a religion which teaches the adoration and love of a God whose character it is to be captious and of high resentment, subject to wrath and anger, furious, revengeful, and revenging himself, when offended, on others than those who gave the offence; and if there be added to the character of this God a fraudulent disposition, encouraging deceit and treachery amongst men, favourable to a few, though for slight causes, and cruel to the rest, 'tis evident that such a religion as this being strongly enforced must of necessity raise even an approbation and respect towards the vices of this kind, and breed a suitable disposition, a capricious, partial, revengeful, and deceitful temper. For even irregularities and enormities of a heinous kind must in many cases appear illustrious to one who considers them in a being admired and contemplated with the highest honour and veneration.

This indeed must be allowed, that if in the cult or worship of such a Deity there be nothing beyond common form, nothing beside what proceeds from mere example, custom, constraint, or fear; if there be, at the bottom, no real heartiness, no esteem or love implied, the worshipper perhaps may not be much misled as to his notion of right and wrong. If in following the precepts of his supposed God, or doing what he esteems necessary towards the satisfying of such his Deity, he is compelled only by fear, and, contrary to his inclination, performs an act which he secretly detests as barbarous and unnatural, then has he an apprehension or sense still of right and wrong, and, according to what has been already observed, is sensible of ill in the character of his God, however cautious he may be of pronouncing anything on this subject, or so thinking of it as to frame any formal or direct opinion in the case. But if by insensible degrees, as he proceeds in his religious faith and devout exercise, he comes to be more and more reconciled to the malignity, arbitrariness, partiality, or revengefulness of his believed Deity, his reconciliation with these qualities themselves will soon grow in proportion, and the most cruel, unjust, and barbarous acts will, by the power of this example, be often considered by him not only as just and lawful, but as divine and worthy of imitation.

For whoever thinks there is a God, and pretends formally to believe that he is just and good, must suppose that there is independently such a thing as justice and injustice, truth and falsehood, right and wrong, according to which he pronounces that God is just, righteous, and true. If the mere will, decree, or law of God be said absolutely to constitute right and wrong, then are these latter words of no significancy at all.[1] For thus, if each part of a contradiction were affirmed for truth by the Supreme Power, they would consequently become true. Thus if one person were decreed to suffer for another's fault, the sentence would be just and equitable. And thus, in the same manner, if arbitrarily and without reason some beings were destined to endure perpetual ill, and others as constantly to enjoy good, this also would pass under the same denomination. But to say of anything that it is just or unjust on such a foundation as this, is to say nothing, or to speak without a meaning.

And thus it appears that where a real devotion and hearty worship is paid to a Supreme Being, who in his history or character is represented otherwise than as really and truly just and good, there must ensue a loss of rectitude, a disturbance of thought, and a corruption of temper and manners in the believer. His honesty will of necessity be supplanted by his zeal, whilst he is thus unnaturally influenced, and rendered thus immorally devout.

To this we need only add, that as the ill character of a God does injury to the affections of men, and disturbs and impairs the natural sense of right and wrong, so, on the other hand, nothing can more highly contribute to the fixing of right apprehensions, and a sound judgment or sense of right and

---

[1] [The reference is probably to Locke, *Essay*, bk. i. ch. iii. § 6. Cp. Spinoza, *Ethics*, part i. Prop. xvii. Scholium.]

wrong, than to believe a God who is ever and on all accounts represented such as to be actually a true model and example of the most exact justice and highest goodness and worth. Such a view of divine providence and bounty extended to all, and expressed in a constant good affection towards the whole, must of necessity engage us, within our compass and sphere, to act by a like principle and affection. And having once the good of our species or public in view, as our end or aim, 'tis impossible we should be misguided by any means to a false apprehension or sense of right or wrong.

As to this second case therefore, religion (according as the kind may prove) is capable of doing great good or harm, and atheism nothing positive in either way. For however it may be indirectly an occasion of men's losing a good and sufficient sense of right and wrong, it will not, as atheism merely, be the occasion of setting up a false species of it, which only false religion or fantastical opinion, derived commonly from superstition and credulity, is able to effect.

Section III

Now as to the last case, the opposition made by other affections to the natural sense of right and wrong.

'Tis evident that a creature having this sort of sense or good affection in any degree must necessarily act according to it, if it happens not to be opposed, either by some settled sedate affection towards a conceived private good, or by some sudden, strong, and forcible passion, as of lust or anger, which may not only subdue the sense of right and wrong, but the very sense of private good itself, and over-rule even the most familiar and received opinion of what is conducing to self-interest.

But it is not our business in this place to examine the several means or methods by which this corruption is introduced or increased. We are to consider only how the opinions concerning a Deity can influence one way or another.

SHAFTESBURY'S CHARACTERISTICS

That it is possible for a creature capable of using reflection to have a liking or dislike of moral actions, and consequently a sense of right and wrong, before such time as he may have any settled notion of a God, is what will hardly be questioned; it being a thing not expected, or any way possible, that a creature such as man, arising from his childhood slowly and gradually to several degrees of reason and reflection, should at the very first be taken up with those speculations or more refined sort of reflections, about the subject of God's existence.

Let us suppose a creature who, wanting reason and being unable to reflect, has notwithstanding many good qualities and affections, as love to his kind, courage, gratitude, or pity. 'Tis certain that if you give to this creature a reflecting faculty, it will at the same instant approve of gratitude, kindness, and pity; be taken with any show or representation of the social passion, and think nothing more amiable than this, or more odious than the contrary. And this is to be capable of virtue, and to have a sense of right and wrong.

Before the time, therefore, that a creature can have any plain or positive notion one way or other concerning the subject of a God, he may be supposed to have an apprehension or sense of right and wrong, and be possessed of virtue and vice in different degrees, as we know by experience of those who, having lived in such places and in such a manner as never to have entered into any serious thoughts of religion, are nevertheless very different among themselves, as to their characters of honesty and worth: some being naturally modest, kind, friendly, and consequently lovers of kind and friendly actions; others proud, harsh, cruel, and consequently inclined to admire rather the acts of violence and mere power.

Now as to the belief of a Deity, and how men are influenced by it, we may consider, in the first place, on what account men yield obedience, and act in conformity to such a supreme Being. It must be either in the way of his power, as presupposing some disadvantage or benefit to accrue from him; or in the way of his excellency and worth, as thinking it the perfection of nature to imitate and resemble him.

If (as in the first case) there be a belief or conception of a Deity who is considered only as powerful over his creature, and enforcing obedience to his absolute will by particular rewards and punishments; and if on this account, through hope merely of reward, or fear of punishment, the creature be incited to do the good he hates, or restrained from doing the ill to which he is not otherwise in the least degree averse, there is in this case (as has been already shown) no virtue or goodness whatsoever. The creature, notwithstanding his good conduct, is intrinsically of as little worth as if he acted in his natural way, when under no dread or terror of any sort. There is no more of rectitude, piety, or sanctity in a creature thus reformed, than there is meekness or gentleness in a tiger strongly chained, or innocence and sobriety in a monkey under the discipline of the whip. For however orderly and well those animals, or man himself upon like terms, may be induced to act, whilst the will is neither gained nor the inclination wrought upon, but awe alone prevails and forces obedience, the obedience is servile, and all which is done through it merely servile. The greater degree of such a submission or obedience is only the greater servility, whatever may be the object. For whether such a creature has a good master or an ill one, he is neither more nor less servile in his own nature. Be the master or superior ever so perfect or excellent, yet the greater submission caused in this case, through this sole principle or motive, is only the lower and more abject servitude, and implies the greater wretchedness and meanness in the creature, who has those passions of self-love so predominant, and is in his temper so vicious and defective as has been explained.

As to the second case. If there be a belief or conception of a Deity who is considered as worthy and good, and admired and reverenced as such, being understood to have, besides mere power and knowledge, the highest excellence of nature, such as renders him justly amiable to all; and if in the manner this Sovereign and mighty Being is represented, or as he is historically described, there appears in him a high and eminent regard to what is good and excellent, a concern for the good of all, and an affection of benevolence and love towards the whole, such an example must undoubtedly serve (as above explained) to raise and increase the affection towards virtue, and help to submit and subdue all other affections to that alone.

Nor is this good effected by example merely. For where the theistical belief is entire and perfect, there must be a steady opinion of the superintendency of a supreme Being, a witness and spectator of human life, and conscious of whatsoever is felt or acted in the universe; so that in the perfectest recess or deepest solitude there must be One still presumed remaining with us, whose presence singly must be of more moment than that of the most august assembly on earth. In such a presence, 'tis evident that as the shame of guilty actions must be the greatest of any, so must the honour be of well-doing, even under the unjust censure of a world. And in this case 'tis very apparent how conducing a perfect theism must be to virtue, and how great deficiency there is in atheism.

What the fear of future punishment and hope of future reward, added to this belief, may further contribute towards virtue, we come now to consider more particularly. So much in the meanwhile may be gathered from what has been said above, that neither this fear nor hope can possibly be of the kind called good affections, such as are acknowledged the springs and sources of all actions truly good Nor can this fear or hope, as above intimated, consist in reality with virtue or goodness, if it either stands as essential to any moral performance, or as a considerable motive to any act, of which some better affection ought alone to have been a sufficient cause.

It may be considered withal, that in this religious sort of discipline, the principle of self-love, which is naturally so prevailing in us, being no way moderated or restrained, but rather

CONCERNING VIRTUE OR MERIT

improved and made stronger every day by the exercise of the passions in a subject of more extended self-interest, there may be reason to apprehend lest the temper of this kind should extend itself in general through all the parts of life. For if the habit be such as to occasion, in every particular, a stricter attention to self good and private interest, it must insensibly diminish the affections towards public good or the interest of society, and introduce a certain narrowness of spirit, which (as some pretend) is peculiarly observable in the devout persons and zealots of almost every religious persuasion.

This, too, must be confessed: that if it be true piety to love God for his own sake, the over-solicitous regard to private good expected from him must of necessity prove a diminution of piety. For whilst God is beloved only as the cause of private good, he is no otherwise beloved than as any other instrument or means of pleasure by any vicious creature. Now the more there is of this violent affection towards private good, the less room is there for the other sort towards goodness itself, or any good and deserving object, worthy of love and admiration for its own sake, such as God is universally acknowledged, or at least by the generality of civilised or refined worshippers.[1]

'Tis in this respect that the strong desire and love of life may also prove an obstacle to piety, as well as to virtue and public love. For the stronger this affection is in any one, the less will he be able to have true resignation, or submission to the rule and order of the Deity. And if that which he calls resignation depends only on the expectation of infinite retribution or reward, he discovers no more worth or virtue here than in any other bargain of interest. The meaning of his resignation being only this, "That he resigns his present life and pleasures conditionally, for that which he himself confesses to be beyond an equivalent: eternal living in a state of highest pleasure and enjoyment."

[1] [Cp. Spinoza, *Ethics*, part ii. (end); part iv. Prop. lxiii; part v. Props. xvii.-xix.]

SHAFTESBURY'S CHARACTERISTICS

But notwithstanding the injury which the principle of virtue may possibly suffer by the increase of the selfish passion in the way we have been mentioning, 'tis certain, on the other side, that the principle of fear of future punishment, and hope of future reward, how mercenary or servile soever it may be accounted, is yet in many circumstances a great advantage, security, and support to virtue.

It has been already considered, that notwithstanding there may be implanted in the heart a real sense of right and wrong, a real good affection towards the species or society, yet by the violence of rage, lust, or any other counter-working passion, this good affection may frequently be controlled and overcome. Where therefore there is nothing in the mind capable to render such ill passions the objects of its aversion, and cause them earnestly to be opposed, 'tis apparent how much a good temper in time must suffer, and a character by degrees change for the worse. But if religion, interposing, creates a belief that the ill passions of this kind, no less than their consequent actions, are the objects of a Deity's animadversion, 'tis certain that such a belief must prove a seasonable remedy against vice, and be in a particular manner advantageous to virtue. For a belief of this kind must be supposed to tend considerably towards the calming of the mind, and disposing or fitting the person to a better recollection of himself, and to a stricter observance of that good and virtuous principle which needs only his attention to engage him wholly in its party and interest.

And as this belief of a future reward and punishment is capable of supporting those who through ill practice are like to apostatise from virtue, so when by ill opinion and wrong thought the mind itself is bent against the honest course, and debauched even to an esteem and deliberate preference of a vicious one, the belief of the kind mentioned may prove on this occasion the only relief and safety.

A person, for instance, who has much of goodness and

natural rectitude in his temper, but withal so much softness or effeminacy as unfits him to bear poverty, crosses, or adversity, if by ill fortune he meets with many trials of this kind, it must certainly give a sourness and distaste to his temper, and make him exceedingly averse to that which he may falsely presume the occasion of such calamity or ill. Now if his own thoughts, or the corrupt insinuations of other men, present it often to his mind "that his honesty is the occasion of this calamity, and that if he were delivered from this restraint of virtue and honesty, he might be much happier," 'tis very obvious that his esteem of these good qualities must in proportion diminish every day as the temper grows uneasy and quarrels with itself. But if he opposes to this thought the consideration "that honesty carries with it, if not a present, at least a future advantage, such as to compensate that loss of private good which he regrets," then may this injury to his good temper and honest principle be prevented, and his love or affection towards honesty and virtue remain as it was before.

In the same manner, where instead of regard or love there is rather an aversion to what is good and virtuous (as, for instance, where lenity and forgiveness are despised, and revenge highly thought of and beloved), if there be this consideration added, "That lenity is, by its rewards, made the cause of a greater self-good and enjoyment than what is found in revenge," that very affection of lenity and mildness may come to be industriously nourished, and the contrary passion depressed. And thus temperance, modesty, candour, benignity, and other good affections, however despised at first, may come at last to be valued for their own sakes, the contrary species rejected, and the good and proper object beloved and prosecuted, when the reward or punishment is not so much as thought of.

Thus in a civil state or public we see that a virtuous administration, and an equal and just distribution of rewards and punishments, is of the highest service, not only by restraining the vicious, and forcing them to act usefully to society, but by making virtue to be apparently the interest of every one, so as to remove all prejudices against it, create a fair reception for it, and lead men into that path which afterwards they cannot easily quit. For thus a people raised from barbarity or despotic rule, civilised by laws, and made virtuous by the long course of a lawful and just administration, if they chance to fall suddenly under any misgovernment of unjust and arbitrary power, they will on this account be the rather animated to exert a stronger virtue in opposition to such violence and corruption. And even where, by long and continued arts of a prevailing tyranny, such a people are at last totally oppressed, the scattered seeds of virtue will for a long time remain alive, even to a second generation, ere the utmost force of misapplied rewards and punishments can bring them to the abject and compliant state of long-accustomed slaves.

But though a right distribution of justice in a government be so essential a cause of virtue, we must observe in this case that it is example which chiefly influences mankind, and forms the character and disposition of a people. For a virtuous administration is in a manner necessarily accompanied with virtue in the magistrate. Otherwise it could be of little effect, and of no long duration. But where it is sincere and well established, there virtue and the laws must necessarily be respected and beloved. So that, as to punishments and rewards, their efficacy is not so much from the fear or expectation which they raise, as from a natural esteem of virtue and detestation of villainy, which is awakened and excited by these public expressions of the approbation and hatred of mankind in each case. For in the public executions of the greatest villains we see generally that the infamy and odiousness of their crime, and the shame of it before mankind, contribute more to their misery than all besides; and that it is not the immediate pain of death itself which raises so much horror either in the sufferers or spectators, as that ignominious kind of death which is inflicted for public crimes and violations of justice and humanity.

And as the case of reward and punishment stands thus in the public, so, in the same manner, as to private families. For slaves and mercenary servants, restrained and made orderly by punishment and the severity of their master, are not on this account made good or honest. Yet the same master of the family using proper rewards and gentle punishments towards his children, teaches them goodness, and by this help instructs them in a virtue which afterwards they practise upon other grounds, and without thinking of a penalty or bribe. And this is what we call a liberal education and a liberal service; the contrary service and obedience, whether towards God or man, being illiberal and unworthy of any honour or commendation.

In the case of religion, however, it must be considered that if by the hope of reward be understood the love and desire of virtuous enjoyment, or of the very practice and exercise of virtue in another life, the expectation or hope of this kind is so far from being derogatory to virtue, that it is an evidence of our loving it the more sincerely and for its own sake. Nor can this principle be justly called selfish; for if the love of virtue be not mere self-interest, the love and desire of life for virtue's sake cannot be esteemed so. But if the desire of life be only through the violence of that natural aversion to death, if it be through the love of something else than virtuous affection, or through the unwillingness of parting with something else than what is purely of this kind, then is it no longer any sign or token of real virtue.

Thus a person loving life for life's sake, and virtue not at all, may by the promise or hope of life, and fear of death or other evil, be induced to practise virtue, and even endeavour to be truly virtuous by a love of what he practises. Yet neither is this very endeavour to be esteemed a virtue. For though he may intend to be virtuous, he is not become so for having only intended or aimed at it through love of the reward. But as soon as he is come to have any affection towards what is morally good, and can like or affect such good for its own sake, as good and amiable in itself, then is he in some degree good and virtuous, and not till then.

Such are the advantages or disadvantages which accrue to virtue from reflection upon private good or interest. For though the habit of selfishness and the multiplicity of interested views are of little improvement to real merit or virtue, yet there is a necessity for the preservation of virtue, that it should be thought to have no quarrel with true interest and self-enjoyment.

Whoever, therefore, by any strong persuasion or settled judgment, thinks in the main that virtue causes happiness and vice misery, carries with him that security and assistance to virtue which is required. Or though he has no such thought, nor can believe virtue his real interest, either with respect to his own nature and constitution, or the circumstances of human life, yet if he believes any supreme powers concerned in the present affairs of mankind, immediately interposing in behalf of the honest and virtuous against the impious and unjust, this will serve to preserve in him, however, that just esteem of virtue which might otherwise considerably diminish. Or should he still believe little of the immediate interposition of Providence in the affairs of this present life, yet if he believes a God dispensing rewards and punishments to vice and virtue in a future, he carries with him still the same advantage and security, whilst his belief is steady and nowise wavering or doubtful. For it must be observed, that an expectation and dependency so miraculous and great as this, must naturally take off from other inferior dependencies and encouragements. Where infinite rewards are thus enforced, and the imagination strongly turned towards them, the other common and natural motives to goodness are apt to be neglected and lose much by disuse. Other interests are hardly so much as computed, whilst

CONCERNING VIRTUE OR MERIT

the mind is thus transported in the pursuit of a high advantage, and self-interest so narrowly confined within ourselves. On this account, all other affections towards friends, relations, or mankind are often slightly regarded, as being worldly and of little moment in respect of the interest of our soul. And so little thought is there of any immediate satisfaction arising from such good offices of life, that it is customary with many devout people zealously to decry all temporal advantages of goodness, all natural benefits of virtue, and magnifying the contrary happiness of a vicious state, to declare " that except only for the sake of future reward and fear of future punishment, they would divest themselves of all goodness at once, and freely allow themselves to be most immoral and profligate." From whence it appears that in some respects there can be nothing more fatal to virtue than the weak and uncertain belief of a future reward and punishment.[1] For the stress being laid wholly here, if this foundation come to fail, there is no further prop or security to men's morals. And thus virtue is supplanted and betrayed.

Now as to atheism; though it be plainly deficient and without remedy, in the case of ill judgment on the happiness of virtue, yet it is not, indeed, of necessity the cause of any such ill judgment. For without an absolute assent to any hypothesis of theism, the advantages of virtue may possibly be seen and owned, and a high opinion of it established in the mind. However, it must be confessed that the natural tendency of atheism is very different.

'Tis in a manner impossible to have any great opinion of the happiness of virtue without conceiving high thoughts of the satisfaction resulting from the generous admiration and love of it; and nothing beside the experience of such a love is likely to make this satisfaction credited. The chief ground and support therefore of this opinion of happiness in virtue must arise from the powerful feeling of this generous moral affection, and the

[1] *Essay on Wit and Humour*, part ii. § 3

knowledge of its power and strength. But this is certain, that it can be no great strengthening to the moral affection, no great support to the pure love of goodness and virtue, to suppose there is neither goodness nor beauty in the Whole itself; nor any example or precedent of good affection in any superior Being. Such a belief must tend rather to the weaning the affections from anything amiable or self-worthy, and to the suppressing the very habit and familiar custom of admiring natural beauties, or whatever in the order of things is according to just design, harmony, and proportion. For how little disposed must a person be to love or admire anything as orderly in the universe who thinks the universe itself a pattern of disorder? How unapt to reverence or respect any particular subordinate beauty of a part, when even the Whole itself is thought to want perfection, and to be only a vast and infinite deformity?

Nothing indeed can be more melancholy than the thought of living in a distracted universe, from whence many ills may be suspected, and where there is nothing good or lovely which presents itself, nothing which can satisfy in contemplation, or raise any passion besides that of contempt, hatred, or dislike. Such an opinion as this may by degrees embitter the temper, and not only make the love of virtue to be less felt, but help to impair and ruin the very principle of virtue, viz. natural and kind affection.

Upon the whole, whoever has a firm belief of a God whom he does not merely call good, but of whom in reality he believes nothing beside real good, nothing beside what is truly suitable to the exactest character of benignity and goodness; such a person believing rewards or retributions in another life, must believe them annexed to real goodness and merit, real villainy and baseness, and not to any accidental qualities or circumstances, in which respect they cannot properly be styled rewards or punishments, but capricious distributions of happiness or unhappiness to creatures. These are the only terms on which the belief of a world to come can happily influence the believer. And on these terms, and by virtue of this belief, man perhaps may retain his virtue and integrity, even under the hardest thoughts of human nature, when either by any ill circumstance or untoward doctrine he is brought to that unfortunate opinion of Virtue's being naturally an enemy to happiness in life.

This, however, is an opinion which cannot be supposed consistent with sound theism. For whatever be decided as to a future life, or the rewards and punishments of hereafter, he who, as a sound theist, believes a reigning mind sovereign in Nature, and ruling all things with the highest perfection of goodness, as well as of wisdom and power, must necessarily believe virtue to be naturally good and advantageous.[1] For what could more strongly imply an unjust ordinance, a blot and imperfection in the general constitution of things, than to suppose virtue the natural ill, and vice the natural good of any creature?

And now, last of all, there remains for us to consider a yet further advantage to virtue, in the theistical belief above the atheistical. The proposition may at first sight appear over-refined, and of a sort which is esteemed too nicely philosophical. But after what has been already examined, the subject perhaps may be more easily explained.

There is no creature, according to what has been already proved, who must not of necessity be ill in some degree, by having any affection or aversion in a stronger degree than is suitable to his own private good, or that of the system to which he is joined. For in either case the affection is ill and vicious. Now if a rational creature has that degree of aversion which is requisite to arm him against any particular misfortune, and alarm him against the approach of any calamity, this is regular and well. But if after the misfortune is happened, his aversion continues still, and his passion rather grows upon him, whilst he rages at the accident and exclaims against his private fortune

---

[1] [Cp. Spinoza, *Ethics*, part v. Prop. xli. and Scholium.]

or lot, this will be acknowledged both vicious in present and for the future, as it affects the temper, and disturbs that easy course of the affections on which virtue and goodness so much depend. On the other side, the patient enduring of the calamity, and the bearing up of the mind under it, must be acknowledged immediately virtuous and preservative of virtue. Now, according to the hypothesis of those who exclude a general mind, it must be confessed there can nothing happen in the course of things to deserve either our admiration and love or our anger and abhorrence. However, as there can be no satisfaction at the best in thinking upon what atoms and chance produce, so upon disastrous occasions, and under the circumstances of a calamitous and hard fortune, 'tis scarce possible to prevent a natural kind of abhorrence and spleen, which will be entertained and kept alive by the imagination of so perverse an order of things. But in another hypothesis (that of perfect theism) it is understood "that whatever the order of the world produces, is in the main both just and good." Therefore in the course of things in this world, whatever hardship of events may seem to force from any rational creature a hard censure of his private condition or lot, he may by reflection nevertheless come to have patience, and to acquiesce in it. Nor is this all. He may go further still in this reconciliation, and from the same principle may make the lot itself an object of his good affection, whilst he strives to maintain this generous fealty, and stands so well disposed towards the laws and government of his higher country.

Such an affection must needs create the highest constancy in any state of sufferance, and make us in the best manner support whatever hardships are to be endured for virtue's sake. And as this affection must of necessity cause a greater acquiescence and complacency with respect to ill accidents, ill men, and injuries, so of course it cannot fail of producing still a greater equality, gentleness, and benignity in the temper. Consequently the affection must be a truly good one, and a creature the more

CONCERNING VIRTUE OR MERIT

truly good and virtuous by possessing it. For whatsoever is the occasion or means of more affectionately uniting a rational creature to his part in society, and causes him to prosecute the public good or interest of his species with more zeal and affection than ordinary, is undoubtedly the cause of more than ordinary virtue in such a person.

This too is certain, that the admiration and love of order, harmony, and proportion, in whatever kind, is naturally improving to the temper, advantageous to social affection, and highly assistant to virtue, which is itself no other than the love of order and beauty in society. In the meanest subjects of the world, the appearance of order gains upon the mind and draws the affection towards it. But if the order of the world itself appears just and beautiful, the admiration and esteem of order must run higher, and the elegant passion or love of beauty, which is so advantageous to virtue, must be the more improved by its exercise in so ample and magnificent a subject. For 'tis impossible that such a divine order should be contemplated without ecstasy and rapture, since in the common subjects of science and the liberal arts, whatever is according to just harmony and proportion is so transporting to those who have any knowledge or practice in the kind.

Now if the subject and ground of this divine passion be not really just or adequate (the hypothesis of theism being supposed false) the passion still in itself is so far natural and good, as it proves an advantage to virtue and goodness, according to what has been above demonstrated. But if, on the other side, the subject of this passion be really adequate and just (the hypothesis of theism being real, and not imaginary), then is the passion also just, and becomes absolutely due and requisite in every rational creature.

Hence we may determine justly the relation which Virtue has to Piety, the first being not complete but in the latter, since where the latter is wanting, there can neither be the same benignity, firmness, or constancy, the same good composure of the affections or uniformity of mind.

And thus the perfection and height of virtue must be owing to the belief of a God.[1]

BOOK II

PART I

Section I

We have considered what virtue is and to whom the character belongs. It remains to inquire, what obligation there is to virtue, or what reason to embrace it.

We have found that, to deserve the name of good or virtuous, a creature must have all his inclinations and affections, his dispositions of mind and temper, suitable, and agreeing with the good of his kind, or of that system in which he is included, and of which he constitutes a part. To stand thus well affected, and to have one's affections right and entire, not only in respect of oneself but of society and the public, this is rectitude, integrity, or virtue. And to be wanting in any of these, or to have their contraries, is depravity, corruption, and vice.

It has been already shown, that in the passions and affections of particular creatures there is a constant relation to the interest of a species or common nature. This has been demonstrated in the case of natural affection, parental kindness, zeal for posterity, concern for the propagation and nurture of the young, love of fellowship and company, compassion, mutual succour, and the rest of this kind. Nor will any one deny that this affection of a creature towards the good of the species or common nature is as proper and natural to him as it is to any

[1] [Cp. Spinoza, *Ethics,* part iv. Prop. xxviii.]

organ, part, or member of an animal body, or mere vegetable, to work in its known course and regular way of growth. 'Tis not more natural for the stomach to digest, the lungs to breathe, the glands to separate juices, or other entrails to perform their several offices, however they may by particular impediments be sometimes disordered or obstructed in their operations.

There being allowed therefore in a creature such affections as these towards the common nature or system of the kind, together with those other which regard the private nature or self-system, it will appear that in following the first of these affections, the creature must on many occasions contradict and go against the latter. How else should the species be preserved? Or what would signify that implanted natural affection, by which a creature through so many difficulties and hazards preserves its offspring and supports its kind?

It may therefore be imagined, perhaps, that there is a plain and absolute opposition between these two habits or affections. It may be presumed that the pursuing the common interest or public good through the affections of one kind, must be a hindrance to the attainment of private good through the affections of another. For it being taken for granted that hazards and hardships of whatever sort are naturally the ill of the private state, and it being certainly the nature of those public affections to lead often to the greatest hardships and hazards of every kind, 'tis presently inferred "that 'tis the creature's interest to be without any public affection whatsoever."

This we know for certain, that all social love, friendship, gratitude, or whatever else is of this generous kind, does by its nature take place of the self-interesting passions, draws us out of ourselves, and makes us disregardful of our own convenience and safety. So that according to a known way of reasoning on self-interest,[1] that which is of a social kind in us should of

[1] [*i.e.* that of Hobbes. See the *Essay on Wit and Humour,* part ii. § 1, and part iii. § 3.]

right be abolished. Thus kindness of every sort, indulgence, tenderness, compassion, and, in short, all natural affection, should be industriously suppressed, and as mere folly and weakness of nature be resisted and overcome; that by this means there might be nothing remaining in us which was contrary to a direct self-end; nothing which might stand in opposition to a steady and deliberate pursuit of the most narrowly confined self-interest.

According to this extraordinary hypothesis, it must be taken for granted "that in the system of a kind or species, the interest of the private nature is directly opposite to that of the common one, the interest of particulars directly opposite to that of the public in general." A strange constitution! in which it must be confessed there is much disorder and untowardness, unlike to what we observe elsewhere in Nature. As if in any vegetable or animal body the part or member could be supposed in a good and prosperous state as to itself, when under a contrary disposition and in an unnatural growth or habit as to its whole.

Now that this is in reality quite otherwise, we shall endeavour to demonstrate, so as to make appear "that what men represent as an ill order and constitution in the universe, by making moral rectitude appear the ill, and depravity the good or advantage of a creature, is in Nature just the contrary. That to be well affected towards the public interest and one's own is not only consistent but inseparable; and that moral rectitude or virtue must accordingly be the advantage, and vice the injury and disadvantage of every creature."

Section II

There are few perhaps who, when they consider a creature void of natural affection and wholly destitute of a communicative or social principle, will suppose him at the same time either tolerably happy in himself, or as he stands abroad, with respect to his fellow-creatures or kind. 'Tis generally thought that such a creature as this feels slender joy in life, and finds little satisfaction in the mere sensual pleasures which remain with him, after the loss of social enjoyment and whatever can be called humanity or good nature. We know that to such a creature as this 'tis not only incident to be morose, rancorous, and malignant; but that of necessity a mind or temper thus destitute of mildness and benignity must turn to that which is contrary, and be wrought by passions of a different kind. Such a heart as this must be a continual seat of perverse inclinations and bitter aversions, raised from a constant ill-humour, sourness, and disquiet. The consciousness of such a nature, so obnoxious to mankind, and to all beings which approach it, must overcloud the mind with dark suspicion and jealousy, alarm it with fears and horror, and raise in it a continual disturbance, even in the most seeming fair and secure state of fortune, and in the highest degree of outward prosperity.

This, as to the complete immoral state, is what, of their own accord, men readily remark. Where there is this absolute degeneracy, this total apostasy from all candour, equity, trust, sociableness, or friendship, there are few who do not see and acknowledge the misery which is consequent. Seldom is the case misconstrued when at worst. The misfortune is, we look not on this depravity, nor consider how it stands, in less degrees. The calamity, we think, does not of necessity hold proportion with the injustice or iniquity. As if to be absolutely immoral and inhuman were indeed the greatest misfortune and misery; but that to be so in a little degree should be no misery nor harm at all. Which to allow, is just as reasonable as to own that 'tis the greatest ill of a body to be in the utmost manner distorted and maimed; but that to lose the use only of one limb, or to be impaired in some one single organ or member, is no inconvenience or ill worthy the least notice.

The parts and proportions of the mind, their mutual

relation and dependency, the connection and frame of those passions which constitute the soul or temper, may easily be understood by any one who thinks it worth his while to study this inward anatomy. 'Tis certain that the order or symmetry of this inward part is in itself no less real and exact than that of the body. However, 'tis apparent that few of us endeavour to become anatomists of this sort. Nor is any one ashamed of the deepest ignorance in such a subject. For though the greatest misery and ill is generally owned to be from disposition and temper; though 'tis allowed that temper may often change, and that it actually varies on many occasions, much to our disadvantage; yet how this matter is brought about we inquire not. We never trouble ourselves to consider thoroughly by what means or methods our inward constitution comes at any time to be impaired or injured. The *solutio continui*, which bodily surgeons talk of, is never applied in this case by surgeons of another sort. The notion of a whole and parts is not apprehended in this science. We know not what the effect is of straining any affection, indulging any wrong passion, or relaxing any proper and natural habit or good inclination. Nor can we conceive how a particular action should have such a sudden influence on the whole mind as to make the person an immediate sufferer. We suppose rather that a man may violate his faith, commit any wickedness unfamiliar to him before, engage in any vice or villainy, without the least prejudice to himself, or any misery naturally following from the ill action.

'Tis thus we hear it often said, "Such a person has done ill indeed; but what is he the worse for it?" Yet, speaking of any nature thoroughly savage, curst, and inveterate, we say truly, "Such a one is a plague and torment to himself." And we allow "that through certain humours or passions, and from temper merely, a man may be completely miserable, let his outward circumstances be ever so fortunate." These different judgments sufficiently demonstrate that we are not accustomed to think with much coherency on these moral subjects; and that our notions in this respect are not a little confused and contradictory.

Now if the fabric of the mind or temper appeared such to us as it really is; if we saw it impossible to remove hence any one good or orderly affection, or introduce any ill or disorderly one, without drawing on, in some degree, that dissolute state, which at its height is confessed to be so miserable; 'twould then undoubtedly be owned that since no ill, immoral, or unjust action could be committed without either a new inroad and breach on the temper and passions, or a farther advancing of that execution already begun, whoever did ill, or acted in prejudice of his integrity, good-nature, or worth, would of necessity act with greater cruelty towards himself than he who scrupled not to swallow what was poisonous, or who with his own hands should voluntarily mangle or wound his outward form or constitution, natural limbs or body.

Section III

It has been shown before, that no animal can be said properly to act otherwise than through affections or passions, such as are proper to an animal. For in convulsive fits, where a creature strikes either himself or others, 'tis a simple mechanism, an engine, or piece of clockwork, which acts, and not the animal.

Whatsoever therefore is done or acted by any animal as such, is done only through some affection or passion, as of fear, love, or hatred moving him.

And as it is impossible that a weaker affection should overcome a stronger, so it is impossible but that where the affections or passions are strongest in the main, and form in general the most considerable party, either by their force or number, thither the animal must incline: and according to this balance he must be governed and led to action.

SHAFTESBURY'S CHARACTERISTICS

The affections or passions which must influence and govern the animal are either—

1. The natural affections, which lead to the good of the public.

2. Or the self affections, which lead only to the good of the private.

3. Or such as are neither of these, nor tending either to any good of the public or private, but contrary-wise; and which may therefore be justly styled unnatural affections.

So that according as these affections stand, a creature must be virtuous or vicious, good or ill.

The latter sort of these affections, 'tis evident, are wholly vicious. The two former may be vicious or virtuous according to their degree.

It may seem strange, perhaps, to speak of natural affections as too strong, or of self affections as too weak. But to clear this difficulty we must call to mind what has been already explained, "That natural affection may, in particular cases, be excessive, and in an unnatural degree." As when pity is so overcoming as to destroy its own end, and prevent the succour and relief required; or as when love to the offspring proves such a fondness as destroys the parent, and consequently the offspring itself. And notwithstanding it may seem harsh to call that unnatural and vicious which is only an extreme of some natural and kind affection, yet 'tis most certain that wherever any single good affection of this sort is over-great, it must be injurious to the rest, and detract in some measure from their force and natural operation. For a creature possessed with such an immoderate degree of passion, must of necessity allow too much to that one, and too little to others of the same character, and equally natural and useful as to their end. And this must necessarily be the occasion of partiality and injustice whilst only one duty or natural part is earnestly followed, and other parts or duties neglected, which should accompany it, and perhaps take place and be preferred.

CONCERNING VIRTUE OR MERIT

This may well be allowed true in all other respects, since even religion itself, considered as a passion, not of the selfish but nobler kind, may in some characters be strained beyond its natural proportion, and be said also to be in too high a degree. For as the end of religion is to render us more perfect and accomplished in all moral duties and performances; if by the height of devout ecstasy and contemplation we are rather disabled in this respect, and rendered more unapt to the real duties and offices of civil life, it may be said that religion indeed is then too strong in us. For how, possibly, can we call this superstition, whilst the object of the devotion is acknowledged just and the faith orthodox? 'Tis only the excess of zeal which in this case is so transporting as to render the devout person more remiss in secular affairs, and less concerned for the inferior and temporal interests of mankind.

Now as in particular cases public affection, on the one hand, may be too high, so private affection may, on the other hand, be too weak. For if a creature be self-neglectful and insensible of danger, or if he want such a degree of passion in any kind as is useful to preserve, sustain, or defend himself, this must certainly be esteemed vicious in regard of the design and end of Nature. She herself discovers this in her known method and stated rule of operation. 'Tis certain that her provisionary care and concern for the whole animal must at least be equal to her concern for a single part or member. Now to the several parts she has given, we see proper affections, suitable to their interest and security, so that even without our consciousness they act in their own defence, and for their own benefit and preservation. Thus an eye, in its natural state, fails not to shut together of its own accord, unknowingly to us, by a peculiar caution and timidity, which if it wanted, however we might intend the preservation of our eye, we should not in effect be able to preserve it, by any observation or forecast of our own. To be wanting therefore in those principal affections which respect the good of the whole constitution, must be a vice and imperfection as great surely in the principal part (the soul or temper) as it is in any of those inferior and subordinate parts to want the self-preserving affections which are proper to them.

And thus the affections towards private good become necessary and essential to goodness. For though no creature can be called good or virtuous merely for possessing these affections, yet since it is impossible that the public good or good of the system can be preserved without them, it follows that a creature really wanting in them is in reality wanting in some degree to goodness and natural rectitude, and may thus be esteemed vicious and defective.

'Tis thus we say of a creature, in a kind way of reproof, that he is too good, when his affection towards others is so warm and zealous as to carry him even beyond his part; or when he really acts beyond it, not through too warm a passion of that sort, but through an over-cool one of another, or through want of some self-passion to restrain him within due bounds.

It may be objected here, that the having the natural affections too strong (where the self affections are overmuch so), or the having the self affections defective or weak (where the natural affections are also weak), may prove upon occasion the only cause of a creature's acting honestly and in moral proportion. For, thus, one who is to a fault regardless of his life, may with the smallest degree of natural affection do all which can be expected from the highest pitch of social love or zealous friendship. And thus, on the other hand, a creature excessively timorous may, by as exceeding a degree of natural affection, perform whatever the perfectest courage is able to inspire.

To this it is answered, that whenever we arraign any passion as too strong, or complain of any as too weak, we must speak with respect to a certain constitution or economy of a particular creature or species. For if a passion, leading to any right end, be only so much the more serviceable and effectual for being strong, if we may be assured that the strength of it will not be the occasion of any disturbance within, nor of any disproportion between itself and other affections, then consequently the passion, however strong, cannot be condemned as vicious. But if to have all the passions in equal proportion with it, be what the constitution of the creature cannot bear, so that only some passions are raised to this height, whilst others are not, nor can possibly be wrought up to the same proportion, then may those strong passions, though of the better kind, be called excessive. For being in unequal proportion to the others, and causing an ill balance in the affection at large, they must of course be the occasion of inequality in the conduct, and incline the party to a wrong moral practice.

But to show more particularly what is meant by the economy of the passions, from instances in the species or kinds below us.[1] As for the creatures who have no manner of power or means given them by Nature for their defence against violence, nor anything by which they can make themselves formidable to such as injure or offend them, 'tis necessary they should have an extraordinary degree of fear, but little or no animosity, such as might cause them to make resistance, or incline them to delay their flight. For in this their safety lies, and to this passion of fear is serviceable, by keeping the senses on the watch, and holding the spirits in readiness to give the start.

And thus timorousness, and an habitual strong passion of fear, may be according to the economy of a particular creature, both with respect to himself and to the rest of his species. On the other hand, courage may be contrary to his economy, and therefore vicious. Even in one and the same species, this is by Nature differently ordered, with respect to different sexes, ages, and growths. The tamer creatures of the grazing kind, who live in herds, are different from the wilder, who herd not, but live in pairs only, apart from company, as is natural and

---

[1] *Infra,* bk. ii. part ii. § 1; *Moralists,* part ii. § 4; *Misc.* iv. ch ii

suitable to their rapacious life. Yet is there found, even among the former inoffensive kind, a courage proportionable to their make and strength. At a time of danger, when the whole herd flies, the bull alone makes head against the lion, or other whatever invading beast of prey, and shows himself conscious of his make. Even the female of this kind is armed, we see, by Nature, in some degree, to resist violence, so as not to fly a common danger. As for a hind or doe, or any other inoffensive and mere defenceless creature, 'tis no way unnatural or vicious in them, when the enemy approaches, to desert their offspring, and fly for safety. But for creatures who are able to make resistance, and are by Nature armed offensively, be they of the poorest insect kind, such as bees or wasps, 'tis natural to them to be roused with fury, and at the hazard of their lives oppose any enemy or invader of their species. For by this known passion in the creature, the species itself is secured, when by experience 'tis found that the creature, though unable to repel the injury, yet voluntarily exposes his life for the punishment of the invader, and suffers not his kind to be injured with impunity. And of all other creatures, man is in this sense the most formidable, since if he thinks it just and exemplary, he may, possibly in his own or in his country's cause, revenge an injury on any one living, and by throwing away his own life (if he be resolute to that degree) is almost certain master of another's, however strongly guarded. Examples of this nature have often served to restrain those in power from using it to the utmost extent, and urging their inferiors to extremity.

Upon the whole, it may be said properly to be the same with the affections or passions in an animal constitution as with the cords or strings of a musical instrument. If these, though in ever so just proportion one to another, are strained beyond a certain degree, 'tis more than the instrument will bear: the lute or lyre is abused, and its effect lost. On the other hand, if while some of the strings are duly strained, others are not wound up to their due proportion, then is the instrument still in disorder, and its part ill performed. The several species of creatures are like different sorts of instruments; and even in the same species of creatures (as in the same sort of instrument) one is not entirely like the other, nor will the same strings fit each. The same degree of strength which winds up one, and fits the several strings to a just harmony and consort, may in another burst both the strings and instrument itself. Thus men who have the liveliest sense, and are the easiest affected with pain or pleasure, have need of the strongest influence or force of other affections, such as tenderness, love, sociableness, compassion, in order to preserve a right balance within, and to maintain them in their duty, and in the just performance of their part, whilst others, who are of a cooler blood, or lower key, need not the same allay or counterpart, nor are made by Nature to feel those tender and endearing affections in so exquisite a degree.

It might be agreeable, one would think, to inquire thus into the different tunings of the passions, the various mixtures and allays by which men become so different from one another. For as the highest improvements of temper are made in human kind, so the greatest corruptions and degeneracies are discoverable in this race. In the other species of creatures around us, there is found generally an exact proportionableness, constancy, and regularity in all their passions and affections; no failure in the care of the offspring or of the society to which they are united; no prostitution of themselves; no intemperance or excess in any kind. The smaller creatures, who live as it were in cities (as bees and ants), continue the same train and harmony of life, nor are they ever false to those affections which move them to operate towards their public good. Even those creatures of prey who live the farthest out of society, maintain, we see, such a conduct towards one another as is exactly suitable to the good of their own species. Whilst man, notwithstanding the assistance of religion and the direction of laws, is often found to live in less conformity with Nature, and by means of religion itself is often rendered the more barbarous and inhuman. Marks are set on men; distinctions formed; opinions decreed under the severest penalties; antipathies instilled, and aversions raised in men against the generality of their own species. So that 'tis hard to find in any region a human society which has human laws. No wonder if in such societies 'tis so hard to find a man who lives naturally and as a man.

But having shown what is meant by a passion's being in too high or in too low a degree; and that "to have any natural affection too high, or any self affection too low," though it be often approved as virtue, is yet, strictly speaking, a vice and imperfection; we come now to the plainer and more essential part of vice, and which alone deserves to be considered as such; that is to say—

1. "When either the public affections are weak or deficient.

2. "Or the private and self affections too strong.

3. "Or that such affections arise as are neither of these, nor in any degree tending to the support either of the public or private system."

Otherwise than thus, it is impossible any creature can be such as we call ill or vicious. So that if once we prove that it is really not the creature's interest to be thus viciously affected, but contrariwise, we shall then have proved "that it is his interest to be wholly good and virtuous," since in a wholesome and sound state of his affections, such as we have described, he cannot possibly be other than sound, good, and virtuous in his action and behaviour.

Our business, therefore, will be to prove—

1. "That to have the natural, kindly, or generous affections strong and powerful towards the good of the public, is to have the chief means and power of self-enjoyment"; and "that to want them, is certain misery and ill."

2. "That to have the private or self affections too strong,

or beyond their degree of subordinacy to the kindly and natural, is also miserable."

3. And "that to have the unnatural affections (viz. such as are neither founded on the interest of the kind or public, nor of the private person or creature himself) is to be miserable in the highest degree."

PART II

Section I

To begin therefore with this proof, "That to have the natural affections (such as are founded in love, complacency, good-will, and in a sympathy with the kind or species) is to have the chief means and power of self-enjoyment; and that to want them is certain misery and ill."

We may inquire first what those are which we call pleasures or satisfactions, from whence happiness is generally computed. They are (according to the common distinction) satisfactions and pleasures either of the body or of the mind.

That the latter of these satisfactions are the greatest, is allowed by most people, and may be proved by this: that whenever the mind, having conceived a high opinion of the worth of any action or behaviour, has received the strongest impression of this sort, and is wrought up to the highest pitch or degree of passion towards the subject, at such time it sets itself above all bodily pain as well as pleasure, and can be no way diverted from its purpose by flattery or terror of any kind. Thus we see Indians, barbarians, malefactors, and even the most execrable villains, for the sake of a particular gang or society, or through some cherished notion or principle of honour or gallantry, revenge or gratitude, embrace any manner of hardship, and defy torments and death. Whereas, on the other hand, a person being placed in all the happy circumstances of outward enjoyment, surrounded with everything which can allure or charm the sense, and being then actually in the very moment of such a pleasing indulgence, yet no sooner is there anything amiss within, no sooner has he conceived any internal ail or disorder, anything inwardly vexatious or distempered, than instantly his enjoyment ceases, the pleasure of sense is at an end, and every means of that sort becomes ineffectual, and is rejected as uneasy and subject to give distaste.

The pleasures of the mind being allowed, therefore, superior to those of the body, it follows "that whatever can create in any intelligent being a constant flowing series or train of mental enjoyments, or pleasures of the mind, is more considerable to his happiness than that which can create to him a like constant course or train of sensual enjoyments or pleasures of the body."

Now the mental enjoyments are either actually the very natural affections themselves in their immediate operation, or they wholly in a manner proceed from them, and are no other than their effects.

If so, it follows that, the natural affections duly established in a rational creature being the only means which can procure him a constant series or succession of the mental enjoyments, they are the only means which can procure him a certain and solid happiness.

Now, in the first place, to explain "how much the natural affections are in themselves the highest pleasures and enjoyments," there should methinks be little need of proving this to any one of human kind who has ever known the condition of the mind under a lively affection of love, gratitude, bounty, generosity, pity, succour, or whatever else is of a social or friendly sort. He who has ever so little knowledge of human nature is sensible what pleasure the mind perceives when it is touched in this generous way. The difference we find between solitude and company, between a common company and that of friends; the reference of almost all our pleasures to mutual converse, and the dependence they have on society either present or imagined; all these are sufficient proofs in our behalf.

CONCERNING VIRTUE OR MERIT

How much the social pleasures are superior to any other may be known by visible tokens and effects. The very outward features, the marks and signs which attend this sort of joy, are expressive of a more intense, clear, and undisturbed pleasure than those which attend the satisfaction of thirst, hunger, and other ardent appetites. But more particularly still may this superiority be known from the actual prevalence and ascendency of this sort of affection over all besides. Wherever it presents itself with any advantage, it silences and appeases every other motion of pleasure. No joy, merely of sense, can be a match for it. Whoever is judge of both the pleasures will ever give the preference to the former. But to be able to judge of both, 'tis necessary to have a sense of each. The honest man indeed can judge of sensual pleasure, and knows its utmost force. For neither is his taste or sense the duller; but, on the contrary, the more intense and clear on the account of his temperance and a moderate use of appetite. But the immoral and profligate man can by no means be allowed a good judge of social pleasure, to which he is so mere a stranger by his nature.

Nor is it any objection here, that in many natures the good affection, though really present, is found to be of insufficient force. For where it is not in its natural degree, 'tis the same indeed as if it were not, or had never been. The less there is of this good affection in any untoward creature, the greater the wonder is that it should at any time prevail; as in the very worst of creatures it sometimes will. And if it prevails but for once in any single instance, it shows evidently that if the affection were thoroughly experienced or known, it would prevail in all.

Thus the charm of kind affection is superior to all other pleasure, since it has the power of drawing from every other appetite or inclination. And thus in the case of love to the offspring and a thousand other instances, the charm is found to operate so strongly on the temper as, in the midst of other temptations, to render it susceptible of this passion alone;

which remains as the master-pleasure and conqueror of the rest.

There is no one who, by the least progress in science or learning, has come to know barely the principles of mathematics, but has found, that in the exercise of his mind on the discoveries he there makes, though merely of speculative truths, he receives a pleasure and delight superior to that of sense. When we have thoroughly searched into the nature of this contemplative delight, we shall find it of a kind which relates not in the least to any private interest of the creature, nor has for its object any self-good or advantage of the private system. The admiration, joy, or love turns wholly upon what is exterior and foreign to ourselves. And though the reflected joy or pleasure which arises from the notice of this pleasure once perceived, may be interpreted a self-passion or interested regard, yet the original satisfaction can be no other than what results from the love of truth, proportion, order and symmetry in the things without. If this be the case, the passion ought in reality to be ranked with natural affection. For having no object within the compass of the private system, it must either be esteemed superfluous and unnatural (as having no tendency towards the advantage or good of anything in Nature) or it must be judged to be what it truly is,[1] "A natural joy in the contemplation of those numbers, that harmony, proportion, and concord which supports the universal nature, and is essential in the constitution and form of every particular species or order of beings."

But this speculative pleasure, however considerable and valuable it may be, or however superior to any motion of mere sense, must yet be far surpassed by virtuous motion, and the exercise of benignity and goodness, where, together with the most delightful affection of the soul, there is joined a pleasing assent and approbation of the mind to what is acted in this good disposition and honest bent. For where is there on earth a fairer matter of speculation, a goodlier view or contemplation,

[1] *Misc.* ii. ch. i.

CONCERNING VIRTUE OR MERIT

than that of a beautiful, proportioned, and becoming action? Or what is there relating to us, of which the consciousness and memory is more solidly and lastingly entertaining?

We may observe that in the passion of love between the sexes, where, together with the affection of a vulgar sort, there is a mixture of the kind and friendly, the sense or feeling of this latter is in reality superior to the former; since often through this affection, and for the sake of the person beloved, the greatest hardships in the world have been submitted to, and even death itself voluntarily embraced without any expected compensation. For where should the ground of such an expectation lie? Not here in this world, surely; for death puts an end to all. Nor yet hereafter, in any other; for who has ever thought of providing a heaven or future recompense for the suffering virtue of lovers?

We may observe withal, in favour of the natural affections, that it is not only when joy and sprightliness are mixed with them that they carry a real enjoyment above that of the sensual kind. The very disturbances which belong to natural affection, though they may be thought wholly contrary to pleasure, yield still a contentment and satisfaction greater than the pleasures of indulged sense. And where a series or continued succession of the tender and kind affections can be carried on, even through fears, horrors, sorrows, griefs, the emotion of the soul is still agreeable. We continue pleased even with this melancholy aspect or sense of virtue. Her beauty supports itself under a cloud and in the midst of surrounding calamities. For thus when by mere illusion, as in a tragedy, the passions of this kind are skilfully excited in us, we prefer the entertainment to any other of equal duration. We find by ourselves that the moving our passions in this mournful way, the engaging them in behalf of merit and worth, and the exerting whatever we have of social affection and human sympathy, is of the highest delight, and affords a greater enjoyment in the way of thought and sentiment than anything besides can do in a way of sense and common appetite. And after this manner it appears "how much the mental enjoyments are actually the very natural affections themselves."

Now, in the next place, to explain "how they proceed from them, as their natural effects," we may consider first, that the effects of love or kind affection, in a way of mental pleasure, are "an enjoyment of good by communication. A receiving it, as it were, by reflection, or by way of participation in the good of others"; and "a pleasing consciousness of the actual love, merited esteem, or approbation of others."

How considerable a part of happiness arises from the former of these effects will be easily apprehended by one who is not exceedingly ill-natured. It will be considered how many the pleasures are of sharing contentment and delight with others; of receiving it in fellowship and company; and gathering it, in a manner, from the pleased and happy states of those around us, from accounts and relations of such happinesses, from the very countenances, gestures, voices and sounds, even of creatures foreign to our kind, whose signs of joy and contentment we can anyway discern. So insinuating are these pleasures of sympathy, and so widely diffused through our whole lives, that there is hardly such a thing as satisfaction or contentment of which they make not an essential part.

As for that other effect of social love, viz. the consciousness of merited kindness or esteem, 'tis not difficult to perceive how much this avails in mental pleasure, and constitutes the chief enjoyment and happiness of those who are, in the narrowest sense, voluptuous. How natural is it for the most selfish among us to be continually drawing some sort of satisfaction from a character, and pleasing ourselves in the fancy of deserved admiration and esteem? For though it be mere fancy, we endeavour still to believe it truth, and flatter ourselves all we can with the thought of merit of some kind, and the persuasion of our deserving well from some few at least with whom we happen to have a more intimate and familiar commerce.

What tyrant is there, what robber, or open violator of the laws of society, who has not a companion, or some particular set, either of his own kindred, or such as he calls friends, with whom he gladly shares his good, in whose welfare he delights, and whose joy and satisfaction he makes his own? What person in the world is there who receives not some impressions from the flattery or kindness of such as are familiar with him? 'Tis to this soothing hope and expectation of friendship that almost all our actions have some reference. 'Tis this which goes through our whole lives, and mixes itself even with most of our vices. Of this, vanity, ambition, and luxury have a share, and many other disorders of our life partake. Even the unchastest love borrows largely from this source. So that were pleasure to be computed in the same way as other things commonly are, it might properly be said, that out of these two branches (viz. community or participation in the pleasures of others, and belief of meriting well from others) would arise more than nine-tenths of whatever is enjoyed in life. And thus in the main sum of happiness there is scarce a single article but what derives itself from social love, and depends immediately on the natural and kind affections.

Now such as causes are, such must be their effects. And therefore as natural affection or social love is perfect or imperfect, so must be the content and happiness depending on it.

But lest any should imagine with themselves that an inferior degree of natural affection, or an imperfect partial regard of this sort, can supply the place of an entire, sincere, and truly moral one; lest a small tincture of social inclination should be thought sufficient to answer the end of pleasure in society, and give us that enjoyment of participation and community which is so essential to our happiness; we may consider first, that partial affection, or social love in part, without regard to a complete society or whole, is in itself an inconsistency, and implies an absolute contradiction. Whatever affection we have towards anything besides ourselves, if it be not of the natural sort towards the system or kind, it must be of all other affections the most dissociable, and destructive of the enjoyments of society. If it be really of the natural sort, and applied only to some one part of society, or of a species, but not to the species or society itself, there can be no more account given of it than of the most odd, capricious, or humorsome passion which may arise. The person, therefore, who is conscious of this affection can be conscious of no merit or worth on the account of it. Nor can the persons on whom this capricious affection has chanced to fall, be in any manner secure of its continuance of force. As it has no foundation or establishment in reason, so it must be easily removable, and subject to alteration without reason. Now the variableness of such sort of passion, which depends solely on capriciousness and humour, and undergoes the frequent successions of alternate hatred and love, aversion and inclination, must of necessity create continual disturbance and disgust, give an allay to what is immediately enjoyed in the way of friendship and society, and in the end extinguish, in a manner, the very inclination towards friendship and human commerce. Whereas, on the other hand, entire affection (from whence integrity has its name) as it is answerable to itself, proportionable, and rational, so it is irrefragable, solid, and durable. And as in the case of partiality, or vicious friendship, which has no rule or order, every reflection of the mind necessarily makes to its disadvantage and lessens the enjoyment, so in the case of integrity, the consciousness of just behaviour towards mankind in general, casts a good reflection on each friendly affection in particular, and raises the enjoyment of friendship still the higher, in the way of community or participation above mentioned.

And in the next place, as partial affection is fitted only to a short and slender enjoyment of those pleasures of sympathy or participation with others, so neither is it able to derive any considerable enjoyment from that other principal branch of human happiness, viz. consciousness of the actual or merited esteem of others. From whence should this esteem arise? The merit, surely, must in itself be mean, whilst the affection is so precarious and uncertain. What trust can there be to a mere casual inclination or capricious liking? Who can depend on such a friendship as is founded on no moral rule, but fantastically assigned to some single person, or small part of mankind, exclusive of society and the whole?

It may be considered, withal, as a thing impossible, that they who esteem or love by any other rule than that of virtue, should place their affection on such subjects as they can long esteem or love. 'Twill be hard for them, in the number of their so beloved friends, to find any in whom they can heartily rejoice, or whose reciprocal love or esteem they can sincerely prize and enjoy. Nor can those pleasures be sound or lasting which are gathered from a self-flattery and false persuasion of the esteem and love of others who are incapable of any sound esteem or love. It appears therefore how much the men of narrow or partial affection must be losers in this sense, and of necessity fall short in this second principal part of mental enjoyment.

Meanwhile entire affection has all the opposite advantages. It is equal, constant, accountable to itself, ever satisfactory and pleasing. It gains applause and love from the best, and in all disinterested cases from the very worst of men. We may say of it with justice, that it carries with it a consciousness of merited love and approbation from all society, from all intelligent creatures, and from whatever is original to all other intelligence. And if there be in Nature any such original, we may add that the satisfaction which attends entire affection is full and noble in proportion to its final object, which contains all perfection, according to the sense of theism above noted. For this, as has been shown, is the result of virtue. And to have this entire affection or integrity of mind is to live according to Nature, and the dictates and rules of supreme wisdom. This is morality, justice, piety, and natural religion.[1]

But lest this argument should appear perhaps too scholastically stated, and in terms and phrases which are not of familiar use, we may try whether possibly we can set it yet in a plainer light.

Let any one, then, consider well those pleasures which he receives either in private retirement, contemplation, study and converse with himself, or in mirth, jollity, and entertainment with others, and he will find that they are wholly founded in an easy temper, free of harshness, bitterness, or distaste; and in a mind or reason well composed, quiet, easy within itself, and such as can freely bear its own inspection and review. Now such a mind and such a temper, which fit and qualify for the enjoyment of the pleasures mentioned, must of necessity be owing to the natural and good affections.

As to what relates to temper, it may be considered thus. There is no state of outward prosperity or flowing fortune where inclination and desire are always satisfied, fancy and humour pleased. There are almost hourly some impediments or crosses to the appetite; some accidents or other from without, or something from within, to check the licentious course of the indulged affections. They are not always to be satisfied by mere indulgence. And when a life is guided by fancy only, there is sufficient ground of contrariety and disturbance. The very ordinary lassitudes, uneasinesses, and defects of disposition in the soundest body; the interrupted course of the humours or spirits in the healthiest people; and the accidental disorders common to every constitution, are sufficient, we know, on many occasions to breed uneasiness and distaste. And this in time must grow into a habit, where there is nothing to oppose its progress and hinder its prevailing on the temper. Now the only sound opposite to ill-humour is natural and kind affection.

[1] [Cp. Spinoza, *Ethics*, part iv. Prop. xxxv.]

CONCERNING VIRTUE OR MERIT

For we may observe, that when the mind upon reflection resolves at any time to suppress this disturbance already risen in the temper, and sets about this reforming work with heartiness and in good earnest, it can no otherwise accomplish the undertaking than by introducing into the affectionate part some gentle feeling of the social and friendly kind, some enlivening motion of kindness, fellowship, complacency, or love, to allay and convert that contrary motion of impatience and discontent.[1]

If it be said, perhaps, that in the case before us, religious affection or devotion is a sufficient and proper remedy, we answer, that 'tis according as the kind may happily prove. For if it be of the pleasant and cheerful sort, 'tis of the very kind of natural affection itself; if it be of the dismal or fearful sort;[2] if it brings along with it any affection opposite to manhood, generosity, courage, or free thought, there will be nothing gained by this application, and the remedy will, in the issue, be undoubtedly found worse than the disease. The severest reflections on our duty, and the consideration merely of what is by authority and under penalties enjoined, will not by any means serve to calm us on this occasion. The more dismal our thoughts are on such a subject, the worse our temper will be, and the readier to discover itself in harshness and austerity. If perhaps by compulsion, or through any necessity or fear incumbent, a different carriage be at any time affected, or different maxims owned, the practice at the bottom will be still the same. If the countenance be composed, the heart, however, will not be changed. The ill passion may for the time be withheld from breaking into action, but will not be subdued, or in the least debilitated against the next occasion. So that in such a breast as this, whatever devotion there may be, 'tis likely there will in time be little of an easy spirit or good temper remaining, and consequently few and slender enjoyments of a mental kind.

---

[1] [Cp. Spinoza, *Ethics*, part iv. Prop. vii.]
[2] *Letter Concerning Enthusiasm*, § 4; *Misc.* ii. ch. iii.

SHAFTESBURY'S CHARACTERISTICS

If it be objected, on the other hand, that though in melancholy circumstances ill-humour may prevail, yet in a course of outward prosperity, and in the height of fortune, there can nothing probably occur which should thus sour the temper and give it such disrelish as is suggested, we may consider, that the most humoured and indulged state is apt to receive the most disturbance from every disappointment or smallest ail. And if provocations are easiest raised, and the passions of anger, offence, and enmity are found the highest in the most indulged state of will and humour, there is still the greater need of a supply from social affection, to preserve the temper from running into savageness and inhumanity. And this the case of tyrants and most unlimited potentates may sufficiently verify and demonstrate.

Now as to the other part of our consideration, which relates to a mind or reason well composed and easy within itself, upon what account this happiness may be thought owing to natural affection, we may possibly resolve ourselves after this manner. It will be acknowledged that a creature such as man, who from several degrees of reflection has risen to that capacity which we call reason and understanding, must in the very use of this his reasoning faculty be forced to receive reflections back into his mind of what passes in itself, as well as in the affections or will; in short, of whatsoever relates to his character, conduct, or behaviour amidst his fellow-creatures and in society. Or should he be of himself unapt, there are others ready to remind him, and refresh his memory in this way of criticism. We have all of us remembrancers enow to help us in this work. Nor are the greatest favourites of Fortune exempted from this task of self-inspection. Even flattery itself, by making the view agreeable, renders us more attentive this way, and ensnares us in the habit. The vainer any person is, the more he has his eye inwardly fixed upon himself, and is after a certain manner employed in this home survey. And when a true regard to ourselves cannot oblige us to this inspection, a false

CONCERNING VIRTUE OR MERIT

regard to others and a fondness for reputation raises a watchful jealousy, and furnishes us sufficiently with acts of reflection on our own character and conduct.

In whatever manner we consider of this, we shall find still, that every reasoning or reflecting creature is by his nature forced to endure the review of his own mind and actions, and to have representations of himself and his inward affairs constantly passing before him, obvious to him, and revolving in his mind. Now as nothing can be more grievous than this is to one who has thrown off natural affection, so nothing can be more delightful to one who has preserved it with sincerity.

There are two things which to a rational creature must be horridly offensive and grievous, viz. "To have the reflection in his mind of any unjust action or behaviour which he knows to be naturally odious and ill-deserving; or of any foolish action or behaviour which he knows to be prejudicial to his own interest or happiness."

The former of these is alone properly called Conscience, whether in a moral or religious sense. For to have awe and terror of the Deity does not, of itself, imply conscience. No one is esteemed the more conscientious for the fear of evil spirits, conjurations, enchantments, or whatever may proceed from any unjust, capricious, or devilish nature. Now to fear God any otherwise than as in consequence of some justly blamable and imputable act, is to fear a devilish nature, not a divine one. Nor does the fear of hell or a thousand terrors of the Deity imply conscience, unless where there is an apprehension of what is wrong, odious, morally deformed, and ill-deserving. And where this is the case, there conscience must have effect, and punishment of necessity be apprehended, even though it be not expressly threatened.

And thus religious conscience supposes moral or natural conscience. And though the former be understood to carry with it the fear of divine punishment, it has its force however from the apprehended moral deformity and odiousness of any act with respect purely to the Divine Presence, and the natural veneration due to such a supposed being. For in such a presence the shame of villainy or vice must have its force, independently on that further apprehension of the magisterial capacity of such a being, and his dispensation of particular rewards or punishments in a future state.

It has been already said, that no creature can maliciously and intentionally do ill without being sensible at the same time that he deserves ill. And in this respect, every sensible creature may be said to have conscience. For with all mankind, and all intelligent creatures, this must ever hold, "That what they know they deserve from every one, that they necessarily must fear and expect from all." And thus suspicious and ill apprehensions must arise, with terror both of men and of the Deity. But besides this, there must in every rational creature be yet farther conscience, viz. from sense of deformity in what is thus ill-deserving and unnatural, and from a consequent shame or regret of incurring what is odious and moves aversion.

There scarcely is, or can be, any creature whom consciousness of villainy, as such merely, does not at all offend; nor anything opprobrious or heinously imputable move or affect. If there be such a one, 'tis evident he must be absolutely indifferent towards moral good or ill. If this indeed be his case, 'twill be allowed he can be no way capable of natural affection; if not of that, then neither of any social pleasure or mental enjoyment as shown above, but on the contrary, he must be subject to all manner of horrid, unnatural, and ill affection. So that to want conscience, or natural sense of the odiousness of crime and injustice, is to be most of all miserable in life; but where conscience or sense of this sort remains, there, consequently, whatever is committed against it must of necessity, by means of reflection, as we have shown, be continually shameful, grievous, and offensive.

A man who in a passion happens to kill his companion,

CONCERNING VIRTUE OR MERIT

relents immediately on the sight of what he has done. His revenge is changed into pity, and his hatred turned against himself. And this merely by the power of the object. On this account he suffers agonies: the subject of this continually occurs to him, and of this he has a constant ill remembrance and displeasing consciousness. If on the other side we suppose him not to relent or suffer any real concern or shame, then, either he has no sense of the deformity of the crime and injustice, no natural affection, and consequently no happiness or peace within; or if he has any sense of moral worth or goodness, it must be of a perplexed and contradictory kind. He must pursue an inconsistent notion, idolise some false species of virtue, and affect as noble, gallant, or worthy that which is irrational and absurd. And how tormenting this must be to him, is easy to conceive. For never can such a phantom as this be reduced to any certain form. Never can this Proteus of honour be held steady to one shape. The pursuit of it can only be vexatious and distracting. There is nothing beside real virtue (as has been shown) which can possibly hold any proportion to esteem, approbation, or good conscience. And he who, being led by false religion or prevailing custom, has learnt to esteem or admire anything as virtue which is not really such, must either through the inconsistency of such an esteem, and the perpetual immoralities occasioned by it, come at last to lose all conscience, and so be miserable in the worst way; or, if he retains any conscience at all, it must be of a kind never satisfactory, or able to bestow content. For 'tis impossible that a cruel enthusiast or bigot, a persecutor, a murderer, a bravo, a pirate, or any villain of less degree, who is false to the society of mankind in general, and contradicts natural affection, should have any fixed principle at all, any real standard or measure by which he can regulate his esteem, or any solid reason by which to form his approbation of any one moral act. And thus the more he sets up honour or advances zeal, the worse he renders his nature, and the more detestable his character. The more he engages in the love or admiration of any action or practice as great and glorious, which is in itself morally ill and vicious, the more contradiction and self-disapprobation he must incur. For there being nothing more certain than this, "That no natural affection can be contradicted, nor any unnatural one advanced, without a prejudice in some degree to all natural affection in general," it must follow, "That inward deformity growing greater by the encouragement of unnatural affection, there must be so much the more subject for dissatisfactory reflection, the more any false principle of honour, any false religion or superstition prevails."

So that whatever notions of this kind are cherished, or whatever character affected, which is contrary to moral equity and leads to inhumanity, through a false conscience, or wrong sense of honour, serves only to bring a man the more under the lash of real and just conscience, shame, and self-reproach. Nor can any one who, by any pretended authority, commits one single immorality, be able to satisfy himself with any reason why he should not at another time be carried further into all manner of villainy, such perhaps as he even abhors to think of. And this is a reproach which a mind must of necessity make to itself upon the least violation of natural conscience, in doing what is morally deformed and ill-deserving, though warranted by any example or precedent amongst men, or by any supposed injunction or command of higher powers.

Now, as for that other part of conscience, viz. the remembrance of what was at any time unreasonably and foolishly done in prejudice of one's real interest or happiness; this dissatisfactory reflection must follow still and have effect, wheresoever there is a sense of moral deformity contracted by crime and injustice. For even where there is no sense of moral deformity as such merely, there must be still a sense of the ill merit of it with respect to God and man. Or though there were a possibility of excluding for ever all thoughts or suspicions of any superior powers, yet considering that this insensibility

CONCERNING VIRTUE OR MERIT

towards moral good or ill implies a total defect in natural affection, and that this defect can by no dissimulation be concealed, 'tis evident that a man of this unhappy character must suffer a very sensible loss in the friendship, trust, and confidence of other men, and consequently must suffer in his interest and outward happiness. Nor can the sense of this disadvantage fail to occur to him, when he sees, with regret and envy, the better and more grateful terms of friendship and esteem on which better people live with the rest of mankind. Even therefore where natural affection is wanting, 'tis certain still, that by immorality, necessarily happening through want of such affection, there must be disturbance from conscience of this sort, viz. from sense of what is committed imprudently and contrary to real interest and advantage.

From all this we may easily conclude how much our happiness depends on natural and good affection. For if the chief happiness be from the mental pleasures, and the chief mental pleasures are such as we have described, and are founded in natural affection, it follows " that to have the natural affections is to have the chief means and power of self-enjoyment, the highest possession and happiness of life."

Now as to the pleasures of the body and the satisfactions belonging to mere sense, 'tis evident they cannot possibly have their effect or afford any valuable enjoyment otherwise than by the means of social and natural affection.

To live well has no other meaning with some people than to eat and drink well. And methinks 'tis an unwary concession we make in favour of these pretended good livers when we join with them in honouring their way of life with the title of living fast. As if they lived the fastest who took the greatest pains to enjoy least of life; for if our account of happiness be right, the greatest enjoyments in life are such as these men pass over in their haste, and have scarce ever allowed themselves the liberty of tasting.

But as considerable a part of voluptuousness as is founded

in the palate, and as notable as the science is which depends on it, one may justly presume that the ostentation of elegance, and a certain emulation and study how to excel in this sumptuous art of living, goes very far in the raising such a high idea of it as is observed among the men of pleasure. For were the circumstances of a table and company, equipages, services, and the rest of the management withdrawn, there would be hardly left any pleasure worth acceptance, even in the opinion of the most debauched themselves.

The very notion of a debauch (which is a sally into whatever can be imagined of pleasure and voluptuousness) carries with it a plain reference to society or fellowship. It may be called a surfeit or excess of eating and drinking, but hardly a debauch of that kind, when the excess is committed separately, out of all society or fellowship. And one who abuses himself in this way is often called a sot, but never a debauchee. The courtezans, and even the commonest of women, who live by prostitution, know very well how necessary it is that every one whom they entertain with their beauty should believe there are satisfactions reciprocal, and that pleasures are no less given than received. And were this imagination to be wholly taken away, there would be hardly any of the grosser sort of mankind who would not perceive their remaining pleasure to be of slender estimation.

Who is there can well or long enjoy anything, when alone, and abstracted perfectly, even in his very mind and thought, from everything belonging to society? Who would not, on such terms as these, be presently cloyed by any sensual indulgence? Who would not soon grow uneasy with his pleasure, however exquisite, till he had found means to impart it, and make it truly pleasant to him, by communicating and sharing it at least with some one single person? Let men imagine what they please, let them suppose themselves ever so selfish, or desire ever so much to follow the dictates of that narrow principle by which they would bring Nature under restraint,

CONCERNING VIRTUE OR MERIT

Nature will break out; and in agonies, disquiets, and a distempered state, demonstrate evidently the ill consequence of such violence, the absurdity of such a device, and the punishment which belongs to such a monstrous and horrid endeavour.

Thus, therefore, not only the pleasures of the mind, but even those of the body, depend on natural affection; insomuch that where this is wanting, they not only lose their force, but are in a manner converted into uneasiness and disgust. The sensations which should naturally afford contentment and delight produce rather discontent and sourness, and breed a wearisomeness and restlessness in the disposition. This we may perceive by the perpetual inconstancy and love of change so remarkable in those who have nothing communicative or friendly in their pleasures. Good fellowship, in its abused sense, seems indeed to have something more constant and determining. The company supports the humour. 'Tis the same in love. A certain tenderness and generosity of affection supports the passion, which otherwise would instantly be changed. The perfectest beauty cannot, of itself, retain or fix it. And that love which has no other foundation, but relies on this exterior kind, is soon turned into aversion. Satiety, perpetual disgust, and feverishness of desire attend those who passionately study pleasure. They best enjoy it who study to regulate their passions. And by this they will come to know how absolute an incapacity there is in anything sensual to please or give contentment, where it depends not on something friendly or social, something conjoined, and in affinity with kind or natural affection.

But ere we conclude this article of social or natural affection we may take a general view of it, and bring it once for all into the scale, to prove what kind of balance it helps to make within,[1] and what the consequence may be of its deficiency or light weight.

There is no one of ever so little understanding in what

[1] *Supra*, p. 289.

belongs to a human constitution who knows not that without action, motion, and employment the body languishes and is oppressed; its nourishment turns to disease; the spirits, unemployed abroad, help to consume the parts within; and Nature, as it were, preys upon herself. In the same manner, the sensible and living part, the soul or mind, wanting its proper and natural exercise, is burdened and diseased. Its thoughts and passions being unnaturally withheld from their due objects, turn against itself, and create the highest impatience and ill-humour.

In brutes and other creatures who have not the use of reason and reflection[1] (at least not after the manner of mankind) 'tis so ordered in Nature that by their daily search after food, and their application either towards the business of their livelihood or the affairs of their species or kind, almost their whole time is taken up, and they fail not to find full employment for their passion according to that degree of agitation to which they are fitted, and which their constitution requires. If any one of these creatures be taken out of his natural laborious state and placed amidst such a plenty as can profusely administer to all his appetites and wants, it may be observed that as his circumstances grow thus luxuriant, his temper and passions have the same growth. When he comes at any time to have the accommodations of life at a cheaper and easier rate than was at first intended him by Nature, he is made to pay dear for them in another way, by losing his natural good disposition and the orderliness of his kind or species.

This needs not to be demonstrated by particular instances. Whoever has the least knowledge of Natural History, or has been an observer of the several breeds of creatures, and their ways of life and propagation, will easily understand this difference of orderliness between the wild and the tame of the same species. The latter acquire new habits, and deviate from their original nature. They lose even the common instinct

---

[1] *Supra*, p. 289; and *Moralists*, part vi. § 4; and *Misc.* iv. ch. ii.

CONCERNING VIRTUE OR MERIT

and ordinary ingenuity of their kind, nor can they ever regain it whilst they continue in this pampered state; but being turned to shift abroad, they resume the natural affection and sagacity of their species. They learn to unite in stricter fellowship, and grow more concerned for their offspring. They provide against the seasons, and make the most of every advantage given by Nature for the support and maintenance of their particular species against such as are foreign and hostile. And thus as they grow busy and employed, they grow regular and good. Their petulancy and vice forsakes them with their idleness and ease.

It happens with mankind that whilst some are by necessity confined to labour, others are provided with abundance of all things by the pains and labour of inferiors. Now, if among the superior and easy sort there be not something of fit and proper employment raised in the room of what is wanting in common labour and toil; if instead of an application to any sort of work, such as has a good and honest end in society (as letters, sciences, arts, husbandry, public affairs, economy, or the like), there be a thorough neglect of all duty or employment; a settled idleness, supineness, and inactivity; this of necessity must occasion a most relaxed and dissolute state: it must produce a total disorder of the passions, and break out in the strangest irregularities imaginable.

We see the enormous growth of luxury in capital cities, such as have been long the seat of empire. We see what improvements are made in vice of every kind where numbers of men are maintained in lazy opulence and wanton plenty. 'Tis otherwise with those who are taken up in honest and due employment, and have been well inured to it from their youth. This we may observe in the hardy remote provincials, the inhabitants of smaller towns, and the industrious sort of common people, where 'tis rare to meet with any instances of those irregularities which are known in courts and palaces, and in the rich foundations of easy and pampered priests.

SHAFTESBURY'S CHARACTERISTICS

Now if what we have advanced concerning an inward constitution be real and just; if it be true that Nature works by a just order and regulation as well in the passions and affections as in the limbs and organs which she forms; if it appears withal that she has so constituted this inward part that nothing is so essential to it as exercise, and no exercise so essential as that of social or natural affection; it follows that where this is removed or weakened, the inward part must necessarily suffer and be impaired. Let indolence, indifference, or insensibility be studied as an art, or cultivated with the utmost care, the passions thus restrained will force their prison, and in one way or other procure their liberty and find full employment. They will be sure to create to themselves unusual and unnatural exercise where they are cut off from such as is natural and good. And thus in the room of orderly and natural affection, new and unnatural must be raised, and all inward order and economy destroyed.

One must have a very imperfect idea of the order of Nature in the formation and structure of animals to imagine that so great a principle, so fundamental a part as that of natural affection, should possibly be lost or impaired, without any inward ruin or subversion of the temper and frame of mind.

Whoever is the least versed in this moral kind of architecture, will find the inward fabric so adjusted, and the whole so nicely built, that the barely extending of a single passion a little too far, or the continuance of it too long, is able to bring irrecoverable ruin and misery. He will find this experienced in the ordinary case of frenzy and distraction, when the mind, dwelling too long upon one subject (whether prosperous or calamitous) sinks under the weight of it, and proves what the necessity is of a due balance and counterpoise in the affections. He will find that in every different creature and distinct sex there is a different and distinct order, set, or suit of passions, proportionable to the different order of life, the different functions and capacities assigned to each. As the operations and effects are different, so are the springs and causes in each system. The inside work is fitted to the outward action and performance. So that where habits or affections are dislodged, misplaced, or changed, where those belonging to one species are intermixed with those belonging to another, there must of necessity be confusion and disturbance within.

All this we may observe easily by comparing the more perfect with the imperfect natures, such as are imperfect from their birth, by having suffered violence within in their earliest form and inmost matrix. We know how it is with monsters, such as are compounded of different kinds or different sexes. Nor are they less monsters who are misshapen or distorted in an inward part. The ordinary animals appear unnatural and monstrous when they lose their proper instincts, forsake their kind, neglect their offspring, and pervert those functions or capacities bestowed by Nature. How wretched must it be, therefore, for man, of all other creatures, to lose that sense and feeling which is proper to him as a man, and suitable to his character and genius? How unfortunate must it be for a creature whose dependence on society is greater than any others, to lose that natural affection by which he is prompted to the good and interest of his species and community? Such indeed is man's natural share of this affection, that he, of all other creatures, is plainly the least able to bear solitude. Nor is anything more apparent than that there is naturally in every man such a degree of social affection as inclines him to seek the familiarity and friendship of his fellows. 'Tis here that he lets loose a passion, and gives reins to a desire which can hardly by any struggle or inward violence be withheld; or if it be, is sure to create a sadness, dejection, and melancholy in the mind. For whoever is unsociable, and voluntarily shuns society or commerce with the world, must of necessity be morose and ill-natured. He, on the other side, who is withheld by force or accident, finds in his temper the ill effects of this restraint. The inclination, when suppressed, breeds discontent, and on the contrary affords a healing and enlivening joy when acting at its liberty and with full scope; as we may see particularly when after a time of solitude and long absence the heart is opened, the mind disburdened, and the secrets of the breast unfolded to a bosom friend.

This we see yet more remarkably instanced in persons of the most elevated stations, even in princes, monarchs, and those who seem by their condition to be above ordinary human commerce, and who affect a sort of distant strangeness from the rest of mankind. But their carriage is not the same towards all men. The wiser and better sort, it is true, are often held at a distance, as unfit for their intimacy or secret trust. But to compensate this there are others substituted in their room, who though they have the least merit, and are perhaps the most vile and contemptible of men, are sufficient, however, to serve the purpose of an imaginary friendship, and can become favourites in form. These are the subjects of humanity in the great. For these we see them often in concern and pain; in these they easily confide; to these they can with pleasure communicate their power and greatness, be open, free, generous, confiding, bountiful, as rejoicing in the action itself; having no intention or aim beyond it; and their interest, in respect of policy, often standing a quite contrary way. But where neither the love of mankind nor the passion for favourites prevails, the tyrannical temper fails not to show itself in its proper colours and to the life, with all the bitterness, cruelty, and mistrust which belong to that solitary and gloomy state of uncommunicative and unfriendly greatness. Nor needs there any particular proof from history or present time to second this remark.

Thus it may appear how much natural affection is predominant: how it is inwardly joined to us, and implanted in our natures; how interwoven with our other passions, and how essential to that regular motion and course of our affections on which our happiness and self-enjoyment so immediately depend.

And thus we have demonstrated that as, on one side, to

have the natural and good affections is to have the chief means and power of self-enjoyment; so, on the other side, to want them is certain misery and ill.

SECTION II

WE are now to prove, that by having the self-passions too intense or strong, a creature becomes miserable.

In order to this we must, according to method, enumerate those home-affections which relate to the private interest or separate economy of the creature, such as love of life; resentment of injury; pleasure, or appetite towards nourishment and the means of generation; interest, or desire of those conveniences by which we are well provided for and maintained; emulation, or love of praise and honour; indolence, or love of ease and rest. These are the affections which relate to the private system, and constitute whatever we call interestedness or self-love.

Now these affections, if they are moderate and within certain bounds, are neither injurious to social life nor a hindrance to virtue; but being in an extreme degree, they become cowardice, revengefulness, luxury, avarice, vanity and ambition, sloth; and as such are owned vicious and ill with respect to human society. How they are ill also with respect to the private person, and are to his own disadvantage as well as that of the public, we may consider as we severally examine them.

If there were any of these self-passions which for the good and happiness of the creature might be opposed to natural affection, and allowed to over-balance it, the desire and love of life would have the best pretence. But it will be found perhaps that there is no passion which, by having much allowed to it, is the occasion of more disorder and misery.

There is nothing more certain or more universally agreed than this, "That life may sometimes be even a misfortune and misery." To enforce the continuance of it in creatures reduced to such extremity is esteemed the greatest cruelty. And though religion forbids that any one should be his own reliever, yet if by some fortunate accident, death offers of itself, it is embraced as highly welcome. And on this account the nearest friends and relations often rejoice at the release of one entirely beloved, even though he himself may have been so weak as earnestly to decline death, and endeavour the utmost prolongment of his own uneligible state.

Since life, therefore, may frequently prove a misfortune and misery, and since it naturally becomes so by being only prolonged to the infirmities of old age; since there is nothing, withal, more common than to see life over-valued, and purchased at such a cost as it can never justly be thought worth; it follows evidently that the passion itself (viz. the love of life, and abhorrence or dread of death) if beyond a certain degree, and over-balancing in the temper of any creature, must lead him directly against his own interest; make him, upon occasion, become the greatest enemy to himself, and necessitate him to act as such.

But though it were allowed the interest and good of a creature, by all courses and means whatsoever, in any circumstances or at any rate, to preserve life, yet would it be against his interest still to have this passion in a high degree. For it would by this means prove ineffectual, and no way conducing to its end. Various instances need not be given. For what is there better known, than that at all times an excessive fear betrays to danger instead of saving from it? 'Tis impossible for any one to act sensibly and with presence of mind, even in his own preservation and defence, when he is strongly pressed by such a passion. On all extraordinary emergencies 'tis courage and resolution saves, whilst cowardice robs us of the means of safety, and not only deprives us of our defensive faculties, but even runs us to the brink of ruin, and makes us meet that evil which of itself would never have invaded us.

But were the consequences of this passion less injurious than we have represented, it must be allowed still that in itself it can be no other than miserable, if it be misery to feel cowardice, and be haunted by those spectres and horrors which are proper to the character of one who has a thorough dread of death. For 'tis not only when dangers happen, and hazards are incurred, that this sort of fear oppresses and distracts. If it in the least prevails, it gives no quarter so much as at the safest, stillest hour of retreat and quiet. Every object suggests thought enough to employ it. It operates when it is least observed by others, and enters at all times into the pleasantest parts of life, so as to corrupt and poison all enjoyment and content. One may safely aver that by reason of this passion alone many a life, if inwardly and closely viewed, would be found to be thoroughly miserable, though attended with all other circumstances which in appearance render it happy. But when we add to this the meannesses and base condescensions occasioned by such a passionate concern for living, when we consider how by means of it we are driven to actions we can never view without dislike, and forced by degrees from our natural conduct into still greater crookednesses and perplexity, there is no one surely so disingenuous as not to allow that life in this case becomes a sorry purchase, and is passed with little freedom or satisfaction. For how can this be otherwise, whilst everything which is generous and worthy, even the chief relish, happiness, and good of life, is for life's sake abandoned and renounced?

And thus it seems evident " that to have this affection of desire and love of life too intense, or beyond a moderate degree, is against the interest of a creature, and contrary to his happiness and good."

There is another passion very different from that of fear and which in a certain degree is equally preservative to us, and conducing to our safety. As that is serviceable in prompting us to shun danger, so is this in fortifying us against it, and enabling us to repel injury and resist violence when offered. 'Tis true that according to strict virtue, and a just regulation of the affections in a wise and virtuous man, such efforts towards action amount not to what is justly styled passion or commotion. A man of courage may be cautious without real fear; and a man of temper may resist or punish without anger; but in ordinary characters there must necessarily be some mixture of the real passions themselves, which, however, in the main, are able to allay and temper one another. And thus anger in a manner becomes necessary. 'Tis by this passion that one creature offering violence to another is deterred from the execution, whilst he observes how the attempt affects his fellow, and knows by the very signs which accompany this rising motion, that if the injury be carried further it will not pass easily or with impunity. 'Tis this passion withal which, after violence and hostility executed, rouses a creature in opposition, and assists him in returning like hostility and harm on the invader. For thus, as rage and despair increase, a creature grows still more terrible, and being urged to the greatest extremity, finds a degree of strength and boldness unexperienced till then, and which had never risen except through the height of provocation. As to this affection therefore, notwithstanding its immediate aim be indeed the ill or punishment of another, yet it is plainly of the sort of those which tend to the advantage and interest of the self-system, the animal himself, and is withal in other respects contributing to the good and interest of the species. But there is hardly need we should explain how mischievous and self-destructive anger is, if it be what we commonly understand by that word: if it be such a passion as is rash and violent in the instant of provocation, or such as imprints itself deeply, and causes a settled revenge and an eager vindicative pursuit. No wonder indeed that so much is done in mere revenge, and under the weight of a deep resentment, when the relief and satisfaction found in that indulgence is no other than the assuaging of the most torturous pain, and the alleviating the most weighty and pressing sensation of misery. The pain of this sort being for awhile removed or alleviated by the accomplishment of the desire in the ill of

CONCERNING VIRTUE OR MERIT

another, leaves indeed behind it the perception of a delicious ease, and an over-flowing of soft and pleasing sensation. Yet is this, in truth, no better than the rack itself. For whoever has experienced racking pains, can tell in what manner a sudden cessation or respite is used to affect him. From hence are those untoward delights of perverseness, frowardness, and an envenomed malignant disposition acting at its liberty. For this is only a perpetual assuaging of anger perpetually renewed. In other characters, the passion arises not so suddenly or on slight causes, but being once moved, is not so easily quieted. The dormant fury, Revenge, being raised once, and wrought up to her highest pitch, rests not till she attains her end; and, that attained, is easy and reposes, making our succeeding relief and ease so much the more enjoyed as our preceding anguish and incumbent pain was of long duration and bitter sense. Certainly if among lovers, and in the language of gallantry, the success of ardent love is called the assuaging of a pain, this other success may be far more justly termed so. However soft or flattering the former pain may be esteemed, this latter surely can be no pleasing one; nor can it be possibly esteemed other than sound and thorough wretchedness, a grating and disgustful feeling, without the least mixture of anything soft, gentle, or agreeable.

'Tis not very necessary to mention the ill effects of this passion in respect of our minds or bodies, our private condition, or circumstances of life. By these particulars we may grow too tedious. These are of the moral sort of subjects, joined commonly with religion, and treated so rhetorically and with such enforced repetition in public as to be apt to raise the satiety of mankind. What has been said may be enough perhaps to make this evident, " That to be subject to such a passion as we have been mentioning, is in reality to be very unhappy"; and " that the habit itself is a disease of the worst sort, from which misery is inseparable."

Now as to luxury, and what the world calls pleasure: were

it true (as has been proved the contrary) that the most considerable enjoyments were those merely of the sense; and were it true, withal, that those enjoyments of the sense lay in certain outward things capable of yielding always a due and certain portion of pleasure, according to their degree and quality, it would then follow that the certain way to obtain happiness would be to procure largely of these subjects to which happiness and pleasure were thus infallibly annexed. But however fashionably we may apply the notion of good living, 'twill hardly be found that our inward faculties are able to keep pace with these outward supplies of a luxuriant fortune. And if the natural disposition and aptness from within be not concurring, 'twill be in vain that these subjects are thus multiplied from abroad, and acquired with ever so great facility.

It may be observed in those who by excess have gained a constant nauseating and distaste, that they have nevertheless as constant a craving or eagerness of stomach. But the appetite of this kind is false and unnatural, as is that of thirst arising from a fever, or contracted by habitual debauch. Now the satisfactions of the natural appetite, in a plain way, are infinitely beyond those indulgences of the most refined and elegant luxury. This is often perceived by the luxurious themselves. It has been experienced in people bred after the sumptuous way, and used never to wait, but to prevent appetite, that when by any new turn of life they came to fall into a more natural course, or for awhile, as on a journey, or a day of sport, came accidentally to experience the sweet of a plain diet, recommended by due abstinence and exercise, they have with freedom owned that it was then they received the highest satisfaction and delight which a table could possibly afford.

On the other side, it has been as often remarked in persons accustomed to an active life and healthful exercise, that having once thoroughly experienced this plainer and more natural diet, they have upon a following change of life regretted their loss, and undervalued the pleasures received from all the delicacies of luxury in comparison with those remembered satisfactions of a preceding state. 'Tis plain that by urging Nature, forcing the appetite, and inciting sense, the keenness of the natural sensations is lost. And though through vice or ill habit the same subjects of appetite may every day be sought with less satisfaction; though the impatience of abstaining be greater, the pleasure of indulgence is really less; the palls or nauseatings which continually intervene are of the worst and most hateful kind of sensation. Hardly is there anything tasted which is wholly free from this ill relish of a surfeited sense and ruined appetite. So that instead of a constant and flowing delight afforded in such a state of life, the very state itself is in reality a sickness and infirmity, a corruption of pleasure, and destructive of every natural and agreeable sensation. So far is it from being true "that in this licentious course we enjoy life best, or are likely to make the most of it."

As to the consequences of such an indulgence: how fatal to the body, by diseases of many kinds, and to the mind, by sottishness and stupidity; this needs not any explanation.

The consequences as to interest are plain enough. Such a state of impotent and unrestrained desire, as it increases our wants, so it must subject us to a greater dependence on others. Our private circumstances, however plentiful or easy they may be, can less easily content us. Ways and means must be invented to procure what may administer to such an imperious luxury as forces us to sacrifice honour to fortune, and runs us out into all irregularity and extravagance of conduct. The injuries we do ourselves, by excess and unforbearance, are then surely apparent, when through an impotence of this sort, and an impossibility of restraint, we do what we ourselves declare to be destructive to us. But these are matters obvious of themselves. And from less than what has been said 'tis easy to conclude "that luxury, riot, and debauch are contrary to real interest, and to the true enjoyment of life."

There is another luxury superior to the kind we have been mentioning, and which in strictness can scarce be called a self-passion, since the sole end of it is the advantage and promotion of the species. But whereas all other social affections are joined only with a mental pleasure, and founded in mere kindness and love, this has more added to it and is joined with a pleasure of sense. Such concern and care has Nature shown for the support and maintenance of the several species, that by a certain indigence[1] and kind of necessity of their natures they are made to regard the propagation of their kind. Now whether it be the interest or good of the animal to feel this indigence beyond a natural and ordinary degree, is what we may consider.

Having already said so much concerning natural and unnatural appetite, there needs less to be said on this occasion. If it be allowed that to all other pleasures there is a measure of appetite belonging, which cannot possibly be exceeded without prejudice to the creature, even in his very capacity of enjoying pleasure, it will hardly be thought that there is no certain limit or just boundary of this other appetite of the amorous kind. There are other sorts of ardent sensations accidentally experienced, which we find pleasant and acceptable whilst they are held within a certain degree; but which, as they increase, grow oppressive and intolerable. Laughter provoked by titillation grows an excessive pain, though it retains still the same features of delight and pleasure. And though in the case of that particular kind of itch which belongs to a distemper named from that effect, there are some who, far from disliking the sensation, find it highly acceptable and delightful, yet it will hardly be reputed such among the more refined sort, even of those who make pleasure their chief study and highest good.

Now if there be in every sensation of mere pleasure a certain pitch or degree of ardour, which by being further advanced

[1] [In the common Latin sense, *indigentia est libido inexplebilis.*—Cicero.]

comes the nearer to mere rage and fury; if there be indeed a necessity of stopping somewhere, and determining on some boundary for the passion; where can we fix our standard, or how regulate ourselves but with regard to Nature, beyond which there is no measure or rule of things? Now Nature may be known from what we see of the natural state of creatures, and of man himself, when unprejudiced by vicious education.

Where happily any one is bred to a natural life, inured to honest industry and sobriety, and unaccustomed to anything immoderate or intemperate, he is found to have his appetites and inclinations of this sort at command. Nor are they on this account less able to afford him the pleasure or enjoyment of each kind. On the contrary, as they are more sound, healthy, and uninjured by excess and abuse, they must afford him proportionate satisfaction. So that were both these sensations to be experimentally compared; that of a virtuous course which belonged to one who lived a natural and regular life, and that of a vicious course which belonged to one who was relaxed and dissolute; there is no question but judgment would be given in favour of the former, without regard to consequences, and only with respect to the very pleasure of sense itself.

As to the consequences of this vice, with respect to the health and vigour of the body, there is no need to mention anything. The injury it does the mind, though less noticed, is yet greater. The hindrance of all improvement, the wretched waste of time, the effeminacy, sloth, supineness, the disorder and looseness of a thousand passions through such a relaxation and enervating of the mind, are all of them effects sufficiently apparent when reflected on.

What the disadvantages are of this intemperance, in respect of interest, society, and the world; and what the advantages are of a contrary sobriety and self-command, would be to little purpose to mention. 'Tis well known there can be no slavery greater than what is consequent to the dominion and rule of such a passion. Of all other, it is the least manageable by favour or concession, and assumes the most from privilege and indulgence. What it costs us in the modesty and ingenuity of our natures, and in the faith and honesty of our characters, is as easily apprehended by any one who will reflect. And it will from hence appear "that there is no passion which in its extravagance and excess more necessarily occasions disorder and unhappiness."

Now as to that passion which is esteemed peculiarly interesting, as having for its aim the possession of wealth, and what we call a settlement or fortune in the world: if the regard towards this kind be moderate and in a reasonable degree; if it occasions no passionate pursuit, nor raises any ardent desire or appetite; there is nothing in this case which is not compatible with virtue, and even suitable and beneficial to society. The public as well as private system is advanced by the industry which this affection excites. But if it grows at length into a real passion, the injury and mischief it does the public is not greater than that which it creates to the person himself. Such a one is in reality a self-oppressor, and lies heavier on himself than he can ever do on mankind.

How far a coveting or avaricious temper is miserable, needs not surely be explained. Who knows not how small a portion of worldly matters is sufficient for a man's single use and convenience; and how much his occasions and wants might be contracted and reduced if a just frugality were studied, and temperance and a natural life came once to be pursued with half that application, industry, and art which is bestowed on sumptuousness and luxury? Now if temperance be in reality so advantageous, and the practice as well as the consequences of it so pleasing and happy, as has been before expressed, there is little need, on the other side, to mention anything of the miseries attending those covetous and eager desires after things which have no bounds or rule; as being out of Nature, beyond which there can be no limits to desire. For where shall we once stop when we are beyond this boundary? How shall we fix or ascertain a thing wholly unnatural and unreasonable? Or what method, what regulation, shall we set to mere imagination, or the exorbitancy of fancy, in adding expense to expense, or possession to possession.

Hence that known restlessness of covetous and eager minds in whatever state or degree of fortune they are placed; there being no thorough or real satisfaction, but a kind of insatiableness belonging to this condition. For 'tis impossible there should be any real enjoyment except in consequence of natural and just appetite. Nor do we readily call that an enjoyment of wealth or of honour when through covetousness or ambition the desire is still forward, and can never rest satisfied with its gains. But against this vice of covetousness there is enough said continually in the world, and in our common way of speaking "a covetous and a miserable temper has, in reality, one and the same signification."

Nor is there less said abroad as to the ills of that other aspiring temper, which exceeds an honest emulation or love of praise, and passes the bounds even of vanity and conceit. Such is that passion which breaks into an enormous pride and ambition. Now if we consider once the ease, happiness, and security which attend a modest disposition and quiet mind, such as is of easy self-command, fitted to every station in society, and able to suit itself with any reasonable circumstances whatever, 'twill on the first view present us with the most agreeable and winning character. Nor will it be found necessary after this to call to mind the excellence and good of moderation, or the mischief and self-injury of immoderate desires, and conceited fond imagination of personal advantage, in such things as titles, honours, precedencies, fame, glory, or vulgar astonishment, admiration, and applause.

This too is obvious, that as the desires of this kind are raised and become impetuous, and out of our command, so the aversions and fears of the contrary part grow proportionably strong and violent, and the temper accordingly suspicious, jealous, captious, subject to apprehensions from all events, and incapable of bearing the least repulse or ordinary disappointment. And hence it may be concluded "that all rest and security as to what is future, and all peace, contentedness, and ease as to what is present, is forfeited by the aspiring passions of this emulous kind; and by having the appetites towards glory and outward appearance thus transporting and beyond command."

There is a certain temper placed often in opposition to those eager and aspiring aims of which we have been speaking. Not that it really excludes either the passion of covetousness or ambition, but because it hinders their effects, and keeps them from breaking into open action. 'Tis this passion which by soothing the mind and softening it into an excessive love of rest and indolence, renders high attempts impracticable, and represents as insuperable the difficulties of a painful and laborious course towards wealth and honours. Now though an inclination to ease, and a love of moderate recess and rest from action, be as natural and useful to us as the inclination we have towards sleep, yet an excessive love of rest, and a contracted aversion to action and employment, must be a disease in the mind equal to that of a lethargy in the body.

How necessary action and exercise are to the body may be judged by the difference we find between those constitutions which are accustomed, and those which are wholly strangers to it; and by the different health and complexion which labour and due exercise create, in comparison with that habit of body we see consequent to an indulged state of indolence and rest. Nor is the lazy habit ruinous to the body only. The languishing disease corrupts all the enjoyments of a vigorous and healthy sense, and carries its infection into the mind, where it spreads a worse contagion. For however the body may for awhile hold out, 'tis impossible that the mind, in which the distemper is seated, can escape without an immediate affliction and disorder. The habit begets a tediousness and anxiety, which influences the whole temper, and converts the unnatural rest into an unhappy sort of activity, ill-humour, and spleen, of which there has been enough said above, where we considered the want of a due balance in the affections.

'Tis certain that as in the body, when no labour or natural exercise is used, the spirits which want their due employment turn against the constitution, and find work for themselves in a destructive way, so in a soul or mind unexercised, and which languishes for want of proper action and employment, the thoughts and affections being obstructed in their due course, and deprived of their natural energy, raise disquiet, and foment a rancorous eagerness and tormenting irritation. The temper from hence becomes more impotent in passion, more incapable of real moderation, and, like prepared fuel, readily takes fire by the least spark.

As to interest, how far it is here concerned: how wretched that state is in which by this habit a man is placed towards all the circumstances and affairs of life when at any time he is called to action; how subjected he must be to all inconveniencies, wanting to himself, and deprived of the assistance of others; whilst being unfit for all offices and duties of society he yet of any other person most needs the help of it, as being least able to assist or support himself; all this is obvious. And thus 'tis evident "that to have this over-biassing inclination towards rest, this slothful, soft, or effeminate temper, averse to labour and employment, is to have an unavoidable mischief and attendant plague."

Thus have we considered the self-passions, and what the consequence is of their rising beyond a moderate degree. These affections, as self-interesting as they are, can often, we see, become contrary to our real interest. They betray us into most misfortunes and into the greatest of unhappinesses, that of a profligate and abject character. As they grow imperious and high, they are the occasion that a creature in proportion becomes mean and low. They are original to that which we call selfishness, and give rise to that sordid disposition of which we have already spoken. It appears there can be nothing so miserable in itself, or so wretched in its consequence, as to be thus impotent in temper, thus mastered by passion, and by means of it brought under the most servile subjection to the world.

'Tis evident, withal, that as this selfishness increases in us, so must a certain subtlety and feignedness of carriage which naturally accompanies it. And thus the candour and ingenuity of our natures, the ease and freedom of our minds, must be forfeited; all trust and confidence in a manner lost, and suspicions, jealousies, and envies multiplied. A separate end and interest must be every day more strongly formed in us; generous views and motives laid aside; and the more we are thus sensibly disjoined every day from society and our fellows, the worse opinion we shall have of those uniting passions which bind us in strict alliance and amity with others. Upon these terms we must of course endeavour to silence and suppress our natural and good affections, since they are such as would carry us to the good of society against what we fondly conceive to be our private good and interest, as has been shown.

Now if these selfish passions, besides what other ill they are the occasion of, are withal the certain means of losing us our natural affections; then (by what has been proved before) 'tis evident "that they must be the certain means of losing us the chief enjoyment of life, and raising in us those horrid and unnatural passions, and that savageness of temper, which makes the greatest of miseries and the most wretched state of life," as remains for us to explain.

Section III

The passions, therefore, which in the last place we are to examine, are those which lead neither to a public nor a private good, and are neither of any advantage to the species in general nor the creature in particular. These, in opposition to the social and natural, we call the unnatural affections.

Of this kind is that unnatural and inhuman delight in beholding torments, and in viewing distress, calamity, blood, massacre and destruction, with a peculiar joy and pleasure. This has been the reigning passion of many tyrants and barbarous nations, and belongs in some degree to such tempers as have thrown off that courteousness of behaviour which retains in us a just reverence of mankind, and prevents the growth of harshness and brutality. This passion enters not where civility or affable manners have the least place. Such is the nature of what we call good breeding, that in the midst of many other corruptions it admits not of inhumanity or savage pleasure. To see the sufferance of an enemy with cruel delight may proceed from the height of anger, revenge, fear, and other extended self-passions; but to delight in the torture and pain of other creatures indifferently, natives or foreigners, of our own or of another species, kindred or no kindred, known or unknown; to feed as it were on death, and be entertained with dying agonies; this has nothing in it accountable in the way of self-interest or private good above mentioned, but is wholly and absolutely unnatural, as it is horrid and miserable.

There is another affection nearly related to this, which is a gay and frolicsome delight in what is injurious to others; a sort of wanton mischievousness, and pleasure in what is destructive; a passion which, instead of being restrained, is usually encouraged in children;[1] so that 'tis indeed no wonder if the effects of it are very unfortunately felt in the world. For 'twill be hard, perhaps, for any one to give a reason why that temper which was used to delight in disorder and ravage when in a nursery,

---

[1] [This is one of the testimonies which prove a distinct change for the better to have taken place in the ordinary parental attitude towards the characters of children. Compare Montaigne, *Essais*, I. xxii. as to the usages of his day: "It is a pastime for mothers to see a child wring

should not afterwards find delight in other disturbances, and be the occasion of equal mischief in families, amongst friends, and in the public itself. But of this passion there is not any foundation in Nature, as has been explained.

Malice, malignity or ill-will, such as is grounded on no self-consideration, and where there is no subject of anger or jealousy, nor anything to provoke or cause such a desire of doing ill to another, this also is of that kind of passion.

Envy too, when it is such as arises from the prosperity or happiness of another creature no ways interfering with ours, is of the same kind of passion.

There is also among these a sort of hatred of mankind and society, a passion which has been known perfectly reigning in some men, and has had a peculiar name given to it. A large share of this belongs to those who have long indulged themselves in a habitual moroseness, or who by force of ill-nature and ill-breeding have contracted such a reverse of affability and civil manners that to see or meet a stranger is offensive. The very aspect of mankind is a disturbance to them, and they are sure always to hate at first sight. The distemper of this kind is sometimes found to be in a manner national, but peculiar to the more savage nations, and a plain characteristic of uncivilised manners and barbarity. This is the immediate opposite to that noble affection which in ancient language was termed hospitality,[1] viz. extensive love of mankind and relief of strangers.

We may add likewise to the number of the unnatural passions all those which are raised from superstition (as before mentioned) and from the customs of barbarous countries; all

the neck of a chicken, and struggle to hurt a dog or cat; and a father can be found fool enough to take it as good promise of a martial spirit when he sees his son beating a peasant or a lacquey who does not resist; and as proof of cleverness when he sees him overreach a companion by some malicious disloyalty or treachery" (Ed. Firmin-Didot, 1882, vol. i. p. 88). Montaigne and Shaftesbury agree in their comment.]

[1] *Misc.* iii. ch. i. in the notes.

which are too horrid and odious in themselves to need any proof of their being miserable.

There might be other passions named, such as unnatural lusts, in foreign kinds or species, with other perversions of the amorous desire within our own. But as to these depravities of appetite we need add nothing here, after what has been already said on the subject of the more natural passion.

Such as these are the only affections or passions we can strictly call unnatural, ill, and of no tendency so much as to any separate or private good. Others indeed there are which have this tendency, but are so exorbitant and out of measure, so beyond the common bent of any ordinary self-passion, and so utterly contrary and abhorrent to all social and natural affection, that they are generally called, and may be justly esteemed, unnatural and monstrous.

Among these may be reckoned such an enormous pride or ambition, such an arrogance and tyranny, as would willingly leave nothing eminent, nothing free, nothing prosperous in the world; such an anger as would sacrifice everything to itself; such a revenge as is never to be extinguished, nor ever satisfied without the greatest cruelties; such an inveteracy and rancour as seeks, as it were, occasion to exert itself, and lays hold of the least subject, so as often to make the weight of its malevolence fall even upon such as are mere objects of pity and compassion.

Treachery and ingratitude are in strictness mere negative vices, and in themselves no real passions, having neither aversion nor inclination belonging to them, but are derived from the defect, unsoundness, or corruption of the affections in general. But when these vices become remarkable in a character, and arise in a manner from inclination and choice; when they are so forward and active as to appear of their own accord, without any pressing occasion; 'tis apparent they borrow something of the mere unnatural passions, and are derived from malice, envy, and inveteracy, as explained above.

It may be objected here that these passions, unnatural as

they are, carry still a sort of pleasure with them, and that however barbarous a pleasure it be, yet still it is a pleasure and satisfaction which is found in pride, or tyranny, revenge, malice, or cruelty exerted. Now if it be possible in Nature that any one can feel a barbarous or malicious joy otherwise than in consequence of mere anguish and torment, then may we perhaps allow this kind of satisfaction to be called pleasure or delight. But the case is evidently contrary. To love, and to be kind; to have social or natural affection, complacency, and good-will, is to feel immediate satisfaction and genuine content. 'Tis in itself original joy, depending on no preceding pain or uneasiness, and producing nothing beside satisfaction merely. On the other side, animosity, hatred, and bitterness, is original misery and torment, producing no other pleasure or satisfaction than as the unnatural desire is for the instant satisfied by something which appeases it. How strong soever this pleasure therefore may appear, it only the more implies the misery of that state which produces it. For as the cruellest bodily pains do by intervals of assuagement produce (as has been shown) the highest bodily pleasure, so the fiercest and most raging torments of the mind do, by certain moments of relief, afford the greatest of mental enjoyments to those who know little of the truer kind.

The men of gentlest dispositions and best of tempers have at some time or other been sufficiently acquainted with those disturbances which, at ill hours, even small occasions are apt to raise. From these slender experiences of harshness and ill-humour they fully know and will confess the ill moments which are passed when the temper is ever so little galled or fretted. How must it fare, therefore, with those who hardly know any better hours in life, and who, for the greatest part of it, are agitated by a thorough active spleen, a close and settled malignity and rancour? How lively must be the sense of every thwarting and controlling accident? How great must be the shocks of disappointment, the stings of affront, and the agonies of a working antipathy, against the multiplied objects of offence? Nor can it be wondered at if, to persons thus agitated and oppressed, it seems a high delight to appease and allay for the while those furious and rough motions, by an indulgence of their passion in mischief and revenge.

Now as to the consequences of this unnatural state in respect of interest and the common circumstances of life; upon what terms a person who has in this manner lost all which we call Nature can be supposed to stand in respect of the society of mankind; how he feels himself in it; what sense he has of his own disposition towards others, and of the mutual disposition of others towards himself; this is easily conceived.

What enjoyment or rest is there for one who is not conscious of the merited affection or love, but, on the contrary, of the ill-will and hatred of every human soul? What ground must this afford for horror and despair? What foundation of fear, and continual apprehension from mankind and from superior powers? How thorough and deep must be that melancholy which, being once moved, has nothing soft or pleasing from the side of friendship to allay or divert it? Wherever such a creature turns himself, whichever way he cast his eye, everything around must appear ghastly and horrid; everything hostile and, as it were, bent against a private and single being, who is thus divided from everything, and at defiance and war with the rest of Nature.

'Tis thus, at last, that a mind becomes a wilderness, where all is laid waste, everything fair and goodly removed, and nothing extant beside what is savage and deformed. Now if banishment from one's country, removal to a foreign place, or anything which looks like solitude or desertion, be so heavy to endure, what must it be to feel this inward banishment, this real estrangement from human commerce, and to be after this manner in a desert, and in the horridest of solitudes even when in the midst of society? What must it be to live in this disagreement with everything, this irreconcilableness and opposition to the order and government of the universe?

Hence it appears that the greatest of miseries accompanies that state which is consequent to the loss of natural affection; and that to have those horrid, monstrous, and unnatural affections is to be miserable in the highest degree.

CONCLUSION

Thus have we endeavoured to prove what was proposed in the beginning. And since in the common and known sense of vice and illness, no one can be vicious or ill except either—

1. By the deficiency or weakness of natural affections;

Or, 2. By the violence of the selfish;

Or, 3. By such as are plainly unnatural;

It must follow that, if each of these are pernicious and destructive to the creature, insomuch that his completest state of misery is made from hence, to be wicked or vicious is to be miserable and unhappy.

And since every vicious action must in proportion, more or less, help towards this mischief and self-ill, it must follow that every vicious action must be self-injurious and ill.

On the other side, the happiness and good of virtue has been proved from the contrary effect of other affections, such as are according to Nature and the economy of the species or kind. We have cast up all those particulars from whence (as by way of addition and subtraction) the main sum or general account of happiness is either augmented or diminished. And if there be no article exceptionable in this scheme of moral arithmetic, the subject treated may be said to have an evidence as great as that which is found in numbers or mathematics. For let us carry scepticism ever so far, let us doubt, if we can, of everything about us, we cannot doubt of what passes within ourselves. Our passions and affections are known to us. They are certain, whatever the objects may be on which they are employed. Nor is it of any concern to our argument how these exterior objects stand: whether they are realities or mere illusions; whether we wake or dream. For ill dreams will be equally disturbing; and a good dream (if life be nothing else) will be easily and happily passed. In this dream of life, therefore, our demonstrations have the same force; our balance and economy hold good, and our obligation to virtue is in every respect the same.

Upon the whole there is not, I presume, the least degree of certainty wanting in what has been said concerning the preferableness of the mental pleasures to the sensual; and even of the sensual, accompanied with good affection, and under a temperate and right use, to those which are no ways restrained, nor supported by anything social or affectionate.

Nor is there less evidence in what has been said of the united structure and fabric of the mind, and of those passions which constitute the temper or soul, and on which its happiness or misery so immediately depend. It has been shown that in this constitution the impairing of any one part must instantly tend to the disorder and ruin of other parts, and of the whole itself, through the necessary connection and balance of the affections; that those very passions through which men are vicious are of themselves a torment and disease; and that whatsoever is done which is knowingly ill must be of ill consciousness; and in proportion as the act is ill must impair and corrupt social enjoyment, and destroy both the capacity of kind affection and the consciousness of meriting any such. So that neither can we participate thus in joy or happiness with others, nor receive satisfaction from the mutual kindness or imagined love of others, on which, however, the greatest of all our pleasures are founded.

If this be the case of moral delinquency, and if the state which is consequent to this defection from Nature be of all other the most horrid, oppressive, and miserable, 'twill appear

SHAFTESBURY'S CHARACTERISTICS

"that to yield or consent to anything ill or immoral is a breach of interest, and leads to the greatest ills"; and "that on the other side, everything which is an improvement of virtue, or an establishment of right affection and integrity, is an advancement of interest, and leads to the greatest and most solid happiness and enjoyment."

Thus the wisdom of what rules, and is first and chief in Nature, has made it to be according to the private interest and good of every one to work towards the general good, which if a creature ceases to promote, he is actually so far wanting to himself, and ceases to promote his own happiness and welfare. He is on this account directly his own enemy, nor can he any otherwise be good or useful to himself than as he continues good to society, and to that whole of which he is himself a part. So that virtue, which of all excellences and beauties is the chief and most amiable; that which is the prop and ornament of human affairs; which upholds communities, maintains union, friendship, and correspondence amongst men; that by which countries, as well as private families, flourish and are happy, and for want of which everything comely, conspicuous, great, and worthy, must perish and go to ruin; that single quality, thus beneficial to all society, and to mankind in general, is found equally a happiness and good to each creature in particular, and is that by which alone man can be happy, and without which he must be miserable.

And thus virtue is the good, and vice the ill of every one.

END OF VOL. I